CRIMINAL BELIEF SYSTEMS

CRIMINAL BELIEF SYSTEMS

An Integrated-Interactive Theory of Lifestyles

Glenn D. Walters

PRAEGER

Westport, Connecticut
London

Library of Congress Cataloging-in-Publication Data

Walters, Glenn D.

Criminal belief systems : an intergrated-interactive theory of lifestyles / Glenn D. Walters.

p. cm.

Includes bibliographical references and index.

ISBN 0–275–97820–6 (alk. paper)

1. Criminal psychology. 2. Developmental psychology. 3. Socialization.
4. Lifestyles—Psychological aspects. 5. Resocialization. I. Title.

HV6080.W25 2002

364.2—dc21 2002070903

British Library Cataloguing in Publication Data is available.

Library of Congress Catalog Card Number: 2002070903
ISBN: 0–275–97820–6

First published in 2002

Praeger Publishers, 88 Post Road West, Westport, CT 06881
An imprint of Greenwood Publishing Group, Inc.
www.praeger.com

Printed in the United States of America

The paper used in this book complies with the
Permanent Paper Standard issued by the National
Information Standards Organization (Z39.48–1984).

10 9 8 7 6 5 4 3 2

Contents

Preface

Lifestyle theory holds that crime is a consequence of the *conditions* to which a person is exposed, the *choices* he or she makes in life, and the *cognitions* he or she invokes in support of an evolving criminal pattern (Walters, 1990). A criminal lifestyle can be formally or structurally defined as an interactive style characterized by irresponsibility, self-indulgence, interpersonal intrusiveness, and social rule breaking. Lifestyles are also defined by their function—which in most cases entails furnishing the individual with a short-cut solution to existential fear and the problems of everyday living (Walters, 2000a). However, neither definition adequately captures the essence of lifestyle process for we must look beyond structure and function to ascertain the true nature of a criminal pattern. It has taken me 14 years, 120 publications, and countless hours of reflection to realize that a lifestyle is a belief system, or more accurately, a series of belief systems. My intent in writing this book is to elaborate on crime-congruent lifestyles by defining them as integrated sets of belief systems that assist people's daily interactions with the internal and external environments.

This book begins with a review of six traditional criminological models, each of which is considered to be of sufficient breadth and profundity to advance our understanding of crime-congruent belief systems. Strain theory elucidates how sociocultural factors impact on crime initiation and maintenance, while differential association/social learning theory offers insight into the role of learning in the initiation and maintenance of a criminal pattern. Social control theory affords criminal justice scholars and practitioners a means of fathoming the socialization process that impedes crime initiation, whereas neutralization/drift theory and the labeling perspective account for crime maintenance. One of the fundamental premises of this book is that the relationships that form between variables are as instrumental as the variables themselves in explaining crime. In his interactional theory of delinquency development, Thornberry (1987) asserts that these relationships are often reciprocal and interactive, a concept that has been incorporated into this book.

The six models reviewed in this opening chapter supply the groundwork for an integrated-interactive theory of crime.

The second chapter of this book explores the sociocognitive roots of belief system development. Belief systems can be conceptualized as epistemological conduits through which a person interacts with the internal and external environments. Rather than serving as pure cognitive functions, belief systems organize and integrate the cognitive, emotional, behavioral, and social aspects of a person's experience. Developmentally, belief systems can be traced to genetic and social cognitive factors that interact to form evolutionary patterns of influence. In this chapter these evolutionary patterns are ordered along a developmental continuum in which interaction/joint attention, attachment/social referencing, language/private speech, and theory of mind/perspective taking serve as major developmental milestones. As such, the individual contributions of Piaget, Bowlby, Vygotsky, and Flavell are emphasized. The chapter closes with a discussion on the manner in which sociocognitive factors interact to create the conditions responsible for self-awareness and later belief system development.

In Chapter 3 efforts are made to organize information from Chapters 1 and 2 into an integrated-interactive theory of crime capable of expounding on the role of belief systems in the initiation and maintenance of habitual law-breaking behavior. Commencing with a review of the process by which people come to construct and defend their own versions of reality, this chapter defines the role of belief systems as the center point of interaction between the individual and his or her internal and external environments. This is followed by a review of six major categories of schematic representations—attributions, outcome expectancies, efficacy expectancies, goals, values, and thinking styles. Over half the chapter, however, is devoted to a review of the five major belief systems that comprise lifestyle theory—self-view, world-view, present-view, past-view, and future-view—and how these belief systems explain a person's progressive involvement in crime-congruent lifestyles.

The next four chapters explore belief systems associated with violent crime, sexual assault, white-collar crime, and drug trafficking, respectively. Detailed case histories are included in each chapter to illustrate and clarify the theoretical constructs described in the first half of the chapter. However, no claims are made for the representativeness of the individual case studies dramatized in this text for each person is a unique, non-reproducible individual. Of major consequence in comprehending the various belief systems that support crime-congruent lifestyles is the individual's current situational context and the avoidance of broad sweeping generalizations that would have all people convicted of a white-collar crime or sexual offense assigned to the same general category and managed in the same identical way. Individualization is important in understanding a person's belief systems and facilitating the person's desistance from criminal conduct.

The final chapter of this book describes belief systems incongruent with crime in an effort to provide guidance on how desistance from crime-congruent lifestyles might be achieved. It is argued in this chapter that belief systems incongruent with crime coalesce around issues of responsibility, confidence, meaning, and community and that criminally congruent belief systems must be altered and replaced by criminally incongruent belief systems before the criminal pattern can be terminated. Micro-level strategies for promoting change in lifestyle-congruent belief systems can be broken down into four phases: initiation, transition, maintenance, and change. The initiation phase is characterized by a crisis, public pronouncement of change, and prolongation of the arresting process through creation of a shaman effect; transition is driven by changes in outcome expectancies and the development of prosocial skills; maintenance is championed by changes in a person's involvements, commitments, and identifications; change draws on the knowledge that change is an ongoing, perpetual process. Macro-level strategies are implemented at the community or societal level and seek to inform, direct, and reorganize values, practices, and policies that support and maintain crime-congruent belief systems.

The purpose of this book is to demonstrate how criminal conduct can be conceptualized as an integrated set of criminal belief systems and how change is dependent on a person's willingness to adopt belief systems antagonistic to crime. Cognitive and behavioral interactions contributing to these belief systems are integrated into a generalized sense of self, the world, the past, present, and future. Information incompatible with one of these belief systems creates anxiety because it disrupts system homeostasis. The conflict or incompatibility can be resolved by altering the belief system or by denying, distorting, or diverting the inharmonious information. Belief systems congruent with crime are characteristically rigid, constrained, and seemingly immutable. Owing to the fact that they are devoid of flexibility and unreceptive to corrective feedback, the belief systems that support crime-congruent lifestyles become repetitive and assume a fragmented appearance. It is my goal in writing this book to shed light on belief systems congruent with crime in hopes of making the lifestyle concept more intelligible to students, researchers, and practitioners.

1

Precursors of an Integrated-Interactive Theory of Crime

There is certainly no lack of theoretical speculation in the field of criminology. Meaningful empirical evaluation of major theories of criminology, on the other hand, is in much shorter supply. Research in criminology continues to be dominated by studies probing minor delinquency in high school students, although in recent years there has been greater diversity in both the severity of offenses examined and age of offenders studied. How a theory fares with respect to both minor delinquency in high school students and more serious criminality in adult offenders is one way to distinguish between the many theories that seek to explain crime. In evaluating traditional criminological paradigms for possible inclusion in an integrated-interactive theory of crime, two criteria were considered: empirical verification and facility of integration. Paradigms accruing a reasonable amount of empirical support and demonstrating amenability to cross-theoretical integration were selected for inclusion in the integrated-interactive theory outlined in this book. Six models were judged to exhibit good empirical verification and facility of integration: strain, differential association, social control, labeling, neutralization, and Thornberry's (1987) integrated approach.

STRAIN

Classic Strain Theory

Strain theory has its roots in Emile Durkheim's (1938) anomie concept wherein traditional social norms and rules lose their authority over behavior during periods of rapid social change and economic-political upheaval. Robert Merton (1957), the father of classic strain theory, held that society instills in its members a desire for certain goals and then establishes the means by which these goals might be attained. If a person is thwarted in his or her attempts to achieve these goals through conventional means, then he or she may respond by finding illegal means to these goals. According to Merton, lower-class individuals are especially prone to strain because the goals–means disjunction is greater for them than it is for middle-class respondents. However, the relationship between social class and crime is relatively weak, particularly when self-report data are examined (Tittle, Villemez, & Smith, 1978). Additionally, strain theory assumes that adverse social conditions and blocked economic opportunities precede and predict crime, at least at the aggregate level, although research has not been entirely supportive of this hypothesis (Vold, Bernard, & Snipes, 1998). As a result, strain theory has lost adherents in the field of criminology over the last several decades (Ellis & Walsh, 1999).

Much of the research published on strain theory prior to 1989 amassed only limited support for classical strain theory (Bahr, 1979; Hirschi, 1969; Thornberry, Moore, & Christenson, 1985). Taking issue with how these studies were conducted, Farnworth and Leiber (1989) argued that much of the disconfirmatory research on strain theory was a consequence of how strain had been defined and measured. Operationalizing strain as the disjunction between economic goals and educational means, Farnworth and Leiber uncovered a moderate relationship between strain and self-reported utilitarian or property crime and a weak, but significant, association between strain and nonutilitarian crime. Jensen (1995), in turn, declared that Farnworth and Leiber had confounded strain and expectations by neglecting to look at the interaction between economic aspirations and education expectations. Reanalyzing Farnworth and Leiber's data with a measure of strain that incorporated the interaction between aspirations and expectations, Jensen found that expectations accounted for the relationship that Farnworth and Leiber had attributed to strain.

Burton, Cullen, Evans, and Dunaway (1994) operationalized strain in three ways—(1) discrepancy between educational aspirations and expectations; (2) perceived blocked economic opportunities; (3) low attainments relative to others in one's reference group—and correlated each measure with self-reported crime in a general population sample of midwestern adults. Zero-order correlations were significant between all three measures of strain and self-reported adult crime. Regression analyses, on the other hand, determined that only relative deprivation and blocked opportunities were statistically related to criminal outcomes after age, gender, and income had been controlled. Even with this, each definition accounted for less than 2% of the total variance in crime. Inequality, a normative form of strain, is known to correspond with self-reported minor delinquency in college students, a relationship that is somewhat stronger in females than males (O'Connor, 1994). Menard (1995) contends that when strain is properly defined, the proportion of variance explained by Merton's model rises several-fold. Agnew, Cullen, Burton, Evans, and Dunaway (1996) likewise discovered that dissatisfaction with one's monetary status, another putative measure of strain, inspired both drug use and income-generating crime.

Whereas traditional strain appears to correlate as well with female delinquency as with male delinquency, questions have been raised about its applicability to African American respondents. Joseph (1995) writes that traditional strain variables like socioeconomic status and blocked or limited opportunities had no apparent effect on the delinquent activities of African American youth. Whereas African American subjects in one study harbored a stronger commitment to the American Dream than whites, high aspirations coupled with low attainment of economic goals were prognostic of criminality in white subjects but not African American subjects (Cernkovich, Giordano, & Rudolph, 2000). Likewise, poverty was associated with a sense of blocked opportunities in white but not African American students in a study by Vowell and May (2000). While blocked opportunities correlated with violent criminality and gang membership in both white and African American students participating in the Vowell and May study, the relationship was stronger for white students. These findings intimate that classic strain theory may be less predictive of crime in African Americans than in white Americans, perhaps because of differences in how the two groups perceive themselves and the world around them.

General Strain Theory

In response to the many limitations and criticisms that have been directed at classic strain theory, Robert Agnew (1985, 1992) has constructed a revised version of Merton's model that he calls general strain theory. Agnew (1992) proposed three primary pathways to strain—(1) failure to achieve positively valued goals; (2) loss of positively valued stimuli; (3) exposure to noxious or negatively valued stimuli—and four dimensions along which strain is said to vary—magnitude, recency, duration, and clustering. Exposure to strain, says Agnew, creates negative affect in the form of anxiety, frustration, depression, and anger. Anger, according to general strain theory, is the affective expression with the greatest likelihood of eliciting an escapist (drug use), expropriative (theft), or retaliatory (violent crime) response. Agnew adds that factors like temperament, intelligence, conventional social support, delinquent peer associations, social skills, and self-efficacy moderate the effect of strain and negative affect on a person's response.

Cross-sectional data gathered by Agnew and White (1992) disclosed that a composite measure of general strain correlated robustly with prior delinquency and drug use even after controlling for social control and differential association. However, longitudinal data from this same study showed that general strain was unrelated to future drug use and only weakly correlated with future delinquency. Gender differences have also been studied with respect to strain. There is a belief among some theoreticians that interpersonal strain may be as salient a motivating factor for delinquency as economic or situational strain, particularly in females. Agnew and Brezina (1997) certified that interpersonal strain is capable of explaining delinquency initiation in both males and females, but contrary to most theoretical views on gender and crime, interpersonal strain was found to be more critical in furthering the delinquent activities of male adolescents than female adolescents. Mazerolle (1998) notes that general strain theory is equally predictive of property crime in male and female juveniles but predicts violent offending only in males. Katz (2000), citing outcomes obtained from the National Longitudinal Study of Youth, concludes that general strain theory may furnish researchers with greater conceptual insight into the general delinquency of minority women than more traditional criminological theories.

General strain may render as powerful an influence over delinquency escalation and maintenance as it does over delinquency initiation. A longitudinal survey of 861 adolescents from 601 families revealed that strain and stressful life events were associated with escalating delinquent activity (Hoffman & Cerbone, 1999). There is also support for Agnew's assertion that strain and negative affect are linked to later delinquency. Brezina (1996) advises that strain augments negative affect and that negative affect increases a person's odds of adopting a rebellious response to strain. Negative affect may be particularly instrumental in initiating and maintaining violent criminality (Agnew, 1990). After controlling for social bonding (moral beliefs) and differential association (deviant peers), Mazerolle and Piquero (1997) affirmed that general strain exerted both a direct and indirect (mediated by anger) effect on assaultive intentions. Mazerolle, Burton, Cullen, Evans, and Payne (2000) likewise recorded a positive association between anger and strain, on the one hand, and self-reported involvement in violent crime, on the other hand. Incongruent with previous research, Mazerolle et al. (2000) were unable to document a mediating role for anger. In fact, they observed the exact opposite: strain appeared to mediate the effect of anger on self-reported violence.

There has been less support for the moderating or conditioning assumptions of general strain theory. Using the first and second waves of the National Youth Survey (NYS: Elliott, Huizinga, & Ageton, 1985), Paternoster and Mazerolle (1994) ascertained that generalized strain had both a direct and indirect effect on a range of delinquent behaviors. Traditional strain (perceived limitations on economic/educational goal attainment) was the only strain measure that did not correlate with, or predict, delinquency. General strain—as represented by negative life events, neighborhood problems, school/peer hassles, and negative relations with adults—conversely, correlated with, and predicted, delinquency. However, the prediction that strain would interact with conditioning factors like delinquent peers, moral inhibitions, self-efficacy, and conventional social support was not confirmed in this study. Hoffman and Cerbone (1999) also failed to corroborate Agnew's position that the strain–delinquency relationship would be moderated by conditioning variables like income, mastery, and self-esteem. Results from the Mazerolle et al. (2000) study, on the other hand, supplied modest support for Agnew's conditioning hypothesis in the sense that the criminologic effects of strain were magnified by weak social bonds and exposure to delinquent peers.

DIFFERENTIAL ASSOCIATION

Differential Association Theory

The French scholar Gabriel Tarde (1912) is often credited with recognizing that delinquency and crime are learned in much the same manner as any other behavior, an observation that launched Edwin Sutherland's (1939) differential association theory of crime and delinquency. According to Sutherland, the extent to which antisocial behavior is adopted is determined by the frequency, duration, primacy, and intensity of a person's associations with lawbreakers. Not only do people learn the techniques of crime from those already engaged in this activity, but they also learn the motives, drives, attitudes, and rationalizations that make crime possible. Sutherland held that individuals acquire definitions favorable to violations of the law as well as definitions unfavorable to violations of the law. When a person holds a greater proportion of definitions favorable to violations of the law than definitions unfavorable to violations of the law, he or she will engage in delinquent and criminal acts (Sutherland & Cressey, 1978).

Differential association has been found to be instrumental in the transmission of attitudes and skills conducive to professional thievery (Letkemann, 1973), computer code violations (Hollinger, 1992), marijuana use (Orcutt, 1987), white-collar crime (Coleman, 1994), and the possession of firearms by students (May, 1999). Tittle, Burke, and Jackson (1986) witnessed a differential association effect for self-reported delinquency, noting that the effect was indirect in the sense that it operated through symbolic channels that affected the individual's motivation to violate the law. McCarthy (1996), on the other hand, uncovered a direct tutelage effect for differential associations in a study on theft and drug dealing. To the theory's credit, a robust differential association effect has been registered in both African American (Joseph, 1995) and female (Mears, Ploeger, & Warr, 1998) respondents, although males may be more reliably and consistently influenced by delinquent peers than females (Erickson, Crosnoe, & Dornbusch, 2000; Mears et al., 1998). Differential association appears to correlate as well with serious crime as it does with minor delinquency. Alarid, Burton, and Cullen (2000) observed that differential association variables (criminal friends, definitions favorable to violations of the law) correlated robustly with violent, property, and drug offenses in a group of newly incarcerated young adult male and female felons, while Burton et al. (1994) discovered that these same differential association variables correlated with utilitarian, nonutilitarian, and assaultive adult crime.

Despite an impressive record of empirical support, there have been a number of criticisms leveled against Sutherland's differential association theory. First, critical aspects of the theory (e.g., definitions) are difficult, if not impossible, to operationalize and consequently test (Costello, 1997). Second, most recidivistic offenders have a history of strained peer associations, which makes the positing of peer relationships as the central cause of initial and subsequent criminal involvement potentially untenable (Wong, 1998). Third, questions have been raised as to why delinquents and criminals take the advice of deviant peers rather than following the example of law-abiding parents and prosocial peers (Wilson & Herrnstein, 1985). Finally, Sutherland has been taken to task for failing to assimilate the larger social structural context in which differential rewards and punishments are dispensed into his theory (Colvin & Pauly, 1983). In partial response to these criticisms, Akers developed and implemented a social learning reinterpretation of the differential association process.

Social Learning Theory

Ronald Akers (1977, 1994, 1998) is the primary architect of the social learning approach to crime. Akers (1977) initially elaborated on the learning bases of differential association theory by merging it with Skinner's (1953) operant conditioning approach. This gave rise to a differential reinforcement version of differential association theory. Next, Akers incorporated aspects of Bandura's (1986) social learning model into his differential reinforcement paradigm of the differential association process, subsequently calling it the social learning theory of crime. The four components of Akers' (1994) social learning theory of crime were differential association, differential reinforcement/punishment, definitions of behaviors, and imitation. Most recently, Akers (1998) has integrated certain social structural considerations and a person's differential position in the social structure into his social learning theory of crime.

Akers and several colleagues tested the social learning theory of differential association on a group of 3,065 male and female high school students from eight communities in the midwestern United States and identified meaningful empirical links between differential association, differential reinforcement, and imitation, on the one hand, and self-reported alcohol and marijuana use, on the other hand. The probability of alcohol and marijuana use increased as the number of substance-using peer associations, rewards for substance use, and definitions favorable to substance use grew (Akers, Krohn, Lanza-Kaduce, & Radosevich, 1979). Akers and his colleagues determined that these three social learning factors accounted for 55% of the variance in alcohol use and 68% of the variance in marijuana use in the juveniles who participated in this study.

Other investigations have also generated support for Akers' social learning reformulation of differential association theory, although in nearly every case the primary investigator was either Akers or one of his followers. Supportive studies include a five-year longitudinal analysis of smoking behavior in junior and senior high school students (Krohn, Skinner, Massey, & Akers, 1985), a four-year longitudinal survey of conforming and deviant drinking behavior in elderly respondents (Akers, LaGreca, Cohran, & Sellers, 1989), and an assessment of rape and sexual coercion in male college students (Boeringer, Shehan, & Akers, 1991). In a recent evaluation of social learning theory, Skinner and Fream (1997) registered a robust positive correlation between associations with friends who had previously committed computer crime, definitions favorable to computer crime, and participation in five illegal computer activities on the part of 581 undergraduate college students.

Gerald Patterson (1996) offers another version of social learning theory in which parents, teachers, and peers are viewed as playing a pivotal role in the initiation and maintenance of conduct disorder in children and young adolescents by unwittingly reinforcing sporadic and often trivial episodes of antisocial behavior. These same individuals also frequently miss opportunities to reinforce prosocial behavior when such opportunities present themselves. Patterson and his colleagues explain how parents often reinforce situational deviance in their children to the point where the deviance evolves into a pattern of serious delinquent conduct (Larzelere & Patterson, 1990). The solution, says Patterson, is to instruct parents in the use of more effective strategies of child management. Research conducted on this supposition has been largely congruent with Patterson's views on the connection between parental disciplinary practice and childhood and adolescent onset conduct disorder (Wells & Rankin, 1988).

SOCIAL CONTROL

Social Control Theory

In his book *The Gang*, Frederic Thrasher (1927) argued that violent delinquency and gang behavior were the consequence of ineffective social control. Thrasher's work laid the groundwork for the development of control theories of criminal behavior, the most influential being Travis Hirschi's (1969) social bond theory. Hirschi asserts that instead of learning to commit crime, as differential association theory postulates, people learn how not to commit crime. Hirschi claims that people learn not to violate the law by bonding to conventional social groups (family, school, prosocial peers), activities, and ideas. Socialization, according to Hirschi, comprises four key elements: attachment, commitment, involvement, and belief. Attachment is the degree to which law-abiding people serve as sources of positive reinforcement for the individual. Commitment connotes an investment in conformity and correlated interest in long-term goals. Involvement subsumes participation in conventional activities like school, church, or employment. Belief, on the other hand, entails an acceptance of the moral validity of societal rules and practices. People who are attached to their family or school, committed to law-abiding goals, involved in conventional social and leisure activities, and faithful to societal norms are much less likely to enter and maintain a pattern of significant criminality than persons lacking such attachments, commitments, involvements, and beliefs (Hirschi, 1969).

Research has consistently confirmed the underlying tenets of social control theory, although there has been a great deal more support for the attachment, commitment, and belief elements than there has been for involvement (Empy & Stafford, 1991; Jenkins, 1997; Jensen & Rojek, 1992; Wiatrowski & Anderson, 1987), findings that have generalized to cultures outside the United States (Junger & Marshall, 1997). Two areas in which the data are less clear are with respect to research on violent offending and the generalizability of social control theory to African American respondents. In a large-scale study of American adolescents Rosenbaum (1987) discerned that social control theory successfully accounted for drug offenses and was moderately predictive of property crimes but could not explain violent outcomes. Bernburg and Thorlindsson (1999), on the other hand, unearthed a significant negative correlation between social bonding and violent delinquency in a group of Icelandic teenagers. With respect to African American subjects, parental attachment appears to have little impact on subsequent delinquency (Cernkovich et al., 2000), although attachment to school (Joseph, 1995) and church (Johnson, Jang, De Li, & Larson, 2000) may serve as buffers against certain types of offenses for at least a portion of African American youth.

As was discussed with respect to strain and differential association, much of the research on social control theory has focused on relatively minor offenses in adolescents. Several evaluations of social control theory, however, have utilized adult samples with reasonably good success. Linquest, Smusz, and Doerner (1985) used three of Hirschi's key elements (attachment, commitment, involvement) to predict probation outcome in male adults. The results established that commitment was strongly correlated, involvement moderately correlated, and attachment largely uncorrelated with success on probation. Surveying 435 executives from a multinational automobile manufacturer, Lasley (1988) discovered that individuals exhibiting the strongest bonds to managers, coworkers, and the corporation were the least likely to participate in white-collar crime. Finally, attachment to parents, involvement in conventional activities, and belief in the law all correlated significantly with self-reported criminality in a group of felony-convicted young adult male and female boot camp residents (Alarid, Burton, & Cullen, 2000).

Hirschi has been criticized for taking a dichotomous approach to an issue, bonding, that may be more properly conceptualized as a continuum (Curran & Renzetti, 1994). Moreover, Hirschi did not properly define many of his terms, including deviance (Bernard, 1987). Agnew (1993) further contends that Hirschi neglected the reciprocal relations that form between social bonding and other relevant variables and ignored research showing that motivation to deviate is not evenly distributed in the population. It is also uncertain why involvement often fails to correlate with, and predict, delinquency and crime. Krohn and Massey (1980) speculate that involvement may actually be a subcomponent of commitment and as such, provides redundant information when all four elements are regressed onto delinquency, whereas Paternoster, Saltzman, Waldo, and Chircos (1983) argue that there is still a great deal of free time available to persons extensively involved in conventional activities that could be used for delinquency. Regardless of the reason for the relatively weak performance of involvement in research on social control theory, the fact that it lags behind the other three elements implies that social control theory may be in need of revision. However, rather than revising his social control theory, Hirschi and sociologist Michael Gottfredson have teamed up to create a general theory of crime that focuses on self-control.

General Theory of Crime

In their general theory of crime Gottfredson and Hirschi (1990) declared that all crime is a function of low self-control. Marked by behavioral impulsivity, interpersonal insensitivity, self-centeredness, poor planning, impatience, and a poverty of long-range goals, low self-control is believed to be a personality trait with high cross-situational consistency and strong cross-temporal stability. According to Gottfredson and Hirschi, people low in self-control are freed from conventional restraints and are therefore at increased risk for engaging in crime when opportunities and incentives conducive to antisocial behavior are in place. Concepts from classical theory like choice and decision making consequently work their way into Gottfredson and Hirschi's general theory of crime. Although there are clear differences between Hirschi's (1969) original social control (bonding) theory and Gottfredson and Hirschi's (1990) general theory of crime, both models share a belief in the primacy of the family as an agent of socialization in preventing crime. However, whereas social control theory focuses on how parents indirectly control their children's behavior through creation of a social bond, the general theory emphasizes the direct control that parents exert by teaching their children self-discipline, tolerance, and personal control.

Low self-control has been found to correlate with self-reported delinquency in adolescents (Le Blanc, 1997), self-reported criminality in adults (Burton et al., 1994), shoplifting offenses (Deng, 1995), fraud (Grasmick, Tittle, Bursick, & Arneklev, 1993), white-collar crime, and sexual assault (Nagin & Paternoster, 1994). A four-nation comparative study of self-control determined that self-control accounted for 10–16% of the variance in specific forms of deviance and 20% of the variance in total deviance (Vazsonyi, Pickering, Junger, & Hessing, 2001). Further empirical evidence for the primacy of self-control in the evolution of crime-related lifestyles is supplied by Mak (1990), who observed that self-control contributed unique variance beyond that associated with social control in accounting for self-reported delinquency. Self-control accounted for a small, but significant, slice of variance in crimes of force and fraud investigated by Longshore and Turner (1998), but only the relationship between self-control and fraud was contingent on criminal opportunity. Longitudinal panel studies also document a role for self-control in predicting later delinquency (Sampson & Laub, 1993; Wright, Caspi, Moffitt, & Silva, 1999). A prospective analysis of 731 early adolescent Canadian boys, however, revealed that while both self-control and social control (supervision) correlated with delinquency and accidents, social control demonstrated a somewhat stronger relationship with both criteria than self-control (Junger & Tremblay, 2000).

It has been suggested that the general theory of crime may rest on a tautological foundation to the extent that low self-control is nothing more than another term for crime. If this is true, then much of the research in this area is suspect, for all it has done is validate self-control against itself (Akers, 1991). Gottfredson and Hirschi can also be faulted for excluding important variables from their general theory—belief (Brownfield & Sorenson, 1993), negative affect (Caspi, Moffitt, Silva, Stouthamer-Loeber, Krueger, & Schmutte, 1994), and situational influences (Nagin & Paternoster, 1993), to name a few. There is the additional problem of oversimplicity, as recognized by Polk (1991), who takes exception to Gottfredson and Hirschi's position that white-collar crime is largely impulsive and unskilled, for it neglects the planning, skills, and specialized knowledge that serve as precursors to many white-collar crimes. Traditional crimes may also not be as impulsive as Gottfredson and Hirschi postulate. Nagin and Tremblay (1999) note that many of the antisocial boys in their sample were not among the most impulsive and that many of the chronically impulsive boys were not among the most antisocial. Although the general theory of crime is probably not as general or inclusive as Gottfredson and Hirschi (1990) have proposed, it nonetheless brings new respectability to the classical concepts of choice and decision making and highlights the role of direct parental control in the development of crime and delinquency.

LABELING

The Labeling Perspective

Frank Tannenbaum (1938) brought attention to the labeling process with his revelation that society, in its zeal to reform perceived acts of evil, paradoxically creates the conditions that bring about the very behavior that reformers seek to eliminate by labeling and isolating young lawbreakers from natural sources of social support. Traditional labeling theorists like Lemert (1951) and Schur (1971) argue that lawbreakers are indistinguishable from nonlawbreakers except for the presence of a deviant label. Initial acts of delinquency (primary deviance) are held to be evenly distributed in the population. The imposition of a deviant label is believed to (1) alter the labeled individual's self-concept and (2) reduce the labeled person's access to legitimate social, occupational, and employment opportunities (Rutter & Giller, 1984). A person's delinquency-sustaining reaction to the deviant label is referred to by labeling theorists as secondary deviance. Drawn to like-labeled peers, the individual goes about reestablishing new behavioral norms and recasts his or her identity in light of the label, a process known as retrospective interpretation. In effect, the label becomes a master status or central defining trait of the person's identity and contributes to a process identified by labeling theorists as deviance amplification (Becker, 1963). It is assumed that deviant labels are differentially applied to disadvantaged, impoverished, and minority subjects.

An early study on official labeling disclosed that juvenile shoplifters referred to the police by store officials were more likely to reoffend than juvenile shoplifters who for some reason were not referred to the police (Klemke, 1978). More recent research suggests that labeling may indirectly affect delinquency by influencing a person's delinquent peer associations (Adams, 1996). It is uncertain what impact official labels have on young offenders' sense of self, however (Klein, 1986). Official labels may have a detrimental effect on the self-images and attitudes of middle-class white youth, nonserious offenders, and persons most heavily invested in the conventional social order (Jensen, 1980) but probably have minimal impact on those individuals with the greatest likelihood of being processed through the criminal justice system (i.e., minority individuals who have committed serious crimes and have little investment in the conventional social order). There is evidence, congruent with the underlying tenets of labeling theory, that official labels may limit a person's job opportunities (Erickson & Goodstadt, 1979) and promote deviance amplification (Young, 1971).

In comparison to official labels, unofficial labels, particularly those held by parents, may have a more substantial and predictable effect on future delinquency. Paternoster and Iovanni (1989) speculate that the negative impact of official labeling may have diminished in recent years because of growing community skepticism toward the integrity of those doing the labeling (i.e., police, courts). Research conducted by both Paternoster and Iovanni (1989) and Triplett and Jarjoura (1994) denote that unofficial labeling is more intimately tied to people's future propensity to commit crime than official labeling. There is also speculation that labeling may facilitate the intergenerational spread of crime. Hagan and Palloni (1990), investigating working-class crime in London between 1950 and 1980, discerned that labeling made it difficult for boys born to criminal fathers to escape the "fate" of following in their fathers' footsteps. Hence, labeling may stigmatize and inhibit even the progress of future generations.

The labeling perspective, despite its attention to issues neglected by other major schools of thought, is limited as a theory and has attracted few adherents in recent years (Ellis & Walsh, 1999). Several factors prevent the labeling perspective from achieving status as a complete and comprehensive theory of crime. First, labeling theorists are uninterested in crime initiation. Proponents maintain that the model's inattention to primary deviance is more than compensated for by its emphasis on secondary deviance (Lemert, 1951). However, research on secondary deviance indicates that official labeling may not have the impact on crime and delinquency that labeling theorists presume (Wellford & Triplett, 1993). Many of the studies that have been used to confirm deviance amplification can be cited for a possible selection artifact in the sense that a higher rate of future offending in court-referred juveniles may simply reflect the fact that intake officers are able to differentiate between high- and low-risk youth (Smith & Paternoster, 1990). Even if the research on official labeling was more favorable to the labeling position, the perspective is limited by its inattention to primary deviance. Furthermore, the weak direct effects of labeling on delinquency challenge the deterministic assumptions of traditional labeling theory. Studies by both Adams (1996) and Hayes (1997) suggest that the effects of labeling on delinquency are largely indirect and mediated by delinquent peer group associations. These limitations have encouraged development of a modern symbolic interactional theory of crime and delinquency.

Symbolic Interactionism

Compared to traditional labeling theory, symbolic interactionism takes a much broader view of crime. Integrating the labeling perspective with features from the social control and social learning traditions, symbolic interactionists like Karen Heimer and Ross Matsueda (1997) contend that delinquency is most apt to occur when people hold attitudes favorable to lawbreaking, participate in groups that condone crime, and are viewed by significant others as delinquent. The symbolic interactional view of crime differs from the labeling perspective in three key respects: (1) symbolic interactionism attempts to explain both primary and secondary deviance; (2) symbolic interactionism defines delinquency as an objective phenomenon; (3) symbolic interactionism examines informal social control and unofficial labeling as well as formal social control and official labeling (Heimer & Matsueda, 1997). Heimer and Matsueda (1994) state that when similar problematic situations are repeatedly resolved with delinquency, the situation becomes progressively less problematic and the delinquency perniciously more nonreflective and habitual. This contributes directly to our understanding of lifestyles because a criminal lifestyle is believed to be a belief system capable of providing the individual with short-term solutions to everyday problems, which through repetition become patterned and automatic.

Much of the validating research on the symbolic interactional theory of crime and delinquency has been conducted by either Matsueda or Heimer and relies almost exclusively on data from the longitudinal National Youth Survey (NYS). Consistent with the symbolic interactional perspective on labeling, definitions, and delinquency as an objective phenomenon, Matsueda (1992) verified that parents were more likely to label their male children lawbreakers if the children were nonwhite, resided in an urban setting, or were guilty of committing previous delinquent acts. In this study parental labels augmented a child's reflected appraisals (view of self as seen through another's eyes) of themselves as lawbreakers. These delinquency-based reflected appraisals were found by Matsueda to have a significant facilitative effect on future delinquency. Matsueda also discovered that a youth's reflected appraisals of parents, teachers, and friends coalesced into a consensual, organized sense of self rather than fragmenting into a series of distinct independent selves. This last finding suggests that there is a unified perspective of self and perhaps a unified belief system that covers major aspects of the self-view, world-view, past-view, present-view, and future-view.

Bartusch and Matsueda (1996) extended Matsueda's (1992) NYS results to females. In this study both male and female adolescents' reflected appraisals as lawbreakers elevated their future risk of delinquent involvement. Informal labeling by parents and reflected appraisals as lawbreakers had a greater impact on boys than girls, but prior delinquent conduct was more apt to result in a negative parental label for girls. Using these same data, Heimer (1996) demonstrated that maintaining traditional gender roles and definitions reduced delinquency in female youth but not male youth. Parental supervision, on the other hand, was more effective in deterring crime in males than females. The implication of the Heimer study is that it is perhaps best to control a girl's behavior indirectly by encouraging the assumption of traditional gender-based roles, values, and attitudes, whereas boys may require more direct control by way of increased parental supervision. Despite the need for additional research by investigators other than Matsueda and Heimer, the symbolic interactional theory of crime holds promise as a vehicle in advancing our understanding of labeling phenomena in ways that are more comprehensive and integrated than can be attained through traditional labeling channels.

NEUTRALIZATION AND DRIFT

Techniques of Neutralization

Arguing against the notion of a delinquent subculture (Cloward & Ohlin, 1960; Cohen, 1955) and borrowing from both the social control tradition and Freudian perspective on defense mechanisms, Gresham Sykes and David Matza (1957) introduced techniques of neutralization into the criminological literature. Sykes and Matza proposed that lawbreakers are not necessarily antagonistic to the larger society. Consequently, those who break the law need to find ways to avoid moral blame and protect their self-esteem prior to committing an act that goes against the grain of society. The individual accomplishes this by neutralizing the guilt associated with future deviance. Neutralization is achieved through cognitive distortion or rationalization. Sykes and Matza identified five techniques of neutralization (see Table 1.1), although five additional techniques have since been added: the metaphor of the ledger (good outcomes outweigh the negative consequences of crime), the defense of necessity, the denial of the necessity of the law, the claim of entitlement, and the belief that "everyone else is doing it" (Collins, 1995; Minor, 1984).

Research reveals that techniques of neutralization can be applied, and have been applied, to a wide variety of offenses. A group of white-collar criminals who had embezzled large amounts of money, for instance, had rationalized that they were simply "borrowing" the money and fully intended on paying it back (Cressey, 1953/1971). Neutralization has also been observed in studies on violence against strangers (Dietz, 1983), murder for hire (Levi, 1981), wife beating (Dutton, 1986), retail theft (Hollinger, 1991), deer poaching (Eliason & Dodder, 1999), and violations of hospital policy by registered nurses (Dabney, 1995). Early studies by Ball (1977, 1983) and Ball and Lilly (1971) challenged some of the underlying assumptions of neutralization theory. Agnew and Peters (1986), however, found fault with Ball's research on the grounds that it overlooked the two principal features of neutralization: (1) belief in a technique of neutralization and (2) perception that one is in a situation where the technique is applicable. When both of these dimensions were taken into account, Agnew and Peters discovered that neutralizations effectively explained cheating and shoplifting in a group of 429 undergraduate students.

Neutralization theory assumes that less delinquent youth will make greater use of techniques of neutralization than more delinquent youth because of the former's greater commitment to the conventional social order. In support of this contention, Agnew (1994) reports that the neutralization of violence rose longitudinally in teenagers disapproving of violence. However, when he examined his data cross-

Table 1.1
Techniques of Neutralization Introduced by Sykes and Matza (1957)

Techniques of Neutralization	**Definition**	**Example**
Denial of Responsibility	Belief that lawbreaking conduct is caused by influences outside a person's control (e.g., poverty, peers, broken home).	"I was raised in poverty, and everyone knows the only way out of the ghetto is through entertainment, sports, or crime."
Denial of Injury	Belief that no one got injured and so even if the behavior is technically a crime, it really is not wrong.	"What's the big deal? Maybe I used a gun when I robbed that store, but I didn't use it, and nobody got hurt."
Denial of Harm	Belief that one is justified in retaliating against the victim because one was victimized first.	"That guy was disrespecting me. I had no choice. I had to put him in his place."
Condemnation of Condemners	Shifting attention to the actions of those who condemn the behavior of the offenders (society, authority figures).	"The government is the real criminal here. Did you see how much time that judge gave me? Child molesters get off with less time than I got."
Appeals to Higher Authorities	Belief that loyalty to a subgroup (gang, family) supersedes loyalty to the rules of the larger society.	"I had to kill that guy when he moved into the neighborhood and started selling drugs; this was *our* corner."

sectionally, neutralization turned out to be stronger in adolescents professing more favorable attitudes toward violence. Shields and Whitehall (1994) discerned that scores on a measure of neutralization were four times higher in young offenders than in nondelinquent high school students, that these scores correlated with other measures of delinquency, and that higher scores successfully predicted recidivism in the young offender group. Neutralization has also been found to correlate with involvement in gang activities (Esbensen, Winfree, He, & Taylor, 2001). One possible interpretation of these findings is that delinquents have more to neutralize than nondelinquents.

Landsheer, Hart, and Kox (1994) determined that the ability to neutralize physical injury to a person with whom one is familiar is difficult, even for a habitual delinquent. Such behavior is therefore deemed unacceptable even for persons heavily committed to a criminal lifestyle. Nondelinquents, unlike delinquents, extend this non-neutralization policy to unfamiliar persons, institutions, organizations, and property. Using factor analysis, Thurman (1984) ascertained that neutralization and moral commitment were conceptually and empirically distinct. In situations where moral commitment was low, neutralization was effective in reducing the guilt associated with a delinquent act and accordingly increased the chances of expected future deviance. However, neutralization had minimal impact on the future expected illegal activities of subjects exhibiting medium to high levels of moral commitment. Therefore, delinquents may rely more on neutralization than nondelinquents—first, because delinquents have more to neutralize and second, because neutralization is more effective in eliminating crime-inhibiting thoughts and feelings in delinquents than in nondelinquents.

Neutralization, like labeling, does not provide a complete explanation of crime. It affords insight into how a pattern of delinquency may be maintained but adds little to our understanding of how the pattern is initiated. Furthermore, there is no empirical evidence to support the assumption that general neutralization protects the self-esteem of juvenile lawbreakers, although police-related neutralization may have a small ameliorative effect on a person's self-view (Costello, 2000). There has also been no empirical corroboration of Sykes and Matza's contention that certain crimes are more effectively neutralized by one technique than another (Shields & Whitehall, 1994). More importantly, neutralization theory assumes that techniques of neutralization are used prior to the commission of a deviant act to neutralize any anticipated guilt; much of the existing research, however, suggests that neutralization more typically follows, rather than precedes, the deviance (Minor, 1984; Pogrebin, Poole, & Martinez, 1992). Some of these issues led Matza (1964) to reformulate his ideas into what is commonly referred to as drift theory.

Drift Theory

David Matza (1964), in presenting his drift theory, railed against the deterministic leanings of traditional criminological theory. According to Matza, many youth drift between delinquency and a conventional lifestyle as a result of situational influences and personal choice. Strongly allied with neither side, they sway back and forth between deviance and conformity. Drift theory, as conceptualized by Matza, encompasses three primary elements. First, novice delinquents learn techniques of neutralization from more experienced delinquents in order to reduce or eliminate the guilt that would otherwise accompany their law-breaking behavior. Second, rather than being deterministically pulled or pushed into delinquency, the individual wills it. Third, the individual wills delinquency through preparation and desperation. Preparation encompasses the skills and attitudes necessary to commit crime, while desperation entails cultivating the beliefs that one's life is uncontrollable and that crime will supply one with greater control and a variety of other benefits, from money, to power, to status.

Matza's drift theory offers a unique perspective potentially capable of informing an integrated-interactive theory of crime. His emphasis on situational factors, nonrational choice, and neutralization all figure prominently in the model outlined in this text. Drift theory also explains, at least in part, why many individuals drop out of crime during the teen years and early adulthood. Unfortunately, many of Matza's ideas have never been tested empirically. Indirect confirmation of drift theory can be found in research tracing the roots of delinquency to the pursuit of adventure, thrills, and excitement rather than the desire for escape from adverse social conditions or acceptance by a criminal subculture (Bernburg & Thorlindsson, 1999) and studies showing that delinquent actions and gang membership are more the result of choice than of peer pressure or collective coercion (Emler & Reicher, 1995). In a more direct test of Matza's theory, Khoo and Oakes (2000) concluded that, congruent with drift theory, delinquents displayed the greatest propensity to endorse neutralization techniques when placed in situations conducive to shame (i.e., their family identity is salient and the hypothetical confrontation takes place in a public, rather than private, setting).

INTERACTIONAL THEORY

Integrating social control, social learning, strain, and cultural conflict theories, Terrence Thornberry (1987) constructed an interactive theory designed to redress the limitations of traditional criminological theory. According to Thornberry, attachment to parents, commitment to school, belief in conventional values, association with delinquent peers, adoption of delinquent attitudes and values, and such social status variables as social class, minority status, and social disorganization interact to facilitate not only the initiation of crime but its maintenance as well. Thornberry criticized past criminological theory for its reliance on unidirectional causal models, its lack of attention to developmental factors, and the assumption of uniform causal effects across the social structure. In its place, he offered an integrated developmental model of crime in which social structure is taken into account and the majority of relationships are assumed to be bidirectional. The primary contributions of Thornberry's model to the integrated-interactive theory of crime propounded in this book are its developmental emphasis and assertion of reciprocal causal relationships.

Peer relations and delinquent behavior have been studied extensively using data from the NYS. Elliott et al. (1985) unearthed a reciprocal relationship between peer delinquency and delinquent behavior in several waves of the NYS to where the peer influence effect (peer delinquency → delinquent behavior) slightly exceeded the peer selection effect (delinquent behavior → peer delinquency). Subsequent research on alternate waves of the NYS have also confirmed the presence of a reciprocal relationship between peer delinquency and delinquent behavior with either the peer influence effect (Menard & Elliott, 1994) or peer selection effect (Reed & Rose, 1998) predominating. A reciprocal relationship is also purported to exist between peer and respondent drug use (Krohn, Lizotte, Thornberry, Smith, & McDowell, 1996). Bauman and Ennett (1994) remark that at least half the commonality in drug use between friends is a consequence of selection factors because people choose whom they want to interact with, peer groups restrict themselves to like-thinking members, and friendships disappear when drug use behaviors become dissimilar.

The association between indirect parental control (attachment) and delinquent behavior is another area in which the reciprocal relations hypothesis has been tested. Liska and Reed (1985) recorded significant bidirectional correlations between attachment to parents, success in school, and delinquency. Burkett and Warren (1987) likewise espied that religious commitment, belief in the sinfulness of marijuana use, association with marijuana-using peers, and self-reported marijuana use were reciprocally related over time. Religious commitment and delinquency also appear to be reciprocally linked (Benda, 1997). Conversely, Agnew (1985) determined that parental attachment significantly influenced later delinquency, although delinquency had little effect on subsequent parental attachment. Jang and Smith (1997), by comparison, discerned that delinquency influenced subsequent affective ties but that affective ties had no bearing on later delinquency. It should be pointed out, however, the Jang and Smith study was conducted with a group of midadolescent subjects. In a survey of early adolescents, attachment and delinquency were found to be reciprocally connected (Thornberry, Lizotte, Krohn, Farnworth, & Jang, 1991).

Direct parental control (supervision), like indirect control, has been studied using structural equation modeling. In one of the earliest studies done in this area, Olweus (1980) ascertained that a strong-willed temperament in infancy predicted greater permissiveness for aggression on the part of the mother during early childhood, which, in turn, predicted increased aggressiveness on the part of the child in later childhood. A review of the literature notes that ineffective discipline and parental irritability are both a cause and an effect of a child's antisocial behavior (Lytton, 1990). Along these same lines, Patterson (1996) asserts that parental use of coercive discipline sets the stage for a child's involvement in antisocial behavior but that the child's antisocial behavior can also evoke high levels of parental coercion. Paternoster (1988) chronicles the presence of reciprocal relations between parental supervision, marijuana use, and petty larceny wherein weak supervision contributes to increased deviance, which then serves to further weaken parental supervision. While Jang and Smith (1997) failed to detect a bidirectional relationship between affective ties and delinquency in midadolescent respondents, there was a reciprocal association between supervision and delinquency. Finally, Brezina (1999) witnessed a countervailing effect between parent and child aggression, with parental slapping leading to increased child aggression and child aggression resulting in reduced parental slapping.

Although not quite definitive, the bulk of research conducted on the reciprocal relations model set forth by Thornberry imparts general support for the prediction that criminologically relevant variables are often bidirectionally linked. Reciprocal associations assume a prominent position in the integrated-interactive theory of crime described in this book. Crime-related lifestyles are a function of many variables, but these variables interact with one another, often in reciprocal fashion. Crime-congruent beliefs, a cardinal feature of the integrated-interactive approach, appear to enter into reciprocal relationships with other criminogenic influences (e.g., delinquent peer associations) to promote criminal behavior (Thornberry, Lizotte, Krohn, Farnworth, & Jang, 1994). As we approach the final section of this chapter, we would do well to remember that relationships are assumed to be reciprocal unless there is strong logical or empirical evidence to the contrary. The integrated-interactive lifestyle theory of criminal belief systems holds firmly to this assumption. In fact, if the assumption of reciprocal influence were to be proven false in a number of investigations, it would severely challenge the scientific credibility of the lifestyle theory of criminal behavior.

CONCLUSION

There have been several integrated theories of crime and delinquency introduced in recent years, and there seems to be a general trend toward integration within the field of criminology itself (Barak, 1998). Concerted attempts at integration can be observed in four of the five traditional models of criminology discussed in this chapter. Agnew's general strain theory, Akers' social learning theory, Matsueda and Heimer's symbolic interactional theory, and Matza's drift theory all provide more integrated and broad-spectrum views of crime and delinquency than their predecessors. The exception appears to be Gottfredson and Hirschi's general theory of crime, which is probably more narrow and parochial than Hirschi's original formulation. The six theories presented in this chapter correspond to one another and to the initiation and escalation/maintenance of crime through unidirectional, bidirectional, or mediated channels. The proposed relationships are outlined in Figure 1.1.

The integrated model pictured in Figure 1.1 construes crime initiation and crime escalation/maintenance as separate, yet related, phases of the criminal development process. Social control, differential association, and strain variables are hypothesized to form bidirectional relationships (primary contribution of the interactional theory) with crime initiation and with one another. Research indicates

Figure 1.1
An Integrated Theoretical Model Showing the Interrelationships Hypothesized to Exist between Six Standard Criminological Theories

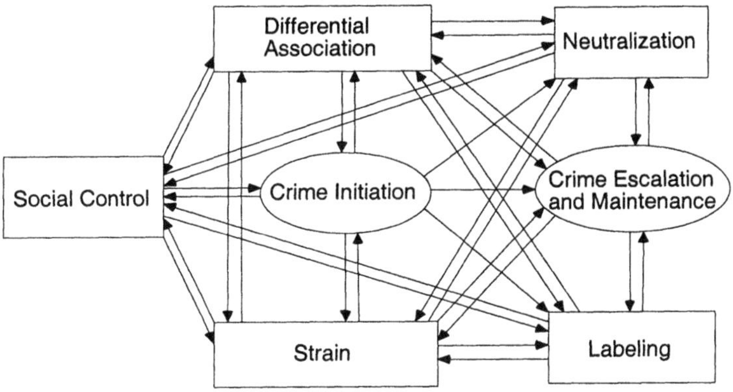

that strain, as defined by Agnew (1992), interacts with, and is modified by, social control and differential association (Mazerolle et al., 2000; Paternoster & Mazerolle, 1994). A number of integrated models have focused on the interrelatedness of social control and differential association variables (cf. Elliott et al., 1985; Thornberry, 1987),and current research strongly confirms the empirical presence of such a relationship (Agnew, 1993; May, 1999). Furthermore, crime initiation has also been known to correlate in reciprocal fashion with strain (Paternoster & Mazerolle, 1994), differential association (Menard & Elliott, 1994), and social control (Sampson & Laub, 1993).

Moving to the escalation and maintenance phase, we can see that the model depicted in Figure 1.1 holds that crime initiation has a unidirectional effect on neutralization, labeling, and crime escalation/maintenance. Neutralization, labeling, differential association, strain, and social control (link not shown) are all believed to enter into a bidirectional relationship with crime escalation/maintenance. The two additions to this stage (neutralization and labeling) are believed to form reciprocal relations not only with crime escalation/maintenance but with strain, differential association, and social control as well. Studies denote that techniques of neutralization can magnify the effect of differential association (Mitchell, Dodder, & Norris, 1990) and social control (Benda & Whiteside, 1995), whereas labeling has been found to promote strain (Hayes, 1997), facilitate differential association (Adams, 1996), and weaken social controls (Paternoster & Iovanni, 1989). Neutralization and labeling are not believed to interact directly but influence one another through the mediating effect of crime escalation/ maintenance, social control, differential association, and strain.

A principal impediment to integration of the six criminological models included in this chapter is that they rest on dissimilar philosophical foundations. Control theory, for instance, is based on the Hobbesian assumption of natural delinquent impulses, whereas differential association theory is grounded in the Lockean presumption of a blank slate that is shaped by environmental experience and learning. In contrast to the deterministic underpinnings of the labeling perspective, drift theory is firmly entrenched in free will and the capacity for choice. How can such widely divergent philosophical assumptions and principles be reconciled in order to bring about effective integration? The solution, according to the present author and the one pursued in this book, is to accept the surface contributions of these disparate criminological models but then fuse and buttress them with an underlying sociocognitive developmental framework. Primary elements of the theoretical infrastructure of an integrated-interactive theory of crime are explored next as part of a discussion on the sociocognitive parameters of belief system organization and development.

2

Sociocognitive Foundations of Belief System Development

Belief is defined in Webster's *Unabridged Third New International Dictionary* as a "conviction of the truth of some statement or the reality of some being or phenomenon" (Merriam-Webster, 2000). A belief system is therefore a group of interrelated convictions of truth or statements of perceived reality. It is argued in this chapter that beliefs and belief systems are not exclusively cognitive but possess vital behavioral, sensory, motivational, and affective features as well. Consequently, emotions, in their role as linchpins of human evolution, are instrumental in shaping and promoting the belief systems that support a person's actions (Abe & Izard, 1999). A second major assumption on which this chapter rests is that human knowledge and information processing cannot be realistically divorced from their environmental context (Thompson & Fine, 1999). Third, it is assumed that a functioning human nervous system is a prerequisite for belief system development, although belief cannot be reduced to brain function (Slavney, 1992). One must therefore take cognitive, behavioral, sensory, motivational, affective, and contextual factors into account when attempting to unravel the mysteries of belief system evolution.

Belief, being something more than what fills a person's head, supplies researchers with an opportunity to visualize the interactive nature of human psychology (Walters, 2000a). Rather than focusing exclusively on dispositional or situational characteristics, the integrated-interactive perspective adopted in this book concentrates on a person's interactions with the internal and external environments. Whereas the internal environment is made up of a person's thoughts, feelings, sensations, and expectancies, the external environment is composed of outside social and nonsocial stimuli. The breakdown of environments into internal and external is, of course, arbitrary since both stem from a person's perceptions. The internal-external distinction is made principally for conceptual reasons. As this discussion intimates, belief systems are multifaceted phenomena that bridge the gap between the individual and his or her internal and external environments. To comprehend how these complex interpretations of reality gain dominion over our actions, we must understand how they develop. In an effort to fathom the emergence of belief systems, we will consider the evolutionary process that sets the stage for belief system formation and the four early sociocognitive influences that help shape incipient belief systems into lifestyle-congruent patterns of interaction: early interaction/joint attention, attachment/social referencing, language/private speech, and theory of mind/perspective taking.

EVOLUTION AND GENETICS

According to the integrated-interactive theory described in this text, the primal incentive for interaction is survival. Living organisms are presumably endowed with an instinct to survive, referred to as the life instinct (Walters, 2000a). However, the life instinct is threatened by the reality of a constantly changing environment. The clash of these two forces creates a global state of strain or discomfort. In organisms with the capacity to perceive themselves as separate from the surrounding environment (i.e., humans eighteen months of age and older: Lewis & Brooks-Gunn, 1979) the unease registers as existential fear. Existential fear comprises two principal elements—(1) a fear of death or nonexistence (Pyszczynski, Greenberg, & Solomon, 1998) and (2) a subject-object duality believed to produce a profound sense of separation or alienation from the external environment (Boss, 1963)—that direct the organism's actions toward certain objectives and goals and away from others. Several general influences, by virtue of their survival-relevance, help cast human fear into a unique expression of a person's current existential condition. These three general experiences or life tasks are referred to as affiliation, predictability, and status.

Through evolution organisms have learned to protect their survival by affiliating with others of their kind, realizing a sense of mastery, control, and predictability over the environment, and acquiring status within their community through territoriality or a particular position in a dominance hierarchy. Groups select individual characteristics that promote survival of the group, and survival of the group promotes survival of the individual group members. This contributes to an evolutionary-based need to belong (Baumeister & Leary, 1995). Ainsworth (1989) further contends that social bonds formed early in life improve an organism's chances of survival. With respect to predictability, it has been noted that achieving and maintaining environmental control and predictability is of evolutionary significance (Shapiro, Schwartz, & Astin, 1996). It is clearly advantageous to be able to predict another's actions, a fact perhaps responsible for a common attributional bias in which people tend to emphasize dispositional attributions over situational ascriptions in assessing other people's behavior (Higgins, 2000). Status, in the form of human territoriality, reinforces identity, which, in turn, nurtures psychological well-being and survival, whether the territory being protected is one's home (Omata, 1995), neighborhood (Marusza, 1997), or a seat in class

(Suzuki, 1990). All three life tasks are therefore critical in the genesis and development of survival-supporting belief systems.

In a comparison of 278 identical and 378 fraternal twins, Scourfield, Martin, Lewis, and McGuffin (1999) recorded a genetic effect for social cognition that was weaker for adolescents than children. These investigators tentatively attributed the observed age-dependent rise in environmental influence on social cognition to a growing awareness of social cues and accentuated social learning opportunities in older children. The genetic link to social cognition and belief system evolution, according to the present formulation, may be found in childhood temperament, although temperament is only exclusively genetic at the moment of conception. After conception, temperament is molded by the organism's interactions with a constantly changing environment, interactions that commence in the womb. Five temperament dimensions, traceable to the three early survival-relevant tasks of affiliation, predictability, and status, can be identified. The temperament dimension of sociability is directly related to the need for affiliation. Information-processing speed and novelty seeking, two other temperament dimensions, furnish increased opportunities for environmental control and predictability, while the temperament dimensions of emotionality and activity level potentially afford a person status and identity within the context of ongoing interactions with salient environmental stimuli (see Figure 2.1).

Sociability, a temperament dimension defined and developed by Buss and Plomin (1984), encompasses a person's response to interpersonal stimuli. Twin (Spinath & Angleitner, 1998) and adoption (Daniels & Plomin, 1985) studies convey strong heritability estimates for sociability. Longitudinal studies, in addition, demonstrate that individual differences in sociability are reasonably stable in children between the ages of 4 and 24 months (Kagan & Snidman, 1991). The influence of early sociability on later adjustment was documented in a study by Caspi, Elder, and Bem (1988), where shy boys exhibited delayed entry into marriage, parenthood, and a stable career thirty years after being tested, and shy girls displayed a more conventional pattern of marriage, homemaking, and child-bearing compared to age-mates assessed as outgoing.

Information-processing speed is the swiftness with which information is detected, processed, stored, and retrieved. Information-processing speed correlates well with information-processing efficiency (Schweizer, 1998) and is much easier to evaluate. This, then, was the rationale for favoring information-processing speed over efficiency as one of two temperamental links to environmental control and predictability. The genetic origins of information-processing speed were established in a twin study by Baker, Vernon, and Ho (1991), and the stability of information-processing speed during the first year of life has been detailed in investigations like the one conducted by Canfield, Smith, Brezsynak, and Snow (1997). The performance-enhancing effects of information-processing speed have been documented for both timed and untimed tests of memory and reasoning ability (Kail & Salthouse, 1994).

Novelty seeking is the tendency to approach novel or unfamiliar stimuli (Clonin-

Figure 2.1
Relationships Presumed to Exist between Evolution (Early Life Tasks) and Genetics (Temperament)

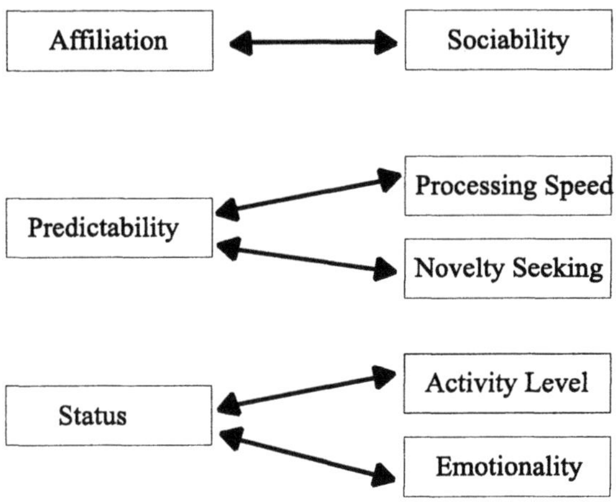

ger, 1987). Like information-processing speed, novelty seeking assists with environmental predictability and control by leading the organism to search for more information about unfamiliar stimuli and situations. As with all five temperament dimensions, novelty seeking demonstrates strong evidence of heritability (Heath, Cloninger, & Martin, 1994) and early temporal stability (Svrakic, Svrakic, & Cloninger, 1996). The relevance of novelty seeking to future adjustment is manifest in studies showing that novelty-seeking tendencies at age 11 predict subsequent aggressive behavior (Sigvardsson, Bohman, & Cloninger, 1987) and problem drinking (Cloninger, Sigvardsson, & Bohman, 1988).

A fourth temperament dimension is activity level. Buss and Plomin (1984) define activity level as the amplitude and rate of motor output and behavioral response. The stability of activity level is reasonably well established during the first several years of life (Goldsmith & Campos, 1990), whereas family (Willerman & Plomin, 1973) and twin (Torgersen, 1985) studies imply that activity level has strong genetic roots. Investigators have discerned that infants and young children with evidence of high activity level frequently experience school academic and disciplinary problems in later childhood (Cowen, Wyman, & Work, 1992). Activity level would appear to make important contributions to both status seeking and identity.

Emotionality, like activity level, plays a leading role in the formation of status and identity and can be defined as a person's emotional/affective response to environmental stimuli (Buss & Plomin, 1984). Heritability for this temperament dimension has been verified in both twin (Plomin & Rowe, 1977) and adoption

(Schmitz, Saudino, Plomin, Fulker, & De Fries, 1996) studies, and Loehlin (1989) reports that emotionality is reasonably stable after the first two to three months of life. Longitudinal data indicate that children evaluated as highly emotional at 7 years of age are rated as significantly more anxious, aggressive, distractible, and depressed ten years later compared to 7-year-old children earning average emotionality scores (Gjone & Stevenson, 1997).

McClelland and his colleagues speak of the interaction that they believe takes place between memory systems. A person's general assumptions about life are stored in the neocortex as semantic memories, while novel or unexpected events are stored in the hippocampus as episodic memories (McClelland, McNaughton, & O'Reilly, 1995). It is hard to imagine survival in the absence of either system. Affiliation, prediction, and status would not be possible without the stability supplied by semantic memory, although the ability to respond and adapt to unanticipated situations and events is equally consequential for survival. Novel information with a possible bearing on future survival is initially recorded in episodic memory but eventually works its way into semantic memory. The complex interplay of these two memory systems illustrates how an organism's genetically programmed evolutionary capacity is shaped by ongoing interactions with the environment.

Before revering genetics as the source of all human interaction, we might want to consider that temperament is never fully genetic except at the moment of conception. In fact, Caporael (1997) takes exception to the history of genocentrism that pervades traditional evolutionary theory. Asserting that evolutionary principles function at several different levels—gene, person, group—Caporael offers a cogent argument in favor of the hypothesis that these differing levels overlap and interact with one another as part of a complex evolutionary process. The levels of selection concept and the possibility that group dynamics may be as critical as genetic inheritance in supporting human survival provide a lead-in to the next four sections in which different aspects of social cognition are discussed with respect to the role that each plays in fostering the belief systems that human organisms use to negotiate their way through life.

EARLY INTERACTION AND JOINT ATTENTION

Jean Piaget's (1952) pioneering work in the field of infant and child intellectual development revealed that a person's interactions with the environment lay the foundation for sensorimotor development (birth–24 months). According to Piaget, newborns rely on their reflexes to interact with the environment during the first substage of the sensorimotor period (birth–1 month). Over the next three months, however, the focus of interaction shifts to the infant's own body and primary circular reactions, patterns of random activity that are repeated because of their pleasurable consequences (e.g., thumb in one's mouth). Secondary circular reactions denote transition to the third substage of Piaget's sensorimotor period (4–9 months), where interactions with the environment are repeated because of their pleasurable consequences (e.g., banging a high-chair tray with one's hands). Intentional behavior surfaces in infants 9 to 12 months of age to the point where goals are established and pursued and object permanence is achieved. Substage 5 of the sensorimotor period (12–18 months) is marked by preliminary understanding of cause-effect relationships through tertiary circular reactions wherein the child employs trial and error to decipher the world and solve problems. A child might drop a wooden block, a metal spoon, and then a dish of oatmeal in order to experience the differing sounds and varying caregiver reactions associated with each event. The child begins to fully internalize the external environment with the construction of schemes during substage 6 (18–24 months).

The guiding principle of Piaget's model is the scheme, reflecting the interactive nature of his theoretical views on human cognitive development. A scheme can be defined as a consistent pattern of interaction stored in a person's semantic memory. The first schemes to emerge are largely visual in nature, but verbal schemata soon begin to dominate one's representations of the external environment. Baldwin (1990) has called attention to a pivotal scheme in the evolution of social cognition in young children—the relational scheme. Relational schemes are cognitive/affective representations of regularities in interpersonal patterns of interaction. The central elements of a relational scheme are (1) a self-scheme of how the self is perceived in the current interpersonal context; (2) schemes of the other people involved in the interaction; and (3) a dynamic transactional script describing the interpersonal relations that transpire between the interacting parties. Recently, Fehr, Baldwin, Collins, Patterson, and Benditt (1999) unearthed evidence of an interactive script for anger in undergraduate psychology students based on relational schemes that anticipate negative or provoking partner responses, even if there was no "objective" evidence for such a malignant interpretation of other people's intentions.

Piaget (1952) described two primary pathways by which schemes grow and develop: assimilation and accommodation. Assimilation involves the incorporation of new information or experience into an existing scheme. Accommodation, on the other hand, requires modification of an existing scheme to symbolize an experience for which no meaningful scheme exists. The dynamic interaction of assimilation and accommodation propagates the cognitive system. Using the analogy of eating, accommodation can be equated with food intake and assimilation with digestion. Both are necessary functions in the sense that food must be digested to have any nutritional value, and digestion cannot occur in the absence of consumption. Problems arise in cognitive development, as they do in nutrition, in the presence of chronic imbalance between assimilation and accommodation. Effective thinking and cognitive growth demand that both assimilation and accommodation be featured in one's interactions with the outside world. These two interrelated processes, with roots in sensorimotor circular reactions, create the mental representations that permit humans to conceive of others as intentional beings with minds of their own and themselves as active negotiators of their own reality.

The social nature of a child's interactions with the environment is portrayed by the concept of joint attention. Joint attention is the incorporation of outside entities into a child's interactions with others and is normally classified in terms of sharing, following, and directing attention. Sharing attention or joint engagement means that the child and an adult simultaneously address the same object, the child often looking back and forth between the adult and object. Joint engagement normally appears by age 8 or 9 months (Saxon, Frick, & Colombo, 1997), grows rapidly from this point, and peaks sometime between the ages of 14 and 18 months (Adamson & Bakeman, 1985). Following an adult's gaze or directional gesture (pointing) is another way that children demonstrate joint attention. This particular manifestation of joint attention is rarely found in children under the age of 9 months (Butterworth & Grover, 1990) and does not consistently appear until a child is 12 to 15 months of age (Morissette, Ricard, & Gouin-Décarie, 1995). Children seek to direct an adult's attention to an object by whining and reaching for the object (imperatives) or by pointing to the object (declaratives). Directing attention initially appears around 9–10 months of age but, like sharing and following attention, does not occur with any degree of regularity until a child is 12 to 15 months old (Bakeman & Adamson, 1986).

Research intimates that joint attention assists with the development of later social referencing, language, and theory of mind skills. It makes sense that joint attention and social referencing, in which a child looks into an adult's face for information about ambiguous events, would be related. In fact, some scholars conceptualize social referencing as a component of joint attention (Tomasello, 1999). A study of children with Down's syndrome, however, showed the presence of social referencing deficits with no corollary joint attention problems (Kasari, Freeman, Mandy, & Sigman, 1995). Language is another skill with roots in joint attention. In one study joint engagement between 15-month infants and their mothers effectively predicted the size of the child's vocabulary three months later (Smith, Adamson, & Bakeman, 1988). Results from a recent study suggest that joint attention may precede and facilitate the development of problem-solving and planning skills (de la Ossa & Gauvain, 2001). Joint attention may also have an effect on a child's ability to conceptualize people as intentional agents with their own thoughts, feelings, and ideas. A longitudinal analysis of two autistic and two normal children 2 to 6 years of age disclosed a strong relationship between earlier joint attention problems and later deficits in theory of mind task performance (Gattegno, Ionescu, Malvy, & Adrien, 1999).

Scrutinizing the responses of twenty-four American middle-class infants to monthly evaluations administered between the ages of 9 and 15 months, Carpenter, Nagell, and Tomasello (1998) determined that 9 to 12 months of age was when joint attention first appeared, followed shortly thereafter by language and communication skills. Although there were individual differences in the sequence of sociocognitive development for children participating in this study, the modal sequence began with attention sharing, followed by communicative gestures, attention following, imitative learning, and referential language. A third major finding uncovered by these investigators was that while the amount of time that children spent in joint attention with their mothers rose from 9 to 15 months, there were major interindividual differences and only modest intraindividual stability in joint attention over the six-month period of observation. Finally, a robust relationship surfaced between mother–infant joint attentional engagement and subsequent development of linguistic and nonlinguistic communication skills. As Tomasello (1999) points out, the significance of joint attention is that it epitomizes the child's ability to perceive other humans as intentional agents, which, in turn, makes cultural learning feasible and language, shared discourse, and tool use attainable.

ATTACHMENT AND SOCIAL REFERENCING

It has been surmised from research conducted on hospital patients anticipating major surgery (Kulik & Mahler, 1989) and college students waiting to participate in anxiety-provoking laboratory experiments (Luminet, Bouts, Delie, Manstead, & Rimé, 2000) that fear and stress elicit affiliation. As was described in an earlier section of this chapter, sociability may have a genetic-evolutionary foundation. Only several hours after birth, neonates display preference for patterned visual stimuli and moving patterns and gaze significantly longer at facial stimuli than nonsocial stimuli (Johnson, Dziurawiec, Bastrip, & Morton, 1992). Innate facial expressions, like smiling, anger, and fear, are designed to keep the caregiver close, aver supporters of attachment theory, for connection to the caregiver is essential for the newborn's survival (Izard et al., 1995). Attachment relationships consequently serve the evolutionary tested function of protecting the vulnerable newborn from perishing in the harsh external environment. Attachment also furnishes one with a secure base from which to explore the world, which, in turn, lays the groundwork for future self-reliance (Bowlby, 1969/1982, 1980).

John Bowlby (1969/1982) called attention to the importance of child–caregiver attachment in the development of later interpersonal relationships. Bowlby's approach is based on two assumptions: (1) a responsive and accessible caregiver provides the child with a secure base from which to investigate the environment; and (2) early bonding experiences are introjected and become working models for future friendships and romantic relationships. There are four phases of attachment, according to Bowlby. Initially, the child engages in indiscriminate social responsiveness marked by a general orientation to all human stimuli. Next, the child becomes increasingly more discriminating in response to social stimuli, distinguishing between familiar and unfamiliar people, something that ordinarily occurs between the ages of 4 and 6 months. The principal objective of the third phase of attachment is proximity seeking, whereby the child actively seeks contact with familiar people, a process normally observed in children between the ages of 7 and 36 months. Finally, a goal-connected partnership is formed in which the child endeavors to predict the caregiver's movements in order to maintain close physical proximity and anticipate the caregiver's absence (Bowlby, 1980).

Building on Bowlby's work, Mary Salter Ainsworth developed a psychometric measure of attachment known as the "strange situation," which assesses the child's reaction to eight increasingly more stressful situations involving the introduction of a stranger and separation from the caregiver (Ainsworth, Blehar, Waters, & Wall, 1978). Scores on the "strange situation" are used to classify children into three global categories of attachment: secure, avoidant, and anxious/ambivalent. Secure infants adaptively endure brief periods of separation from the caregiver and allow strangers to approach provided the caregiver is in close proximity. Children classified as secure are described by others as curious, happy, and confident and normally enjoy positive intimate relationships in adolescence and adulthood. Avoidant children, on the other hand, seem unaffected by the approaching stranger or separation from the caregiver. These children are more often characterized as detached, aloof, and emotionally uninvolved and generally avoid intimate relationships in later life. Finally, anxious-ambivalent children experience extreme separation anxiety when the caregiver leaves, and strong stranger anxiety when a stranger approaches and are difficult to comfort once upset. Anxious-ambivalent children are often deathly afraid of unfamiliar situations and as adults have trouble maintaining long-term intimate relationships because they demand closeness yet resist others' overtures for intimacy (Ainsworth, 1979, 1989; Hazan & Shaver, 1987).

Attachment style is determined by characteristics of both the child and caregiver and is shaped by a plethora of contextual factors. The mothers of securely attached children tend to be more affectionate (Bates, Maslin, & Frankel, 1985), accepting (Benn, 1986), and positive (Roggman, Langlois, & Hubbs-Tait, 1987) in their interactions with their child than the mothers of less securely attached children. Alternatively, maternal alcohol consumption (O'Connor, Sigman, & Brill, 1987) and depression (Field, Healy, Goldstein, & Guthertz, 1990) correspond with insecure attachment in affected offspring. Attachment has been known to correlate inversely with later delinquency, but research suggests that lack of closeness to the father is a better predictor of male delinquency than lack of closeness to the mother (Johnson, 1987). Certain characteristics of the child also influence the quality of child–caregiver relationship. Goldsmith and Alansky (1987) ascertained that child temperament was as effective in predicting child–mother attachment as a cross-section of maternal characteristics in a meta-analysis of the attachment literature. Irritability and attention—corollaries of emotionality and activity level, respectively—may be two of the more salient features of temperament with relevance to attachment (Bell, 1990). Contextual factors from family dysfunction (Mothersead, Kivlighan, & Wynkoop, 1998), to the quality of the mother–father relationship (Gloger-Tippelt, & Huerkamp, 1998) also effect the strength of the child–caregiver bond. Attachment, then, is a dynamic consequence of the reciprocal child–caregiver relationship established within a specific social context.

Beginning around the tenth or twelfth month of life, infants start looking to adults when faced with an ambiguous object or event. By monitoring their parents' emotional reactions to ambiguous stimuli, children learn how to think, feel, and act (Feinman, 1985). This process, commonly referred to as social referencing, is firmly grounded in joint attentional skills and is typically studied in three stages. First, a novel stimulus like a stranger, mechanical toy, or moderate visual cliff is presented to the child. Next, an adult, typically the child's mother, is instructed to simulate a positive or negative emotional response. Once this is accomplished, the child's emotional and behavioral response to the stimulus is measured. A group of 8- to 9-month-old infants whose mothers were instructed to show joy upon seeing a stranger were more likely to approach the stranger than infants whose mothers feigned worry (Boccia & Campos, 1989). Likewise, 76% of the 12-month-old infants whose mothers smiled as the child approached a twelve-inch visual cliff crossed the cliff as compared to none of the infants whose mothers simulated fear (Sorce, Emde, Campos, & Klinnert, 1985). Social referencing occurs in familiar (day care) as well as unfamiliar (laboratory) settings (Walden & Baxter, 1989), whether the caregiver's reactions are constrained or freely given (Rosen, Adamson, & Bakeman, 1992).

Bowlby maintains that close physical proximity to the mother affords the child a secure base from which to explore the environment. However, the mother's emotional response, as communicated in her face and voice, must also be widely available to the child. Without access to the mother's emotional reaction, the child will be confused as to how to interpret many of the ambiguous stimuli to which he or she is exposed. Social referencing, perhaps because it merges affect, cognition, and behavior, appears to facilitate a child's preliminary understanding of causal relationships (Desrochers, Ricard, Décarie, & Allard, 1994). It should also be noted that even though mothers have been studied nearly exclusively in research on social referencing, children also look to their fathers and friendly strangers to make sense out of life's uncertainties. Hirshberg and Svejda (1990) report that 12-month-old infants seek greater physical proximity to their mothers when highly stressed but divide their attention equally between their mothers and fathers when searching for guidance on how to interpret ambiguous situations. Klinnert, Emde, Butterfield, and Campos (1986) learned that friendly strangers can also serve a social referencing function for young children.

Individual differences appear to influence and interact with the social referencing process. Ten-month-old infants projecting an "easy" temperament evinced greater responsiveness to maternal facial/emotional cues than children classified as "difficult" (Feinman & Lewis, 1983). Bradshaw, Goldsmith, and Campos (1987), in contrast, failed to detect a consistent relationship between a global measure of temperament and self-referencing in a group of 12-month-old children. Employing a more specific estimate of temperament and dividing their sample into two age groups (11–15 months, 16–22 months), Blackford and Walden (1998) discovered that the parents' reactions were colored by a consideration of their child's temperament and gender and that they typically tailored their messages to the individual child's fearfulness and gender. Blackford and Walden uncovered an interaction between gender and temperament, with parents supplying higher-quality positive and lower-quality fear messages to temperamentally fearful boys. Younger children in the high temperamental fear group did not use social information transmitted by parents as well as children assigned to the low temperamental fear group. Older temperamentally fearful children, however, failed to differ from their less fearful age-mates on the social referencing task, perhaps because the child or parent had learned to compensate for the interference engendered by a fearful temperament.

Two competing theoretical explanations have been offered as explanations for the social referencing effect. The social referencing hypothesis holds that the effect is specific to the object or event targeted by the referring adult, whereas the mood modification hypothesis posits that the referee institutes a general emotional climate that helps configure the child's attitude toward the overall environment. Research upholding the social referencing hypothesis should indicate an effect specific for the referenced object or event that does not extend to the rest of the child's environment; backing for the mood modification hypothesis, on the other hand, should reveal a generalized emotional effect. Hornik, Risenhoover, and Gunnar (1987) marshaled support for the social referencing interpretation in a survey of infants confronted with a new toy in that the emotional response did not generalize to other objects in the environment. Zarbatany and Lamb (1985), by way of contrast, unearthed support for the mood modification hypothesis. In a recent evaluation of forty-eight 1-year-old infants randomly assigned to one of four maternal message conditions, Stenberg and Hagekull (1997) found that vocally and facially delivered messages directed at a target provoked a specific effect, in line with the social referencing hypothesis, but that general, facially delivered messages produced a general effect, congruent with the mood modification hypothesis. It would seem that social referencing and mood modification both occur, their relative impact depending on the nature of the referee's communication.

LANGUAGE AND PRIVATE SPEECH

Language is a structured system of sounds used by a group of individuals to communicate among themselves. Language consists of phonemes (sounds), morphemes (meaning), and syntax (rules). A child goes from babbling and cooing to holophrastic speech at 10–12 months, when meaning is conveyed through word-action couplings, to speaking simple two-word sentences at 18–24 months, to communicating in multiword sentences shortly after the second birthday (Bigner, 1994). There are two major theories of language development. First, there are the nativistic theories in which language structure is viewed as innate and highly modularized. This is perhaps most clearly represented by Chomsky's (1968) inherent language acquisition device (LAD), which is said to structure the child's early verbalizations. A second theoretical perspective on language acquisition holds that language is an associational process in which words are paired with salient environmental stimuli and that syntax is learned through reinforcement, shaping, and modeling (Smith, 1995). The position adopted in this book is that innate structures and learning interact to form the syntax for speech and that content is a function of social influences to the extent that language creates a shared reality for those who use it to communicate with one another (Krauss &

Fussell, 1996).

Language not only promotes a shared reality but actually contours a person's belief systems. The linguistic relativity hypothesis asserts that "language embodies an interpretation of reality and language can influence thought about that reality" (Lucy, 1997: 294). Cultures invent language, which affects belief systems, which, in turn, affect culture. Miller (1984) asked urban children and adults from the United States and India to narrate and explain two prosocial and deviant behaviors and noted that the 8-year-old children in both cultures named dispositional and situational causes equally, whereas American adults stressed disposition causes, and Indian adults made more situational attributions, especially when deviant behavior was being discussed. The Asian mentality, based largely on Buddhist and Confucian teachings, is more situationally inclined than that of the United States, where an Occidental doctrine prevails (Lillard, 1999). Interestingly, children from rural America give more situational explanations for behavior than children from urban America, denoting that their attributional styles are more similar to that of Asian adults than to that of American adults (Lillard, Zeljo, & Harlan, 1998). This would seem to suggest that culture, language, and belief systems are enmeshed in a complex web of reciprocal influences that can be disentangled only by taking into account developmentally based changes in social cognition.

Lev Semenovich Vygotsky (1934/1986), the Russian developmental psychologist, rejected Piaget's conceptualization of private speech as a sign of presocial egocentrism, choosing instead to view it as an instrument of social and intellectual development. Vygotsky construed private speech as a species-specific interaction between thought and language that assists young children in mastering both their behavior and the environment. Using the analogy of a two-sided mirror, Vygotsky argued that private speech reflects a child's history of social linguistic interactions, on one side, and potential for cognitive self-direction in the form of planning and monitoring, on the other side. This illustrates how a social process (communication with an adult) can be transformed into a cognitive process (interaction with oneself). Private speech has been observed in children as young as 2 years of age and as old as 10 years of age (Berk & Garvin, 1984) but peaks between the ages of 4 and 5 years, typically becoming completely internalized by the time a child is 7 to 8 years of age (Diaz & Lowe, 1987). Berk (1992) estimates that private speech accounts for 20% to 50% of the total audible utterances of children 4 to 8 years of age. Adults can help children make more effective use of private speech through a technique known as scaffolding, a nondirective interactive style designed to facilitate a child's problem-solving skills by encouraging autonomy and self-reliance (Berk & Winsler, 1995).

Scaffolding and private speech mediate the transition between collaborative and independent problem solving, while maturity bridges the gap between overt private speech and covert private speech. Winsler (1998) advises that the internalization of private speech is associated with increased behavioral self-regulation. The internalization of private speech grows rapidly between early and middle childhood and is instrumental in promoting effective task performance (Berk & Spuhl,

1995). Failure to internalize private speech may produce a higher than average rate of overt private speech in late preschool children. This has been witnessed in children with attention deficit disorders (Berk & Potts, 1991) and in children identified by their preschool teachers as exhibiting significant behavioral problems (Winsler, Diaz, McCarthy, Atencio, & Chabay, 1999). Children judged by their kindergarten teachers as autonomous and academically advanced, by comparison, generate significantly more task-relevant metacognitive (self-monitoring, self-reinforcing) private speech than their more dependent and less academically inclined peers (Manning, White, & Daugherty, 1994).

Girls and middle-class children manifest more mature forms of private speech than boys and lower-class children (Berk, 1986; Berk & Garvin, 1984). Creative children also tend to display higher levels of private speech (Daugherty, White, & Manning, 1994). Patrick and Abravanel (2000) studied a small group of 3- to 5-year-old children and discovered that private speech served an adaptive function by helping the children focus their attention, rehearse their plans, pace their activities, and reassure themselves. Older children participating in this study used less overt private speech than younger children, an outcome attributed to the fact that the older children had made the transition to covert private speech. Contextually, private speech increases with task difficulty, implying that children make extensive use of private speech when attempting to overcome obstacles (Berk & Landau, 1997). Certain environments may be more conducive to the production of private speech than other environments. In an observational study of preschool children, Krafft and Berk (1998) determined that children attending a traditional preschool generated twice as much private speech as children enrolled in a Montessori school which provided fewer opportunities for unstructured play and fantasy activity. Open-ended play and free fantasy evoke more private speech because they challenge the child to set new goals and construct self-regulatory strategies in a manner similar to that of children exposed to effective parental scaffolding.

Language and private speech serve vital sociocognitive functions. In order to act purposefully, the human organism must possess stable internal representations or mental models of the external environment (Johnston & Hawley, 1994). The internalization process that begins with early interactions and joint attention and is fostered by attachment relationships and social referencing comes to fruition with the introduction of language and private speech. Language furnishes the symbols that open up lines of communication with other people and afford children the opportunity to benefit from the cultural experiences of the wider social environment. Private speech begins as a social interaction but soon becomes an internalized process through which children learn to monitor and regulate their behavior. Sociocognitive development, as represented by language and private speech, means joining the inner and outer worlds with symbolic mental representations. Without these representations there would be no shared experience, cultural learning, or belief system development.

We know that private speech becomes internalized as a child matures. However, there has been a conspicuous lack of scientific speculation on the role of private speech in the lives of older children, adolescents, and adults. Dennett's (1991) theory of brain function and Blachowicz's (1998) philosophical treatise on inner speech are two noteworthy exceptions to this general trend. Blachowicz maintains that inner speech is a genuine dialogue between independent interests of experienced meaning, one typically better articulated than the other, with neither subordinate to the other. Dennett contends that brain lateralization holds the key to discerning inner speech, with the serial processing of the left hemisphere being the more articulate partner in the internal dialogue and the parallel processing of the right hemisphere serving as the "silent" partner. The private speech of early and middle childhood evolves into the self-talk that cognitive-behavioral therapists seek to comprehend and challenge in clients. Based on the work of Blachowicz and Dennett, it is speculated that self-talk is grounded in an active dialogue between two parties dialectically engaged in basic problem solving. The problem may be nothing more than an ambiguous situation, but given the impact that private speech has on a child's metacognitive and executive skills, it would seem that self-talk is of cardinal significance in supplying people with a sense of environmental control and predictability.

THEORY OF MIND AND PERSPECTIVE TAKING

By the time most children have turned 4 years old, they have formed a preliminary understanding of mind to where they conceptualize a person's actions in terms of thoughts, feelings, and motives (Cadinu & Kiesner, 2000). Imputing intentions and other mental states to other people is commonly referred to as theory of mind. John Flavell (2000) traces a child's theory of mind to acquisition of intentionality late in the first year of life, made possible by a child's mastery of joint attention. Social referencing and language are additional steps in configuring a child's theory of mind (Bretherton, 1991). Bartsch and Wellman (1995) outline the four primary elements of a theory of mind: (1) appreciation of the difference between mental events and physical objects; (2) discernment of the causal connection between mental states and the external world; (3) comprehension that how we view the world and how the world really is are not the same and that two people can perceive the same object or situation differently; (4) acknowledgment that people represent their own views and perceptions of the world in a process known as meta-representation.

A child's theory of mind is ordinarily evaluated using one of three principal research strategies: false beliefs, appearance-reality, or level 2 visual perspective taking (Flavell, 2000). In a false belief task the child is presented with an event that conflicts with perceived reality (e.g., cookies in a pencil box; object is moved to a new location when a third party is not present) and asked what another child might think the box contains or where the third party will look for the object once he or she returns. A child who responds by stating that another child would probably think that there were pencils in the box or that the third party would look for the object in the place where it was before it was moved is demonstrating an appreciation of mind. Appearance-reality tests, on the other hand, confront the child with an object that appears to be something other than what it is (e.g., a sponge made to look like a rock). A child passes the appearance-reality test if he or she can identify the object as a sponge, even though it has been made to look like a rock. Finally, level 2 visual perspective taking entails asking the child to estimate how a stimulus (e.g., picture book that is face up to the child but upside down to an observer sitting across the table from the child) might be perceived by another person. Children who are able to successfully solve these theory of mind tests fathom that belief is independent of reality, that appearances can sometimes be deceiving, and that people retain differing perspectives of the same object or event.

Theory of mind, as the reader may have already gathered, is an evolving concept. According to Perner (1991), a child goes from a copy theory of mind, marked by the assumption of direct correspondence between belief and reality, to an interpretive representational theory of mind in which it is understood that belief and reality are not the same thing. Flavell and his colleagues report that children normally realize that other people have desires different from their own before they surmise that other people have beliefs different from their own (Flavell, Green, & Flavell, 1990). Concluding that people act on the basis of their wants and desires is not the same as recognizing that they are motivated by intricate and sometimes contradictory thoughts and beliefs. Research indicates that by age 3 years there is a discernible shift in which the child moves from a simple desire theory of mind to a more complex belief-desire theory of mind (Wellman, 1990). Emotional understanding is another way that children demonstrate an appreciation of mind. Research discloses that while perceiving the relationship between emotion and behavior and solving a false belief task are clearly related, they are probably best viewed as distinct aspects of social cognition (Cutting & Dunn, 1999). The alleged continuity of these sociocognitive skills is reinforced by longitudinal data revealing stable patterns of individual differences in a child's appreciation of emotions and false beliefs (Hughes & Dunn, 1998).

Contextual factors may be particularly crucial in encouraging an evolving theory of mind in young children. Cooperation with siblings (Dunn, Brown, Slomkowski, Tesla, & Youngblade, 1991) and social pretend play with mothers and siblings (Youngblade & Dunn, 1995) measured at 33 months of age reliably predicted false belief performance and emotional understanding at 40 months. Young children who simply have more siblings to interact with experience greater success on false belief tasks than children with few or no siblings (Perner, Ruffman, & Leekam, 1994). More deaf children than normal preschoolers, handicapped children, or mentally retarded children fail theory of mind tests. Peterson and Siegel (2000) speculate that deaf children have trouble with theory of mind tasks because they are prevented from participating in the abstract family discussions on mental states to which most non-hearing-impaired children are exposed. Early attachment is another contextual factor with implications for development of a child's theory of mind. Secure attachment corresponds with strong performance on false belief tasks at 4 years and superior mentalizing ability at 5 years (Meins, Fernyhough, Russell, & Clark-Carter, 1998). The authors of this study postulate that the outcomes that they obtained reflect a tendency on the part of the securely attached child's mother to treat the child as an individual with a mind. The mother's education and occupational class as well as the father's occupational class may also facilitate a child's acquisition of theory of mind (Cutting & Dunn, 1999).

Language skills (Hughes & Dunn, 1997) and verbal ability (Happé, 1995) are person characteristics associated with theory of mind development and a child's performance on false belief tasks. As was mentioned in Chapter 1, the integrated-interactive theory of lifestyles assumes that relationships are reciprocal in the absence of convincing evidence to the contrary. Astington and Jenkins (1999) tested the reciprocity hypothesis in fifty-nine preschoolers administered language and theory of mind measures on three separate occasions, 3.5 months apart, over the course of the nursery school year. The results of this investigation showed that language competence predicted theory of mind but that theory of mind did not predict language competence. The syntactic or structural features of language seemed to be the best predictors of theory of mind performance in this study. Although more research is necessary to properly evaluate the relationship between language competence and theory of mind, the outcome of the Astington and Jenkins study suggests that language is an important precursor of a child's theory of mind and that the structural aspects of language permit children to impute intentionality to fellow humans. Accordingly, the presence of mental terminology in a child's vocabulary has been found to correlate meaningfully with performance on false belief tasks (Brown, Doneland-McCall, & Dunn, 1996).

Three families of theory have been advanced to explain theory of mind phenomena. Proponents of nativist-modular theory contend that humans are equipped with an innate processing mechanism that fosters awareness of mental states (Scholl & Leslie, 1999). Improved performance on theory of mind tasks with age is attributed to maturational changes in this innate processor. The principal argument against nativist-modular theories is that they fail to account for the wide cross-cultural variations that have been documented with respect to theory of mind (Lillard, 1999). Simulation theory subscribes to a contrary view. From the perspective of simulation theorists, people grasp the concept of mind by role taking or imagining themselves in another person's situation (Harris, 1995). Developmental changes in theory of mind occur because people's simulation skills improve as they gain experience with role taking. The primary criticism leveled against simulation theory is that it is based on a Cartesian view that would have children achieving introspective insight into their own mental states (Perner & Howes, 1992). The third major model used to explain theory of mind research is theory theory. According to patrons of theory theory, people use folk psychology to construct a theorylike body of knowledge about mental processes that helps them interpret other people's behavior (Wellman & Gelman, 1998). Development emanates from the accumulated experience achieved through interaction with the environment. Even though it has been criticized for mistaking personal relatedness for theory (Hobson, 1991), theory theory is the explanation believed to have the most to offer an integrated-interactive theory of crime.

George Herbert Mead (1934) once argued that role taking underlies all social interaction, for it makes person perception possible. Children as young as 2 and 3 years of age direct simpler speech to a younger sibling than to a parent (Dunn & Kendrick, 1982), and children who are 3 and 4 years of age have been known to adjust their language and vocabulary when communicating with a mildly delayed peer (Guralnick & Paul-Brown, 1989). A child's ability to construct meaning from a wordless picture book rests, in part, on his or her ability to assume another person's perspective (Crawford & Hade, 2000). These findings denote the presence of an incipient capacity for social perspective taking in children 2 to 4 years of age. Social perspective taking, which can be defined as the ability to view a situation from the perspective of another, may be a necessary prerequisite for the development of emotional empathy. Conduct-disordered children (Happé & Frith, 1996) and adults classified as psychopathic (Blair et al., 1996) perform within the normal range on false belief tasks, although this does not mean that their sociocognitive skills are intact. A more finely tuned analysis is required with an emphasis on perspective taking.

Deborah Richardson and her colleagues note that perspective taking inhibits aggressive responding under conditions of moderate threat (Richardson, Hammock, Smith, Gardner, & Signo, 1994) and that perspective taking not only inhibits aggressive/negative responding but also maintains nonaggressive/positive responding in the face of attack (Richardson, Green, & Lago, 1998). Chronic peer rejection may interfere with the maturation of perspective-taking skills by encouraging the formation of aggressive biases and attributions (Badenes, Estevan, & Bacete, 2000). Through repeated interaction with the environment, children labeled with conduct disorders and adults diagnosed with psychopathy may forge attributions that interfere with their perspective-taking ability and make antisocial acting out seem a reasonable solution to their problems.

A robust relationship has been recorded between social perspective taking, on the one hand, and emotional empathy and prosocial behavior, on the other hand, in primary school children (Bengtsson & Johnson, 1992; Garner, 1996). Distinguishing between cognitive perspective taking—defined as the ability to recognize and understand another person's thoughts—and affective perspective taking—defined as the ability to recognize and understand another person's feelings—Oswald (1996) surveyed a group of working adults enrolled in evening college classes. Oswald found that participants who engaged in affective perspective taking were more willing to volunteer their time to counsel fellow students than participants adopting a cognitive approach to perspective taking. Whereas affective perspective takers were more likely to engage in altruistic helping than cognitive perspective takers, there were no group differences in empathy. Hughes, White, Sharpen, and Dunn (2000) discovered that neither performance on a false belief task nor affective perspective taking differentiated between "hard-to-manage" preschoolers and a group of control children, although the "hard-to-manage" children did exhibit weaker executive control. There is evidence from another study that perspective taking may correspond with executive control and metacognition (Tarshis & Shore, 1991). These latter two findings hint at a possible link between theory of mind and people's ability to control their actions through private speech.

CONCLUSION

The principal aim of this chapter was to illustrate how evolution/genetics, early interaction/joint attention, attachment/social referencing, language/private speech, and theory of mind/perspective taking form a sequence responsible for the development of belief systems and people's views of reality (see Figure 2.2). The elements of this sequence interact with one another, sometimes in unidirectional fashion but, more often than not, reciprocally to erect the sociocognitive conditions conducive to the creation of criminal belief systems. Genetics and evolution merge to produce an organism prepared for social contact. This innate motivational trend is contoured around early interactions with the social and nonsocial environments, particularly interactions of a joint attention nature, between the ages of 6 and 18 months. Between 9 and 24 months of age attachment and social referencing rise to prominence. The nascent belief systems that ensue from these interactions then receive additional input from the child's developing language skills and growing ability to engage in private speech between 24 and 48 months. Early belief systems begin to solidify around the age of 48 to 60 months, when the child acquires a theory of mind and learns how to adopt another's perspective. Through an interaction of these differing developmental tasks and influences, the child attains self-awareness, considered by the integrated-interactive theory to be the forerunner of the guiding belief system, the self-view.

Self-awareness is not viewed as an exclusive characteristic of the individual. Rather, it is an evolving construct with origins in people's interactions with the internal and external environments. In studies where mothers were instructed to surreptitiously place rouge on their child's nose and then turned the child to face a mirror, only the 18- to 24-month-old children were able to reliably locate the mark on their noses, thereby signaling the presence of an objective self-concept (Lewis & Brooks-Gunn, 1979). Povinelli, Landau, and Perilloux (1996) had experimenters surreptitiously place stickers on the foreheads of 2-, 3-, and 4-year-old children and then after a three-minute delay presented the child with a videotaped recording of the marking event. Whereas 75% of the 4-year-olds reached up to touch the sticker, none of the 2-year-olds did so, and only 25% of the 3-year-olds reached up to touch the area where the sticker had been placed. These authors concluded that young children have a temporally restricted sense of self that does not achieve reasonable continuity until a child is at least 4 years of age. Making a number of methodological refinements, Zelazo, Sommerville, and Nichols (1999) repeated the Povinelli et al. study and determined that a 3-year-old child's lack of ability to use delayed feedback may not be confined to the self and that children this age may have trouble reasoning about all delayed representations. Findings from the Zelazo

Figure 2.2
Proposed Sequence of Sociocognitive Developmental Influences

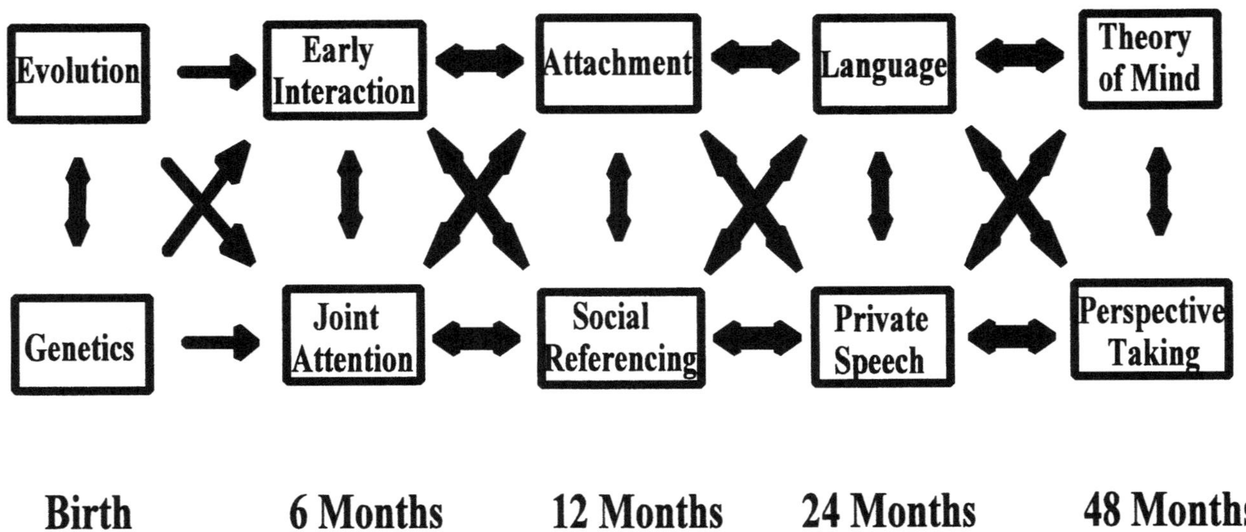

et al. study imply that the self is represented in a manner similar to how external objects and events are represented. The difference, according to the integrated-interactive theory outlined in this text, is that most external representations are organized around, or referenced, by self representations.

Self-awareness, being the framework around which other belief systems are configured, is of paramount significance in clarifying the inner workings of the criminal mind. Beliefs about self relative to crime are what fuels the lifestyle. Each of the five major developmental milestones described in this chapter impacts self-awareness. Separation from the external environment supplies the evolutionary motivation for both self-awareness and existential fear. Early social interactions and joint attention support self-awareness by linking the child to others through shared observation. Seibert, Sliwin, and Hogan (1986), in fact, identified a connection between joint attention and social schemes of self in a group of 6- to 27-month-old children. Attachment and social referencing promote self-awareness, as was demonstrated by a group of 3-year-old children who used social referencing to concoct and access internal representations of parental affect as a means of regulating their own behavior and making sense of ambiguous stimuli (Emde, Biringen, Clyman, & Oppenheim, 1991). Language and private speech likewise contribute to the development of self-awareness. Morin (1995) reports that self-awareness was mediated by private speech and self-talk in a group of eighty five Canadian college students whereby high rates of self-talk were associated with more complex self-concepts. Theory of mind is no less important in organizing self-awareness. Frith and Happé (1999) note that children with autism normally perform poorly on false belief and introspective tasks but that higher-functioning autistic children display stronger theory of mind and self-consciousness skills than lower-functioning autistic children.

In closing this chapter, it may be helpful to review what we have learned about belief systems in the course of early sociocognitive development. First, a belief system is a person's view or perception of reality through which he or she acts on the internal and external environments. A belief system, rather than being a characteristic of the individual, mirrors a person's interactions with the environment. Second, belief systems are the embodiment of schemes comprising sensory, affective, behavioral, motivational, and cognitive elements. These schemes interact, and their interactions spawn global and increasingly more integrated belief systems. Third, belief systems evolve and develop within a social context. As such, people's interactions underpin their perceptions of self, world, past, present, and future. Social interaction drives personal and collective meaning (Ickes & Gonzalez, 1994), while self-awareness, a product of sociocognitive development, is the reference point for future belief system development. Fourth, the relationships that form between different schemes within a belief system are often reciprocal. As a case in point, Teasdale (1993), in presenting his interacting cognitive subsystems (ICS) model of depression, describes how a depressed mood can have as much effect on a person's thinking as thinking has on a person's mood. This same relationship has been obtained with emotion-driven violent assault (Lopez &

Emmer, 2000). Finally, belief systems are dynamic processes that self-alter in response to changing environmental contingencies. In fact, belief system stagnation is the hallmark of a lifestyle. The manner in which belief systems congruent with crime evolve and take root is explored in the next chapter.

3

Belief Systems and Crime

There is a growing trend on the part of criminologists to treat delinquency and adult crime as separate and distinct categories of rule-violating behavior. While it is true that a majority of delinquent careers last less than a year (Elliott, Huizinga, & Morse, 1988) and that a fair number of adult criminals have no record of prior juvenile arrest (Walters, 1990), there is evidence of a temporal link between the two patterns. In a cohort of Philadelphian males followed for twenty years beginning at age 10, it was discerned that 51% of the cohort members with a juvenile record also had an adult arrest record, whereas just 18% of cohort members with no juvenile record had been arrested as adults. Furthermore, participants with more extensive histories of juvenile delinquency were responsible for more severe adult crimes (Wolfgang, Thornberry, & Figlio, 1987). In a related study, three-fifths of a large cohort of juvenile offenders from Columbus, Ohio, made the transition to serious adult law-breaking (Hamparian, Davis, Jacobson, & McGraw, 1985). An earlier study had found that 61% of a group of young male Londoners with juvenile convictions were later convicted of an adult offense, relative to a 13% rate of adult conviction for young males with no prior record of juvenile convictions (Farrington, 1979).

Continuity may go back even further than adolescence since research shows that children who suffer from early onset conduct disorder are at increased risk for severe and "life-course persistent" patterns of antisocial behavior (Moffitt, 1993a). Even with a number of turning points and transitions marking the progression from early onset conduct disorder to later criminality (Sampson & Laub, 1993), there is undoubtedly some degree of continuity in the behavioral patterns that evolve from criminal belief systems. Since a lifestyle is, in essence, a series of interrelated belief systems, it would make sense that these belief systems are instrumental in promoting continuity between conduct disorders, delinquency, and adult crime. The general attitude that permeates criminal belief systems (Reicher & Emler, 1985) is what positions conduct disorders, delinquency, and adult crime along the same continuum. This general attitude and the belief systems that spring from it are described next, using examples borrowed from the conduct disorder, delinquency, and adult criminality literatures.

SEEING IS BELIEVING AND BELIEVING IS REALITY

It is a fundamental tenet of the integrated-interactive theory that people construct their own realities and then proceed to defend these realities against alternative perspectives. Objective reality has no real value or meaning in this model, for people view themselves, the surrounding environment, and time through a prism fashioned from their personal dispositions and experiences. Consequently, we all believe that our particular brand of reality is the correct one; metaphorically, our very existence depends on it. As research to be reviewed later in this chapter suggests, a negative self-view is much less threatening than disconfirmation of a negative self-view. The point at which people believe their version of reality to be incorrect is the point at which they begin to change their view of reality. In this section we examine how people construct and defend their personalized versions of reality and how this leads to the creation of belief systems.

Reality Construction and Defense

Constructing Reality

The integrated-interactive approach holds that reality is invented rather than discovered. As such, there is no such thing as objective reality, just the separate realities of each individual person (Hare-Mustin & Marecek, 1988). In keeping with the overall theme of Chapter 2, it is postulated that people construct reality via a social interactive process. The child initially adopts the constructed realities of others—primarily parents and older siblings—using impressions recounted in stories, fables, directives, and teachings, the validity of which the child accepts on faith. These are called mythical constructions. Mythical constructions are sources of shared meaning, inspiration, and personal empowerment (Krippner, 1986) that connect or join the individual to a larger collective. Indeed, mythical constructions are never totally abandoned, though they are supplemented by other forms or levels of construction as the child matures.

As a direct consequence of perceptual development and the acquisition of executive cognitive skills, the child attains the ability to internalize environmental experience on which he or she forges a personalized view of reality. An empirical level of reality construction is henceforth procured whereby children employ their personal experiences to shape their belief systems. George Kelly (1955), in outlining the hypothesis-testing parameters of reality construction, proclaimed that children compare and contrast the various aspects of their experience to produce personalized constructs that permit more effective interaction with the surrounding environment.

Some people do not move beyond an empirical level of reality construction. Those who do will make use of a third constructional style modeled after the teleological perspective. Teleological constructions attempt to organize and integrate one's mythical and empirical knowledge in an effort to make sense of larger patterns and ascertain wider meanings. Joseph Rychlak (1992) considers himself a teleologist and relies heavily on the dialectic approach in constructing his own version of reality, whereby a concept (thesis) is contrasted with its opposite (antithesis) to form a more integrated and meaningful whole (synthesis).

The fourth level of reality construction is dedicated to acquiring an epistemological understanding of one's experience. Epistemology is the study of the nature and origins of knowledge, and an epistemological construction is based on an appreciation of the relativity of knowledge and the natural limitations of any single method of data collection and analysis. An epistemological construction provides for humility and balance—humility in the sense that the person acknowledges that his or her perception of reality is only one of many possible views and balance in the sense that the person appreciates the necessity of using all four levels of reality construction (mythical, empirical, teleological, epistemological) to achieve superior results (survival).

Difficulties arise when one particular level of construction consistently reigns over the other three in a person's everyday decision making. There may be no such thing as objective reality, but some constructional arrangements are more congruent with the prime objective of life (survival) than others. An unbalanced constructional configuration, particularly one governed by mythical or empirical constructions, provokes constructional errors. Common errors of construction include arbitrary inference, dichotomous reasoning, magnification, minimization, overgeneralization, and personalization (Beck, Wright, Newman, & Liese, 1993), although other possibilities exist. The thinking of those who habitually engage in crime is marred by a number of these constructional errors.

Defending Reality

People not only construct their own realities, but also defend these realities against information incompatible with the underlying tenets of their belief systems. Whereas reality construction places a premium on accommodation, defense is predicated on the assimilation of new information into an existing scheme (Piaget, 1952). Incorporating some of the work of Freud (1894/1962) and Adler (1927) on defense mechanisms into the integrated-interactive approach, this book defines defense as a cognitive/affective process in which an internal or external stimulus incompatible with an existing scheme or belief system is identified and then reconciled with, and assimilated into, the incongruous scheme or belief system. Defense is designed to safeguard the integrity of existing schemes and belief systems and maintain continuity.

Just as there are four developmentally defined levels of construction, there are also four developmentally informed levels of defense. However, unlike the philosophy of science bent of the constructive function, defenses are organized along information-processing lines. The first and most primitive level of defense is denial. By ignoring and not symbolizing information incompatible with an existing belief system, one forecloses on the decision to use a higher-order defense or change the belief system. Denial allows us to ignore many of the stimuli that impinge on our senses each day and selectively direct our attention to those stimuli that we believe possess the most relevance to our survival, while simultaneously enhancing our self-esteem and identity (Janoff-Bulman & Timko, 1987). As long as it does not become excessive, denial can be a highly effective coping strategy.

The next rung of the defense ladder is occupied by the defensive style of distortion. This is because distortion requires a greater number of information-processing steps to enact than denial. In any event, distortion occurs when information incompatible with a belief system is modified or reinterpreted to augment its congruence with the belief system. Distortion can certainly promote survival, particularly in situations where people are confronted by information and experiences over which they have no control. Swann (1987) notes that distortion is a chief component of the self-verification process, which finds people distorting and reinterpreting feedback that clashes with their self-view in order to make the feedback more congruent with their self-view.

Diversion falls on a slightly higher plane than distortion to the extent that it typically requires several additional information-processing steps to enact. People use diversion to defend their view of reality by redirecting feelings meant for one target onto a more accessible or less threatening target, projecting blame onto another person, externalizing responsibility for a particular outcome onto an outside situation, or shifting attention to an alternative reality. Diversion can therefore be used to compensate for failure in one area by focusing on success in another area. As a case in point, Brown and Smart (1991) determined that participants who failed a test of intellectual ability were especially beneficent when given the opportunity to help another person.

The highest level of defense, owing to the fact that it requires the greatest number of information processing steps to enact, is justification/application. Information incompatible with an existing belief system does not have to be denied, distorted, or diverted to be neutralized. It can also be rationalized and incorporated into one's self- or world-view. Excuse making, although we often consider it an avoidance of responsibility, has been known to foster good physical health, guard against anxiety and depression, and improve performance on a variety of tasks (Snyder & Higgins, 1988). In many respects, excuse making and other forms of justification/application can be highly beneficial provided they do not become excessive and interfere with the daily operations of the constructive function.

The key to survival is balance: balance between the construction and defensive functions and balance within each function. A lack of balance, on the other hand, is an invitation to poor adaptability as personified by a rigid pattern or lifestyle. In the case of a criminal lifestyle, as with many lifestyles associated with the rebel family (Walters, 2000a), the defensive function prevails over the constructive function, mythical constructions govern the constructive function, and primitive defenses (denial, distortion) reign over more sophisticated defenses (justification/application). Imbalance lays the groundwork for constructional errors, rigid defenses, and criminal belief systems. The process by which these belief systems crystallize into a lifestyle congruent with crime may span several weeks, months, or even years but is believed to conform to the same basic, three-stage developmental sequence.

Belief System Development

The belief systems that protect a crime-congruent lifestyle from information incompatible with continuation of the lifestyle evolve in three phases: an initiation phase, a transitional phase, and a maintenance phase.

Initiation Phase

Lifestyle initiation is the combined result of three variables: incentive, opportunity, and choice. The incentive for lifestyle initiation is existential fear. As was mentioned in Chapter 2, three early life tasks are instrumental in molding a person's experience of existential fear: affiliation, prediction/control, and status. People in search of affiliation, control, or status are at increased risk for experimenting with a lifestyle to secure these outcomes since a lifestyle holds promise of acceptance and belonging, as might be achieved in interactions with fellow gang members; control, as might be realized in robbing another person at gunpoint; and status, as might be found in the respect that one's criminal reputation earns in the neighborhood. Incentive in the form of existential fear is thus integral to the construction of belief systems congruent with crime.

A second major influence on lifestyle initiation is opportunity. Opportunity can be realized through temperament, stress, socialization, and availability. It is speculated that temperaments high in emotionality and activity level and low in sociability and novelty seeking set the stage for interactions that could eventually lead to the advent of criminal belief systems. Environmental stress and strain may also play a major role in initiating a crime-congruent lifestyle, in part, because of the way it interacts with temperament. Socialization to criminal goals and lack of socialization to conventional goals also inspire criminal belief systems. Finally, growing up in an environment with easy access to criminal opportunities markedly improves a person's odds of experimenting with crime. It is important to remember that three of these factors correspond to four of the criminological theories described in Chapter 1: that is, stress-strain theory, poor socialization-social control theory, deviant socialization-differential association theory, and availability-drift theory.

No matter what incentive or opportunity factors may be operating in any particular situation, the individual is ultimately responsible for the choices that he or she makes in life, the third prong of the lifestyle initiation process. The choices that an individual makes and that give birth to lifestyles congruent with crime are often made relatively early in life, when people's decision-making skills are underdeveloped and they do not yet appreciate the full ramifications of their actions. This does not mean, however, that the individual did not make a decision or that he or she should not be held accountable for his or her actions. The integrated-interactive approach outlined in this book does not accentuate choice in an effort to place blame, but rather as a means of assigning responsibility to the only person capable of altering the destructive path he or she has taken—namely, the individual himself or herself. Accepting responsibility, according to the integrated-interactive theory, is the first step in the change process.

Transitional Phase

During the transitional phase of lifestyle development belief systems constructed during the initiation phase are reinforced and advanced. Though typically brief, the transitional phase is indispensable to the evolution of criminal belief systems in that it serves as a bridge between the initiation and maintenance phases; hence, the term transition. Outcome expectancies are a principal feature of the transitional phase of lifestyle development. People expect certain outcomes as a consequence of their involvement in criminal activity, some of which are positive and others of which are negative. A preponderance of positive over negative outcome expectancies for crime, particularly if the positive expectancies promise to resolve personal fears in the areas of affiliation, control, and status, will frequently spark the transition from crime initiation to crime maintenance. The formation of crime-congruent skills is equally significant in facilitating the transition from a pattern to a lifestyle. By becoming skilled in crime, the individual is rewarded for antisocial conduct and develops increased self-efficacy for crime.

Maintenance Phase

Belief systems during the maintenance phase of a lifestyle are rigid and self-perpetuating. Whereas the constructive function presides over the initiation phase, the defensive function prevails during the maintenance phase. Particulars that help maintain the belief systems hypothesized to underpin a crime-congruent lifestyle are fear of change, affect regulation, low self-efficacy for crime-incongruent activities, enabling interpersonal relationships, self-attributions and labeling, conditioning, possible physiological alterations, rituals, criminal thinking styles, and atrophy of crime-incongruent skills (Walters, 2000d). It should be noted that self-attributions and criminal thinking styles relate directly to two of the precursor theories described in Chapter 1—labeling and neutralization, respectively.

During the maintenance phase of a lifestyle four interactive styles emerge, two of which relate to a person's interactions with the internal environment and two of which pertain to a person's interactions with the external environment. The first of the two "internal" interactions concerns how internal standards of conduct are handled, which in the case of a criminal lifestyle involves regular bouts of *irresponsibility*. The second "internal" interaction is one's habitual manner of coping with affective stimuli, with a criminal lifestyle reflecting *self-indulgence* and the pursuit of immediate gratification. *Interpersonal intrusiveness*, the first of the two "external" interactive styles, is marked by a hostile, intrusive manner of social interaction. The second "external" interactive style is *social rule breaking*, whereby one habitually violates the rules of the home, neighborhood, school, or larger society. The four interactive styles can be assessed using the Lifestyle Criminality Screening Form (LCSF: Walters, White, & Denney, 1991).

CRIME-CONGRUENT SCHEMES

Schemes have traditionally been defined as cognitive phenomena, but this is a simplistic view that fails to due justice to the richness and complexity of schemes. Where schemes may be the foundation for what is commonly referred to as cognition, they are actually composed of interdependent sensory, behavioral, affective, and motivational elements. Each element of a scheme can be represented by a neuron or group of neurons, and each scheme is conceptualized as a node in a neural network. Circuits of schemes or nodes engender belief, and a series of interrelated beliefs constitutes a belief system. It is further reasoned that a single scheme may be embodied in two or more divergent beliefs and so may be distributed across different belief systems. Several of the principal categories of belief or schematic subnetworks are covered in this section, while the major belief systems are explored in the final section of this chapter.

Before reviewing attributions, expectancies, goals, values, and thinking styles, we would be well advised to consider the dimensions on which schemes are organized. One dimension on which a scheme can be ordered is valence. Valence is an evaluative dimension that can vary from extremely positive to extremely negative. In addition to an evaluative dimension, schemes can be organized by their complexity, from highly integrated and complex schemes, to schemes that are unintegrated and simple. Focus is a third dimension along which schemes are ordered. The dimension of focus assesses whether the scheme covers a broad range of topics or restricts itself to a narrow band of information. Each scheme and every belief system that is based on a scheme can be classified according to these three key dimensions of valence (positive-negative), complexity (high-low), and focus (narrow-broad).

A scheme is defined for the purposes of this book as a basic unit of meaning. As schemes develop, meanings change. Take, for instance, the scheme of dog. Small children will often categorize all four-legged animals as dogs since this is often the animal with whom they are most familiar. Initially, then, the scheme of dog is a simple construct broadly applied to all four-legged creatures, which may have positive or negative valence depending on the child's experience with four-legged animals. As the child grows, he or she learns to differentiate between animals and, may, in fact, learn to distinguish between dogs, constructing individual schemes for successive differentiations, each with its own associated valence. There is a tendency on the part of the evolving human organism to construct more narrow and integrated schemes as he or she interacts with the environment, particularly the social environment. This was illustrated in Chapter 2 by a child's realization of joint attention, social referencing, private speech, and theory of mind.

Attributions

Attributions are schemes designed to explain the causes of one's own or another's behavior. These schematic subnetworks have been traditionally organized along four dimensions: internal versus external, global versus specific, stable versus unstable, and controllable versus uncontrollable (Weiner, 1990). Compared to families of delinquents rated high in conflict, families of delinquents low in conflict manifest a shift in attributional style whereby they attribute each other's more positive actions to internal, global, and stable causes and less positive actions to external, specific, and unstable causes (Mas, Alexander, & Turner, 1991). Guerra, Huesmann, and Zelli (1993) add that attributing social failure to stable and controllable factors encourages the belief that physical aggression is justified in response to social failure. These two studies show that attributions may make a distinct contribution to the belief systems that initiate and sustain criminal and antisocial behavior. What needs to be clarified is which specific attributions are most supportive of crime.

According to the actor-observer hypothesis (Jones & Nisbett, 1971), people tend to attribute their own actions to external influences and other people's behavior to internal causes. Blaming external conditions can also be seen as reflecting a self-serving attributional bias in which one ascribes negative outcomes to factors outside oneself (Snyder, Stephan, & Rosenfield, 1978). Henderson and Hewstone (1984) witnessed both biases in forty-four violent offenders asked to explain their involvement in 226 separate incidents of violence. In this study 80% of the attributions for responsibility were externalized to the victim or situation. Fondacaro and Heller (1990) likewise determined that adolescent offenders made more external attributions of blame in an ambiguous problem situation than nonoffending youth. Studies by Di Fazio, Kroner, and Forth (1997) and Dolan (1995), as a point of contrast, were unable to document the presence of a consistent relationship between external attributions and aggressive criminality.

One variable that may moderate the relationship between external attributions and aggression is the perceived relevance of the situation. It is well known that aggressive children display perceptual and attributional biases in which they over-perceive hostile intentions on the part of others (Dodge, Pettit, McClasky, & Brown, 1986; Waas, 1988), but only when they feel personally threatened (Dodge & Frame, 1982). Externalization, it would seem, may embody a defensive reaction to a perceived threat to one's belief systems. Once responsibility has been externalized, the next step is to attribute hostile intentions to others. Viewing others as harboring hostile intent may reflect developmental obstacles in the evolution of an offender's theory of mind to where future offenders construct a suspicious and hypervigilant theory of "nasty minds" (Happé & Frith, 1996), which then handicaps their ability to accurately infer the motivations and intentions of others.

External attributions can lead to irresponsibility, the first of the four core interactional styles associated with a criminal lifestyle. Other attributional styles can preserve the criminal pattern through labeling. The internal, global, stable attributions that accompany a self-label of criminal or psychopath can set a series of nefarious events into motion that then make it extremely difficult for the labeled individual to abandon a life of crime. Official labeling, as was pointed out in Chapter 1, has little bearing on a person's attitudes and actions. Unofficial labeling and the self-labeling that frequently ensues from the practice of official and unofficial labeling, on the other hand, can be truly devastating. The internal, global, stable self-attributions that accompany self-labeling keep people locked in lifestyles and interfere with their ability to view themselves in a more positive light. Attributions, then, are schemes that can both initiate and maintain a crime-congruent lifestyle which must be altered if one is to successfully abandon this lifestyle.

Outcome Expectancies

For every action there is an equal and opposite reaction. When Sir Issac Newton formulated his third law of motion, he probably did not have the behavioral consequences of social interaction in mind, though they are clearly relevant here. Not only do our actions have consequences, but we also learn to anticipate these consequences. The anticipation of such consequences comes under the heading of outcome expectancies. As we all know, crime yields both positive and negative results. Research denotes that aggressive children and youthful offenders anticipate more positive than negative outcomes from violence. Aggressive children retain the belief that aggression will lead to positive consequences and tangible rewards to a much greater extent than do their nonaggressive peers (Perry, Perry, & Rasmussen, 1986). Delinquent adolescents, by comparison, are more inclined to endorse the expectancy that involvement in crime will enhance their self-esteem and decrease negative social evaluations than nondelinquent youth (Slaby & Guerra, 1988). Crane-Ross, Tisak, and Tisak (1998) contend that teenage aggression and rule breaking correlate with the anticipation of positive outcomes but that the effects are specific in that expectancies for aggression predict only aggression and expectancies for rule breaking predict only rule breaking.

Recent evidence connotes that outcome expectancies may make a significantly larger contribution to planned aggression, what is commonly known as proactive aggression, than to undersocialized or reactive aggression. After presenting eighty-six incarcerated adolescent offenders with audiotaped hypothetical vignettes,

Smithmyer, Hubbard, and Simons (2000) detected a moderately strong association between positive outcome expectancies for aggression and proactive aggressive behavior, although a relationship failed to surface between positive outcome expectancies for aggression and reactive aggressive behavior. Reactive aggression, it would seem, is more apt to be triggered by hostile attributional biases (Dodge, Price, Bachorowski, & Newman, 1990). Whether these preliminary findings generalize to proactive and reactive forms of adult crime remains to be seen, but this is a question that certainly warrants further study.

Using structural equation modeling, Walters (2000c) explored the relationship between existential fear, outcome expectancies for crime, and the actual consequences of past criminal conduct. The results of this investigation disclosed that outcome expectancies correlated significantly better with existential fear than they did with the consequences of past criminal conduct. On the basis of these results, Walters concluded that outcome expectancies gain their potency, at least in part, by interfacing with existential fear in that crime-congruent lifestyles metaphorically promise satisfaction of people's desire for affiliation, control, or status. In order that change might take place, negative expectancies for crime (anticipation of jail, death, loss of family) may need to replace positive expectancies for crime. Although this has been observed with the cessation of an alcohol-abusing lifestyle (Jones & McMahon, 1994), it remains to be seen if these relationships generalize to crime-related lifestyles.

Efficacy Expectancies

Whereas outcome expectancies are an anticipation of the potential aftermath of one's actions, efficacy expectancies underwrite one's belief that personal actions are responsible for a desired outcome. Efficacy expectancies, or self-efficacy, as it is more commonly called, help shape a person's choices and decisions (Bandura, 1986). Self-efficacy is a process with roots in early attachment relationships but with branches that extend well into adulthood. Mikulincer (1997) comments that securely attached children are confident in their abilities and accordingly are more open to information that conflicts with their present belief systems. Consequently, they are more willing to modify and correct erroneous beliefs. Low self-efficacy, poor academic performance, weak purpose in life, and low self-esteem form a cluster that facilitates adolescent deviant behavior, including delinquency, according to the results of a study by Dukes and Lorch (1989). It would seem well within the realm of possibility that self-efficacy and confidence—the former being more narrow in scope than the latter, although both make use of reasonably complex and positively valenced schemes—protect a person from initial involvement in criminal activity.

The proposed negative association between efficacy expectancies and antisocial behavior is well documented. Allen, Leadbeater, and Aber (1990) calculated a robust inverse correlation between self-reported delinquency and self-efficacy across twelve problem situations in males and a moderate inverse relationship in females.

In conjunction with his general strain theory of crime and delinquency Agnew (1992), proposed that self-efficacy conditions or alters the sequels of strain, although this supposition has yet to be verified empirically (Hoffmann & Cerbone, 1999; Paternoster & Mazerolle, 1994). Self-efficacy and a drive for mastery may be especially critical in protecting against delinquency when prosocial values are low (Ludwig & Pittman, 1999) and have been found to forecast positive prison adjustment in adult offenders enrolled in an anger management program (Sappington, 1996). Self-efficacy apparently is an avenue through which people achieve agency, defined as the capacity to produce, control, and regulate events in one's life (Bandura, 1997).

Although chronic offenders may experience low self-efficacy for prosocial conduct, they invariably possess high self-efficacy for crime. Okamoto (1998), for instance, reports that Japanese juvenile delinquents attained lower self-efficacy ratings for jobs but higher self-efficacy ratings for delinquency than did nondelinquent Japanese youth. Participants in this study who experienced attenuated self-efficacy and outcome expectancies for delinquency tended to have higher outcome expectancies for legitimate jobs. The Okamoto study underscores the value of inspecting the situational context of a behavior and the overlap that exists between different schematic subsystems, in this case, outcome and efficacy expectancies. The association between low self-efficacy and delinquency may have its origins in early childhood. Perry et al. (1986) note that aggressive children feel more efficacious about performing aggressive behavior than nonaggressive children. It would seem that in order to change crime-congruent efficacy expectancy schemes, it may be necessary to lower people's high efficacy appraisals of their criminal actions and elevate their low efficacy appraisals for prosocial conduct.

Goals

Goals are the objectives that guide a person's actions and decisions. Research on delay of gratification has shown that as children mature, their ability to forgo a small, immediate reward in exchange for a larger, less immediate reward improves, although significant individual differences nevertheless exist between same-aged peers (Mischel, Shoda, & Rodriguez, 1989). Early learning experiences within the home are one avenue by which individual differences in delay of gratification are formed. Mauro and Harris (2000) advise that preschoolers whose mothers employed an authoritative (directive) approach when instructing their children to refrain from touching a brightly wrapped present were better able to delay gratification than children whose mothers adopted a permissive (nondirective) teaching model. Given the possibility that learning to delay gratification in early childhood fortifies a person's later coping skills, it follows that weak learning for delay of gratification in childhood may be associated with delinquency and criminal behavior in adolescence and adulthood.

In a large-scale study of early adolescent boys it was determined that failure to delay gratification was more common in boys evincing externalized disorders (aggression, delinquency) than in boys manifesting internalized disorders (anxiety, depression) or nondisordered boys (Krueger, Caspi, Moffitt, White, & Stouthamer-Loeber, 1996). Young adult male parolees with histories of violent criminality selected more impulsive options in a laboratory investigation than young adult male parolees with a history of nonviolent criminality, signaling weaker ability to delay gratification on the part of the former group (Cherek, Moeller, Dougherty, & Rhoades, 1997). Elevations on the Psychopathic Deviate (Pd) scale of the Minnesota Multiphasic Personality Inventory (MMPI), conversely, failed to predict delay of gratification in a group of medium-security male inmates (Brown & Gutsch, 1985). There is some conjecture that delay of gratification may reflect a culturewide change in attitude. As a case in point, delinquents tested in 1974 displayed shorter time horizons and less of an ability to delay gratification than a cohort of delinquents tested at the same facility fifteen years earlier (Davids & Falkof, 1975).

Given the eminence that Gottfredson and Hirschi (1990) assign self-control in their general theory of crime, it should come as no surprise that delay of gratification assumes a prominent position in their views on the etiology and remediation of crime. Gottfredson and Hirschi, however, are pessimistic about the prospect of teaching youthful offenders self-control skills and believe that "such teaching is highly unlikely to be effective unless it comes very early in development" (269). Instead, they seem content to rely on imperfect and highly flawed predictions of future violence and serious criminality (Monahan, 1984; Walters, 1992) to administer a formal program of selective incapacitation and incarceration. Others, at any rate, believe that self-control and delay of gratification can be taught beyond the first few years of life. Potential interventions for weak impulse control include the modeling of self-talk strategies (Mischel et al., 1989), lengthening time horizons (Wilson & Herrnstein, 1985), and engaging clients in cognitive skills training in which goal-setting and problem-solving skills are emphasized (Ross & Fabiano, 1985).

Values

Rokeach (1973) defines values as the enduring beliefs that reflect personally or socially preferred priorities. With respect to the criminological application of values, there has been some speculation that prosocial values are deficient in those who habitually commit crime. Simons, Whitbeck, Conger, and Conger (1991) declare that adolescents with low prosocial values are at increased risk for delinquency. Also, self-reported delinquency in a large cross-section of junior and senior high school students was found to correlate negatively with prosocial values (Ludwig & Pittman, 1999). Several earlier investigations propagated support for Matza's (1964) drift theory to the extent that delinquents were often indistinguishable from nondelinquents in their endorsement of conventional values (Elizur, 1979; Heather, 1979), although there are also indications that delinquents may subscribe to subterranean values—where adventure, excitement, and thrills are accentuated—more than their nondelinquent peers (Heather, 1979; Regoli & Poole, 1978). These findings imply that the value systems of delinquents may not substantially differ from the value systems of nondelinquents, with the exception of a greater emphasis on hedonistic goals in the former. Of interest is whether this difference in value structure is the cause or effect of involvement in criminal activity. From the standpoint of the integrated-interactive theory, values and crime are believed to be both a cause and effect of one another.

Walters (1998b) divides values into four general categories or clusters: social values, work values, visceral values, and intellectual values. Social values assess the value that a person invests in interpersonal relationships, while work values reflect a person's willingness to devote time and energy to productive activity. Visceral values encompass personal pleasure and self-gratification, whereas intellectual values place a premium on understanding oneself and the surrounding environment. Research demonstrates that the self-centeredness and immediacy of visceral values are underscored by those involved in crime (Welch, 1990). This suggests that people may enter a criminal pattern in search of visceral satisfaction, although long-term involvement in such a lifestyle can also stimulate visceral interests. The fact that visceral values are widely pursued in the routine activities of persons engaged in crime-related lifestyles does not mean that visceral values must be eliminated or repressed for change to occur. Rather, a dynamic balance needs to be struck between the four value clusters. Balance can be achieved through values clarification (Rokeach, 1983), value skills instruction (Walters, 1998b), autonomy- and responsibility-engendering interventions (Martin & Osgood, 1987), and integration of the cultural symbolic foundations of value commitment through analysis of cultural stories, myths, and fairy tales (Holton, 1995).

Thinking Styles

Barriga, Landau, Stinson, Liau, and Gibbs (2000) ascertained that self-serving and self-debasing cognitive distortions were more prominent in delinquents than nondelinquents and that self-serving distortions like projection of blame were associated with higher levels of externalizing behavior and poorer institutional adjustment in the delinquent group. Working with self-reported delinquents, Guerra (1989) discerned that a larger number of delinquent youth held beliefs that minimized the importance, probability, and severity of the negative consequences of deviance than less delinquent youth. In both samples learning seemed to play a salient role in the genesis of these cognitive distortions. Congruent with differential association theory, Crick and Dodge (1994) asseverate that interaction with aggressive peers encourages the attainment of aggressive schemes, aggressive responses to ambiguous situations, and justifications and excuses for aggressive behavior. As Sutherland and Cressey (1978) have certified, it is not just the act of crime that is learned through intimate association with those already involved in crime; people also acquire the attitudes and rationalizations that facilitate the antisocial process in their interactions with delinquent peers.

The constructional errors and rigid defenses described earlier interact to form thinking styles. These thinking styles systematically vary from one family of lifestyle to the next, although the eight thinking styles that protect a criminal lifestyle are listed in Table 3.1. The Psychological Inventory of Criminal Thinking Styles (PICTS: Walters, 1995) now makes it possible to assess the eight criminal lifestyle-supporting thinking styles. Research conducted with the PICTS indicates that scales designed to measure the eight thinking styles are moderately internally consistent, with test-retest reliability ranging between .73 and .93 after two weeks and .47 and .86 after twelve weeks (Walters, 1995; Walters, Elliott, & Miscoll, 1998). In addition to correlating with criminal history (Walters, 1995; Walters et al., 1998), the PICTS enjoys a reasonably good relationship with the LCSF (Walters et al., 1991), Hare (1991) Psychopathy Checklist-Revised, and masculinity scale of the Bem (1981) Sex Role Inventory (Walters, in press-b). Several of the PICTS thinking style scales display a reasonable degree of predictive validity in studies prognosticating disciplinary adjustment and release outcome in male (Walters, 1996a, 1997) and female (Walters & Elliott, 1999) offenders, and the overall inventory seems sensitive to reduced criminal thinking in response to counseling (Walters, Trgovac, Rychlec, Di Fazio, & Olson, 2002) and increased criminal thinking attributed to incarceration (Walters, in press-a).

The six crime-congruent schematic subnetworks surveyed in the present section figure prominently in the evolution of criminal and other crime-congruent lifestyles through the construction and defense of crime-supporting belief systems. Adopting the basic outline from Figure 1.1 and replacing the five precursor models listed in the figure with the six aforementioned schematic subnetworks, we can see how these schematic subnetworks may serve as proxies for the precursor theories in accounting for the construction and defense of criminal belief systems (see Figure 3.1). Poor socialization to conventional values and goals, as proposed by social control theory, can stimulate preliminary development of crime-congruent belief systems. Outcome expectancies, peer reinforcement (differential association), and efficacy expectancies (strain) may further raise a person's chances of constructing belief systems congruent with crime. Thinking styles (neutralization) and self-attributions (labeling) are viewed to be primary avenues of belief system defense, although goals and values, outcome expectancies, and efficacy expectancies are also of major consequence in maintaining a lifestyle compatible with crime.

CRIME-CONGRUENT BELIEF SYSTEMS

Although the number of possible belief systems is infinite, there is a need to limit ourselves to a finite number of constructs for the sake of probity and heuristics. The decision was therefore made to divide major belief systems along the time-space continuum. Space was partitioned into the self and the world outside the self to form the self- and world-views, while time was parceled into the past, present, and future to yield the past-, present-, and future-views, respectively. To under-

Table 3.1
Definitions and Examples of the Eight Thinking Styles That Support a Criminal Lifestyle

Thinking Style	Definition	Example
Mollification	Justifying, rationalizing, making excuses, or externalizing responsibility for criminal actions.	"That woman was looking to be raped; did you see how she was dressed?"
Cutoff	Rapid elimination of common deterrents (fear, sanctions) to crime.	"Fuck it! I'm tired of trying; I'm going back to stealing."
Entitlement	Sense of privilege and ownership; misidentification of wants as needs.	"After all those years in prison, they owe me."
Power Orientation	Exerting power and control over aspects of one's social environment, other people in particular.	"There is nothing more life-affirming than robbing someone at gunpoint."
Sentimentality	Performing a good deed in order to compensate for the negative consequences of crime; also known as the "Robin Hood" syndrome.	"I can honestly say that I took the welfare of people whose homes I burglarized into account."
Superoptimism	The belief that one can indefinitely avoid the negative consequences of a criminal lifestyle.	"There is no way the police are going to catch me; they don't even know who I am."
Cognitive Indolence	Thinking in a lazy and uncritical fashion; marked by liberal and habitual use of shortcuts.	"Why work when dealing drugs is so much easier and I can pick my own work hours."
Discontinuity	Lack of congruence or consistency in one's thinking and actions; can give rise to a "Jekyll & Hyde" persona.	"I leave prison with the best of intentions, but it's usually only a matter of time before I fall back into my old patterns."

Figure 3.1
Schematic Subnetworks in the Construction and Defense of Crime-Congruent Belief Systems

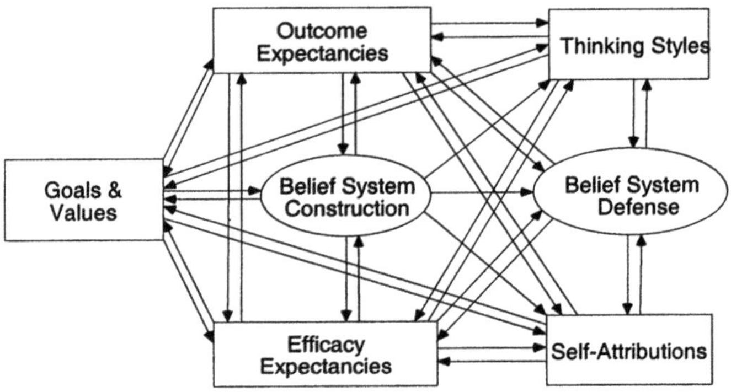

stand a crime-congruent lifestyle is to understand criminal belief systems, and the self-view, world-view, past-view, present-view, and future-view are belief systems that enable and support crime-congruent interactive styles. Just as a scheme can be ordered along the lines of valence (positive-negative), focus (broad-narrow), and complexity (high-low), so, too, can a belief system be organized along these same three dimensions. The purpose of the present discussion is to clarify the primary functions and attributes of each of the five major belief systems.

Self-View

The self-view communicates how a person perceives himself or herself. Being the most intricate and richly featured of the five major belief systems, there is no way a single chapter, let alone a section of a chapter, could do justice to the complexity of the self-system. For this reason, only those aspects of the self-view directly related to crime are covered in this section. The significance of the self-view has not been lost on personality and social psychologists, who believe that the self-view organizes and structures the other major belief systems, from a person's world-view to his or her view of the past and future (Markus & Wurf, 1987). Besides reviewing the four primary functions of the self-view, this section explores development of the self-view with respect to reflected appraisals, social comparisons, self-representations, role identity, and possible selves.

Four Functions

The integrated-interactive theory of lifestyles holds that the self-view serves four primary functions: a self-monitoring function, a self-organizing function, a self-referencing function, and a self-verifying function. The self-monitoring function represents a person's openness to information inconsistent with his or her current self-view. This function gives rise to a working self-concept whereby the self is considered to be in dynamic interaction with the surrounding environment and subject to continually shifting emphases and priorities (Markus & Wurf, 1987). High self-monitoring individuals are able to flexibly construct and modify self-schemes in response to the demands and requirements of a particular situation; low self-monitoring individuals, by comparison, are insensitive to environmental input and consequently manifest minimal change in self-view across situations (Snyder, 1983). Dodge and Tomlin (1987) noticed that a group of aggressive children, perhaps because they had already entered the early stages of an aggressive or delinquent lifestyle, were less sensitive to environmental cues and information than nonaggressive children. The aggressive children relied more on previously assembled schemes and self-schemes in responding to a potential conflict situation than a group of more flexible and environmentally attuned nonaggressive children.

Whereas the self-monitoring function highlights the situational specificity of the self-view, the other three functions account for the unity of self-identity through increased complexity, integration, and consistency of self-schematic material. Appreciation of the self-organizing function requires that one keep the developmental nature of self-awareness in mind. It has been argued that the self-view is global and undifferentiated in young children but becomes more complex and differentiated in adolescence (Rosenberg, 1986). With maturity the self-view becomes more complex and integrated and protects self-esteem by allowing maintenance of a positive self-view despite specific life failures. Hence, possessing a range of identities portends superior psychological adjustment provided these different identities are integrated rather than isolated (Pietromonaco, Manis, & Markus, 1986). People who adopt a lifestyle, all the same, tend to compile a reduced number of self-schemes (low cognitive complexity) and/or suffer from poor integration of existing self-schemes. As Brewer (1993) discovered in a group of injured athletes, this can become problematic. Participants in the Brewer study who identified exclusively with the social role of athlete experienced significantly more depression following an injury than participants less tied to the athlete role.

Rogers, Kuiper, and Kirker (1977) called attention to the self-referencing function of the self-view by describing how recall is enhanced by relating the target information to the self. Klein and Loftus (1988) developed this notion further and proposed that self-referencing facilitates recall by promoting an organizational context for self-referenced words. This hypothesis is corroborated by research showing that the self-reference effect is strongest on tasks requiring greater conjecture and inference on the part of the subject (Catrambone & Markus, 1987). In a review of research on the self-reference effect, Higgins and Bargh (1987) concluded that processing information relative to the self may lead to deeper symbolization, patterning, and storage of information than when the self is not referenced, for the self-view is more elaborately defined and data in it more eloquently encoded than is the case with other belief systems. Some researchers have even identified a self-referencing effect for nonverbal images (Brown, Keenan, & Potts, 1986). Building on this research, Keenan, Golding, and Brown (1992) established that self-referencing occurred on evaluative tasks (assessing information stored in memory) but not on factual tasks (direct retrieval of stored factual information) irrespective of the type of stimulus (noun, non-noun) or source of information referenced (autobiographical, nonautobiographical).

People search for information about themselves and others that fits with their self- and world-views and go about interpreting environmental and personal data in a manner congruent with these conceptualizations (Markus, 1980). This process is referred to as self-verification, and it fosters selective attention and biased interpretations of information pertinent to oneself and others. With roots in self-consistency theory (Festinger, 1957; Lecky, 1945), the self-verification hypothesis asserts that people seek self-confirmatory feedback, even if the feedback is negative. Proponents of the self-verification model contend that people do not pursue consistency for its own sake but rather seek to authenticate their self-conceptions as a means of reinforcing their ability to predict and control the environment (Kelly, 1955). Studies betoken that people with negative self-views are disposed to seek unfavorable evaluations (Swann, Hixon, Stein-Seroussi, & Gilbert, 1990) and interact with partners who supply them with negative feedback (Swann, Pelham, & Krull, 1989), while people with positive self-views tend to do the exact opposite. Self-verification has also been observed in subclinical depression (Swann, Wenzlaff, Krull, & Pelham, 1992). Swann (1987) maintains that self-verification is the combined result of selective interaction (we associate with those who view us as we view ourselves), identity cues (we portray ourselves in ways that tell others who we are and how we should be treated), and interpersonal prompts (interactive strategies that encourage others to respond in ways congruent with our self-view).

Reflected Appraisals

A gesture like a smile or frown has meaning only in interaction with others, for an actor perceives an emotional experience based on a shared symbolic reality with his or her audience (Mead, 1914/1982). Nowhere is the effect of the social environment on the evolution of a person's self-view more profound than with the concept of reflected appraisals. Grounded in Charles Horton Cooley's (1902/1964) views on the looking-glass self and George Herbert Mead's (1934) ideas on self as object, reflected appraisals convey how we believe others perceive us. The internal audience that directs the reflected appraisal process is one of the three components of the looking-glass self described by Cooley. An external audience or others' actual appraisals and one's self-appraisal are the two other components of the looking-glass self. These three components interact with one another to create self-awareness from which the self-view emerges. It should be mentioned that the social context can exert a powerful impact on the reflected appraisal process, as exemplified by the outcome of a study in which the salience of a teen's identity as a family member weakened the antiauthority attitudes of youthful delinquents confronted by an authority figure in the presence of family members (Khoo & Oakes, 2000). Perceived status may also moderate the reflected appraisal process, with the reflected appraisals of higher-status people having more influence on the self-appraisals of lower-status individuals than the reflected appraisals of lower-status people have on the self-appraisals of higher-status individuals (Cast, Stets, & Burke, 1999).

Labeling is one of the principal consequences of the reflected appraisal process. A founding tenet of labeling theory is that deviant labels promote future crime by damaging a person's self-esteem (Rutter & Giller, 1984). Studies employing the Tennessee Self Concept Scale (TSCS: Fitts, 1965) as an estimate of self-esteem seemly substantiate this view. Al-Talib and Griffin (1994) determined that British adolescents labeled delinquent scored significantly lower on the majority of TSCS scales than nonlabeled delinquent juveniles. Levy (1997) recorded a similar outcome in a group of institutionalized and noninstitutionalized adolescents from Queensland, Australia. There are two problems with these studies. First, incarceration (Levy) or educational placement (Al-Talib & Griffin) could have directly influenced delinquency independent of labeling. Second, neither study matched labeled and nonlabeled participants on prior level of delinquency. Chassin and Stager (1984) conclude on the basis of their own study that a label of delinquency has a negative effect on self-esteem only when the labeled individual perceives the delinquent role as relevant to himself or herself, is aware of the negative views that others have of delinquency, concurs with these negative appraisals, and respects the opinions of the evaluating other. The Chassin and Stager investigation indicates that self-labeling is a necessary step in the chain of events leading from an official label to the formation of crime-congruent belief systems.

Social Comparisons

Another way that social factors shape a person's self-view is through a process known as social comparison. We learn about the world by comparing the known with the unknown, and we learn about ourselves by comparing ourselves against others. Glaser, Calhoun, and Horne (1999) report that relative to abused and control children, aggressive children derive less favorable self-views when comparing themselves to their parents. Social comparisons serve three primary functions: self-enhancement, self-improvement, and self-evaluation. Self-enhancement goals are advanced by downward comparisons (with an inferior target), self-improvement by upward comparisons (with a superior target), and self-evaluation by parallel comparisons (with an equivalent target). Festinger (1954) postulated that the social comparison process is a direct result of the similarity between the self and target other in performance and that people compare themselves with those whose ability they view as being similar to their own. In a reformulation of Festinger's theory, Goethals and Darley (1977) declared that the similarity sought in social comparisons is for attributes correlated with performance rather than for performance per se. Presently, most social psychologists adopt Goethals and Darley's perspective that social comparison is a contrast of attributes rather than performance.

People generally make downward comparisons when their self-view is threatened (Wood, 1989). The actual strategy differs, nonetheless, depending on whether the individual enters the situation with high or low self-esteem. People with low self-esteem typically seek a downward comparison after failing a task in order to enhance their self-view (Wood, Giordano-Beech, Taylor, Michela, & Gaus, 1994). High self-esteem individuals, alternately, are more apt to choose a parallel comparison or even one that is slightly upward in an attempt to restore the positive valence of their self-view through superior performance (Wood, Giordano-Beech, & Ducharme, 1999). In situations where self-improvement may not be a viable or realistic option, high self-esteem individuals may deal with a threatening social comparison by shifting their attention to aspects of their identity that they do not share with a superior other. Persons with low self-esteem take a different tack, focusing even more on the attributes that they share in common with the superior other (Mussweiler, Gabriel, & Bodenhausen, 2000). The degree to which criminal offenders display self-protection, self-enhancement, and self-improvement is uncertain in that there is little research on this issue. It is hypothesized that like someone with low self-esteem, persons committed to a lifestyle congruent with crime engage in more self-protection and self-enhancement than self-improvement.

Howard Kaplan's (1980) countervailing theory of delinquency states that low self-esteem encourages an initial delinquent pattern through self-defense but that continued involvement in delinquency causes self-esteem to rise through self-enhancement. Kaplan's theory, while intriguing, has met with mixed empirical support: some studies conducted on Kaplan's theory uphold the self-defense aspect of his theory (Owens, 1994; Rosenberg, Schooler, & Schoenbach, 1989), other studies corroborate the self-enhancement aspect (Bynner, O'Malley, & Bachman, 1981), but few studies support both aspects. One possible explanation for these mixed findings is that other variables not initially included in Kaplan's theory may moderate the relationship between delinquency and self-esteem. In an empirical test of the proposed moderating effect of delinquent associations on the esteem–delinquency relationship, Jang and Thornberry (1998) remark that while low self-esteem does not appear to contribute directly to delinquent outcomes or association with delinquent peers, delinquent associations do have a self-enhancing effect on later self-esteem. There is also evidence that a deviant identity may moderate the relationship between low self-esteem and delinquency (Kaplan & Lin, 2000). Besides seeking downward comparisons—for example, "at least I'm not a sex offender"—offenders may use their interactions with like-thinking peers and a deviant identity to justify their actions and feel good about themselves.

Besides the agentic drive for self-enhancement and self-improvement there is also a communal drive for self-evaluation in which the person seeks a common bond with others (Locke & Nekich, 2000). In a classic study on this issue Schachter (1959) compared students waiting to participate in a study where they believed they would receive painful electrical shocks with students waiting to participate in a less threatening procedure and determined that the former group affiliated more with one another than the latter group. Schachter concluded that the students affiliated for social comparative reasons, that is, to compare their emotional reactions with one another. Twenty-nine years later Kirkpatrick and Shaver (1988) replicated this study and discerned that social support provided a direct fear reduction effect and social affiliation an information-seeking or self-referencing effect. The self-evaluation process makes use of a "proxy" to evaluate and make predictions about one's performance (Smith & Sachs, 1997) and relies more on stable attributes than unstable ones given the former's greater reliability (Arnkelsson & Smith, 2000). Offenders, it is hypothesized, engage in self-evaluation in an effort to justify their continued involvement in crime and to measure themselves against other criminals.

People not only measure themselves against others, but also measure themselves against themselves. The social comparison model (Festinger, 1954; Goethals & Darley, 1977) asserts that people compare themselves to others whom they view as similar to themselves on various relevant dimensions. What happens, though, when a relevant social comparison cannot be found? Past selves might furnish the best comparison under such circumstances. Owing to the fact that people generally see themselves as improving with age (Ross & Wilson, 2000), comparing the current self with a past self is likely to be more self-enhancing and less threatening than comparing oneself to a competent contemporary other. Wilson and Ross (2000) generated support for the prediction that people would favor temporal-past self-comparisons when motivated to enhance themselves and social comparisons when inclined to evaluate themselves. Regarding offenders, it is surmised that downward social comparisons (informants and child molesters) and temporal-past self-comparisons (prior mistakes) are used for self-enhancement purposes, parallel social comparisons ("everyone else is doing it") serve self-evaluation and self-protection motives, and upward social comparisons (emulation of older and more "successful" criminals) are designed for self-improvement.

Self-Representations

Self- and social awareness may be so intertwined as to be practically indistinguishable. As such, perspective taking may be as crucial to forming a thorough understanding of the self as it is in clarifying our perceptions of others. High school seniors and college students asked to construct elaborate perspectives of others erected more complex self-views than a group of control students given no such instructions (Enright, Olson, Ganiere, Lapsley, & Buss, 1984). By the same token, students given perspective-taking instructions attributed a larger number of personal characteristics to another person, the effect being particularly pronounced for positive attributes (Davis, Conklin, Smith, & Luce, 1996). Still, people's inferences about others are rarely as prolific or complex as their inferences about themselves. According to research, the private aspects of self are more available and distinct in memory than the public aspects, whereas the public aspects of others are more available, distinctive, and accessible in memory than the private aspects (Anderson, Glassman, & Gold, 1998). There were more private aspects of significant others available to, and distinctive in, the memories of participants in the Anderson et al. study than private aspects of nonsignificant others. On the basis of these results it is ventured that external attributions and other information relating to others is processed relative to self-attributions and other self-schemes which are then coded and stored in the self-view. Self-representations, then, are the personal attributes and environmental stimuli with which we identify and eventually incorporate into our self-views.

Self-representations, in addition to being classified on a private-public continuum, can also be classified along a personal-collective continuum. People from individualistic cultures like the United States typically retrieve more personal self-representations and fewer collective self-representations than persons from collectivist cultures like China (Triandis, McCusker, & Hui, 1990), although individuals growing up in collectivist cultures do have access to personal self-representations (Trafimow, Silverman, Fan, & Law, 1997). These culturally based differences in self-representation are acquired early in life. Chao (1995) noticed that 64% of the European American mothers, compared to 8% of the Chinese mothers whom she interviewed, underscored building their child's "sense of themselves" as the single most important goal of child raising. Mothers from collectivist cultures, rather than stressing a child's sense of personhood, emphasize sensitivity to others (Okimoto & Rohlen, 1988). Socialization of such belief systems is reinforced by advertising that appeals to nonconformity and uniqueness in Western nations and group harmony and social connection in Eastern countries (Mueller, 1987). In contrast to the Western (individualistic) accent on choice, originality, and personal contributions, Eastern (collectivist) cultures feature a person's duties to the collective (Hideo, 1988). Since a culture's standing on individualism and its rate of serious crime demonstrate a moderately strong relationship (Walters, 1999), it may well be that offenders have greater access to their personal self-representations than they do to their collective self-representations.

As the current discussion suggests, self-representations are not a series of disparate, isolated schemes but exist within a larger identity structure. A recent investigation ascertained that social validation of an intrinsic sense of self was superior to self-value based on personal accomplishments in reducing defensiveness (Schimel, Arndt, Pyszczynski, & Greenberg, 2001). Two different models have been offered in an attempt to account for the effect of social perception on the structure of the self: the "one-basket" or integration model and the "two-basket" or segregation model. The segregation model posits that social or collective identities are represented separately from personal attributes (Trafimow, Triandis, & Goto, 1991), in contrast to the integration model, which holds that social identities and personal attributes are connected through a series of interlocking identity clusters (Deaux, 1992). In a conceptual replication of Trafimow et al.'s (1991) original study, Reid and Deaux (1996) enlisted support for both the segregation and integration models of self-representation schematic organization. Although personal attributes clustered more with other attributes and social identities with other social identities, there were significant linkages between attributes and identities. It therefore seems likely that personal attributes and social identities are inextricably linked through a complex system of interacting nodes to where personal attributes inspire as much meaning in a person's social or collective identity as a person's social or collective identity ascribes to his or her personal attributions.

Role Identity

The roles that we assume in life can have as far-reaching an effect on our self-views as the internal and external attributes with which we identify. Each role is defined by a set of role expectations, and some of the actions that people take in the performance of a role are done as a result of these perceived expectations. Someone adopting a maternalistic role will act nurturing if he or she defines nurturance as an expectation of that role. Assumption of a business role requires standards of dress and conduct that differ greatly from those that define a maternalistic role, and while it is possible to juggle these conflicting roles and responsibilities, such efforts invariably take their toll on the individual. Labeling and personal acceptance of a label, self-labeling, can lead to overidentification with a role. The internal, stable, global self-attributions that accompany acceptance of a criminal identity are conducive to maintaining crime-congruent belief systems. Whether a person labels himself or herself a criminal, drug dealer, bank robber, or gangster, the outcome is much the same: crystallization of the criminal role identity and slavish adherence to its associated role expectations. Gender-role identity also exerts leverage over criminal conduct.

A person's identification with the masculine or the feminine gender role may help explain the chasm that separates male and female criminality. Research reveals that males are arrested at a rate four to nine times that of females (Bureau of Justice Statistics, 1999). It has been proposed that delinquency is incompatible with the female gender-role, and so cognitive dissonance is produced each time a person with a feminine gender identity commits a crime or delinquent act. The dissonance motivates the individual to either change the identity or alter the behavior. Generally, it is easier to modify a behavior than an identity, and so most females are law-abiding. To the extent that delinquency is compatible with the male gender role, boys with strong masculine identities may seek to diminish conformity-induced dissonance by engaging in delinquency (Matsueda, 1992). Research addressing this supposition indicates that differential role expectancies and role-taking behaviors in interaction with parental labeling account for a substantial portion of the gender gap in delinquency (Bartusch & Matsueda, 1996; Heimer, 1996).

A significant rise in the number of women incarcerated for violent crimes in the early 1970s led to speculation that the women's movement may have instigated a change in the female gender role (Adler, 1975), but research conducted since that time finds little evidence of a meaningful connection between either masculinity or femininity and crime in females (Horowitz & White, 1987; Huselid & Cooper, 1994). In fact, violent and younger female offenders tend to be more feminine that nonviolent and older female offenders (Campbell, MacKenzie, & Robinson, 1987; Erez, 1988). A longitudinal panel study of 120 incarcerated women administered the Bem Sex-Role Inventory (BSRI) on two separate occasions fourteen months apart disclosed small increases in both masculinity and femininity, with changes on the femininity scale being somewhat larger than changes on the masculinity scale (Trice & Lamb, 1996). Research has been fairly consistent, however, in portraying the presence of a positive correlation between masculinity and delinquency in men (Horowitz & White, 1987; Huselid & Cooper, 1994; Shover, Norland, James, & Thorton, 1979).

Opting for a somewhat different approach to the study of gender-role identity and crime, Walters (2001a) correlated the masculinity and femininity scales of the BSRI with the four factor scales of the PICTS (problem avoidance, interpersonal hostility, self-deception/assertion, denial of harm). As predicted, the BSRI masculinity scale correlated negatively with the PICTS problem avoidance scale and positively with the self-assertion/deception scale in male adult felony offenders. The PICTS denial of harm factor scale, by comparison, correlated positively with both masculinity and femininity in a sample of female offenders. What these data show is that gender-role identity enters into complex associations with criminal thinking and perhaps with criminal behavior. Whereas masculinity may protect against those facets of criminal thinking that impute irresponsibility (problem avoidance) they appear to facilitate the more agentic-intrusive features of criminal thinking (self-assertion/deception). Femininity as well as masculinity appear to facilitate beliefs that one's actions do not harm others and so may be instrumental in sustaining criminal conduct.

Possible Selves

Possible selves are the roles that people envision themselves fulfilling at some point in the future. By virtue of their future orientation, possible selves link people's self-views to their future-views and bridge the gap between an adolescent sense of self and an adult self-view (Markus & Nurius, 1986). These possible selves can be either positive or negative. In a cross-sectional analysis of adolescent attitudes toward law-abiding behavior, Oyserman and Saltz (1993) discovered that weak social competence and heightened impulsiveness interfered with the ability to negotiate and maintain a positive possible self of oneself as an adult and were associated with higher rates of delinquency. Investigating the roots of these positive and negative possible selves, Mikulincer (1995) ascertained that securely attached individuals had positive self-views that were balanced by access to negative possible selves. Avoidant individuals also held positive self-views but had limited access to negative possible selves, while anxious/ambivalent individuals held negative self-views with little access to positive possible selves. The balance that access to both positive and negative possible selves apparently affords people may facilitate human adaptation.

Negative or feared possible selves are most effective as sources of motivation when paired with a self-relevant positive or expected possible self. The self-relevant positive possible self supplies direction to one's efforts to avoid a negative or feared possible self. For example, a feared possible self of being alone may be compensated for by a positive possible self marked by attributions, outcome expectancies, and efficacy expectancies that reinforce the notion that one possesses the requisite skills and attitudes to be successful in intimate social relationships. Oyserman and Markus (1990) studied four groups of lower-middle-class and working-class youth in Detroit, Michigan, each group representing an increasing level of delinquent involvement, to determine whether poor balance between positive and negative possible selves correlated with delinquency. Findings from this study indicated that while 81% of the nondelinquents had at least one match between their expected and feared selves, only 37% of the most delinquent group achieved such balance. Oyserman and Markus subsequently followed subjects in two of their four subsamples and observed that those individuals with the least amount of balance between their feared and expected selves were the ones most likely to have participated in delinquent activities over the course of the three-month follow-up.

A noted existential psychoanalyst has argued that human agency is essential for effective integration of the various situational selves that arise as a result of self-monitoring (von Broembsen, 1989). It is possible, nevertheless, that human agency is also potentiated by integration of the different possible selves in a self- or future-view. Oyserman (1993) reports that in the absence of adult influence youth may define themselves and their future goals according to the deviant images furnished by peers. Conversely, in the presence of adult influence adolescents are more disposed to internalize, integrate, and actualize the conventional attitudes and beliefs of their parents and prosocial peers. Along similar lines, Leung and Lau (1989) failed to distinguish a relationship between delinquency and general self-esteem but did note that delinquency correlated negatively with academic self-concept and adolescent–adult relationships and positively with social and physical abilities. This implies that while there is a tendency to experience the self as a whole rather than as a medley of individual selves (Matsueda, 1992), the self-views of delinquents and criminals are perhaps more compartmentalized and discontinuous than are the self-views of persons less committed to a criminal way of life and that such poor integration may be both a cause and effect of weak agency.

World-View

Montgomery, Fine, and James-Myers (1990) define the world-view as a "structure of philosophical assumptions, values, and principles upon which a way of perceiving the world is based" (38). Sewall (1998) compares the world-view to a perceptual filter formed from expectations and assumptions that help people organize environmental information. Janoff-Bulman (1989) states that people are reluctant to alter their world-views because a world-view grants them predictability, stability, and clarity. The world-view is conceptualized by the integrated-interactive theory of lifestyles as a belief system designed to make sense of the outside world, just as the self-view is intended to make sense of one's inner world. As such, it serves a variety of functions, can be ordered along several dimensions, and comprises components known as prototypes.

Four Functions

Like the self-view, the world-view serves four major functions. These four functions are borrowed directly from the work of Walsh and Middleton (1984) and can be posed as questions. The first function is designed to answer the question, who are we? This question addresses the related issues of human autonomy, equality, and the nature of a person. A second function seeks answers to the question, where are we? The moral and historical status of the world as well as the nature of reality are subsumed under this particular function. Why are we suffering? is the question that defines the third function, which seeks to conceptualize the problems confronting humanity and attribute causality to factors presumed to be responsible for these problems. The fourth and final function of a world-view is to identify prescriptions for alleviating the problems of humanity. This function is summed up in the question, what is the remedy? World-views can be either personal or collective, and often they are both. Pyszczynski, Greenberg, and Solomon (1997) contend that adopting a collective or cultural world-view renders concerns over mortality, one facet of existential fear, impotent through achievement of a protective sense of symbolic immortality.

Jensen (1997) unearthed support for Walsh and Middleton's (1984) system in a survey of fundamentalist and mainline Baptists. Asked about human autonomy, fundamentalists stressed divine agency and human obedience, while mainline Baptists underscored human agency and self-determination. When queried about the nature of reality, fundamentalists focused on the world beyond the one that we perceive, whereas mainline Baptists emphasized the perceived world. Fundamentalists averred that we suffer out of a disregard for God's plan; mainline Baptists, by comparison, attributed human suffering to societal injustice and lack of concern. Finally, fundamentalists considered living in harmony with the divine order of God the solution to the problems currently facing human civilization, in contrast to mainline Baptists, who indicated that moving society along a more progressivist path was the solution to the problems of modern-day life. As intriguing as these findings are, they pale in comparison to the attitudinal and behavioral correlates of each world-view. Mainline Baptists interviewed for this study were more likely to approve of divorce and were, in fact, divorced more often than fundamentalists. Fundamentalists, for their part, often viewed society and its institutions as morally bankrupt and were more inclined to have removed their children from public school so that they could be home-schooled.

Four Dimensions

World-views have been classified in several different ways, each with its own set of theoretical assumptions, strengths, and biases. Perhaps the most famous classification is Pepper's (1942) system, in which world-views are categorized into one of four groups: organicism, mechanism, formism, and contextualism. Much of the research on Pepper's system, in any event, has focused on organicism and mechanism as two poles of a single dimension. Janoff-Bulman (1991) proposes a system of three orthogonal dimensions—benevolence-malevolence, distribution of positive and negative outcomes, and self-worth—while Epstein (1991) offers an alternative system also composed of three dimensions—benevolence-malevolence, meaningful-meaningless, and self worthiness-unworthiness. Dropping the self from the world-views of Janoff-Bulman and Epstein because it is already subsumed under the self-view and synthesizing unique and common features of the three models, a four-dimensional system for classifying world-view was constructed: mechanistic-organismic, fatalistic-agentic, justice-inequality, and malevolence-benevolence.

People falling at the mechanistic end of the mechanistic-organismic continuum conceive of the world as a machine that can be reduced to its constituent parts. Individuals adopting an organismic philosophy of life generally perceive the world and the people in it as dynamic systems of complex, interrelated processes. An Afrocentric world-view features such organismic concerns as cooperation, cohesion, and spirituality and contrasts sharply with the mechanistic bent of the Eurocentric world-view (Robinson & Howard-Hamilton, 1994). Hatter and Ottens (1998) discovered that African American college students who adopted an Afrocentric world-view were better able to adjust to the stress and strain of attending a predominantly white midwestern university. As one might anticipate, Eastern cultures espouse a more organismic philosophy of life than Western cultures (Chapell & Takahashi, 1998) and students rated as organismic are viewed to be more creative, intuitive, and socially skilled than mechanistic students, who come across as conventional, realistic, and interpersonally detached (Johnson, Germer, Efran, & Overton, 1988). The mechanistic-organismic continuum also distinguishes between academic disciplines, with social science staff avowing a more organismic world-view and natural science staff assuming a more mechanistic world-view (Babbage & Ronan, 2000).

Fatalism is the belief that all events are induced by fate and are accordingly inevitable. Agenticism, by comparison, champions free choice and a belief that many of the consequences that we face in life are of our own creation. Fatalism is often equated with an external locus of control, and research intimates that presuming one's life is dictated by fate or other outside forces may augment one's risk of substance abuse (Olmstead, Guy, O'Mally, & Bentler, 1991), suicidal thinking (Roberts, Roberts, & Chen, 1998), and sexually transmitted diseases

(Kalichman, Kelly, Morgan, & Rompa, 1997). Encouraging self-reliance in both high school students (Davis, 1986) and adult male workers (Kohn & Schooler, 1982), antithetically, has been shown to reduce fatalistic beliefs. Gluhoski and Wortman (1996) assessed the possibility that people who experienced a trauma are more fatalistic than those able to avoid traumatic experiences. Reevaluating participants after three years, Gluhoski and Wortman failed to detect a significant correlation between trauma and subsequent performance on a fatalism scale. In fact, fatalism scores seemed to drop in the three years between the two testings for the sample as a whole.

Lerner (1980) maintains that some people have a need to believe that the world in which they live is just. Those who profess strong just world beliefs experience distress in the face of unfair outcomes, which is reduced by the opportunity to explain the causes of the unfair event. Lupfer, Doan, and Houston (1998) report that people who believe in a just world have an attributional style that motivates them to fathom the causes of unfair events. Belief in a just world may help people cope with accidents (Janoff-Bulman & Wortman, 1977) and serious medical conditions (Agrawal & Dalal, 1993) but may also make them less sensitive to the plight of AIDS patients (Conners & Heaven, 1990), rape victims (Furnham & Boston, 1996), criminal defendants (O'Quin & Volger, 1989), and the poor (Furnham & Gunter, 1984). There is also proof that belief in a just world may ignite an egocentric fairness bias in which the person believes that his or her actions are fairer than the actions of others (Tanaka, 1999). As might be anticipated, minorities (Glennon, Joseph, & Hunter, 1993), the unemployed (Retowski, 1995), and those with less social power (Bègue & Fumey, 2000) typically emit weak just world beliefs. There would appear to be both advantages and disadvantages to belief in a just world, although exclusive accent on either justice or inequality is a recipe for personal disaster.

The final dimension along which a world-view can be ordered is the ratio of benevolence to malevolence that the person believes exists in the world. Securely attached college students proclaim a more benevolent view of the world than students classified with an avoidant attachment style (Levy, Blatt, & Shaver, 1998). Maltreatment in childhood portends subsequent malevolent world-views (Ornduff, 2000) and many Israeli survivors of the Holocaust understandably hold a malevolent world-view (Prager & Solomon, 1995). Yet, when Calhoun, Cann, Tedeschi, and McMillan (1998) explored the relationship between traumatic life events and beliefs about world justice and benevolence they, like Gluhoski and Wortman (1996) before them, failed to discern a connection between world-view beliefs and psychological trauma. One implication of these findings is that while protracted maltreatment as a child in an abusive home or as a prisoner in a Nazi concentration camp may influence a person's world-view, isolated traumatic events have much less impact on how the person perceives reality. This also confirms Janoff-Bulman's (1989) contention that for the sake of stability people prefer to assimilate new information into their world-view rather than dramatically alter their belief systems, with changes occurring gradually over time rather than abruptly after a single traumatic episode.

The mechanistic-organismic, fatalistic-agentic, justice-inequality, and malevolence-benevolence dimensions of a world-view, while stable, are not immutable. People move up and down the length of each continuum depending on the current situational context and other factors, the degree of movement reflecting the relative flexibility of the person's composite world-view. Although research on the world-views of delinquents and criminal offenders is limited, it has been observed that such groups retain world-views that strike a decidedly mechanistic (Coleman, 1992), fatalistic (Parrott & Strongman, 1984), and malevolent (Jankowski, 1991) pose. With respect to the justice-inequity dimension, it is posited that people committed to a criminal way of life are vulnerable to the egocentric fairness bias in the sense that they believe that others get what they deserve but that they themselves have been treated unjustly. This attitude may be both a cause and effect of their well-documented problems with social perspective taking (Foglia, 2000).

Prototypes

People use prototypes or exemplars to judge whether an object belongs to a particular cognitive class or category. A prototype is a schematic ideal or template with a graded internal structure and fuzzy boundaries used to make comparisons with environmentally perceived objects and experiences. The person compares the perceived object or experience to the prototype in an effort to make sense of a confusing array of internal and external stimuli. Prototypes are used not only for cognitive comparisons but for affective comparisons as well (Karniol & Ben-Moshe, 1991). Information gathered from subjects representing eight different nations revealed that the prototype of a business leader varied widely between countries (Gerstner & Day, 1994). This outcome implies that prototypes are catalyzed by sociocultural learning and, as is the case with all facets of a belief system, are an extension of a person's active interactions with the internal and external environments. Prototypes are necessary for human survival in that they help decipher events and make sense of the world; however, they can have certain unforeseen negative side effects. This may be particularly true when people use their prototyping skills to pigeonhole, label, and stereotype themselves and others.

Data touching on possible prototypes that might initiate, fortify, and sustain crime are in short supply. Rogers, Salekin, Sewell, and Cruise (2000) found that compared to forensic experts, criminal offenders asked to describe antisocial personality disorder emphasized behavioral manifestations over emotional and interpersonal patterns. These results may be the consequence of differences in how offenders and forensic experts construct prototypes, or they may simply reflect the fact that experts have more formal education and greater experience with diagnostic categories. Given the paucity of research on the prototypes that constitute the world-views of adolescent and adult offenders, we are left to speculate on the structure and content of such prototypes. Conceptualizing low cognitive complexity as both a cause and effect of criminal involvement and revisiting the proposed role of the four dimensions in shaping world-view content, it is theorized that the prototypes employed by persons committed to crime are simplistic and stereotypic and stress the mechanistic, fatalistic, and malevolent sides of life. Quite obviously, additional research is required to substantiate these claims. It should be noted that the criminal lifestyle and other crime-congruent patterns are themselves construed to be prototypes, ideals with graded internal structures and fuzzy boundaries used to assess a person's level of lifestyle commitment as defined by the four interactive styles discussed in an earlier section of this chapter.

Present-View

With respect to the two previous belief systems the individual functions and content of the self- and world-views were distinguished. In the case of the present-view the functions are the belief system. The two primary functions of the present-view are to (1) perceive information and (2) act on this information. Information does not remain in the present-view long because once it is coded into memory, it resides in one of the other belief systems. This review commences with a critique of the perceptual function, followed by a discussion on the executive function.

Perceptual Function

Sensory, affective, behavioral, and motivational stimuli must be processed before they can be represented in a scheme, and schemes must be stored and accessed to have an effect on the decision-making process. The perceptual function that makes this possible is considered a general integrated process. In support of this hypothesis, Borod et al. (2000) witnessed significant correlations between three modes of emotional perceptual processing (facial perception, prosodic perception, lexical perception), denoting the presence of a general processor of emotional perceptual stimuli. It is further reasoned that perception and initial perceptual processing are largely automatic and independent of intellectual ability, an assumption corroborated by research (Moore, Hobson, & Anderson, 1995). Other studies indicate that children who inaccurately perceive and code nonverbal stimuli have fewer friends and more problems with self-esteem than children who perceive and code nonverbal stimuli normally and that this may ignite a negative chain of events that eventually engulf the child in a self- and other-destructive lifestyle (Whalen, Henker, & Granger, 1990). One possible repercussion of poor perceptual functioning is aggression and conduct disorder. Cadesky, Mota, and Schachar (2000), while discerning no conduct disorder-control differences in intelligence, noticed that conduct-disordered children were more apt to misinterpret emotional cues than non-conduct-disordered children.

Crick and Dodge (1994) delineate six stages of social information processing: (1) encoding cues, (2) interpreting encoded cues, (3) establishing goals, (4) formulating responses, (5) evaluating responses, and (6) enacting selected behaviors, the first two of which deal with the perceptual function of the present-view.

Habitually aggressive children selectively attend to hostile stimuli (Dodge & Frame, 1982), encode others' intentions as hostile (Matthys, Cuperus, & Van Engeland, 1999), base their decisions on fewer social cues (Dodge & Tomlin, 1983), and view aggression more positively (Dodge, 1993) than nonaggressive children. According to Crick and Dodge, aggressive children have a social information-processing deficit in which they project hostile intentions onto others in ambiguous situations. These perceptual abnormalities may extend beyond childhood, as the outcome of a study by Williamson, Harpur, and Hare (1991) suggests. In this study psychopathic or more criminally oriented offenders displayed less of a differential emotional response to affective and neutral words than nonpsychopathic or less serious criminals, which Williamson et al. interpret as evidence of a genetically based neurological deficit. Initial perceptual processing may therefore be instrumental in both initiating and maintaining belief systems congruent with crime.

Executive Function

Once perceived and initially processed, information must be analyzed, stored, and accessed to have meaning. The analysis, integration, and use of information to initiate and sustain efficient goal attainment is the principal responsibility of the executive function of the present-view. The executive function entails planning, problem solving, selective attention, inhibitory control, cognitive-set shifting, response flexibility, and working memory. Zelazo, Carter, Reznick, and Frye (1997) conceptualize the executive function as a macroconstruct encompassing subfunctions that interact with one another to accomplish their higher-order function (i.e., problem solving). As with the perceptual function, the executive function is postulated to be a single, general integrated process rather than a series of disparate functions, and like the perceptual function, it does not correspond well to traditional measures of intellectual ability (Ardila, Pineda, & Rosselli, 2000). Although the executive function encompasses both procedural and declarative memory, it highlights the episodic features of the latter in the construction of belief systems. As with all functions of a belief system, the executive function evolves from an active interaction between the person and his or her social environment. On this point, Newcomb and Bagwell (1996) relate that children acquire social problem-solving skills by observing their parents and interacting with friends.

Choice and decision making are the principal goals of the executive function. The integrated-interactive theory adopts Clarke and Cornish's (1986) limited rationality assumption, which asserts that a criminal act is the consequence of a rational decision made within certain constraints imposed by time, cognitive ability, and data access. This has been verified in studies showing that choice in juvenile delinquents (Cimler & Beach, 1981) and adult property offenders (Carroll & Weaver, 1986) is a psychological process subject to heuristics, shortcuts, and errors of both omission and commission. Executive function problems have been observed in physically aggressive children (Séguin, Pihl, Harden, Tremblay, &

Boulerice, 1995), conduct-disordered preadolescents (Toupin, Déry, Pauzé, Mercier, & Fortin, 2000), juvenile delinquents (Moffitt & Silva, 1988), and adult criminals (Kandel & Freed, 1989). All the same, the relationship between executive dysfunction and crime may be mediated by other variables. Moffitt (1993b) reasons that mild cognitive deficits and subclinical neurological impairment set the stage for a difficult temperament, which complicates the childrearing process and makes it more likely that the child will turn to antisocial peers and delinquent solutions when faced with the problems of everyday living. Participation in a budding criminal pattern might then interfere with the inception of age-dependent executive skills, thereby feeding into a vicious cycle of criminal activity and poor decision making.

Past-View

The primary function of the past-view is to reflect on prior events, personal as well as impersonal. This, of course, allows each person to profit from, and correct, past mistakes. There is a general feeling among many criminologists and research psychologists that habitual lawbreakers do not learn from their mistakes due to neurophysiological deficits that block or weaken pain and punishment signals (Ellis, 1987). Using heart rate and skin conductance measures as indicators of autonomic response, researchers calculated that low autonomic arousal, a prime index of poor conditionability, in a group of 15-year-olds predicted an elevated rate of adult conviction nine years later (Raine, Venables, & Williams, 1990). In another study children exhibiting low autonomic arousal at age 10 years received higher ratings on disruptiveness and conduct disorder from teachers, employers, and other adults at age 17 or 18 years compared to children displaying normal automatic arousal at age 10 (Venables, 1987). If the past-views of criminal offenders are not storing information designed to correct past mistakes, then what is their function? One possibility is that the past-views of people committed to a crime-congruent lifestyle are dedicated to maintaining the lifestyle by highlighting certain memories and schemes and discounting other memories and schemes.

The past-view is rich in personalized historical schemes known as recollections. Early recollections are an assessment tool originally devised by Alfred Adler (1927), the father of individual psychology, to assess a person's style of life. Scrutinizing and comparing the early recollections of delinquent and nondelinquents boys, Bruhn and Davidow (1983) determined that the recollections of the delinquent group were imbued with themes of injury, rule breaking, and victimization. These same investigators recorded parallel results in a study of 14- to 18-year-old boys, with delinquents recalling more encounters with serious rule breaking, injury, and mastery—coupled with fewer documented successes—than nondelinquents (Davidow & Bruhn, 1990). Hankoff (1987) acknowledges that the early recollections of thirty-two incarcerated adult male criminals were unpleasant and dramatic, with a common motif of interpersonal conflict. Comparing maximum-security male prison inmates with non-criminal controls of similar age, education, and ethnic background, Elliott, Fakouri, and Hafner (1993) ascertained that the early recollections of inmates were dominated by themes of death, punishment, and physical activity and expressed much less mutuality than the recollections of noncriminals.

In comprehending the primary function of the past-view in someone committed to a life of crime, it is vital that it be acknowledged how Alfred Adler conceptualized early recollections. Adler (1927) was of the opinion that early recollections are impacted by current attitudes and beliefs to the extent that people selectively attend to memories and recollections that are most relevant to their current situations. From research conducted on early recollections in delinquent and criminal populations it would seem that the past-views of persons committed to a life of crime are saturated with negativity. It is very possible, then, that criminally committed individuals use their past-views to justify continued criminal involvement (e.g., "after all, I've had a rough life"). Heavy representation of rule breaking and dramatic themes in the early recollections of offenders suggests that a second function of the past-view is to reminisce about one's glorious criminal past (e.g., "the good old days"). In either case, a change in recollections can lead to a change in behavior. Positive recollections predicted success in mainstreaming violent and assaultive youth originally assigned to a special school for disruptive students (Roth & Nicholson, 1990).

Future-View

The primary function of the future-view is to establish goals for the individual to pursue. Schemes located in the future-view are designed to anticipate future possibilities, reactions, and outcomes. As such, outcome expectancies are often included in a person's future-view. Data gathered from a group of Japanese adolescents revealed that delinquent boys possessed more optimistic future-views than nondelinquent high school boys and that delinquent youth anticipated more favorable results from delinquent action than did their nondelinquent peers (Kono, 1994). It may henceforth be necessary to challenge the positivity bias that exists in the future-views of people habitually involved in crime so that they can take the negative aspects of their lifestyle into account when making decisions and setting goals. Forming positive anticipations for alternatives to crime is another potential avenue by which change in a criminal pattern might be realized. Youthful German apprentices enrolled in a training program who exuded a strong sense of attachment and bonding to their adult supervisors held less favorable views of delinquency and more optimistic attitudes toward the future occupations for which they were training than apprentices demonstrating weaker attachment and bonding to their adult supervisors (Silverberg, Vazsonyi, Schlegel, and Schmidt, 1998).

Optimism is another facet of anticipations that helps shape a person's future-view. Arnett (2000), in a survey of 140 American 21- to 28-year-olds, discovered that while these young adults were pessimistic about their generation's future, they were much more optimistic about their own ability to live a happy and productive life. The position adopted by these individuals seems to reflect a cognitive bias similar in kind to the attributional biases described earlier. Harris and Middleton (1993) found that people make downward comparisons when assessing risk and assume that people with whom they are not familiar suffer more risk factors than they or those with whom they are familiar suffer. Thus, people tend to be more optimistic about their own situations than they are about other people's circumstances, particularly if these other people are strangers. Like the bias that finds positive expectancies more accessible than negative expectancies, optimism bias (Weinstein & Klein, 1996) may be adaptive to some extent. What is not adaptive is optimism predicated on fantasy, known in lifestyle circles as superoptimism (Walters, 1998b). Superoptimism and confidence/self-efficacy both involve positive or optimistic appraisals of the future. The difference is that while superoptimism is based on illusion, confidence and self-efficacy are grounded in skills that the individual utilizes to achieve his or her stated goals.

CONCLUSION

Belief systems have their origins in a child's interactions with the social environment. The realization of developmental milestones along the lines of joint attention, social referencing, private speech, and perspective taking are meanwhile central to the formation of self-awareness, beliefs, and belief systems. Figure 3.2 depicts the parallel development hypothesized to occur in the evolution of sociocognitive skills and belief systems. Self-awareness, as described in Chapter 2, is considered the precursor of belief system development, and the self-and present-views are postulated to emanate directly from self-awareness. The self-view is presumed to provide the impetus for the world-view, and the present-view putatively spawns the past- and future-views, although all five of these belief systems eventually enter into reciprocal relationships (Sedikides & Brewer, 2001). We would also do well to remember that human experience can be organized into belief systems other than the five described here and that the five belief systems that constitute the core of the integrated-interactive theory of crime-based lifestyles overlap extensively to the point where they share many of the same schemes. Furthermore, the developmental epochs referenced in Figure 3.2 are broadly estimated time frames in which the five major belief systems surface in an organized and integrated fashion. Hence, there may be important schemes in each belief system that predate the belief system by months or even years.

The perspective advanced in this book takes nonlinear dynamical systems theory as its conceptual framework (Walters, 1999). Within nonlinear dynamical systems theory there is the belief that different levels of a phenomenon tend to replicate one another through what is known as fractals. Benoit Mandelbröt (1990) determined that the irregularities of coastlines were constant whether one viewed the entire west coast of the United States or only a small section of coastline in northern California. Mandelbröt concluded that these repeated patterns or fractals operate through self-similarity to the extent that the individual components of a system resemble the larger system from whence they originate. The current chapter

Figure 3.2
Parallel Development of Sociocognitive Skills and Belief Systems

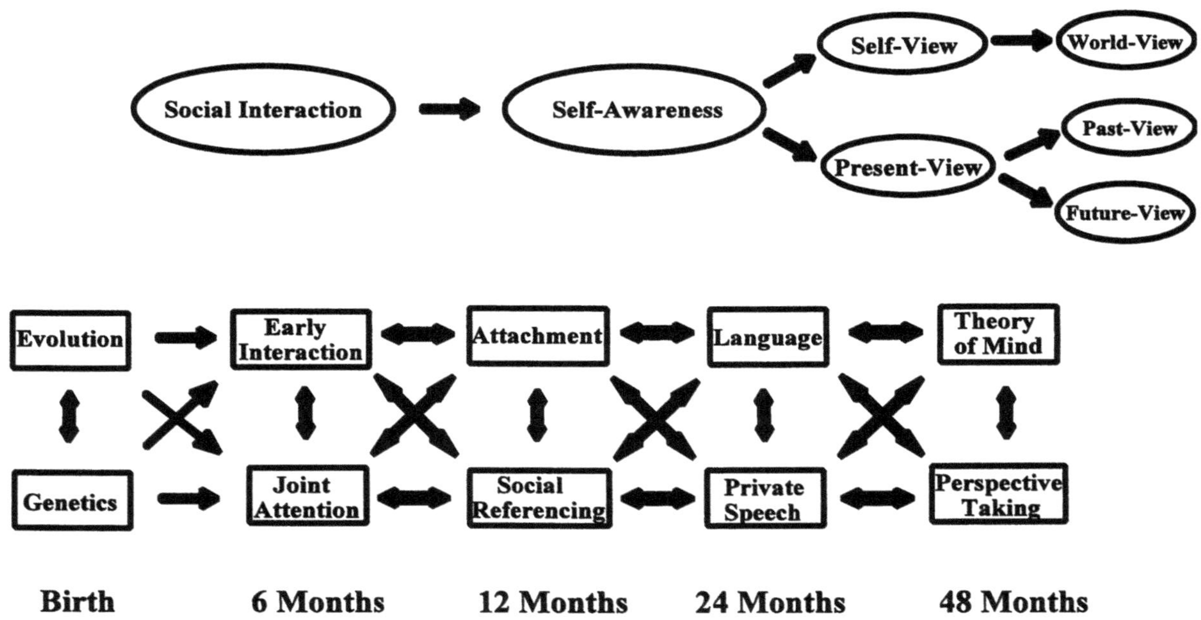

focused on crime-congruent belief systems in individuals. Even so, belief systems may be just as pivotal in perpetuating crime at the group (gang), organizational (La Costa Nostra), or national (Nazi Germany) levels. It is hard to imagine Hitler coming to power, let alone wielding the kind of influence that he did, had he not been able to tap into, and mold, a collective belief system and shared reality that endeared him to a large segment of the German populace. Likewise, gangs and organized crime could not exist in the absence of a common bond or belief system.

Before moving to the next chapter I think it is important that the reader understand that belief systems are not solely a function of the individual because they are not exclusively dispositional; nor are belief systems entirely situational as behaviorists have traditionally claimed. Rather, belief systems evolve from the ongoing interaction that takes place between a person's existing psychological state and current situational context. Disposition characteristics influence this psychological state, but only as part of a complex, never-ending interaction. The integrated-interactive theory proposed in this book adopts the view that human experience is the product of a person's transactions with the internal and external environments and that these person × person and person × situation interactions culminate in, and define, the belief systems that support crime-congruent lifestyles. The purpose of this chapter has been to demonstrate how belief systems act to promote and preserve crime-congruent lifestyles, with the constructive function directing the initiation phase and the defensive function governing the maintenance phase. Illustrating how belief systems account for the development of four major categories of crime—violent crime, sexual assault, white-collar crime, and drug trafficking—is the goal of the next four chapters of this book. Our journey would be incomplete, however, if mention were not at least made of how belief systems can be made less congruent with crime, the subject of the final chapter of this text.

4

Belief Systems and Violent Crime

The theories described in Chapter 1 have been unilaterally applied to general delinquency and adult property crime. Questions have accordingly been raised as to the generalizability of these findings to nonproperty adult offenses. Violence, sexual assault, white-collar crime, and drug trafficking are four offense categories that have received only a modicum of attention from theorists promoting the six models described in the opening chapter of this text. In the next four chapters these crimes and their supporting belief systems are explored, with each chapter covering a different crime. The present chapter reviews the problem of violent crime and considers how the integrated-interactive theory may shed light on this complex interactive pattern. As research to be reviewed later in this chapter suggests, people who perpetrate violence often participate in a large number of nonviolent criminal acts as well. For this reason, the next four chapters take as their focus the criminal act rather than the criminal offender. As such, the current chapter examines the correlates, possible causes, and theoretical implications of violent crime. In addition to gauging the relevance of the six traditional criminological models to violent crime and offering an integrated-interactive interpretation of aggressive crime, this chapter presents the case history of an individual who has forged a lifestyle around violent and nonviolent crime. The chapter begins, however, with a survey of the demographic correlates of violent crime.

DEMOGRAPHICS OF VIOLENT CRIME

Data from the FBI's Uniform Crime Reports (UCR) indicate that, in 1997, 17.2% of all persons arrested for violent offenses in the United States were under the age of 18 years. Even more alarming is the fact that the rate of arrest for violent crime in people under 18 climbed 48.9% from 1988 to 1997, as opposed to a 19.0% rise in violent crime for persons 18 years of age and older (Bureau of Justice Statistics: BJS, 1999). Aggression can be observed as early as the first or second year of life, but the impact of aggression multiplies as children enter adolescence, due in part to an increase in physical strength and in part to an increase in the availability of firearms (Berkowitz, 1994). Firearm availability is augmented by drug trafficking (Li & Feigelman, 1994), and there has been a sharp rise in the number of juveniles participating in drug trafficking since the mid-1980s. Because juveniles are less likely to be arrested, convicted, and incarcerated, older individuals have actively recruited children and preadolescents into their drug organizations in hopes of concealing their operations from the authorities (Bush & Iannotti, 1993). As a consequence of this and other factors juvenile violent crime is expanding at an alarming pace, with undertones of future growth in the violent crime rate of adults.

The UCR also indicates that female involvement in violent crime is rising faster than male involvement. While only 16.2% of all persons arrested for violent crime in 1997 were females, a 53.8% increase in female violent crime took place between 1988 and 1997, in contrast to a 3.0% rise in male violent crime (BJS, 1999). Official (Kruttschnitt, 1994) and self-report (Bjorkvist, Lagerspetz, & Kaukiainen, 1992) data reveal a remarkable similarity in the age structure of violent delinquency for boys and girls, whereas the absolute number of adolescent boys who participate in violent crime is several times the rate attained by girls. From an early age boys deploy more physical force and aggression in their interactions with others than girls (Coie & Dodge, 1997); girls, for their part, express aggression in ways that are more indirect, verbal, and relational than boys (Crick, 1995). Where parental supervision appears to be of major consequence in reducing violence in boys, family bonding and accepting traditional gender roles have a hardier inhibitory effect on violence in girls (Heimer & De Coster, 1999). It may therefore be the manner in which aggression is expressed and controlled that accounts for the large gender gap that continues to exist for violent crime.

Minority status is another demographic characteristic that is not equally distributed between high and low violent crime groups. African American males are twice as likely to be arrested for a violent crime as Hispanic males and thirteen, sixteen, and six times more likely than white males to be arrested for homicide, robbery, and aggravated assault, respectively. The rate of arrest for violent crime in African American females is three times that of Hispanic females and thirteen, fifteen, and fourteen times that of white females for homicide, robbery, and aggravated assault, respectively. In fact, African American females are arrested for homicide, robbery, and aggravated assault at a rate on par with white males (Sommers & Baskin, 1992). Attempting to make sense of these outcomes, Sommers and Baskin discerned that 69% of the black female offenders whose records they reviewed lived in areas personified by high concentrations of poverty as compared to 20% of the Hispanic women and 11% of the white women. This suggests that the environment in which a person is raised and currently resides may be a deciding factor in construing the discrepancies noted in the rate of violent crime between white and African American respondents.

Poverty, as Sommers and Baskin (1992) discovered, is another demographic variable pertinent to violent crime. In a meta-analysis of thirty four aggregate level studies, Hsieh and Pugh (1993) detected a link between poverty and income inequality, on the one hand, and violent crime, on the other hand. An N-weighted mean effect size of .44 was obtained in this meta-analysis, with assault and homicide achieving weighted mean effect sizes twice the magnitude of what was found with rape and robbery. Social class may also affect a person's propensity to engage in violent criminality. Heimer (1997) reasons that boys originating from lower socioeconomic status homes experience less legitimate power and are more apt to learn definitions favorable to violence than boys hailing from higher socioeconomic status homes. Socioeconomic status may further mold violent criminality, advises Heimer, by providing opportunities for learning definitions favorable to violent crime outside the home and because lower socioeconomic status parents tend to use more coercive disciplinary techniques than higher socioeconomic parents.

Violent crime may be as much of a problem in other Western nations as it is in the United States, and statistics show that some European countries are experiencing an even greater growth in violent crime than in the U.S. Victim surveys indicate that while the U.S. robbery rate was nearly double Great Britain's in 1981, Great Britain experienced a robbery rate 1.4 times higher than America's in 1995. Likewise, the rate of victim-reported assault was slightly higher in Great Britain in 1981, but by 1995 it had risen to more than twice the rate obtained in the United States. In 1981 the assault rate, as measured by official police statistics, was 1.5 times higher in the United States, but by 1996 the English rate of assaults reported to police had surpassed the American rate. Police statistics further specify that in 1981 the U.S. murder rate was 8.7 times higher than the English rate, but by 1996 the difference had fallen to 5.7 times. Similar drops were recorded in reported rapes, which were 17 times higher in the United States in 1981 but just 3 times higher in 1996, and the U.S. robbery rate, which was 6 times higher in 1981 and 1.4 times higher in 1996 (Langan & Farrington, 1998). Violent crime, it would seem, is a problem that extends beyond the boundaries of the United States and one for which cultural factors play a leading role.

CULTURAL FACTORS AND VIOLENT CRIME

In an attempt to explain the unequal distribution of violence across cultures, Wolfgang and Ferracuti (1967) formulated the subculture of violence hypothesis. The subculture of violence hypothesis, as outlined by Wolfgang and Ferracuti, makes three broad assumptions: (1) some subcultures do not consider violence illegitimate; (2) expectations of violence characterize some subcultures; and (3) penalties and sanctions may be administered for failing to adhere to culturally prescribed beliefs concerning the necessity of violence under specific circumstances. As elegant and interesting as the subculture of violence hypothesis may be, it has accrued very little in the way of empirical support in the handful of studies that have addressed its basic assumptions (Ball-Rokeach, 1973; Hartnagel, 1980).

Tedeschi and Felson (1994), for instance, were unable to identify a community or subculture that placed a positive value on violence. Furthermore, the subculture of violence hypothesis has been criticized on the grounds that it makes a circular argument (Messner, 1988). Several more specific applications of the subculture of violence hypothesis, it would seem, have fared better than the original Wolfgang and Ferracuti thesis.

Hackney (1969) and Gastil (1971) attribute the elevated prevalence of violent crime in the American South to a southern subculture of violence in which violence is sanctioned in defense of honor, family, and property. In one of the more recent studies on this issue, McCall, Land, and Cohen (1992) generated support for a southern subculture of violence with situational violent crimes (assault, homicide) but not violent crime in general. McCall et al. unearthed modest support for the supposition that this southern subculture of violence has diminished to the point of nonsignificance in modern times from its peak period in the mid-1800s. Viewing crime among American blacks as a reflection of exaggerated perceptions of manliness, Curtis (1975) offers a subculture of violence interpretation of African American male aggressive crime. Even though he did not restrict himself to African American men, Donald Mosher has produced evidence showing that hypermasculinity is a central concomitant of violent crime (Mosher & Tomkins, 1988; Zaitchick & Mosher, 1993).

THEORIES OF VIOLENT CRIME

In advancing his general strain theory, Agnew (1985, 1992) isolates three primary causes of strain (failed aspirations, removal of positively valenced stimuli, presentation of noxious stimuli) and three categories of response (escape, instrumental, retaliatory). The retaliatory response is believed to be the progenitor of violent crime through the mediating influence of negative affect (Agnew, 1990). Mazerolle and Piquero (1997) assert that strain exerts both a direct and indirect (via anger) influence over an adolescent's intention to assault. Results from another study substantiated that anger and strain both correlate with violent crime, but anger did not mediate the strain–violence relationship in this particular study (Mazerolle, Burton, Cullen, Evans, & Payne, 2000). Other investigators report that strain theory is predictive of violent offending in male adolescents but not female adolescents (Mazerolle, 1998) and may be more effective in expounding on gang membership and violent criminality in white students than in black students (Vowell & May, 2000). Roitberg and Menard (1995) ascertained that while strain variables had no direct effect on felony assault in a group of acting-out youth, these variables exerted an indirect influence through their interaction with delinquent peer group associations.

As with research on general strain theory, differential association has received authentication in studies on violent crime in juvenile offenders (Friedman & Rosenbaum, 1988; Roitberg & Menard, 1995). There is also evidence that gang membership, a principal means of differential association, correlates well with violent crime in both male and female offenders (Esbensen & Winfree, 1998). Longitudinal data signify that an individual's involvement in violent crime rises dramatically after he or she joins a gang and does not subside until after he or she leaves the gang. Besides unveiling a relationship between differential association and violent youth crime, research also connotes that differential association is helpful in deciphering violent crime in adult offenders. Burton, Cullen, Evans, and Dunaway (1994) verified the presence of a relationship between differential association and adult assaultive crimes. More recently, Alarid, Burton, and Cullen (2000) confirmed a connection between differential association in the form of criminal friends and definitions favorable to violations of the law and violent crime in a mixed-gender sample of late adolescent and young adult felons. In one of the few studies not fully supportive of differential association, Fagan, Piper, and Moore (1986) impart that peer delinquency may not be as salient a force in the generation of violent delinquency as it is in other forms of delinquency.

Research on social control theory as an explanation for violent crime is neither as profuse nor as corroboratory as research on the general strain and differential association theories. Whereas Bernburg and Thorlindsson (1999) calculated a substantive negative correlation between social bonding and violent delinquency, Deschenes and Esbensen (1999) found that only one of the six social control variables that they investigated covaried significantly with self-reports of violent offending in a large sample of eighth grade students. Rosenbaum (1987), while encountering moderate correlations between social control variables and both property and drug crimes, failed to discern a connection between social control variables and violent crime in a group of juvenile offenders. Testing Gottfredson and Hirschi's (1990) self-control theory, Wood (1993) distinguished higher levels of self-reported fighting in juveniles achieving low as opposed to high scores on a measure of self-control. Likewise, Longshore and Turner (1998) employed a sample of adults enrolled in several Treatment Alternatives to Street Crime (TASC) programs to document a negative relationship between self-control and participation in crimes of force (homicide, rape, assault, robbery); in any event, the effect was significant for males only.

Few published accounts explore violent crime from a labeling perspective, which is somewhat surprising given that psychopathy is at the heart of what labeling theorists refer to as secondary deviance. Harris, Rice, and Quinsey (1994) maintain that psychopathy is a taxon with discrete, mutually exclusive categories (psychopath, nonpsychopath) and that many of the predictors of violent recidivism observed in this group of individuals support an offender's membership in the taxon. It has been reasonably well established that people classified as psychopaths commit more aggressive and violent crimes than people classified as nonpsychopaths (Hare & McPherson, 1984; Kosson, Smith, & Newman, 1990). Although a fair number of individuals experience impulsivity or overattribute hostile intentions to others, psychopaths are said to do both (Serin & Kuriychuk, 1994). It remains to be seen whether attributions of psychopathy adversely affect a person's self-concept and limit his or her opportunities for participation in conventional activities and pursuits. Being labeled a juvenile delinquent can have a profound effect on a person's self-concept and opportunities for conventional involvements (Kaplan, Martin, & Johnson, 1986); there is every reason to believe that the psychopathy label might do likewise.

Not to be overlooked as possible explanations for aggression and violent crime are the rationalizations and excuses that people make in an effort to mollify their criminal actions. Neutralization is evident in spousal abusers (Dutton, 1986), people who perpetrate violence against strangers (Dietz, 1983), and professional contract killers (Levi, 1981). Deschenes and Esbensen (1999) identified past victimization as the top correlate of self-reported violent offending in a group of juveniles, followed by neutralization of social norms against fighting and guilt. Mixed support for neutralization was procured in a study by Agnew (1994). In contrast to cross-sectional comparisons, which showed that neutralization was strongest in people approving of violence, longitudinal analyses signified that neutralization was higher in people who disapproved of violence. Further study is required to determine whether the anomalous findings recorded by Agnew are attributable to his research procedures or are an indication that neutralization theory is limited with respect to explaining violent crime.

Thornberry's (1987) reciprocal interaction perspective has been studied only indirectly in regard to violent crime. Even so, the results are encouraging. Several years before Thornberry proposed his reciprocal interaction hypothesis, Olweus (1980) observed that a "strong-willed" temperament interacted reciprocally with maternal permissiveness to promote aggression in later childhood. More recently, Liska and Bellair (1995) witnessed a bidirectional relationship between the violent crime rate (robbery) and the racial composition of inner-city neighborhoods. As it turns out, a larger minority population is associated with more robberies, and a higher rate of robbery has led to "white flight," in which many white families move out of the inner city. Consequently, the violent crime rate and racial composition of inner-city neighborhoods are reciprocally connected. Additional studies in which Thornberry's ideas and assumptions are tested directly in terms of their generalizability to violent crime would seem warranted at this time.

AN INTEGRATED-INTERACTIVE THEORY OF VIOLENT CRIME

Each of the four chapters in which specific offenses (violent crime, sexual assault, white-collar crime, drug trafficking) are described offers an integrated-interactive model of that crime from which belief systems congruent with that crime are thought to evolve. There are three principal components and a number of ancillary variables associated with each crime, and in many instances there is overlap between the four offense categories. The three principal components represent the initiation, transition, and maintenance phases of lifestyle-congruent belief system development. The initiation phase is focused primarily on incentive, the transition phase on outcome expectancies and expanding opportunities for lifestyle involvement, and the maintenance phase on the distorted cognitions that protect the lifestyle and allow it to continue. The three primary components of an integrated-interactive theory of violent crime are believed to be threatened egotism, anger/hostility, and cognitive distortion.

Threatened Egotism

Traditional theories of crime causation often place low self-esteem at the root of violence and aggression (Schoenfeld, 1988; Toch, 1969/1993). Roy Baumeister and his colleagues, however, are working on a different theory in which high self-esteem is construed to be the driving force behind violent crime and aggressive behavior. According to Baumeister, violence is motivated by verbal abuse, disrespect, insults, strain, or a whole host of other variables that threaten the person's sense of control and self-worth. Ego threats trigger negative affect, which, under the right circumstances, can lead to violence. Whether the individual's self-esteem is genuinely high or has been artificially inflated through application of various defense mechanisms, the key to violent crime, claims Baumeister, is threatened egotism. Self-enhancement and self-verification motives gradually converge to provoke a retaliatory response to the perceived threat or insult (Baumeister, Smart, & Boden, 1996).

A factor that appears to contribute to the initiation of violent crime, either by creating conditions conducive to the formation of an inflated sense of self-esteem or by directly challenging a person's sense of self-worth, is physical, sexual, and psychological abuse. Physical abuse in childhood correlates well with later violence in adolescence (Malinosky-Rummell & Hansen, 1993) and adulthood (Becker et al., 1995). Sexual (Greenwald, Leitenberg, Cado, & Tarran, 1990) and psychological (Payne & Gough, 1995) abuse may also foster future aggression and violent criminality. The well-known association between modeling and media violence may, in fact, require exposure to physical abuse within the home before it translates into actual physical aggression (Heath, Kruttschnitt, & Ward, 1986). It should be pointed out, all the same, that while early abuse is a risk factor for violent criminality, it is neither necessary nor sufficient for aggression since the majority of violent offenders do not report childhood abuse, and most people who experience childhood abuse do not resort to violent crime (Widom, 1989).

Biased attributions are another ancillary variable that may interact with early childhood abuse to provide the requisite conditions necessary for construction of belief systems congruent with violent crime. Aggressive children seemingly possess an attributional bias in which they ascribe hostile intentions to ambiguous situations significantly more often than do nonaggressive children (Dodge & Frame, 1982). Relational schemes and scripts, formed through interaction with a rejecting early environment, can lead to attributional biases, which then boost the child's chances of producing an aggressive response (Crick & Dodge, 1994). In a recent investigation on this matter, Gomez and Gomez (2000) established that maternal control corresponded with attributions of hostile intent and hostile response selection in a group of 9- and 10-year-old aggressive boys. Whereas

Copello and Tata (1990) found attributional biases for hostile intent in both violent and nonviolent offenders, inferences of violent threat correlated robustly with an offender's hostility level.

Social rejection is a common occurrence in the family and peer relationships of aggressive children. According to the integrated-interactional approach advanced in this book, the relationship between aggression and social rejection is bidirectional in the sense that aggression can have as much impact on social rejection as social rejection has on aggression. Kupersmidt and Coie (1990) note that aggressive children experience social rejection as early as 6 years of age, and Dishion, Patterson, Stoolmiller, and Skinner (1991) remark that peer rejection encourages aggressive children to associate with antisocial peers. A relationship has been posited between biased attributions and peer rejection whereby socially maladjusted and rejected children display a proclivity for attributing hostile intentions to peers (Dodge & Somberg, 1987; Quiggle, Garber, Panak, & Dodge, 1992). Hence, children who feel rejected at home, in part because of their own temperamentally based interactive styles and their parents' inability to handle these styles, experience biased attributions of hostile intent, which, in turn, trigger aggression toward peers, resulting in social rejection and further hostility, eventually leading the child to affiliate with similarly aggressive peers.

Anger and Hostility

In the formation of belief systems congruent with violent crime the transitional phase defines one's reaction to the threatened egotism of belief system initiation. Anger and hostility in response to ego threats can occur as a single event or as part of a larger pattern. The former is exemplified by youth who assault peers whom they perceive as "disrespectful," the latter by a long history of abuse and social rejection leading to escalation of hostility and anger and a pattern of strong-arm robbery. Research shows that physical (Sappington, Pharr, Tunstall, & Rickert, 1997) and sexual (Greenwald et al., 1990) abuse during childhood correlates with later hostility. We still do not know, however, what links abuse and other initiating factors to subsequent aggression. Exploring this issue in a group of forensic hospital patients, Welsh and Gordon (1991) determined that arousal and trait anger had a measurable effect on subsequent incidents of assaultive behavior. Anger and hostility can lead to a reactive response, like that observed in the Welsh and Gordon study, or it can lead to a proactive response. Reactive aggression is an immediate retaliatory response designed to correct a perceived wrong. Proactive aggression, by comparison, is a calculated response designed to achieve some larger goal.

Several factors amplify opportunities for violence in the transition to belief systems congruent with violent crime. Chief among these facilitative conditions is alcohol intoxication. Substance abuse and crime overlap appreciably, although the exact nature of this linkage is open to speculation and debate (Walters, 1998b). If there is a causal connection between substance abuse and violent crime, the evidence is strongest for an alcohol-violent crime nexus. Several studies indicate that alcohol exerts a powerful effect on violent crime; other drugs, heroin and marijuana in particular, apparently have little or no impact on violent crime and may actually reduce aggression under some circumstances (Dawkins, 1997; Franklin, Allison, & Sutton, 1992). On the basis of a meta-analysis of thirty experimental studies Bushman and Cooper (1990) conclude that alcohol is a causal agent in many forms of aggression. Aggregate studies also verify the existence of an association between the sale of alcohol and assaultive incidents (Stevenson, Lind, & Weatherburn, 1999). Contrasting 345 burglars with 310 violent offenders, Farrington and Lambert (1994) discovered that burglars generally committed their offenses for material gain, compared to violent offenders, who were more often under the influence of alcohol at the time of the offense and operated on the basis of anger and provocation in response to various annoyances.

Outcome expectancies are vital to the alterations that occur during the transitional phase of belief system development. Two categories of outcome expectancy assist with the evolution of violent crime-congruent belief systems. First, there are outcome expectancies for alcohol that indirectly impinge on crime as mediators of alcohol use and intoxication (Walters, 1998a). Second, there are outcome expectancies specific to aggression. Aggressive children characteristically accentuate the benefits (control, status) while downplaying the costs (peer rejection, victim suffering) of violence relative to their nonaggressive age-mates (Boldizar, Perry, & Perry, 1989). Compared to nonaggressive adolescents, aggressive youth are more apt to believe that aggression will reduce negative self-evaluations (Slaby & Guerra, 1988) and terminate aversive treatment from others (Perry, Perry, & Rasmussen, 1986). Investigating youth aggression, Crane-Ross, Tisak, and Tisak (1998) ascertained that placing a premium on the perceived benefits of aggression coupled with low concern for peer disapproval of violence successfully predicted aggression in students enrolled in grades 9 through 12. Outcome expectancies for alcohol would appear to have an indirect effect on violent crime by interacting with alcohol use and intoxication; outcome expectancies for aggression, on the other hand, seem more directly linked to violence through increased anticipation of the benefits and decreased anticipation of the costs of aggression and violent crime.

Situational cues can either increase or decrease the probability of a violent criminal event. Felson and Steadman (1983) narrate that specific actions on the part of a victim and various bystanders can have a direct bearing on whether a violent assault turns lethal. In this study victims were more likely to be killed if they were physically aggressive, intoxicated, or in possession of a weapon during the assault. Third parties can further influence the outcome of an assault by serving as mediators or antagonists (Felson, Ribner, & Siegel, 1984). Henderson and Hewstone (1984) add that the presence of third parties acts to diffuse responsibility for an assault by reducing attributions to the self and increasing attributions to the situation. Having access to a firearm may also heighten opportunities for violent crime. A recent aggregate study conducted in South Carolina denotes that, inasmuch as illegal gun availability promotes violent crime, legal gun ownership had neither a facilitative nor inhibitory effect on aggressive criminal acts (Stolzenberg & D'Alessio, 2000). A study by May (1999), in which fear of victimization encouraged students to bring guns to school, even after controlling for social control and differential association, unmasked a connection between incentive (fear of victimization) and opportunity (bringing firearms to school) that can lead to violent crime.

Cognitive Distortion

A plethora of factors maintains belief systems congruent with violent crime. Near the top of the long list of factors responsible for belief system maintenance are various forms of cognitive distortion. A common class of cognitive distortion is neutralization. As a consequence of neutralization, someone can remain in a pattern of violent criminality indefinitely, even when the violent pattern clashes with the person's basic morals, values, and beliefs. Having the capacity to neutralize social proscriptions against fighting effectively predicted violent offending in the Deschenes and Esbensen (1999) study described earlier. Furthermore, the spousal abusers interviewed by Dutton (1986) and the professional hit men surveyed by Levi (1981) used neutralization to continue with their lives after committing their violent acts. The cognitive distortion that underlies neutralization, along with high levels of stress and poor coping ability, are intrinsic features of belief system maintenance in the service of violent criminality.

Biased attributions of hostile intent are pivotal in initiating belief systems congruent with violent crime. Biased attributions are also one of the distorted cognitions that help maintain violent crime-congruent belief systems. In a study of forty-five male offenders serving time for serious violence, Henderson and Hewstone (1984) discerned that these individuals were nearly exclusively external in their attributions of responsibility for the various violent acts that they had committed in their lives. They either justified their actions or manufactured excuses designed to minimize their culpability for the violence. It is postulated that these external attributions may have served to sustain patterns of violent offending. Guerra, Huesmann, and Zelli (1990) studied the attributional dimensions of locus, stability, and controllability in a group of incarcerated delinquent youth and found that physical aggression in these youth correlated with the tendency to attribute social failure to controllable factors. Hence, while biased attributions may well play a role in maintaining belief systems congruent with violent crime, the precise nature of these biased attributions requires further study.

Overview

Figure 4.1 illustrates the complex reciprocal relationships proposed to exist between variables in the initiation and maintenance of violent crime. The initiation of violent crime-congruent belief systems begins with threatened egotism and the associated issues of inflated self-esteem, physical, sexual, and psychological abuse, hostile attributional biases, and social rejection. It should be pointed out that the four factors that impinge on threatened egotism are believed to be reciprocally related to one another, though this is not portrayed in the diagram. The transitional phase of belief system development is configured around anger and hostility. Alcohol use and intoxication, outcome expectancies for alcohol and aggression, and situational cues assist with the transitional process. Other factors like ambient temperature (Anderson, 1987) and intelligence (Moffitt, Gabrielli, Mednick, & Schulsinger, 1981) either increase or decrease opportunities for violence-congruent belief system development. Maintenance, which follows transition, is prompted by cognitive distortion in combination with ineffective coping skills and mounting life stress. These three forces interact to sustain and solidify nascent belief systems congruent with violent crime that emerge during the initiation and transition phases.

Figure 4.1
An Integrated-Interactive Model of Violent Crime

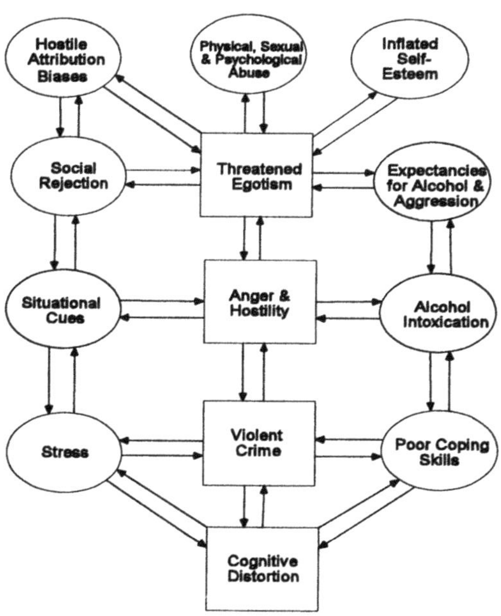

IS THERE A DIFFERENCE BETWEEN VIOLENT CRIME AND OTHER CRIMES?

In presenting their general theory of crime, Gottfredson and Hirschi (1990) emphasize versatility over specialization and argue that people who participate in violent offending do not specialize in violent crime and may actually indulge in more nonviolent than violent acts of law-breaking. Research conducted on juvenile offenders largely authenticates Gottfredson and Hirschi's (1990) views on versatility. Violent offenders are a heterogeneous group who engage in a wide diversity of crimes (Elliott, Huizinga, & Morse, 1986; Fagan et al., 1986). Mednick, Brennan, and Kandel (1988), by way of contrast, report that first-time violent offenders were 1.9 times more likely to perpetrate future acts of serious violence than first-time property offenders. Two studies by David Farrington serve as testament to the modest specialization that exists in relatively heterogeneous groups of violent and nonviolent offenders. The first study represents a follow-up of fifty violent offenders who committed eighty-five violent criminal acts and 263 nonviolent offenses during the follow-up period, with only 14% of the sample not participating in at least one subsequent nonviolent offense (Farrington, 1991). In the second study the criminal backgrounds of persons convicted of burglary and violent offenses were scrutinized. Fifty-one percent of the burglars and 25% of the violent offenders had a history of prior burglaries, whereas 32% of the burglars and 47% of the violent offenders had a prior record of violence (Farrington & Lambert, 1994).

Results from the Farrington and Lambert (1994) investigation insinuate that people convicted of violent offenses present with more extensive histories of violence than persons convicted of burglary. By the same token, the majority of violent offenders had no prior record of violence, and one-third of the burglars did. A study by Sommers and Baskin (1994) suggests that the onset of violence may play a role in whether specialization or versatility predominates. Probing the backgrounds of eighty-five inner city women arrested for nondomestic violent felonies, Sommers and Baskin conclude that early onset violent offending is accompanied by a variety of different offending patterns and other deviant lifestyles. Later onset violent offending, conversely, is associated with greater specialization and a focus on nonviolent, gender-congruent crimes like prostitution and shoplifting. In all probability, a number of factors in addition to the onset of violent offending moderate the versatility of violent crime. At this time the most that can be said is that violent crime embodies features of both specialization and versatility. Even with this, it is likely that several delimiting variables like age of onset determine the relative degree of heterogeneity in the offending pattern.

VIOLENT CRIME AS A PERSONALITY TRAIT

Walters (2000b) questions the existence of a violence-prone personality and offers in its place an interactional view of pattern development and maintenance.

In scrutinizing the advisability of conceptualizing violent crime as a personality trait, it is imperative that the reader understands that personality trait abstractions rest on two primary assumptions: (1) consistency across situations and (2) stability over time. In this section we evaluate the serviceability of a personality trait account of violent crime by investigating these two assumptions.

Cross-Situational Consistency

Research previously reviewed on situational cues and violent crime demonstrates that external events are intimately involved in many aggressive and violent incidents. Even before Mischel (1968) wrote his scathing critique of personality trait theory, questions were being raised about the cross-situational consistency of presumed personality traits like honesty (Hartshorne & May, 1928) and extroversion (Newcomb, 1929). Studies directly assessing the cross-situational consistency of aggressive behavior, on the other hand, have produced mixed outcomes. Thus, Campbell, Bibel, and Muncer (1985) uncovered powerful trans-situational correlations in adolescents asked to respond to twenty-four potential conflict situations, while Pollack, Gilmore, Stewart, and Mattison (1989) detected wide situational variations in ratings of actual aggressive behavior. Salient situational shifts in rated aggression were also noted in a group of behaviorally disturbed children attending a residential summer camp, with improved predictions of cross-situational consistency occurring when the similarity between situations was taken into account (Shoda, Mischel, & Wright, 1993). Cross-situational consistency, it would seem, is especially weak when prescribed roles constrain a person's behavioral options, as epitomized by Zimbardo's (1972) mock prison exercise or Milgram's (1974) obedience studies.

Cross-Temporal Stability

The stability of aggressiveness over the life span has been documented in several longitudinal investigations (Caspi, Elder, & Bem, 1987; Eron & Huesmann, 1990). The mean correlation between aggression in childhood and adolescence and violence in adulthood was .63 in several early research studies on this subject (Olweus, 1979). Despite the presence of a reasonably solid relationship between juvenile and adult aggression, correlations demarcate only a person's ranking on a particular measure in relation to other members of the sample. Consequently, they may conceal important developmental shifts and changes over time. Other studies indicate that a substantial portion of aggressive youth desist over time (Loeber & Hay, 1997). Using information gathered from the Vietnam Experience study, Windle and Windle (1995) ascertained that 19.4% of the veterans exhibited significant childhood aggression but had terminated the pattern before entering adulthood, 6.2% of the sample reported adult onset aggression, and 6.5% of the sample displayed continuity in aggressiveness between childhood and adulthood. Longitudinal studies conducted on criminal violence in California (Haapanen,

1991) and Philadelphia (Weiner, 1989) show that serious aggressiveness is neither stable nor highly predictable. Lattimore, Visher, and Linster (1995) enjoyed greater success using past aggression to predict rearrests for violence in a group of male adolescents released from the California Youth Authority, although a wide diversity of outcomes was nevertheless observed.

Overview

This brief review confirms that violence and aggression are sensitive to situational cues and less than fully stable over time, results that challenge the view that violent crime is a personality trait. If violent crime is not a personality trait, then to what do we ascribe the modest to moderate consistency and stability that have been reported in studies on aggression? One possibility is cumulative continuity. As the negative consequences of violence and aggression mount, a person finds himself or herself stuck in a pattern that begins to assume a life of its own and may contribute to a "knifing off" of future opportunities for conventional living (Caspi & Moffitt, 1993). A second possibility is that there may be several different patterns of violent crime, only some of which are stable over time or consistent across situations. Moffitt (1993a) contends that aggression is most stable and consistent in what she refers to as "life-course persistent" delinquency. A third possible explanation for the modest to moderate stability and consistency of violence is that certain dispositional characteristics (e.g., impulsivity) enter into complex interactions with situational factors (e.g., social context) to create patterns of reciprocal influence that maintain themselves over time. This was observed in an analysis of longitudinal data from the Pittsburgh Youth Study (Loeber, Farrington, Stouthamer-Loeber, Moffitt, & Caspi, 1998). Therefore, we need not resort to a personality trait description of violent crime to account for the modest to moderate levels of cross-situational consistency and cross-temporal stability that have been posted in research on aggression and violent crime.

LIFESTYLES CONGRUENT WITH VIOLENT CRIME

As was previously mentioned, aggression can be thought of as proactive or reactive. The lifestyles that support violent crime can also be divided into those that use aggression in a proactive manner to achieve some larger end and aggression as a reaction to perceived provocation. The criminal lifestyle enlists aggression to accomplish an objective, whether that objective is money, status, power, or intimidation. Robbing someone with the intent of taking that person's money or possessions is consistent with the proactive use of aggression. Even when the goal is to assume power over others, the aggression derives from a criminal pattern. The reactive-hostile lifestyle comes into play only in situations where a person experiences threat and acts directly on that threat. Research denotes that outcome expectancies facilitate proactive aggression but have little effect on reactive aggression (Smithmyer, Hubbard, & Simons, 2000). Offenders who rob or murder for money often view the money as their reason for committing the crime. In any event, the true motive is what the money represents to the individual; be it power, status, or the freedom to do whatever he or she desires. Whatever the reason, it is vital that the true motives behind an offender's proactive aggression be explored and clarified.

Many individuals engage in violence, even violent crime, for reasons other than a criminal lifestyle to where biased attributions of hostile intent play a central role. Reactive forms of aggression are believed to emanate from a reactive-hostile lifestyle. The spousal abuser may use aggression to intimidate and control, although spousal abuse is more often conceptualized, at least from the standpoint of the perpetrator, as a reaction to the abused spouse's actions (Stamp & Sabourin, 1995). The child or adolescent who has been continually bullied and decides to retaliate by bringing a weapon to school and settling the score through violence is probably operating out of a reactive-hostile lifestyle. What needs to be understood with respect to violent crime is that while it may be the consequence of a criminal or reactive-hostile lifestyle, more often than not, it is the consequence of both lifestyles. There is nothing to preclude a person from enacting several lifestyles simultaneously, and there is much to suggest that multiple lifestyle execution is more often the rule than the exception. Since lifestyles are, in essence, belief systems, the interrelated and overlapping belief systems that support these lifestyles are responsible for violent criminal acts.

CASE ILLUSTRATION: HAKEEM—HOODLUM

Background

Hakeem was born into a "blue-collar," working-class family, the oldest of five children, in the predominantly African American section of north Philadelphia. His father, who worked as a cook, was rarely home, and when he was home, he did not hesitate to discipline young Hakeem with physical violence. Whereas Hakeem's mother worked days and was more available than his father, even she was not particularly affectionate. Sensing that he could never measure up to his father's expectations and feeling neglected by his mother, Hakeem endured escalating levels of anger and resentment. Both parents are described by Hakeem as violent, and it would not be uncommon to find them embroiled in a fistfight, either with one another or with Hakeem as he got older. The death of a younger brother when Hakeem was 6 years old shook his faith in his parents' omnipotence and caused him to become introverted and doubting of authority. Later, when he adopted Islam and informed his parents that he no longer believed in Christmas, his parents responded by refusing to buy him any presents during the holidays or at any other time of the year.

Feeling rejected at home, Hakeem looked to the streets for support. He had already been adopted by the neighborhood gang after the death of his brother. Now they took him under their collective wing and taught him how to fight, hustle, and stick up for himself. He was one of the youngest members of the gang, and though he had to prove himself to the other gang members, the gang served as a kind of surrogate family for him. During the era in which Hakeem grew up there were many neighborhood gangs in Philadelphia, each of which attempted to protect its "turf" against intruders and rival gangs. Consequently, Hakeem grew up on a steady diet of gang wars. At any rate, gang wars were fought with fists, chains, and knives when Hakeem was young rather than with firearms, as is more often the case today. When he was 12 years of age, Hakeem began hanging around with the "old heads," adults in the neighborhood who were often involved in serious crime. These individuals helped him refine his fighting skills and taught him how to survive on the streets.

Hakeem formally left home when he was 14 years old after spending most of his later childhood on the streets. By associating with older individuals who were actively involved in criminal activity, Hakeem learned to pick pockets, shoplift, and steal in order to both survive and prosper. The crime that he found most appealing, however, was robbery. Hakeem notes that he was initially attracted to robbery for the power and control it afforded him. As he gained experience in the lifestyle, Hakeem spent increasingly more time polishing his robbery technique and honing his hustling skills so that he could follow in the footsteps of the professional gangsters whom he idolized. This shift in motivation for robbery reflects Allport's (1961) concept of functional autonomy. His change in heart and motive notwithstanding, the youthful Hakeem would roam the streets armed with an ice pick looking for easy targets to rob. When he was 13 years old, Hakeem accompanied some of the "old heads" on a major heist, from which he received $10,000 despite the fact he did not actively participate in the robbery. He spent most of the money on luxury items for himself and treated the entire neighborhood to ice cream and the cinema where a gangster movie was playing. In fact, Hakeem maintains that he grew up on a steady diet of gangster movies "from James Cagney to the Godfather." When his mother learned that he had spent $10,000 in ill-gotten gains, she beat him, not because of his criminal activities but because he failed to inform her that he had that much money on him.

Out on his own at age 14, Hakeem lived with friends. When the parents of these friends grew tired of his hanging around the house, he began sleeping in dryers in the basements of apartment complexes. Supporting himself by picking pockets and selling marijuana that he financed through strong-arm robbery, he eventually graduated to armed robbery. He states that he used a tear-gas gun in the commission of many of his robberies because he had assimilated from the "old heads" that it was not the gun but the person behind the gun that effected a successful heist. Hakeem also tried his hand at legitimate employment, and, despite average to above average intelligence, he possessed neither the training nor patience to remain in a regular job for longer than a few weeks. During this period Hakeem's crime-supporting belief systems began to jell. His self-view, molded by personal (gang) and symbolic (movies) interaction with the environment, was that of a gangster or hoodlum. He contends that his goal was to be seen as a hoodlum rather than as a thug. A hoodlum, advises Hakeem, is someone who makes a life out of crime and is loyal, committed, and respectful to others inside and outside the lifestyle. A thug, by comparison, commits crimes without benefit of respect, dignity, or loyalty. The rise in people testifying for the government, "rats" as they are commonly called, is an outgrowth of the influx of thugs into the criminal population, retorts Hakeem.

When he was 16 years old, Hakeem was placed in juvenile detention for auto theft. What began as a twenty eight-day study turned into a thirteen-month confinement. This is when he began viewing the system as corrupt, which in Hakeem's mind gave him license to continue with his law-violating activities. Hakeem observed guards smuggling drugs and other contraband items to inmates and insists that when he refused to supply staff with information on a case that they were investigating, they threw him out of a window. Paroled to a halfway house run by a woman renowned for gang prevention, Hakeem was being driven back to the house after picking up some clothes when the staff member driving the car at the time allegedly stopped the vehicle, got out, and robbed a telephone company employee. The staff member blamed the robbery on 17-year-old Hakeem, who was adjudicated as an adult and placed on five years' probation. Sensing rejection again, he rationalized that nobody cared about what happened to him, which only served to fuel his mounting hatred of society. In retaliation he started stealing payroll bags and was sent to prison for three to seven years after being caught in another stolen car. Originally sentenced to a state prison for young offenders, he soon received a disciplinary transfer to a major adult penitentiary, where he served the majority of his sentence and witnessed violence and predation on a daily basis.

Having lost all respect for the system, Hakeem did not even try to put on appearances when he was released from adult prison at 21 years of age. On the day that he was released from prison, he got locked up for auto theft. He made bail later that evening and from there went on a six-month supermarket robbing spree. Eventually caught and convicted Hakeem received twenty years in a state penitentiary. During this incarceration Hakeem became involved in the "Scared Straight" program and learned that he had a talent for rap singing. Along with several other inmates he constructed a makeshift recording studio where he recorded a demo tape. Hakeem sent the demo out to several record producers, and it was not long before he received news that one of the producers wanted to sign him to a recording contract. Also around this time Hakeem married his first wife while still in prison. After serving ten years of the twenty-year sentence, Hakeem was granted parole. He left prison with big plans and honestly believed that he had left his criminal past behind.

Something that Hakeem had not counted on when he made the decision to abandon crime was the stress associated with responsible living. He had never really acquired the skills to cope with stress and had grown accustomed to acting out violently or criminally in response to bad feelings. For one, his music career had not taken off as he had hoped. Dissatisfied with his manager and the recording contract that he had signed, Hakeem fired the manager and started his own record label. He was making ends meet by cutting hair and doing an occasional interview, but stress and uncertainty were beginning to take their toll. What's more, he was having problems on the home front. Married in prison, Hakeem had no real understanding of the intricacies and responsibilities of marriage. After six months he filed for and was granted a divorce; then, like a man jumping from the frying pan into the fire, he married two other women without benefit of a second divorce. Referencing his adherence to Islamic principles, Hakeem insists that he is entitled to more than one wife. He was being stretched thin by his personal life and an "addiction" that he couldn't see, let alone understand. While he had used drugs during adolescence, commensurate with his Muslim beliefs, Hakeem now eschewed all forms of drug use. It was not drugs to which he was addicted, however, but life on the streets, and he comments on how the 1979 Crusader's song "Street Life" depicts the attraction that the streets held for him.

Two years after his release from state prison an old friend approached Hakeem with a plan that could send both of them to jail. The friend had just lost his job and refused to go on welfare despite having a wife and young child to support. The plan entailed robbing a bank, and while Hakeem was hesitant to re-involve himself in crime he felt a profound sense of loyalty to his old friend that in his mind would not allow him to just walk away. He tried to help his friend with money that he had saved from cutting hair but could not support himself and his friend's family on the money that he was making. After consulting with both wives, he decided to go along with his friend's plan. Murphy's law was operating the day of the robbery: everything that could go wrong did go wrong. For one, the stocking that Hakeem wore over his face was so tight that it revealed his facial features. For another, the police response time, for whatever reason, was faster than usual. Third, the police did not initially pursue Hakeem because they were preoccupied with his partner; who had absconded as soon as the police arrived. Not until the assistant branch manager came out of the bank and identified Hakeem, who had nearly walked away from the scene, was he recognized and apprehended by the police. Hakeem received a 204-month sentence for armed bank robbery and was sent to a federal penitentiary. Unlike past incarcerations, he was no longer blaming the system; it was himself with whom he was most angry. "I knew better," he laments.

After spending half his life in juvenile detention, the federal Bureau of Prisons, and two different state prison systems, Hakeem insists that he is tired of the criminal lifestyle. Although some of the violence that he has perpetrated over the course of his life has been of the reactive-hostile type, the vast majority of violent acts he has committed appear to stem from a criminal lifestyle. Hakeem violates the laws of society and the rights of others in order to acquire that to which he believes he is entitled, namely, financial security and a sense of power. It has become increasingly more difficult for him to blame his life on "the system," for as he has grown older and wiser, he has come to realize that the bad decisions that he has made in life are responsible for his past and present legal predicaments. The immediate gratification that defines a criminal lifestyle has been replaced by a consideration of long-term goals as Hakeem looks to resume his rap career upon his release from prison. Unlike when he left prison the last time, Hakeem is not superoptimistically putting all his hopes in one basket. He recently entered a program of religious study in an effort to learn more about Islam, the Koran, and his responsibilities to his faith so that he can practice his religion properly and eventually instruct others in its principles. Along with this, he is pursuing formal training in cosmetology so that he can be licensed to cut and style hair once he returns to the community.

Lifestyle Assessment

The Lifestyle Criminality Screening Form (LCSF: Walters, White, & Denney, 1991) is a 17-item chart audit form used to score an individual's pre-sentence investigation (PSI) report. Subscale scores on the LCSF selectively summarize the four interactive styles that define a criminal lifestyle: irresponsibility, self-indulgence, interpersonal intrusiveness, and social rule breaking. The most important score furnished by this instrument is the total score, which can range from a low of 0 to a high of 22. The reliability and predictive validity of the LCSF have been confirmed in groups of federal and state inmates released from prison and followed up for periods of one to three years (Walters, 1998c). Scores in the range of 0 to 6 imply low risk for criminal lifestyle involvement, scores of 7 to 9 place an individual at moderate risk for criminal lifestyle involvement, while scores of 10 or higher signify high or elevated risk of criminal lifestyle involvement. A total score of 13 on the LCSF denotes that Hakeem is at high risk for involving himself in criminal lifestyle activities based on his past history (see Table 4.1). Aside from earning two points on each subscale, Hakeem resonated best to the interpersonal intrusiveness and social rule breaking styles, elevations on the former subscale demarcating his propensity for violence.

One limitation of the LCSF is that it based on past criminality. As such, scores on this measure will never fall, though they may rise. With this in mind, a more change-sensitive measure, the Psychological Inventory of Criminal Thinking Styles (PICTS: Walters, 1995), was constructed. The PICTS is an 80-item, four-choice (strongly agree, agree, uncertain, disagree) Likert-type scale that yields scores on two validity scales—confusion-revised (Cf-r), defensiveness-revised (Df-r)—eight thinking style scales—mollification (Mo), cutoff (Co), entitlement (En), power orientation (Po), sentimentality (Sn), superoptimism (So), cognitive indolence (Ci), and discontinuity (Ds)—and two content scales—current criminal thinking (CUR) and historical criminal thinking (HIS). Items and statements marked strongly agree are awarded a score of 4, items marked agree receive a score of 3, items marked uncertain earn a score of 2, and items marked disagree obtain a score of 1 for all scales except defensiveness (Df-r). On the defensiveness scale strongly agree responses receive 1 point, agree responses 2 points, uncertain responses 3 points, and disagree responses 4 points. The total raw score on each scale is then converted to a normative T-score with a mean of 50 and standard deviation of 10. The reliability and validity of the PICTS validity, thinking style, and content scales

Table 4.1
Hakeem's Scores on the Lifestyle Criminality Screening Form (LCSF)

Irresponsibility	3
Self-Indulgence	2
Interpersonal Intrusiveness	4
Social Rule Breaking	4
TOTAL LCSF SCORE	13

have been verified in groups of male and female offenders (Walters, 1995, 1996a, 1997, in press-b; Walters & Elliott, 1999; Walters, Elliott, & Miscoll, 1998).

Clinical interpretation of the PICTS relies on the configuration of T-scores registered on the validity, content, and thinking style scales. T-scores of 55–59 identify areas requiring closer inspection, whereas scores of 60 or higher are considered clinically meaningful. The validity scales are examined first, followed by the content scales, after which the thinking style scales are interpreted. Hakeem's PICTS profile is reproduced in Figure 4.2. His scores on the two validity scales are within average limits. Nevertheless, there is some indication that he may have been mildly to moderately defensive during this particular administration of the PICTS. Content scale analysis catalogs a possible elevation on the historical criminal thinking scale (T-score= 57), compared to Hakeem's current criminal history score (T-score= 44). These findings can be interpreted in one of two ways. First, it may be that Hakeem's current thinking is less criminally oriented than it has been in the past. However, the current and historical scale also load differentially on two of the primary PICTS factors: problem avoidance and self-deception/assertion, respectively. Therefore, a second interpretation is that Hakeem's criminal thinking involves asserting himself over others more than it does being irresponsible. Either way, a score of 55 or higher on at least one of the content scales justifies a closer review of the thinking style scales, where Hakeem achieves a clinically significant elevation on the power orientation scale (T-score= 60) and a subclinical elevation on the sentimentality scale (T-score= 57).

Belief System Analysis

This analysis of Hakeem's belief system is divided along the lines of the five major belief systems proposed by the integrated-interactive approach and described in detail in Chapter 3: the self-view, the world-view, the present-view, the past-view, and the future-view.

Self-View

Major components of the self-view are reflected appraisals, social comparisons, self-representations, role identities, and feared selves. As he was growing up, Hakeem's reflected appraisals were based on his interactions with older gang

Figure 4.2
Hakeem's Scores on the Psychological Inventory of Criminal Thinking Styles (PICTS)

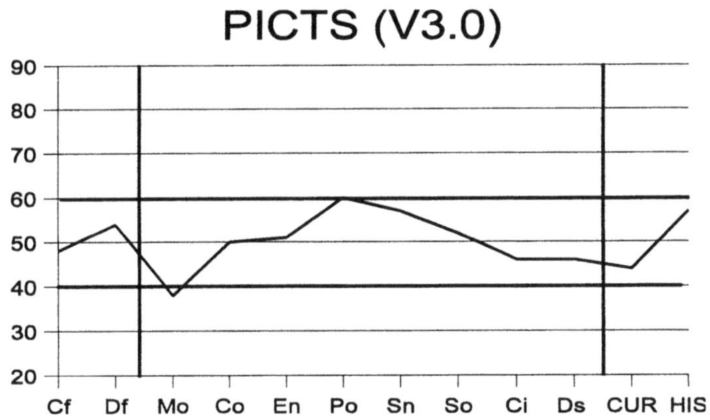

Note. Cf = confusion scale; Df = defensiveness scale; Mo = mollification scale; Co = cutoff scale; En = entitlement scale; Po = power orientation scale; Sn = sentimentality scale; So = superoptimism scale; Ci = cognitive indolence scale; Ds = discontinuity scale; CUR = current content scale; HIS = historical content scale.

members. He had all but given up trying to impress his father and so assembled a real and imaginary audience composed of individuals who he believed accepted him for who he was. Seeing himself as he perceived the older gang members saw him, Hakeem set out to prove that he belonged in the gang, with the ultimate goal being to earn a reputation as a "stand-up" hoodlum. He wanted to be seen as a "thorough" and "solid-hearted" gangster in the eyes of people whom he held in high regard. A man in a boy's body, he was treated like an adult by the older gang members. These reflected appraisals were reinforced further by watching old gangster movies and trying to mold his actions around the values and ideals portrayed in these films. Hakeem acknowledges that to this day he still mentally blocks out the final scenes of many of these movies because he does not like to watch the gangster meet his end in a hail of bullets or with 2,000 volt of electricity coursing through his body.

Hakeem made upward comparisons with the "old heads" in the neighborhood. It was these individuals, not his father, after whom he modeled himself. Hakeem found himself emulating adults who were accorded the respect of other gang members. Respect in this context was earned by showing superior fighting skills, displaying undying loyalty, and performing crime with finesse. Their magnetic character, confidence, and flamboyance drew Hakeem to them and made them the object of his upward comparisons. Downward comparisons, on the other hand, were made with those whom he perceived to be cowards. A coward, according to Hakeem, is someone who does not stand up for what he or she believes. These were the individuals Hakeem looked down upon, and a comparison with someone whom Hakeem saw as a coward was an automatic boost to his self-esteem. Parallel comparisons were made with other gang members at the same level of the gang hierarchy as Hakeem, who were often older than he. Hakeem used parallel comparisons to evaluate his competition and judge what he had to do in order to move up the gang and criminal hierarchies.

There is evidence of both personal and collective self-representations in Hakeem's self-view. His self-representation as a gangster reflects both a personal sense of accomplishment in the lifestyle as well as a sense of bonding and collective identity with the gang. His successes in life were attributed to internal, unstable, and global causes; he would often tell himself that he was successful in crime because he was "thorough" and constantly remind himself that he had to remain vigilant in the face of environmental change so that he did not lose his "edge." Failure, in contrast, was attributed to external, stable, and global causes. When he was younger, it was not uncommon for Hakeem to blame his legal troubles on racism and a corrupt legal system. As he has matured, he has made more internal attributions for the legal and disciplinary problems that he has encountered in the community and prison system. A certain degree of externality persists, nonetheless, in that he ascribes his last two, albeit minor, disciplinary infractions in the federal prison system to "misunderstandings."

Role identity is another key facet of a person's self-view, according to the perspective adopted in this book. Violence is one way that male youth affirm their masculinity (Messerschmidt, 1993). Thus, while traditional gender roles may inhibit aggression in girls, they tend to foster aggression in boys (Heimer & De Coster, 1999). When repeatedly questioned about homosexuality and related issues by a psychologist conducting an evaluation of him at the time, a teenage Hakeem grew angry and assaulted the psychologist. His masculine role identity was manifest in his preoccupation with the gangster stereotypes depicted in the media. Hakeem learned to walk, talk, and dress like a gangster, down to the pinkie ring, knife, and holstered pistol. Later, when he was confined in adult prisons during late adolescence and early adulthood, he sought to project a masculine image in order to avoid being preyed on by older, larger, and more con-wise inmates.

Three feared selves have been instrumental in shaping Hakeem's self-view. First, there is the feared self of becoming a coward or "rat." Hakeem has compensated for this feared self by adopting a gangster persona and remaining loyal to those with whom he commits crime, including the friend who approached him about robbing the bank for which he is currently serving time. Second, there is the feared self of being seen as weak. Hakeem has tried to compensate for this particular feared self by projecting an air of confidence, strength, and power. Third, Hakeem feared turning out like his father, particularly with reference to his treatment of women. Hakeem's father had always been violent with his mother, and Hakeem wanted very much to avoid repeating this pattern. In fact, he compensated for this particular feared self by becoming more compassionate toward females than most of his friends or criminal associates. To this day he expresses pride that he has never raised his hand in anger toward a woman.

World-View

The world-view encompasses four dimensions and derives from schemes known as prototypes. On the organismic-mechanistic dimension of his world-view Hakeem takes an integrated approach in the sense that he perceives the world as both or-ganismic and mechanistic. He harbors certain mechanistic views, gained in part from his studies in Islam, although he also conceptualizes change and development as essential components of his world-view. In integrating the two poles of the organic-mechanistic dimension, Hakeem puts himself in a position to improve his adaptive skills to the extent that synthesis is a cardinal feature of adaptation. This aspect of his world-view would seem to bode well for future change.

Hakeem also relies on both poles of the fatalism-agenticism dimension. However, the poles are not nearly as well integrated as are the two poles of the organismic-mechanistic dimension. Taking his cue from Islam, Hakeem argues that all actions are decreed by Allah, but people still make a choice. The theological determinism that runs through Islam, Judaism, and Christianity is difficult to reconcile with scientific principles and is why religion is based on faith rather than fact. Believing that one's actions are controlled by an omniscient and omnipotent higher power, yet insisting that people have a choice, can be traced to the conflict between the practical necessity of making people responsible for their actions and the ideological requirements of creating a God worth worshiping. The contradictions and internal inconsistencies introduced by a religious doctrine of predestination are as unapparent to Hakeem as they are to most loyal worshipers.

Hakeem clearly favors the justice end of the justice-inequity dimension. Events happen in accordance with the will of Allah, asserts Hakeem. This is another way of saying that negative circumstances exist for a reason; even so, God may be the only one who knows the reason. The core of Hakeem's beliefs on this subject is that people reap what they sow and generally get what they deserve. Belief in a just world is consistent with Hakeem's contention that people have a choice and that we live in a just and ordered universe. Hakeem's endorsement of the just world metaphor, it should be noted, may make him less sympathetic to the plight of others. Even with this particular element of the world-view working against him, seeing as it would appear to facilitate discounting a potential victim's feelings, Hakeem's religious beliefs make no allowances for violent crime and serve as a counteraggression measure as long as he remains true to these beliefs.

Whereas Hakeem incorporates aspects of malevolence and benevolence into his world-view, he conceives of Western culture in general and the government of the United States in particular as hypocritical and corrupt. Such a system, reasons Hakeem, undermines individual choice and freedom. At any rate, Hakeem makes allowances for benevolence in individual actors. On balance, he considers larger social systems malevolent and self-serving but is more open-minded when evaluating individuals. Hakeem takes each person on a case-by-case basis and attempts to weigh the person's positive and negative attributes in assessing his or her overall level of malevolence/benevolence. With respect to Hakeem's malevolent view of society, it is interesting that anthropological research (Huber, 1972), psychological surveys (Altemeyer, 1988), and criminological studies (Wright, Sheley, & Smith, 1992) all distinguish a connection between physical aggression and the belief in a dangerous or malevolent world.

The prototypes that have served as building blocks for Hakeem's world-view are rigid and simplistic and have traditionally emphasized such issues as strength versus weakness and authenticity versus inauthenticity. His elevated score on the power orientation scale of the PICTS reveals that strength versus weakness is a key dimension along which he evaluates himself and others. In addition, he deliberates whether he and others are being genuine and true to their beliefs and values. This characterization transcends criminal involvement since Hakeem respects people who live a noncriminal way of life provided they are willing to stand up for what they believe. It is people who profess one thing and then do another for whom Hakeem has no respect. Criminal and noncriminal lifestyles offer divergent rules for survival, but people who stand up for their beliefs, regardless of the lifestyle that they lead, earn Hakeem's admiration.

Present-View

The present-view consists of both perceptual processing and executive functions. As is the case with many individuals who participate in violent offending, Hakeem displays signs of perceptual distortion. His scores on the PICTS indicate that power-oriented thinking and sentimentality color his perceptions to the point where he seeks to maintain control over situations and then excuses his actions by pointing out the good deeds that he has performed in the past. The attributional misperceptions of hostile intent referred to in the literature on aggression (Crick & Dodge, 1994) were evident in the young Hakeem. He relates that if people bump into him, they had better apologize, or they will receive a severe beating. Any such incident would be interpreted as a sign of disrespect by Hakeem, a deliberate challenge to his manhood. These were insults that he was fully prepared to vindicate with violence. In the eyes of the youthful Hakeem, violence was justified if it meant standing up for one's family or reputation, lessons that he assimilated from his days as a gang member in the neighborhood.

Problem-solving deficits are commonly observed in those who habitually engage in violent criminality (Guerra & Slaby, 1989). Despite average to above average intelligence, Hakeem's life story reveals a string of poor choices. The decision to involve himself in the offense for which he is currently serving time is a case in point. He let loyalty to a friend cloud his judgment and override any misgivings that he had about his friend's robbery plans. Prior to agreeing to accompany his friend to the bank, he spoke with both wives. Although they did not encourage him to participate in the crime, neither did they try to dissuade him. He could not rely on his own judgment and he had no one in his life to give him guidance and encourage him to more thoroughly evaluate his options. It is interesting that cultural research shows that polygymy corresponds with higher levels of crime, while crime is reduced in cultures where the ratio of males-to-females is high, and women can demand greater economic investment and responsibility from their husbands (Barber, 2000). Conceivably, had one of Hakeem's wives felt more secure in her role as his wife, perhaps she would have exercised greater positive control over his eventual decision.

Past-View

At this point in time Hakeem's past-view is centered around the mistakes that he has made in life as he strives to learn from these errors in judgment so that he can avoid repeating them in the future. In reviewing past recollections, Hakeem is struck by the ignorance that he has exhibited throughout his life; still, he tries to avoid "kicking himself" for past mistakes because to do so would only invite relapse and recidivism as he seeks to relieve the bad feelings that would likely ensue. Despite a willingness to acknowledge his own ignorance, Hakeem continues to put himself a rung or two above the younger individuals who are now coming to prison, many of whom he describes as "crack heads" for their lack of criminal professionalism. Reflecting on the past is something that Hakeem is not all that accustomed to because when he was most extensively involved in crime, he was almost exclusively present-oriented. In fact, he made a concerted effort to block out his past, perhaps because to focus on his past would have interfered with his ability to carry out his criminal plans in the present.

Future-View

As is the case with most teenagers, criminal or otherwise, Hakeem thought very little about the future when he first started committing crime. Everything was geared toward the immediate gratification of his aggressive and criminal urges. Therefore, with the exception of short-term positive outcome expectancies for aggression, Hakeem's future-view was barren. As he grew older and entered young adulthood, he expanded his time horizon to include several more long-term benefits of crime, like having a nice car, purchasing a home, and owning his own business. Still, he did not look too far into the future and disregarded all information pertaining to the future negative repercussions of his actions. He recalls spending $30,000 in two days, though he cannot actually remember what he purchased with the money, and $25,000 in one night at the craps tables in Atlantic City. As he has matured, Hakeem has extended his time horizon to where his current plans are to have children, raise them according to Islamic principles, and live a life based on morality, commitment, and respect rather than instant gratification, power, and egotism.

CONCLUSION

Despite the fact that empirical support for Wolfgang and Ferracuti's (1967) subculture of violence hypothesis has been slow in coming, cultural factors are viewed to be vital in the construction of belief systems congruent with violent crime. Culture supplies a context within which belief systems evolve. The self-view, world-view, present-view, past-view, and future-view of someone like Hakeem would likely have been very different had he been raised in another culture. American society and the African American subculture of north Philadelphia helped mold many of Hakeem's beliefs, but not everyone who grows up in north Philadelphia turns to violent crime. In fact, available research indicates that the majority of people raised in such environments do not engage in habitual aggressive criminality (Piper, 1985). What, then, determines who advances to the next phase of violent criminal belief system development? The home environment and immediate neighborhood in which one is raised would appear to be likely candidates for shaping a person's belief systems. With reference to Hakeem, he observed violence in the home and was accepted by neighborhood gang members for executing his own program of violence. This still falls short of providing a complete explanation since many children brought up in violent homes in high crime rate areas do not go on to commit violent crime. Thus, a third factor in the ordering of crime-congruent belief systems is choice and the self-reinforcing nature of patterned interaction.

Choice is critically important when it comes to initiating and maintaining belief systems congruent with crime. Despite making significant strides toward self-improvement, Hakeem still blames some of his past criminal actions on a racist society and corrupt political system. Until he fully acknowledges that it was the choices that he made in life that led him down the present path, he will continue experiencing problems functioning in society and dealing with the many pressures, frustrations, and temptations that he is likely to encounter upon release. Whereas the theological determinism of Islam may produce certain scientific inconsistencies, Hakeem can make practical use of his religious beliefs through reinforcement of the twin notions of choice and responsibility which together form one of the core elements of change (see Chapter 8). Besides choice, the self-reinforcing nature of a lifestyle is also crucial in promoting belief systems congruent with violent crime. With each successive robbery Hakeem became increasingly more confident in his ability to succeed criminally. He also received positive attention from gang members and from various neighbors whom he would periodically help out with proceeds from his criminal lifestyle. These influences combined to create a self-reinforcing pattern that was difficult for Hakeem to abandon because it instilled in him the confidence, meaning, and sense of identity that he lacked prior to entering the lifestyle. Breaking the pattern necessitates finding alternative avenues of confidence, meaning, and identity attainment incongruent with crime. Before considering belief systems incongruent with crime, however, three more crimes must first be discussed—sexual assault, white-collar crime, and drug trafficking.

5

Belief Systems and Sexual Assault

Many acts can be classified under the rubric of sexual assault. In this chapter sexual assault is defined as (1) unlawful sexual contact with an unwilling adult or same-age peer or (2) improper sexual advances made by an adult or older adolescent to a juvenile or child. The first criterion covers such crimes as indecent assault and forcible rape, whereas the latter criterion describes familial and non-familial forms of child molestation. It is a fundamental premise of the integrated-interactive approach that sexual assault, like violent offending, is more meaningfully classified according to the offense rather than with respect to the offender. This is because people categorized as rapists or child molesters often engage in crimes other than rape and child molestation. For the sake of both completeness and uniformity, sexual assault is defined by the act rather than by the perpetrator. Such an approach is believed to hold the greatest promise of clarifying the belief systems that underlie sexual assault.

EXTENT AND SEVERITY OF SEXUAL OFFENDING

There were 32,060 arrests for forcible rape and 101,900 arrests for other sex offenses in the United States in 1997 (BJS, 1999). Because only about half of all rapes are cleared by arrest and only a fraction of rapes and other sexual offenses are ever reported to the police, there is every reason to believe that these figures greatly underestimate the total occurrence and extent of sexual assault. Indeed, the National Crime Victimization Survey apprises that 330,000 rapes and sexual assaults took place in the United States in 1998 (Rennison, 1999). An accurate estimate of the number of children molested each year may be even more elusive. Many child victims are either too young, afraid, embarrassed, or confused to report molestation. With good reason, then, researchers judge the rate of child molestation to be many times the official rate (Finkelhor & Lewis, 1988). Even with a considerable number of sexual assaults not being reported to the police, these acts are relatively infrequent compared to other violent offenses like robbery and aggravated assault. Current estimates indicate that forcible rape represents less than 5% of the total number of Federal Bureau of Investigation (FBI) Uniform Crime Report violent crimes reported to the police each year in the United States (BJS, 1999). This does not mean, however, that sexual assault is any less deserving of national attention than other categories of violent crime.

Sexual assault wrecks havoc on a victim, the victim's family, and society in general. A review of the literature on adult female victims of rape denotes that many of these victims suffer augmented levels of fear, anxiety, depression, post-traumatic stress disorder (PTSD), self-doubt, and sexual dysfunction (Resick, 1993). The negative repercussions of a sexual assault can linger for years and in some cases never remit. Likewise, the victims of child sexual abuse are at elevated risk for lifetime diagnoses of major depression, conduct disorder, panic disorder, and alcoholism, and many such individuals show evidence of heightened suicidal ideation (Dinwiddie et al., 2000). The problem is no less severe in Canada (Hanson, 1990) and Great Britain (West, 2000). As 49% to 97% of sex offenders report that they themselves had been sexually abused as children (Aljazireh, 1993), sexual assault, whether perpetrated against a child or adult, constitutes a problem of epic proportions. The cross-generational transfer of sexual offending, coupled with the fact that three-quarters of all attempted and completed rapes are committed by nonstrangers, one-quarter of whom are husbands or boyfriends (Rennison, 1999), details the scope of the problem introduced by sexual assault.

DEMOGRAPHICS OF SEXUAL CRIME

In 1997, 17% of those arrested for rape and 18% of those arrested for other types of sexual crimes were under 18 years of age (BJS, 1999). There is reason to believe, however, that juveniles account for a higher percentage of sexual crime than is reflected in these figures. Becker (1988) estimates that 20% of all rapes and 30–50% of all cases of child molestation are perpetrated by juveniles. There are also indications that in a fair number of cases sexual offending begins at a relatively early age. A majority of 12- to 15-year-old delinquents adjudicated for sex crimes reported that they had been offending for years, with an average of 69.5 sex offenses and 16.5 victims each (Wieckowski, Hartsoe, Mayer, & Shortz, 1998). Age of onset, in fact, has been found to predict future offending and recidivism. Individuals with onset in childhood or adolescence account for a greater portion of general deviance (Abel, Becker, Cunningham-Rathner, Mittelman, & Rouleau, 1988), poor outcomes (Romero & Williams, 1985), and expressions of weak remorse (Ward, Hudson, & Marshall, 1995) than persons whose sexual offending began in adulthood.

Females were responsible for 1.3% and 9.1% of the arrests for rape and other sexual offenses, respectively, in 1997 (BJS, 1999). There is speculation that, as with juveniles, these official figures underestimate female involvement in sexual assault (Condy, Templer, Brown, & Veaco, 1987). As it stands, females convicted of a sexual offense were less often married and more likely to have made a suicide attempt than male sex offenders and female non-sex offenders and more apt to report sexually transmitted diseases, life stressors, and episodes of psychological treatment than non-sex-offending females (Miccio-Fonseca, 2000). The primary difference between male and female sex offenders, according to Groth (1979), is that females manifest less anger and aggression in the course of their offending and overwhelmingly prefer child victims. Power and control may therefore be less instrumental in motivating sexual assault in women than is the case with men. Contrasting male and female sex and non-sex offenders, Allen and Pothast (1994) determined that females, regardless of offender status, and child sex offenders, irrespective of gender, conveyed stronger emotional and sexual needs than males and non-child sex offenders, respectively. Females may accordingly engage in sexual assault for reasons of emotional and sexual gratification rather than out of a desire for power and control.

Abel and Rouleau (1990) summarize the demographic and background characteristics of a group of 561 males who voluntarily sought assessment and/or clinical services at one of two treatment centers for sexual offending. With an average age of 31.5 years, this group was somewhat younger than the general populations from which it was sampled. The ethnic and socioeconomic composition, on the other hand, paralleled general population estimates. Marital status, educational level, and occupational attainment were also comparable to breakdowns found in the general population, with one-half of the sex-offending sample currently or formally married, 40% possessing one or more years of college, and two-thirds presently employed. Slightly more than half the sample had formed a deviant sexual interest prior to age 18, and those individuals who first engaged in deviant sexuality before age 18 had committed an average of 380 offenses. Whether a subject began offending in childhood, adolescence, or adulthood, simple or isolated paraphilias were rare. In short, more than half the sample had previously participated in, or were currently engaged in, three or more different paraphilias.

THEORIES OF SEXUAL ASSAULT

Social strain theory, like most sociological theories of crime, has not been specifically applied to sexual assault. Nonetheless, several studies have examined the relationship between stress and sexual abuse. Pithers (1990), for one, asserts that sexual offending is most likely to occur under conditions of high stress. There is also evidence that people convicted of sexual assault experience accelerated self-denigrating thoughts under stress (Neidigh & Tomiko, 1991) and frequently cope with stress by withdrawing into fantasy (Marshall, Serran, & Cortoni, 2000; Proulx, McKibben, & Lusignan, 1996). The Proulx et al. study suggests that when faced with interpersonal conflict and negative emotional experiences, people classified as sex offenders generate deviant fantasies to which they masturbate in an effort to manage the inner tension induced by the stress. Ward et al. (1995) enlist Baumeister's (1990) cognitive deconstruction concept to explain how stress and negative affect encourage a breakdown in planning and a focus on short-term, often physical goals. The eventual outcome is an individual who deals with the negative consequences of his or her actions by shifting attention to more concrete levels of awareness and meaning.

Differential association theory may also elucidate certain aspects of sexual assault. Data drawn from large national surveys conducted in the United States and Canada reveal that men who commit violence against women tend to fraternize with like-thinking and similarly acting peers (Schwartz & DeKeseredy, 1997). Male peer support may be one of the strongest predictors of date rape (DeKeseredy & Kelly, 1995), particularly when endorsed by such chauvinistic institutions as social fraternities and male sports (Humphrey & Kahn, 2000). Hanson and Scott (1996) asked 126 men charged with, or convicted of, a sexual offense and 57 nonsexual offenders whether they personally knew any perpetrators of sexual crime. The individuals in the sexual offense group reported significantly more association and identification with people convicted of sexual assault compared to the nonsexual offending group. Of particular interest in advancing a differential association theory of sexual assault is the fact that the affiliations were specific to the offense so that child molesters associated primarily with people who had previously molested children and rapists with people who had previously committed rape.

Labeling an individual a sex offender has the power to perpetuate a pattern of sexual offending. The 1970s saw a growing trend toward the medicalization of deviance and criminal behavior. In an effort to facilitate involuntary civil commitment to mental hospitals for persons suspected of sexual assault, many of the behaviors linked to sexual offending, the so-called paraphilias, were redefined as symptoms of serious mental disorder (Alexander, 1997). These legal developments resonate with attitudes expressed by the general public (Hollin & Howells, 1987) and echoed by many offenders (Fowler, Bray, & Hollin, 1992) that rape and other forms of sexual assault are manifestations of serious mental instability, despite the fact that there is no proof that sex offenders present with greater levels of nonparaphilic psychopathology than other offender groups (Hall, Shepherd, & Mudrak, 1992; Jacobs, Kennedy, & Meyer, 1997). Judges, in an effort to protect the public, rely on these definitions and have been known to treat psychiatric diagnoses in persons charged with sexual assault as aggravating conditions (Dinovitzer, 1997). Thus, instead of receiving leniency from the court, as one might anticipate if one's criminal actions were, in fact, the product of a mental disorder or defect, sex offenders often receive harsher sentences when their behavior has been labeled by mental health experts as indicative of significant psychopathology.

Neutralization is another criminological theory with the potential to advance our understanding of sexual assault. Cognitive distortions have received a fair amount of attention in research on child sex offending. In a prototypic study on this issue Pollock and Hashmall (1991) reviewed the clinical records of eighty-six individuals convicted of child molestation and identified twenty-one different excuses, which the authors then organized into six themes. These themes are similar, and in some cases identical, to the neutralizations described by Sykes and Matza (1957) and include denial of fact ("it didn't happen"), denial of responsibility ("it wasn't may fault"), denial of sexual intent ("it wasn't sexual"), denial of wrongfulness ("it wasn't wrong"), denial of self-determination ("it was done under extenuating circumstances"), and denial of the victim ("it was the child's fault"). Neutralization was also evident in the publications of three pedophile organizations with designs on rationalizing and legitimating sexual contact with young children (Young, 1988).

Although there is a dearth of empirical research on social control theory or Thornberry's (1987) interactional theory in the literature on sexual offending, there is good reason to believe that these approaches may also shed light on sexual assault. First, there is growing consensus that early infant attachment relationships, similar but not identical to Hirschi's (1969) concept of social bonding, influence a person's proclivity for sexual offending. Second, Gottfredson and Hirschi's (1990) general theory of crime assumes that sexual crime is no different than other forms of criminality. The first issue is addressed in the next section, and the second issue is examined in the section after that. Thornberry's (1987) interactional theory emphasizes the prominence of reciprocal associations, and there is speculation that such interconnections may play a leading role in sexual offending. Barbaree and Marshall (1991), for instance, propose the existence of a bidirectional relationship between negative affective states like anger and frustration and inhibitory cognitive-affective states like empathy, guilt, and moral conviction that helps maintain the sexual assault pattern.

AN INTEGRATED-INTERACTIONAL THEORY OF SEXUAL ASSAULT

Stephen Hudson of the University of Canterbury in Christchurch, New Zealand, Tony Ward of the University of Melbourne in Melbourne, Australia, and William Marshall of Queens University in Ontario, Canada, have collaborated to construct a general cognitive-behavioral model of sexual offending with relevance to the integrated-interactive theory outlined in this text. The components of Ward, Hudson, and Marshall's (1996) model most relevant to the integrated-interactional theory are intimacy, empathy, and cognitive distortion. Ward, Hudson, and Marshall maintain that sexual offenders are more lonely than most offenders, experience substantial difficulty empathizing with others, and engage in cognitive distortions to justify continued involvement in sexual crime. Each of these components is discussed in turn.

Intimacy

Research has consistently shown that people convicted of child molestation or rape are lonely compared to non-sex offenders and community respondents and that they suffer pronounced intimacy problems as a result (Bumby & Marshall, 1994; Seidman, Marshall, Hudson, & Robertson, 1994). Self-esteem has also been found to be low in people classified as sex offenders (Marshall, Barbaree, & Fernandez, 1995). Hence, a drop in self-esteem preceded sexual assault in 56% of the subjects convicted of rape and 61% of the subjects convicted of child molestation in a study by Pithers, Beal, Armstrong, and Petty (1989). There is further evidence that psychological forms of intervention are capable of enhancing self-esteem and that a rise in self-esteem is normally accompanied by reductions in deviant fantasies and arousal in habitual sexual offenders (Marshall, 1997). Of cardinal significance in understanding these social and personal skill deficits is determining their origin. One possibility is that these skill deficits spring from an insecure attachment style such as has been described in the writings of John Bowlby (1969/1982, 1980) and Mary Salter Ainsworth (1979, 1989).

Bartholomew (1990) has contributed to our understanding of attachment by organizing Ainsworth's (1979) three styles of attachment (secure, anxious/ambivalent, avoidant) into a four-category classification scheme. People expressing positive views of themselves and others are classified as secure, whereas subjects holding positive views of others but negative views of themselves are categorized as preoccupied. Ainsworth's avoidant style is characterized by a negative view of others and subdivided into a dismissing style when paired with a positive self-view and a fearful style when paired with a negative self-view. Insecure attachment is commonly observed in offenders, whether or not they offend sexually. Even so, persons convicted of child-sex offenses are more likely to be classified as preoccupied and fearful, while individuals convicted of rape are more often dismissing (Ward et al., 1996). In comparing men serving time for sexual crimes against children, men serving time for sexual offenses against adult females, nonsexual violent offenders, and nonsexual non-violent inmates, Hudson and Ward (1997a) noticed that attachment style was a much stronger predictor of loneliness than offense category, with the preoccupied and fearful styles achieving the highest correlations. A person's level of differential attachment to mother versus father may also be important. Smallbone and Dadds (2000) assert that problematic attachment to the mother predicts antisocial behavior and that problematic attachment to the father is more closely tied to sexually coercive behavior.

Loneliness and intimacy problems may stem from attachment style, but what gives rise to insecure attachment styles, and what is unique about people who offend sexually? It has been speculated that childhood sexual abuse disrupts future adult attachments by adversely affecting self-perception and affect regulation (Alexander, 1992). Empirical research signifies that people convicted of sexual assault entertain more negative recollections of their parents and experience much higher rates of psychological abuse and slightly higher levels of physical and sexual abuse during childhood than violent nonsexual offenders (Haapasalo & Kankkonen, 1997). Findings from another study revealed that familial sexual deviance and abuse corresponded to the severity of the offspring's sexual aggression and that physical abuse and neglect were linked to the severity of nonsexual aggression (Prentky et al., 1989). Factors other than sexual and physical abuse that may help shape attachment style include peer relations and parental identification. Sex offenders report fewer friendships and close peer relationships (Blaske, Borduin, Henggeler, & Mann, 1989) and less identification with their mothers and fathers (Levant & Bass, 1991) than non-sex offenders.

Empathy

Marshall, Hudson, Jones, and Fernandez (1995) conceptualize empathy as a four-step process: (1) accurately identifying emotional cues, (2) adopting another's perspective, (3) evoking the appropriate emotion, and (4) forming and delivering an empathic response. It has been proposed that people who engage in sexual assault have difficulty with all four steps of the empathy production process, starting with accurately perceiving emotional cues. The majority of studies on this issue take note of deficits in the ability to decode emotional cues in other people's facial expressions and demeanor (Hudson et al., 1993; Racey, Lopez, & Schneider, 2000). Insomuch as one study found that nonadjudicated rapists were superior to age-matched controls in deciphering nonverbal emotional cues (Giannini & Fellows, 1986), convicted rapists have been found to perform worse on this task than controls. Men serving time in a maximum security federal penitentiary for rape, as a case in point, experienced greater difficulty reading cues in a simulated first date scenario than violent non-sex offenders and nonviolent non-sex offenders (Lipton, McDonel, & McFall, 1987). More sexually aggressive college males also have trouble decoding women's communications and are more apt to interpret assertiveness as a sign of aggression and friendliness as an indication of seduction in comparison to less sexually aggressive male students (Malamuth & Brown, 1994). Persons convicted of child sex offenses also misinterpret innocent cues, like a child sitting on an adult's lap, as invitations to sexual contact (Ward, 2000).

With regard to the second step of the empathy process, perspective taking, there is ample evidence that sex offenders have trouble adopting the perspective of a potential victim. Scully (1988) relates that over half of her sample of rapists acknowledged no feelings for their victims during or after the assault. Hanson and Scott (1995), on the other hand, advise that while people charged with child molestation performed as well as non-sex offenders on a general measure of empathy, the former group displayed specific perspective-taking deficits for child victims of sexual assault. Other studies confirm that child sex offenders perform as well as non-sex offenders on measures of general empathy but that their performance deteriorates when they are asked to assume the perspective of a child who has been sexually abused, particularly if the child is their own victim (Beckett, Beech, Fisher, & Fordham, 1994; Marshall, Champagne, Brown, & Miller, 1997). The highly specific nature of these performance anomalies implies that the empathy deficits traditionally ascribed to child molestation may be more properly attributed to cognitive distortion than to weak perspective taking. In line with this reasoning, Phelen (1995) discovered that incestuous fathers often expressed sentiments insinuating that they believed that their daughters welcomed their incestuous advances, when, in fact, none of the daughters described the encounters as enjoyable.

The evocation of emotion similar to that observed in the victim of a sexual offense is the third step in the empathy process outlined by Marshall et al. (1995). No studies directly assessing this third step could be identified in the published literature. However, results from the aforementioned Scully (1988) investigation connote that while over half the rapists interviewed felt little empathy for their victims, three-quarters of the sample stated that if their wife, girlfriend, sister, or mother had been raped, they would have responded with anger and violence. It would seem that these individuals are capable of evoking the emotions of persons who have been sexually victimized by someone like themselves but that they are unable to apply this knowledge to their own situations because of cognitive distortion.

The fourth step of the empathy process entails responding appropriately to another person's distress or emotional pain, which means assuming responsibility for one's actions. A review of the research on this issue suggests that many sex offenders avoid responsibility by blaming their actions on external factors like the victim (Loza & Clements, 1991; Webster & Beech, 2000). An attributional style that ascribes offending to external, stable, global, and uncontrollable factors is highly conducive to sexual assault (Kennedy & Grubin, 1992). Intervention can be helpful in modifying sex crime-congruent attributions, however. Larsen, Hudson, and Ward (1995) verified that a group of individuals convicted of child molestation began attributing their sexual offending behavior to internal, unstable, specific, and controllable factors following their participation in an organized program of cognitive restructuring. Private speech is another cognitive mechanism potentially useful in modifying a person's propensity to engage in sexual assault through modification of his or her empathic response. Sexually aggressive men habitually produce disinhibitory self-talk, which, in turn, augments their arousal to forced sex cues. Conversely, non-sexually aggressive men were more skilled at differentiating between consensual and forced cues and engaged in more inhibitory self-talk when confronted with forced sex cues that served to attenuate their arousal to the forced cues (Porter & Critelli, 1994).

Cognitive Distortion

It has been argued that the specific empathy deficits that surface when child sex offenders are asked to comment on their own victims or other victims of sexual assault can be traced to cognitive distortion rather than weak perspective taking (Ward, Hudson, Johnston, & Marshall, 1997). Individuals convicted of a child sex offense endorse more cognitive distortions when discussing sexual contact with children than persons convicted of rape or non-sex crimes who have been asked to provide an account of the offense for which they are currently serving time (Blumenthal, Gudjonsson, & Burns, 1999; Stermac & Segal, 1989). Bumby (1996) detected a reasonably robust relationship between the magnitude of cognitive distortion and the number of victims and duration of sexual assault in a group of persons serving time for child sex offenses. Sexual entitlement, in which the offender believes that his or her sexual needs supersede the needs of the victim, is especially prominent in incestuous offending males (Hanson, Gizzarelli, & Scott, 1994). In an effort to clarify the role of cognitive distortion in child sex offending, Abel, Becker, and Cunningham-Rathner (1984) determined that many people convicted of child sex crimes initially began modifying their thoughts and belief systems in an effort to justify their continued involvement in the deviant activity—from the belief that sexual activity increases a child's sexual knowledge, to the belief that if a child fails to report sexual abuse, then he or she must condone such activity. Ward and Keenan (1999) list five implicit theories that they say account for much of the cognitive distortion witnessed in people who sexually abuse children. These implicit theories appear to reflect both the individual's world-view and potential information-processing deficits: (1) children are sexual beings; (2) sexual activity is harmless; (3) sexual entitlement; (4) belief in a dangerous or malevolent world; and (5) uncontrollableness or fatalism.

Offenders who sexually assault children may exhibit greater cognitive distortion than offenders who sexually assault adults (Abel et al., 1988), but the latter group is by no means free of cognitive distortion. First, men who rape adult women tend to make extreme external attributions for their actions, frequently blaming the victim for her predicament (Blumenthal et al., 1999; Loza & Clements, 1991). Externalization or transferring blame to the victim can be accomplished in many different ways, though some of the more popular mollifications are to insist that the woman was looking to be raped because of the revealing clothing that she was wearing, that she didn't do everything within her power to prevent the rape, or that se was in the wrong part of town at the wrong time of day. Another component of the cognitive distortions found in men who rape is sex-role stereotyping. Burt (1983) asserts that rapists and men in general share many of the same attitudes about violence toward women but that rapists more often act on these beliefs and use them to justify their sexually aggressive intentions. One of these rape-supporting beliefs is sex-role stereotyping in which women are seen as property or possessions that men must aggressively pursue and dominate. Males scoring high on a likely-to-sexually-harass scale perceived a stronger connection between dominance and sexuality than men scoring low on this measure (Pryor & Stoller, 1994). There is additional evidence that college males high in sex-role stereotyping are more aroused by rape vignettes than are low sex-role-stereotyping males (Check & Malamuth, 1983). It would seem that whether a child or adult is the target of a sexual assault, cognitive distortion plays a critical role in maintaining the deviant pattern.

Overview

Figure 5.1 depicts the complex reciprocal relations hypothesized to exist between variables considered prominent in initiating and maintaining sexual assault. It is proposed that sexual and physical abuse, poor parental identification,

Figure 5.1
An Integrated-Interactive Model of Sexual Assault

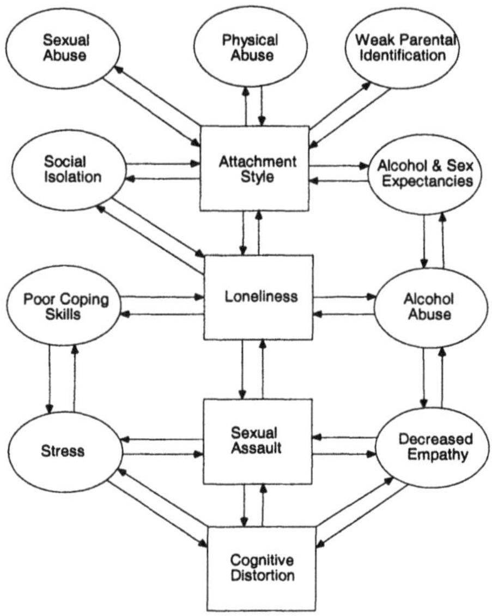

and social isolation encourage development of an attachment style conducive to criminally oriented thinking in general and belief systems congruent with sexual assault in particular. Attachment style, in conjunction with social isolation, forms a reciprocal relationship with loneliness, which, in turn, interacts reciprocally with poor coping ability. While the abuse of alcohol directly affects a person's propensity to commit sexual assault (Langevin & Lang, 1990), it may exert an even more profound indirect effect by interacting with loneliness/social isolation and empathy. Positive outcome expectancies for sexual and social enhancement with the use of alcohol may further promote alcohol misuse through increased consumption designed to further sexual goals (Monson, Jones, Rivers, & Blum, 1998). Environmental stress, aggravated by coping skill deficits and alcohol misuse (although this is not pictured in the diagram), in concert with weak empathy for potential victims, is believed to impact directly on a person's inclination to offend sexually. Cognitive distortion, which includes both distorted thinking and attributional styles that ascribe sexual assault to external, stable, and global factors, helps maintain the pattern directly as well as indirectly through interaction with weak empathy and environmental stress.

IS THERE A DIFFERENCE BETWEEN SEXUAL ASSAULT AND OTHER CRIMES?

Before tackling the task of differentiating between sexual assault and nonsexual crime, it may be instructive to consider whether sexual offending itself is general or specific. In a study previously described, Abel and Rouleau (1990) witnessed substantial overlap between different paraphilias and categories of sexual offending and took note of the fact that single or isolated paraphilias were relatively rare. Weinrott and Saylor (1991) also uncovered versatility in the offense patterns of ninety-nine sex offenders, particularly when self-report data were used instead of official data. Official records showed that 85% of the sample specialized in a single class of victim. Self-report, by contrast, painted a very different picture, with 32% of the official rapists claiming prior sexual contact with children, 12% of the official child molesters confiding participation in at least one attempt at forced sexual activity with an adult female, 34% of nonfamilial child molesters conceding one or more acts of incest, and 50% of familial child molesters confessing to an undetected episode of molestation outside the home. Furthermore, whereas only 4% of the offenders had ever been officially arrested for exhibitionism, 23% acknowledged that they had engaged in this behavior at least once in the past year.

Not only do many sex offenders fail to restrict themselves to a particular type of paraphilia or victim, they also fail to confine themselves to sexual crime. Retrospective accounts suggest that 40–60% of adult and adolescent sex offenders have a history of nonsexual criminal behavior (Aljazireh, 1993). To be sure, both the prevalence and frequency of nonsexual crime in this group can be high. In the twelve months preceding incarceration, rapists participating in the Weinrott and Saylor (1991) study committed an average of 10.5 nonsexual offenses. Subjects serving time for child sex offenses reportedly engaged in an even larger number of nonsexual offenses (mean = 121) during this same period. Prospective studies also detail the presence of moderate versatility in sex offender populations. Hanson, Scott, and Steffy (1995) ascertained that 41% of the child sex offenders whom they followed were subsequently reconvicted of nonviolent crimes and that 14% were reconvicted of nonsexual violent crimes. In a meta-analysis of recidivism studies on sex offending it was discerned that sexual and total recidivism were 13.4% and 36.3%, respectively, and that contrary to what has been traditionally assumed, intervention significantly reduced both forms of recidivism (Hanson and Bussière, 1998). Alternatively, differences surfaced between juveniles adjudicated sexually and violently delinquent, with the former group recounting fewer delinquent acts, less substance abuse, and stronger beliefs in the law yet weaker internal behavioral controls than the latter group (Fagan & Wexler, 1988).

LIFESTYLES CONGRUENT WITH SEXUAL ASSAULT

It is speculated that sexual assault is a function of three interrelated lifestyles: the criminal, sexual, and relationship lifestyles. Although it can be reasonably assumed that people who habitually engage in sexual assault operate out of two or all three of these lifestyles, it is proposed that in most cases one of the lifestyles predominates. Whether the victim is an adult or child, aggressive rape appears most congruent with a hostile-criminal lifestyle. Sixty percent of a group of individuals incarcerated for rape attributed their motivation for committing the offense to their desire to humiliate and degrade the victim (Darke, 1990). The role of power and control in rape is reminiscent of other violent crimes. Like violent and property criminals but unlike child molesters, rapists attribute their sexual arousal and behavior to external, stable, and controllable influences (McKay, Chapman, & Long, 1996). Rapists also model greater similarity to violent offenders than child molesters on a range of dispositional characteristics, to include accentuated social confidence, decreased anxiety, enhanced aggressiveness (Marshall et al., 1995), and a propensity to experience anger rather than sadness prior to offending (Hudson & Ward, 1997b).

The sexual lifestyle is a second pattern into which persons who habitually commit sexual assault generally fall. A sexual lifestyle is enacted in hopes of securing immediate gratification with little regard for the negative long-term consequences of one's actions (Walters, 1996b). Multiple paraphilias, a pattern more characteristic of people who offend sexually against children than of persons who offend sexually against adults (Abel et al., 1988), may signal the presence of a sexual lifestyle. The use of alcohol in conjunction with sexual offending may also identify someone who has embraced a sexual lifestyle in the sense that the individual uses alcohol to cut off or eliminate common deterrents to continued deviant sexuality (Walters, 1996b). Conversely, the use of alcohol in sexual situations may reveal the presence of a coexisting drug lifestyle. Either way, a sexual lifestyle should be seriously considered when entertaining possible alternative explanations for sexual assault, particularly in situations where a child has been victimized.

A third lifestyle that may account for sexual assault is the relationship pattern. A relationship lifestyle may be particularly prominent in people who commit child sex offenses. Men who habitually engage in sexual contact with young girls perceive an adult woman's romantic interest and social desire as weak compared to offenders who target young boys or adult females or whose crimes are nonsexual in nature (Stahl & Sacco, 1995). Men who find themselves attracted to young males, in addition to holding negative views of adult females, perceive themselves as sexually inadequate and physically unattractive (Horley & Quinsey, 1994). It may well be that a certain percentage of people who perpetrate sexual assault, particularly when a child is involved, suffer social isolation as an outgrowth of negative self-appraisals, weak interpersonal ties, and a fear of adult females. It has been determined that people with a sexual interest in children often put themselves in positions where they have close contact with children, either through a particular line of work or a volunteer organization like Scouting and youth sports. The consensus has been that this is done solely for the purpose of sexual predation. Another interpretation is that some such individuals feel more comfortable around children and are to some degree concerned with the welfare of children, though they then allow their desire for companionship to overflow into an inappropriate sexual relationship.

CASE ILLUSTRATION: SID—THE MENTOR

Background

Sid was adopted shortly after birth by a 21-year-old woman whose husband was twenty years her senior. Apparently the adoptive mother had hoped for the perfect child, and Sid, due to no fault of his own, fell short of perfection and thoroughly disappointed her. To make matters worse, Sid suffered from what appears to have been an attention deficit disorder with hyperactivity. This made it difficult for him to sit still, concentrate, and respond appropriately to instructions. The fact that he was an active, inquisitive child did not endear him to his mother who wanted a quiet well-mannered little man whom she could show off to her friends and neighbors. Sid declares that anytime there was a problem, his mother would blame him. Once when he went over to a neighbor's house to get his hair cut, he discovered the neighbor lying dead of a heart attack in the middle of the floor. Sid's mother accused the boy of being responsible for the neighbor's death because of all the running around he did the last time he was there to get his hair cut. She also blamed Sid for his father's periodic absences from home, arguing that the only reason that his father wasn't home was that he was trying to avoid Sid. It seems more likely that it was Sid's mother he was trying to avoid.

When Sid was 7 years old, his mother informed him that he had been adopted, calling him a "son of a bitch . . . who should be damn thankful" she and her husband saw fit to rescue him from the orphanage, where he would surely have spent the remainder of his childhood had they not intervened. As might be expected, Sid's mother had no tolerance for Sid's budding sexuality. On one occasion Sid's mother caught him masturbating in the bathtub. She responded by yanking him out of the tub and dragging him down two flights of stairs to the basement where she proceeded to burn his penis with a hot iron, leaving a lifelong physical and mental scar. There is every indication that Sid's mother was suffering serious psychiatric problems in the form of an undiagnosed and untreated bipolar disorder. Sid recites a litany of bizarre acts that his mother would perform routinely, to include putting on airs despite her humble roots and periodically spending well beyond the family's means. The other children in the neighborhood also found her weird, and, as youngsters are prone to do, they took it out on Sid. Neighborhood children referred to him as the ugly fat kid with the strange mother, and he soon became a social outcast. Of course, his mother blamed him for this as well.

When Sid was 9 years of age, his mother had a "nervous breakdown," and his father arranged to have him placed in a child study center under the guise of an ongoing psychiatric evaluation. Unfortunately for Sid, the evaluation lasted three years. At the child study center Sid was introduced to sex with other boys. Some of the incidents were consensual and pleasurable; others were forced and terrifying.

After being raped by one of the older boys, Sid would sometimes run away from the center, but the authorities would always find him and bring him back. He never informed staff about the assaults because he feared retaliation from his tormentors and didn't think the staff would believe him anyway. When Sid tried to inform the psychiatrists and psychologists at the center about his mother's erratic behavior, he was advised that adoptive mothers love their children, for why else would they go to the trouble of adopting. He reasoned that the staff at the center either couldn't or wouldn't understand him. In any event, he began questioning his own perception. After all, he reasoned, these were professionals whose job was to analyze patients, one of whom was Sid; perhaps they were right, and everything that went wrong in his life was his fault.

Sid's father died when he was in a training school for delinquent boys where he had been sent after running away from the child study center too many times. Following his release from the training school, he returned home to find that his mother had moved out of the house into an apartment, sold or thrown away nearly all of Sid's and his father's possessions, and had arranged for Sid's dog to be put to sleep. The boy felt as if there was nothing of his old life, pitiful as it was, upon which to construct a coherent sense of identity. Sid never really had any role models when he was growing up. He envied boys on television shows like *The Adventures of Rin Tin Tin* and *My Friend Flicka* for the idyllic life that he wished he had, although he never actually looked to the boys as role models. He did, however, identify with "Piggie," the overweight boy in the book *Lord of the Flies* who was the target of teasing and ridicule from the other boys on the island. Sid has felt like "Piggie" for a good portion of his life. Notwithstanding the confusion that he felt as a consequence of the uncertain and chaotic tenor of his life, there was one thing that Sid was not confused about—he didn't like women and deliberately avoided any movies or television shows that featured adult females.

After landing a summer job as a caddy at a local country club, Sid finally began saving money. However, his mother, who received ample funds in the form of a Social Security check, wanted the 15-year-old to pay for his food and rent. He tried to compromise with her by offering her half the money, but she wanted the entire paycheck. When he refused, she took him to court and had him recommitted to the training school as an incorrigible juvenile. Within a year he was paroled to the care of a Pentecostal minister who employed a wide variety of social unfortunates to collect and bale paper. During the week Sid worked for the minister baling paper, and on the weekends he toiled around the minister's house. One of the first chores that the minister assigned Sid was cutting his eleven-acre lawn with a hand mower. The minister would think nothing of beating Sid with the rubber hose that he kept stored in the basement if the 16-year-old did not work as quickly or as efficiently as the minister thought prudent or brought home a report card that did not meet with the older man's approval. Sometime later at a court appearance the abuse became public, leading to the minister's arrest and his mother's semi-coerced agreement to sign the necessary papers for Sid to join the army, as the boy had just turned 17.

Sid's military career was cut short after eighteen months. He was discharged under honorable conditions due to character and behavioral problems that made him unsuitable for military service. The issue was primarily one of immaturity, and Sid admits that he went AWOL on several occasions when he was confronted with problems that he could not handle. Following his discharge from the army, Sid's mother had him committed to a psychiatric hospital, where he remained six months until he was called to Washington, D.C., to get reinstated into the military. He never went back into the military but never went back to the hospital either. Instead, he moved to California, where he survived by hustling and offering his body to older men. As a young adult he became involved in activities that gave him proximity to young children. Capitalizing on his interest in the outdoors, Sid helped out with Scouting and took great pleasure in establishing memorable camping experiences for the boys. He also accompanied them to ball games, museums, zoos, and the circus. In 8½ years of Scouting, several years of which were spent without any direct contact with the Scouts themselves, he recounts having sexual relations with only one child and insists that the boy initiated the contact. Despite the fact that Sid labels himself a pedophile, he sees his actions as fulfilling the role of mentor instead of sexual predator.

Recalling that he first became sexually attracted to young boys in early adolescence, Sid described a sexual preference for young boys between the ages of 9 and 12, his age at the time that he was living at the child study center. This suggests that Sid's sexual interests and maturity may have become fixated at the preadolescent stage. He admits that as he was growing up, he had trouble envisioning himself assuming adult responsibilities and to this day has an immature self-image despite being 53 years of age. Prior to coming to prison, Sid would spend hours each day creating and embellishing sexual fantasies with young boys and states that he felt addicted to these fantasies. He adds that he has unsuccessfully tried to cultivate an interest in both male and female adults and went so far as to rent adult sex videos in hopes of reconditioning his sexual desire. However, he found viewing the adult films as exciting as watching a documentary on "the mating habits of the paramecium." Like many others who sexually offend against children Sid was sexually abused at an early age and responded by forming elaborate sexual fantasies, perhaps in an effort to make sense of the experience. Unlike many others who sexually offend against children, Sid does not abuse alcohol or drugs, nor does he use substances to facilitate his offending behavior or mollify his guilt.

Even though Sid does not employ alcohol to mollify his behavior, he has developed an elaborate system of rationalization and emotional isolation that affects all areas of his life. Even his lifelong interest in the Civil War is not immune from its influence. What draws Sid to the Civil War era of American history is the belief that honor and duty predominated over all else in the lives of the individuals who fought in this war. Sid asserts that he tries to uphold these ideals in his own life and relegates his sexual interest in children to a separate, unrelated compartment in his life (discontinuity). From an early age Sid learned that he could escape his problems by reading. As a consequence, he has become an ardent consumer of fictional as well as nonfictional writings. Tom O'Carroll's (1980) *Paedophilia: The Radical Case* is a book that particularly piqued Sid's interest because it supplied him with logical and historical justification for his sexual interest in children. In his book O'Carroll contends that sex with young boys was an accepted practice in ancient Greece, where adult males sought to promote the physical, intellectual, and emotional development of younger males through a mentoring process in which sexuality was only one component. Perhaps the greatest means of justification, however, came from Sid's interactions with other self-proclaimed pedophiles over the Internet.

Sid's interest in the Internet eventually landed him in prison. After a 9-year-old boy who had been helping Sid paint buildings for his model railroad set reported to police that Sid had kissed him on the lips and pinched his buttocks, an investigation was initiated. The investigation revealed that Sid had, in actuality, engaged in these actions and that he was also in possession of pictures depicting adult males and teenagers in various sexual poses with young male children. Sid eventually pleaded guilty to receiving and distributing child pornography over the Internet and was sentenced to seventy months in federal prison. Before serving his federal sentence, he completed ten months in a county jail for sexually abusing the 9-year-old boy. While confined in jail and prison, Sid began meeting with psychologists in an effort to understand his sexual interest in children and his aversion to women. Although prison is a difficult place to make changes, particularly for someone with a sex offender label, if Sid does not change, he is subjecting himself to continued frustration and legal difficulty.

Lifestyle Assessment

Sid earned a total score of 6 on the LCSF (see Table 5.1), which signifies moderately low involvement in, commitment to, and identification with the criminal lifestyle. Since irresponsibility (section score = 2) and social rule breaking (section score = 3) account for 90% of Sid's score on the LCSF, these two interactive styles should be emphasized in future interventions with Sid. Elevated irresponsibility reflects Sid's lifelong pattern of immaturity, whereas social rule

Table 5.1
Sid's Scores on the Lifestyle Criminality Screening Form (LCSF)

Irresponsibility	2
Self-Indulgence	0
Interpersonal Intrusiveness	1
Social Rule Breaking	3
TOTAL LCSF SCORE	6

Figure 5.2
Sid's Scores on the Psychological Inventory of Criminal Thinking Styles (PICTS)

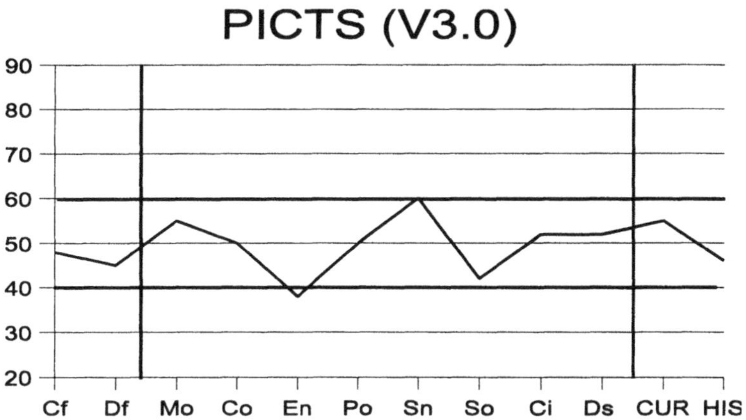

Note. Cf = confusion scale; Df = defensiveness scale; Mo = mollification scale; Co = cutoff scale; En = entitlement scale; Po = power orientation scale; Sn = sentimentality scale; So = superoptimism scale; Ci = cognitive indolence scale; Ds = discontinuity scale; CUR = current content scale; HIS = historical content scale.

breaking demonstrates a disregard for social rules and conventions. These findings are consistent with Sid's self- and world-views in which he has trouble seeing himself as an adult and views himself as being at the mercy of a repressive society. Results from the LCSF denote that the criminal lifestyle does not fully explain Sid's interest in children. His intense sexual fantasies are fueled by an enduring interest in child pornography, which suggests that the sexual lifestyle may have as much to do with his sexual interest in children as the criminal lifestyle. More central perhaps than either the criminal or sexual lifestyles is the relationship lifestyle. Sid is a sad and lonely individual who craves companionship and feels that young boys are the only social group that will accept him. The sexual and criminal lifestyles appear to be responsible for Sid's sexual offending behavior, in contrast to the relationship lifestyle, which supports his abiding interest in prepubescent boys.

Sid completed the PICTS several months after his arrival at the federal correctional institution, where he is now serving a seventy-month sentence for receiving and sending child pornography over the Internet. A subclinical elevation on the mollification scale (T-score = 55) and a clinically significant elevation on the sentimentality scale (T-score = 60) imply that mollification and sentimentality are how Sid justifies his sexual acting-out behavior (see Figure 5.2). In describing his reasons for making sexual advances to the 9-year-old boy whom he recently molested, Sid states that his intention was to mentor the boy but the situation spiraled out of control. It would seem that Sid's principal goal is to grant children whom he views as neglected or unwanted the attention that he never received as a child. In this way he is trying to resolve his own childhood traumas by helping someone else. Seeking to resolve one's own issues by focusing on others is not unique to Sid or those who sexually abuse children, and as most people who have followed this path can attest, not only is one's own problem not solved, but the other person's situation is often made worse. What is more, Sid lacks the impulse control necessary to keep his sexual fantasies under control when he interacts with young boys. Therefore, any time that he tries to "mentor" a young boy, he runs the risk of losing control over his sexual desires and fantasies.

Belief System Analysis

Self-View

Like many people who become sexually involved with children, Sid lacks self-confidence. The reflected appraisal process for Sid seems to operate through his mother despite the fact that he has not seen her in over thirty years. He has even given a name to these reflected appraisals. For two and one-half years prior to coming to prison Sid met regularly with a psychologist who subscribed to the approach developed by Eric Berne (1964) known as transactional analysis. From his contacts with this psychologist Sid began referring to his mother-based negative reflected appraisals as his critical parent. He recalls his mother telling him that he would end up like a cousin who had spent the majority of his young life in various mental hospitals. He tried to challenge these reflected appraisals, but Sid's critical parent is both insidious and ubiquitous. Whenever he fails at something, the critical parent is there to castigate him for being a failure and whenever he succeeds, it is there to remind him that the good feelings are not deserved and will not last. Though Sid periodically tries to resist the messages conveyed by the critical parent, much of the time it dictates the valence of his self-schemes. In working with Sid, the author retained the term critical parent because it was meaningful to Sid, while at the same time prompting him to understand that no matter what foundation his mother may have laid, the critical parent is his own creation, and he is ultimately responsible for extricating himself from its negative influence.

The social comparisons that Sid makes are primarily downward in nature. Not only does he identify more with young children than adults, but he also feels more comfortable around children than adults. It has been recognized for some time that people who molest children often suffer from a fear of negative social evaluation (Overholser & Beck, 1986). Sid has learned to deal with this fear by comparing himself with children because in contrast to adults, children are more accepting and less judgmental. Through downward comparisons Sid is able to access more positively valenced self-schemes and simultaneously relieve some of his loneliness through contact with the object of these comparisons (i.e., young boys). Upward social comparisons can be threatening to someone like Sid, and so he normally avoids such comparisons, choosing instead to make downward comparisons with young children and people who he feels are beneath him (e.g., violent child sex offenders). It should be noted, however, that in his own mind he relates to children as peers: "it is not a power or control thing, we are equals."

Sid's self-representations can be traced to his negative physical self-appraisal, his lifelong interest in the Civil War, and his conflicting self-attributions. McKay and his colleagues (1996) determined that a group of adult males convicted of various child sex crimes ascribed their sexual arousal and offending to internal, stable, and uncontrollable factors. The self-attributions that constitute Sid's self-representations vary according to their ultimate outcome. If he perceives that he has failed at something, he will attribute the cause to internal, stable, and global factors. From this he concludes that he fell short of his goals because he is stupid, dumb, or a loser. Alternately, Sid credits success to largely external, unstable, and specific factors and believes that the fruits of his success will neither last nor generalize to other areas of his life. Helping Sid change his self-representations requires modification of his attributions for success and failure, specifically, helping him develop more stable and global attributions for success and more unstable and specific attributions for failure. Whereas the integrated-interactive approach to change underscores internal attributions for their responsibility-engendering properties, Sid should be encouraged to attribute failure to unstable and specific causes that can be changed and mastered, while success is ascribed to more stable and global factors that afford him a general sense of confidence in his own ability to cope with the problems of everyday living.

Sid's gender-role identity is confused and intimately tied to his sexual offending behavior. Without a strong male role model to emulate and with a father who was either absent or psychologically emasculated by Sid's domineering mother, Sid was uncertain about his place in the world. Doing what comes naturally in modern-day America, he turned to role models supplied by the media. Perhaps because he saw his parents as unhappy, Sid feared growing up, or maybe he just lacked the confidence in his ability to eventually fulfill adult responsibilities. Either way, Sid admits that he could never quite see himself as an adult and found himself drawn to young male leads in television shows like *Lassie*, *The Adventures of Rin Tin Tin*, and *The Rifleman*. However, instead of searching for who he would like to be in the future, Sid was searching for who he would like to be in the present. He wanted the life that Timmy had on *Lassie* or that Mark had on *The Rifleman*. What Sid did not realize at the time was that even children growing up in homes much healthier than his own didn't have lives reminiscent of those portrayed on television. This did nothing, however, to preclude him from blaming himself for the sorry state of his own life; he would often think to himself that if television depicts how mothers are supposed to treat their sons, then he must be downright evil to be treated the way he was by his own mother.

Fear has reigned supreme in Sid's life, and various feared selves have not been as effectively balanced by positive possible selves as they might be. Several feared selves have played a crucial role in the development of Sid's self-view. For one, he fears becoming the loser that his mother so often predicted he would become. As a matter of fact, failure and success are both salient sources of fear for Sid—failure because it confirms his negatively valenced self-view and success because it invokes increased expectations for future success. As was already mentioned, Sid could never envision himself growing into adulthood when he was younger. He henceforth lacked a positive possible self of himself as a mature, well-functioning adult that he could use to offset his fears. Accordingly, he regularly engages in self-handicapping behavior whereby he sets himself up for failure so that his own and other people's expectations are never beyond what he can comfortably handle. One feared self that has haunted Sid since adolescence is his fear of becoming a pedophile. This is a negative possible self that has become a reality in Sid's mind for he presently considers pedophilia to be a defining characteristic of his personal identity.

World-View

Sid has adopted a largely mechanistic world-view and perceives the external environment as logical, orderly, and machinelike. Frightened by intense emotions like anger and depression, Sid has apparently retreated into a linear world of pure reason and rationality. Temper tantrums were Sid's childhood response to an environment lacking in warmth and compassion. Due in part to his mother's overreaction to his fits of rage, he learned to suppress his feelings. His quelled response had little impact on his home environment, however. It remained, at least from his perspective, cold and indifferent, whether he was living with his mother, at the child study center, or in the juvenile home. In fact, he reports that he was raped by the house parent in charge of protecting his welfare within several weeks of his arrival at the juvenile home. Sid's response was to withdraw even further into a mechanistic, intellectual world where books were his only friends.

A review of Sid's beliefs on fatalism-agenticism indicate that he leans toward the fatalism pole of this dimension. Throughout his life Sid has presumed that it was his fate to be a loser as his mother had prophesied. Presently, he takes a fatalistic view of his pedophilia and believes that he was probably born this way. When he was around 30 years of age, Sid began challenging some of the fatalistic beliefs that he had held since childhood in an effort to take greater control of his life. This appears to have moved him further toward the center of the fatalism-agenticism continuum, but there are still issues on which he remains highly fatalistic. One such issue is his self-labeled pedophilia. Sid believes that it was his fate to be a pedophile, and he blames his gender-role confusion on his mother. Whereas his beliefs in this regard are understandable and probably accurate to some extent, they also help maintain his fatalistic world-view and may be preventing him from making important changes in his world-view. Sid admits that he is afraid that if he forgives his mother, he will no longer have her to blame for the pedophilia and would then be forced to assume responsibility for his own decisions in this regard.

Sid is a firm believer in a just world. "What goes around, comes around" is a motto he lives by. When his dog got sick or his father failed to come home at the appointed time, it was his fault. More than this, these negative events were his retribution for being "bad." These were lessons recited so often by his mother that he began to believe them. As he grew older, Sid tried to incorporate inequity into his world-view. Unfortunately, his efforts were insufficient to overcome the belief that the world was just and that he was receiving his just deserts for the real and imagined wrongs that he had perpetrated in life. Looking at other children in an overidealized (Porter, 1990), though not altogether inaccurate, manner, he observed that their lives were better than his. More than once he asked himself, "Why me?" The answer that made the most sense to him at the time was that he was a bad person who warranted such treatment. Pedophilia simply reinforced Sid's negative self-view and belief that if others in society knew of his pedophilia, they would think of him as a "monstrous gargoyle."

It should be fairly obvious by now that Sid's position on the malevolence-benevolence dimension favors the malevolent side of the continuum. There is much in his life that Sid doesn't control, and such events are interpreted by him as evidence of malevolence in the world. Intellectually, he sees a balance between malevolence and benevolence, but in his daily life he stresses the more malevolent aspects of his environment. If we take all of the children that Sid has molested in his lifetime, there is at least one common denominator. There was something missing in each child's life that Sid tried to address through mentoring and, of course, sex. If he wishes to be an effective mentor instead of a catalyst for a new generation of sex offenders he must learn to distinguish between his desire to help young boys who may be suffering from some of the same insults that he suffered as a child and his desire to engage in sexual activity with these same boys. What Sid has done in the past is use his belief in a malevolent world to justify imposing his sexual will on children and betraying their trust, thereby destroying anything positive that may have transpired over the course of their relationship.

The prototypes that compose Sid's world-view appear to be oversimplified for someone as intelligent as Sid. He tends to divide people into categories based largely on such physical traits as age and gender. If you are a male below the age of 14 or 15, you can be trusted. If you are a male over the age of 14 or 15, you are to be feared. With respect to females, intimate relationships are to be avoided, though females under the age of 14 or 15 are less threatening and therefore more tolerable than adult females. Sid may not abide by these guidelines exclusively; still, they represent how he defines his sexual preferences and inclinations for companionship and social interaction. If he could have it his way, Sid would prefer to live in a world populated principally by young boys. He understands that this is not feasible, but it is one of his fantasies. Sid has few adult friends and so the principal goal of any assisted change program should be developing his social skills and helping him overcome his irrational fear of adults so that he is able to expand his adult contacts and relationships.

Present-View

Research demonstrates that males who engage in sexually assaultive behavior have trouble accurately identifying social-emotional cues (Malamuth & Brown, 1994; Racey et al., 2000). The perceptual distortions that appear to have had the greatest impact on Sid's present-view are reflected on the PICTS in the form of mollification and sentimentality. Sid frames his actions as benevolent mentoring, thereby downplaying and minimizing the sexual aspects of his behavior and the harm that he has inflicted on the boys with whom he has come into sexual contact. Forcing Sid to adopt a more candid view of his sexual activities and allowing him to become more cognizant of the harm that he has done to his young victims would probably only serve to heap more guilt onto his already fragile ego and validate his self-view as an evil person. Thus, before implementing a program of intervention designed to help Sid experience the full brunt of damage for which he is responsible, he will need to develop skills that improve his ability to tolerate negative feelings and learn from new experiences.

Stone and Thompson (2001) administered a series of executive function tasks to persons classified as sexual offenders and discerned that these individuals performed significantly worse on a majority of the executive function tasks than the normative sample. Another study found that those individuals who target children and are more impulsive have more executive function deficits than rapists and less impulsive offenders (Martin, 1999). The executive function on which Sid is weakest is his interpersonal problem-solving ability. Despite above average intelligence Sid has engaged in impulsive decision-making throughout his life. Be this as it may, he was able to work for the same company as a locksmith for twenty years. There is an inconsistency in Sid that allows him to persist in a job yet make very impulsive decisions in his personal life. This inconsistency also explains Sid's sexual offending behavior. By his own admission he is more inclined to act out when feeling lonely. Sid realizes intellectually that acting out sexually with a child is harmful to both himself and the child. However, when beset by loneliness, he does not think of the long-range consequences of his actions; rather, he is more inclined to focus on the immediate issue of reducing his sense of social isolation.

Past-View

In many respects Sid's past-view is the most highly developed, integrated, and accessible of the three temporal belief systems (past-view, present-view, future-view). He reports being interested in history from an early age, particularly the Civil War. Reading about historical events is a truly enjoyable experience for Sid, who finds reading an ideal means of escape from the problems of everyday living. Hobbies involving model railroading and Civil War reenacting have given him the opportunity to express his interests in ways other than reading. The downside to Sid's interest in the past is that it has allowed him to retreat from the present and disregard the future. A fully functional relationship between the temporal belief systems requires balance between the past-, present-, and future-views. Sid obviously lacks such balance. Without a strong present-view and hardy future-view to offset the emphasis that Sid has placed on the past, he runs the risk of withdrawing from the outside world into a universe dominated by his fantasies and rationalizations.

Sid's personal life also figures prominently in his past-view. One recollection in particular forges a poignant link between his past- and self-views. He recalls a small pond in one corner of his classroom where he attended kindergarten on which a fleet of small plastic boats likely to attract a young boy's attention floated. One day he climbed onto the ledge of the pond in order to get a closer look at one of the boats. Unfortunately, he lost his balance and fell in the water. The teacher escorted the soaked boy to the boiler room, where the school janitor stripped him naked and placed him in front of two huge boilers, which in the eyes of an imaginative 5-year-old looked not unlike two hideous monsters. After drying off, Sid was given a smock and sent back to his classroom. While listening to a story later that day, he was spotted by the teacher touching his genitals through the smock. His mother was called down to the principal's office and informed that Sid was no longer welcome at that particular school. As his mother dragged him out of the principal's office, she took the opportunity to remind him just how stupid he was and how much trouble it would be for her to find him a new school.

Future-View

Sid never spent much time contemplating the future as a young child, he was too worried about surviving in the present to think much about the future. A weak future orientation is a pattern that has been played out repeatedly in Sid's life. As a result, his future-view is best described as sparse, barren, and underdeveloped. The schemes that constitute Sid's future-view are also meager and rarely extend beyond the immediate moment. Of course, he has formed expectancies for many of his actions, including sexual relations with children, but these anticipations typically focus on the expected short-term gratification provided by his participation in these activities. One future aspiration that Sid held as an adolescent and that loomed large in his future-view at the time was his desire to attend college and major in history. However, his math skills were poor, in part because he suffers from a learning disability for calculating numbers known as dyscalculia and in part because his mother had convinced him that he was inept at math. At 53 years of age Sid enrolled in a general equivalency diploma (GED) course at the federal prison where he was serving time for downloading child pornography from the Internet and passed all sections of the GED test, including the math, on his first attempt. This furnished him with additional incentives and opportunities for developing his future-view in that he now wants to take several college-level history courses and perhaps teach a class on the Civil War.

CONCLUSION

Labeling is an issue germane to all forms of crime and is especially relevant to sexual assault. Individuals who commit sexual assault are more likely to be labeled perverts, pedophiles, and psychopaths than their peers who commit nonsexual crimes despite the presence of moderately high versatility in persons traditionally classified as sex offenders. Some people specialize in rape or child molestation, but many others cross over to other forms of sexual and nonsexual offending. What, then, separates the sex offender from a more conventional offender who just happened to commit one or two sex crimes? In this chapter every effort was made to keep terms like rapist and child molester to a minimum because of their labeling connotations. When these terms do appear, they are used solely for the sake of convenience and literary style in that one of the founding tenets of the integrated-interactive model is that labeling can have a detrimental effect on people so classified. Not only do labels encourage people to think in overly simplistic ways about themselves and their world, but they also place limits on a person's identity and self-view. Labeling may be one of the linguistic shortcuts that we use to make sense of our world, but when applied to people, labels can become self-fulfilling prophecies with the power to interfere with a person's ability to grow and change.

Hopefully, once we acknowledge that all people who commit sex crimes are not cut from the same cloth we can begin the process of understanding the individual offender. Nothing strikes fear in the hearts of parents more than knowledge that a child sex offender is loose in their neighborhood. Such fear is understandable, but when politicians and scientists use this fear to create laws and policies that promote the very behaviors that they are designed to impede, something is wrong. The roots of rape can be traced to the ambivalent attitudes that many societies harbor toward women, the group most often victimized by sexual assault. We must work as hard at changing our own beliefs and practices as we do in assisting those who sexually assault children and women to change their beliefs and practices. Contrary to popular opinion, most people who commit sexual offenses against children do not snatch the child from the mother's arms. Instead, children are put in positions of befriending those who eventually molest them because they feel, as did Sid, that they are unwanted and misunderstood. When someone takes an interest in a neglected child, the child will in all likelihood respond. In no way is this meant to excuse Sid's actions, for his conduct is a violation of trust between a young child and adult with the potential to breed new generations of sexual predators. We as a people must therefore do everything within our power to prevent this pattern from continuing, and we can start by doing a better job of valuing the two groups most often victimized by sexual assault, women and children.

6

Belief Systems and White-Collar Crime

Edwin Sutherland, the founder of differential association theory, first coined the term white-collar crime in 1939 in an address before the American Sociological Society. It was Sutherland's intent to show how theories of crime causation popular at the time (e.g., biological determinism, poverty) were inadequate for the purpose of clarifying offending in the well-to-do. Later, Sutherland (1949/1983) would define white-collar crime as "crime committed by a person of respectability and high social status in the course of his occupation" (7). Debate continues to rage over whether white-collar crime should be defined according to the offender, as did Sutherland, or with reference to the offense, as Coleman (1987) and Shapiro (1990) have proposed. In defining white-collar crime, Sutherland focused on crimes committed by the individual and spent little time discussing crimes committed by organizations and groups. This motivated Clinard and Quinney (1986) to construct a two-group classification scheme in which they divided white-collar into occupational and corporate subcategories, with occupational crime covering offenses committed by an employee against a company or employer and corporate crime being reserved for violations committed by a corporate official, executive, or company in the furtherance of organizational goals. In this chapter white-collar crime is defined as an illicit act, punishable by law, committed by an individual or organization in the course of a legitimate occupation wherein a public or employee–employer trust is violated.

THE EXTENT AND SERIOUSNESS OF WHITE-COLLAR CRIME

White-collar crime of both the occupational and corporate variety is surprisingly common. Data gathered from retail, hospital, and manufacturing employees reveals that one-third acknowledge having stolen something from work over the past year (Clark & Hollinger, 1983). Though many of these acts were probably instances of petty larceny, even minor theft can add up over time. Surveys suggest that American employers lose an estimated $1 billion per annum in stolen pens, pencils, paper clips, postage, and stationery (Wells, 1994). Health care fraud costs the public $70 billion a year, nearly 10% of the total health care budget (Andrews, 1994). Computer crime, embezzlement, corporate crime, and fraud also exact a heavy toll on society, with the losses being measured in more than just dollars and cents. The Ivan Boeskys and Michael Milkins of the world may get the lion's share of media attention, but the vast majority of white-collar crime is committed by everyday people who end up with a few hundred dollars instead of several million. Not to be overlooked are the organizational and corporate crimes that adversely affect the economy, eliminate people's jobs, pollute the environment, and defraud the public. Unfortunately, these expressions of white-collar crime are also extremely common (Coleman, 1994).

There has been increased public outcry over white-collar crime since Rossi, Waite, Bose, and Berk (1974) asked Baltimore residents to evaluate the severity of 140 illegal acts and found that white-collar crimes were uniformly ranked near the bottom of the list in terms of severity. More recent studies conducted in the United States (Cullen, Link, & Polanzi, 1982), Canada (Goff & Nason-Clark, 1989), and Australia (Holland, 1995) have discerned that white-collar crimes leading to injury or death, even though injury and death are not the intended outcomes, are viewed as serious by the general public. The primary costs of white-collar crime in death, injury, and financial loss are seven to twenty-five times the cost of street crime (Donziger, 1996). However, the secondary costs may be even greater. To the extent that white-collar crime is a violation of trust, it breeds mistrust and may contribute to low social morale. If the public loses faith in the ethics and morality of corporate, business, and governmental leaders, it may be inclined to withdraw its pecuniary support from the institutions upon which a nation's economy is based, which, in turn, could precipitate a collapse of the entire capitalistic system (Moore & Mills, 1990). Quite obviously, white-collar crime is both common and serious.

THE DEMOGRAPHICS OF WHITE-COLLAR CRIME

As is the case with most forms of social deviance, white-collar crime is more pervasive in males than females. When women do commit white-collar crime, they normally do so from low-echelon positions, for reasons of economic survival sooner than greed, and with only a modicum of success in terms of material gain (Daly, 1989). It would seem that women enjoy fewer opportunities to profit from white-collar crime than men due, in part, to the fact that they are often consigned to lower-status jobs in the business community. While this may explain the wide discrepancy in the number of males and females who participate in white-collar crime, it is also possible that females are less motivated to commit white-collar crime than males. Investigating youthful white-collar offenses in the form of patent and copyright law violations, Hagan and Kay (1990) determined that compared to boys, girls were more instrumentally controlled by their parents, less interested in taking risks, more likely to perceive that they would get caught and punished for illegally copying eight-track tapes, and therefore less apt to violate patents and copyright laws.

Contrasting eight federal white-collar crimes—securities fraud, antitrust violations, bribery, tax evasion, bank embezzlement, postal and wire fraud, false claims and statements, and credit and lending institution fraud—with two nonviolent, non-white-collar, federal property offenses—postal theft and postal forgery—Wheeler, Weisburd, Waring, and Bode (1988) identified a number of important demographic correlates of white-collar crime. In addition to the observation that the white-collar group was nearly always employed at the time of the offense, white-collar crimes were more often committed by older, better-educated, Caucasian males. There was also an overrepresentation of Jewish subjects in the white-collar group. The two groups were further distinguished by certain characteristics of the crimes committed by group members. White-collar crimes generated more money, took place over a longer period of time, and were more liable to victimize organizations than individuals relative to non-white-collar property offenses (Wheeler et al., 1988).

THEORIES OF WHITE-COLLAR CRIME

Four of the six theories described in Chapter 1 have been applied to white-collar crime with varying degrees of success and not without certain problems and limitations. Merton's (1957) classic strain theory maintains that white-collar crime occurs when the means to satisfy a desire for success are insufficient to achieve one's stated aims. Strain, in the form of means/desire disjunction, is construed to be the motivating force behind white-collar crime by proponents of classic strain theory. Although there is some support for Merton's position that people who commit white-collar crime report high levels of job dissatisfaction and situational strain (Jeyasingh, 1985; Sherwin, 1963), Merton's views are far from satisfactory in rendering a consummate exposition on white-collar crime. A major limitation of classic strain theory is that it fails to explain why persons who indulge in white-collar crime possess a stronger desire for success than white-collar workers who do not resort to crime as a means to an end. Furthermore, poverty and low social class, linchpins of Merton's theory of street crime, do not appear to apply in the case of white-collar crime.

Sutherland (1949/1983) not only coined the term white-collar crime, but also advanced the first formal theory of white-collar offending. According to Sutherland, a person learns white-collar crime from those already involved in this activity. As with strain theory, there is some support for a differential association interpretation of white-collar crime (Coleman, 1994; Cressey, 1953/1971). The principal problem with Sutherland's differential association theory of white-collar crime, it would seem, is that it fails to resolve why some, but not all, people are drawn to criminogenic influences in the work environment where they learn the requisite attitudes and behaviors for white-collar offending. There is also evidence that most white-collar workers receive little support or guidance from coworkers in the performance of white-collar crime and recurrently seek to conceal their crimes from others in the workplace (Vaughn, 1983). Unless we are willing to concede that the overall business environment is criminogenic, in which case one would still need to explain why some people are better able to resist these temptations than others, differential association theory falls short of furnishing a complete rationale for white-collar crime.

Resisting negative environmental influences calls attention to the possible effects of social control on white-collar offending. Some people may be able to avoid business-related criminogenic temptations inasmuch as they have been socialized to have a stake in conformity, as suggested by Hirschi's (1969) social control theory. Lasley (1988) finds support for Hirschi's views in a survey of business executives. Executives with stronger attachment to their corporations, supervisors and coworkers, commitment to corporate lines of action, involvement in corporate activities, and belief in the legitimacy of corporate rules were less likely to report antecedent engagement in work-related white-collar crime than executives with less corporate attachment, commitment, involvement, and belief. The question that needs to be addressed in regard to the social control theory of white-collar crime is why these bonds form or fail to form in the first place. One possible interpretation of individual differences in social bonding is that people vary widely in their level of self-control (Gottfredson & Hirschi, 1990), an issue taken up in a later section of this chapter.

Neutralization theory is the model that has received the greatest amount of attention from researchers looking to unravel the mysteries of white-collar crime. Cressey (1953/1971) identified neutralizations in the comments made by persons serving time for embezzlement. Many of these individuals insisted that they were simply borrowing the money and that they had every intention of paying it back. Others relied on denial of harm to neutralize a guilty mind, as embodied in assurances that no one was injured during the offense. Employees fired from their jobs for stealing used both denial of harm and the belief that the stolen objects were an occupational fringe benefit to neutralize any negative outcomes that they may have encountered as a consequence of their actions (Zeitlin, 1971). A study by Benson (1985) also accrues evidence of neutralization in the accounts of federal white-collar offenders asked to list their reasons for participating in crime, with denial of criminal intent being the most common sentiment expressed by this group of individuals. The primary limitation of neutralization theory as an explanatory device is the assumption that neutralization antedates the criminal act, white-collar or otherwise, for, as research outlined in Chapter 1 suggests, neutralization, at least in some instances, may follow rather than precede the crime.

The labeling and interactional approaches have not been formally applied to white-collar crime, though both may have something to offer a comprehensive theory of white-collar crime. As many people convicted of white-collar crime resist the criminal label, it is speculated that such individuals enjoy higher self-esteem and weaker criminal identification than persons convicted of more conventional crimes. Waegel, Ermann, and Horowitz (1981) detected such resistance on an organizational level whereby the Central Intelligence Agency's (CIA) unwillingness to label itself criminal has resulted in increased levels of collective esteem. An unfortunate side effect of this resistance is that it opens the door to additional crime as manifest in the quasi-legal/ethical operations and practices that have become the CIA's legacy as an organization. Interactional theory may contribute to our understanding of white-collar crime because of its emphasis on bidirectional relationships, particularly the ones that form between white-collar crime and techniques of neutralization. In sum, none of the six theories afford a complete accounting of white-collar crime, but each may elevate our understanding of white-collar crime as part of an overarching integrated-interactive theory.

AN INTEGRATED-INTERACTIONAL THEORY OF WHITE-COLLAR CRIME

James William Coleman (1987, 1992) of California Polytechnic State University offers an integrated subcultural theory of deviance in which two primary factors—motivation and opportunity—are viewed to be instrumental in establishing the conditions necessary for white-collar crime. Taking Coleman's ideas on motivation and opportunity and merging them with the concept of cognitive distortion, the present section offers a three-part theory of white-collar crime comprising incentive, opportunity, and cognitive distortion, which are believed to represent and mediate the initiation, transition, and maintenance of belief systems congruent with white-collar crime.

Incentive

According to the perspective adopted in this text, the incentive for white-collar crime, as with all behavior, is existential fear. Hence, the motivation for white-collar crime can be traced to the affiliation, control, and status that such crimes promise. What makes white-collar crime so unique is the diversity of influences that impinge on the criminal motive. Like violent crime, situational factors are important; like sexual assault, cultural factors are critical; and like drug trafficking, personal ambition is vital. Add corporate goals to the mix, and we can see that the incentive for white-collar crime is formidably complex. An example of situational factors augmenting the incentive for white-collar crime would be what Cressey (1953/1971) refers to as a "nonshareable financial problem" or cash flow predicament that requires an immediate response. Cultural factors are represented by Coleman's (1987) "culture of competition" observed in industrial capitalistic societies where money becomes the yardstick against which a person's worth is gauged. Personal or group ambition, personal ambition being most evident in Western cultures and group ambition taking center stage in Eastern cultures (Kerbo & Inoue, 1990), also supplies incentive for white-collar crime. Finally, corporate culture may encourage or even demand that employees commit white-collar crime in order to advance corporate goals (Braithwaite, 1989).

Opportunity

A person may have the incentive for white-collar crime, but without the opportunity such crime will not take place. Coleman (1987) maintains that the active intersection of motivation and opportunity creates the conditions conducive to white-collar crime. Calavita and Pontell (1991) note that large-scale embezzlement in the U.S. savings and loan and insurance industries is a function of structures of opportunity specific to an individual's position in finance capitalism. The savings and loan or insurance company's role as trustee of other people's money in what has been described as a "casino" economy where profits are made through speculation instead of production affords the opportunity for such high-level and widespread white-collar offending. Differential opportunity also plays a leading role in the white-collar crime of income tax evasion (Mason & Calvin, 1978). People working in positions of trust are automatically at elevated risk for violating this trust, although other factors must be in place before an individual acts on a criminal opportunity. Given the proper combination of motivation, opportunity, and the belief that the potential gains of offending outweigh the anticipated costs, a person is likely to participate in white-collar crime.

Cognitive Distortion

Research previously reviewed on neutralization theory indicates that people who engage in white-collar crime often distort their thinking in order to justify and maintain ongoing criminal activity. An individual indicted in a heavy electric equipment price-fixing scheme rationalized his involvement in a series of white-collar crimes by convincing himself that "if I didn't do it, I felt someone else would" (Geis, 1977: 124). Zeitlin (1971) reports that a group of employees fired for stealing from their employers justified their actions by reinterpreting stealing as a fringe benefit of the job that the employer was more than capable of absorbing with no loss in profit. Statements such as these, the first reflecting mollification and the second entitlement, can be instrumental in initiating and maintaining white-collar crime. Cognitive distortion can also facilitate white-collar offending by influencing the cost-benefit decision-making process. Hagan and Kay (1990) note that youth who reportedly disregarded patents and copyright laws were less likely to believe that their violation would be detected than youth who denied indulging in such activities.

Overview

Figure 6.1 outlines a model of white-collar crime marked by multiple reciprocal relationships. As was previously mentioned, cultural influences, personal ambition, corporate goals, and situational factors interact with a person's natural drive for affiliation, control, and status to create the incentive for white-collar crime. Incentive then interacts with opportunity, the latter of which is influenced by a person's

Figure 6.1
An Integrated-Interactive Model of White-Collar Crime

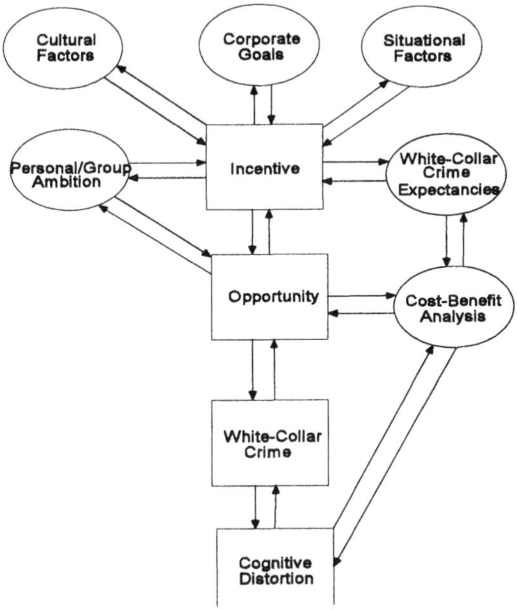

analysis of the relative costs and benefits of committing a particular offense. Crime expectancies are believed to play an important mediating role in this relationship by interacting with the cost-benefit analysis and incentive features of white-collar crime. Finally, cognitive distortion interacts directly with white-collar offending to effect the initiation and maintenance of the criminal act and indirectly through its influence on a person's decision-making ability (cost-benefit analysis).

IS THERE A DIFFERENCE BETWEEN WHITE-COLLAR CRIME AND STREET CRIME?

Traditionally, white-collar crime has been treated separately from what is commonly referred to as street crime—offenses like assault, robbery, rape, larceny, and drug dealing. In the construction of their general theory of crime, Gottfredson and Hirschi (1990) broke with tradition by asserting that all crime, whether of the street or white-collar variety, is a product of low self-control. Whether a person steals cars, television sets, or little old ladies' life savings, Gottfredson and Hirschi hold that the perpetrator's actions are a consequence of low self-control. Advancing low self-control as the cause of white-collar crime, Gottfredson and Hirschi contend that white-collar offenders are as criminally versatile—meaning that they do not specialize in specific crimes—and deviant as street criminals. Empirically, Nagin and Paternoster (1994) have documented that white-collar crime and low self-control correlate significantly, and Weisburd, Waring, and Chayet (1995) note that imprisonment has no more of a deterrent effect on white-collar crime than it does on other forms of criminality, findings that substantiate Gottfredson and Hirschi's claim that white-collar crime is not fundamentally different from other forms of crime inasmuch as both are motivated by low self-control.

Weisburd, Chayet, and Waring (1990) generated circumscribed support for Gottfredson and Hirschi's general theory of crime in a large-scale investigation of eight categories of white-collar crime. With the exception of antitrust violations, persons convicted of federal white-collar crimes did not fit the general stereotype of a white-collar offender. Two out of five of these individuals had at least one prior arrest, one in three had at least one prior conviction, and one in seven had been previously incarcerated. Even when Weisburd et al. restricted their sample to persons holding elite positions or significant assets during the period in which they committed their crimes, one in four had a prior arrest, and one in ten had at last one former conviction. Despite the presence of moderate versatility and deviance in the overall sample, age of onset was later and frequency of offending lower than what has conventionally been observed in street criminals. On the other hand, when Weisburd et al. examined the most chronic offenders in their sample of white-collar offenders (three or more prior arrests) they uncovered a career pattern that was difficult to differentiate from that of the average street criminal.

Benson and Moore (1992) compared federal white-collar offenders with persons convicted of narcotics violations, bank robbery, and postal forgery in an effort to test Gottfredson and Hirschi's versatility and deviance hypotheses. First, white-collar criminals were four times more likely to have been previously arrested for a white-collar crime than common criminals. This reflects greater specialization in the white-collar group and offers challenge to Gottfredson and Hirschi's versatility hypothesis. Second, the common criminal group was significantly more deviant on measures of problem drinking, drug use, poor grades, and social maladjustment than white-collar offenders. A subsample of high-rate white-collar criminals with four or more prior arrests, however, displayed a level of versatility and prior deviance similar to that attained by common criminals.

Like Wheeler et al. (1988) and Benson and Moore (1992) before them, Walters and Geyer (2002) identified several different pathways to white-collar crime in a group of federal prisoners serving time for a variety of white-collar offenses. Walters and Geyer determined that white-collar offenders with no prior history of non-white-collar crime earned significantly lower scores on measures of criminal thinking and identity than white-collar offenders with a history of prior non-white-collar crime. Thus, besides a low self-control group of high-rate white-collar offenders largely indiscernible from criminals convicted of other offenses, there appears to be a high self-control group that engages in white-collar crime as an extension of their egos or in response to powerful situational forces.

LIFESTYLES CONGRUENT WITH WHITE-COLLAR CRIME

There appear to be at least two major categories of white-collar crime: one associated with low self-control and another with high self-control. Embedded within the low self-control group are individuals who identify with the goals of a criminal lifestyle and who find white-collar positions ideal for generating criminal opportunities. The belief systems of these individuals are largely indistinguishable from the belief systems of persons who partake in other forms of criminality. Collins and Schmidt (1993) appear to have captured aspects of this subcategory in a study of 365 incarcerated white-collar offenders and 344 white-collar workers, the results of which revealed lower social conscientiousness, as represented by irresponsibility, poor dependability, and a general disregard for rules and social norms, in the offender group. These characteristics correspond to two of the four interactive styles associated with a criminal lifestyle: irresponsibility and social rule breaking. The two remaining interactive styles—self-indulgence and interpersonal intrusiveness—are implied in the outcome of the Benson and Moore (1992) study, where the high-rate white-collar group not only engaged in more problem drinking and drug use (self-indulgence) but also performed a wider array of offenses—to include ones that were violent (interpersonal intrusiveness)—than low-rate white-collar offenders.

If the first subcategory of white-collar crime tends to corroborate Gottfredson and Hirschi's general theory of crime, the second category clearly disputes it. In contrast to the first subcategory of white-collar crime, the second subcategory is marked by high self-control and weak identification with a criminal lifestyle. Individuals falling into this second subcategory identify with a business lifestyle rather than a criminal lifestyle and, spurred by the "culture of competition" endemic to industrial capitalism (Coleman, 1987), participate in white-collar crime for reasons of personal advancement (Benson, 1989), corporate subservience (Kerbo & Inoue, 1990), or flight from a "nonshareable financial problem" (Cressey, 1953/1971). Whereas these individuals identify more with the business lifestyle than with the criminal pattern, significant overlap nonetheless exists between the two lifestyles by virtue of their common elevation on the dominance dimension of the model used to classify families of lifestyles. As portrayed in Figure 6.2, both the business and criminal lifestyles are situated at the dominant end of the dominance–submission continuum, with the criminal lifestyle falling into the dominant-low control quadrant and the business lifestyle into the dominant-high control quadrant. It is also possible that with time a person's allegiance shifts from a business lifestyle to a criminal lifestyle as he or she becomes increasingly more involved in white-collar offending, irrespective of his or her reasons for initial criminal involvement.

This section would be incomplete without a discussion of crimes committed by occupational groups, companies, and corporations. Given the fractal nature of lifestyles, it is anticipated that the high-low self-control breakdown may be as applicable to groups as it is to individuals. Some businesses operate as criminal enter-

Figure 6.2
Four Lifestyles Arranged According to the Dimensions of Dominance and Control

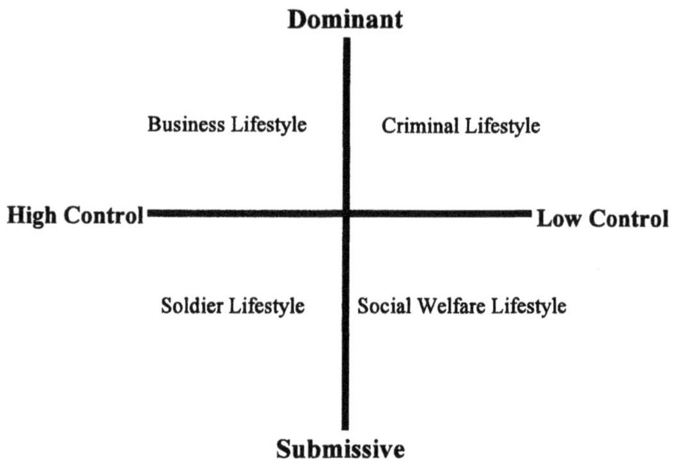

prises (Croall, 1989). Organized crime groups, for instance, will sell stolen property and launder money through legitimate businesses but also operate quasi-legitimate companies with visible criminal intent. This low self-control variant of group white-collar crime approximates a criminal lifestyle more than it does a business lifestyle. Situated at the high self-control end of the group white-collar continuum are corporations known to cut corners and encourage, or even demand, illegality from their employees to meet production goals, quotas, and deadlines. This is sometimes referred to as corporate culture (Braithwaite, 1989), which supplies the group with a high self-control/personal advancement motive for white-collar crime. Corporations that find themselves in financial difficulty may cut corners and condone illegality as a means of extricating themselves from unfavorable economic conditions. Such appears to have been the case, to some extent, in the Orange County (California) bankruptcy fiasco of 1994 (Will, Pontell, & Cheung, 1998). In contrast to low self-control white-collar crime, both high self-control group variants, like their individual counterparts, are more allied with the business lifestyle than criminal lifestyle.

CASE ILLUSTRATION: RANDY—JEKYLL AND HYDE

Background

Randy is an only child born to working-class parents. His blue-collar father was Randy's role model until the boy reached midadolescence. After this, it was his rich uncle with whom he identified and whose behavior he sought to emulate. From his uncle Randy learned that money opens doors and that image is everything, lessons that would serve him well in his future occupation as a stockbroker. Randy spent several summers living with his uncle and witnessed him bribing judges and public officials. He also paid close attention when his uncle discussed the importance of traveling in the proper circles and hanging around with the right people. Randy committed to memory the salience of political connections after another uncle, a local politician, bailed him out of trouble with the local authorities when he got caught by the police drinking and smoking marijuana at age 17. Randy graduated from high school and attended college for three years, but his interests lay elsewhere. At this point Randy entered the business world intent on following in his rich uncle's footsteps.

Randy's first job out of college was to sell real estate in a resort community. It was only a matter of time before Randy became the corporation's top salesperson. He parlayed his success with real estate into a position with a small brokerage firm selling stocks. Opening forty-three accounts in his first month on the job, he was soon touted as the office superstar. Randy reports that he soon became aware of how intoxicating sales could be and relates that he felt a sense of exhilaration each time he closed a major deal. From here he moved to a large national brokerage firm, where he began climbing the ladder of success. His wife of several months could not believe how much their standard of living had improved since Randy accepted the job with the larger firm. She also noticed that Randy was beginning to change in subtle and insidious ways.

Randy had been indoctrinated into the world of big business by his rich uncle. Stealing other people's clients was standard practice, according to Randy, and instilled a mindset that facilitated further rule breaking in exchange for economic success. Misappropriation of client funds for the purpose of covering debts or personal investments was also common, says Randy. Many of the stockbrokers jokingly referred to these unabashed acts of embezzlement as "no-interest loans." If the client detected the missing money before it could be returned to his or her account, the firm would ordinarily reimburse the client, with interest, to shield the broker from any negative repercussions. What is viewed as white-collar crime by society is perceived as a rite of passage by many brokers. Being a broker in a large brokerage firm is akin to belonging to an exclusive club in which members are entitled to violate the laws and rules of society so long as no one gets hurt physically. This gave Randy license to do whatever gave him immediate gratification with little regard for the long-term consequences of his actions.

It should be noted that stockbrokers are viewed as assets by brokerage firms, seeing as the firm receives a percentage of what each broker earns. Hence, high-producing brokers are often bailed out of legal trouble and enabled in other ways by brokerage houses whose very survival depends on a broker's ability to bring money and new accounts into the firm. In a capitalistic society money translates into power, and, given the amount of money that brokerage firms control, their power seems almost limitless. Ordinances are changed and legal actions squelched as the bonds that keep municipalities solvent and police pension plans afloat are typically underwritten by large brokerage firms. Consequently, a brokerage firm enjoys significant leverage when it comes to guarding its most valuable asset, the high-producing broker. The brokers, according to Randy, share in the power and influence and are frequently taken care of in other ways, to include tax-free cash bonuses and access to female interns who spend more time doing sexual favors for the brokers than researching the stock market.

As Randy describes it, life in the brokerage firm was like the movie *Goodfellas* without the killing, all the way down to two Christmas parties, one for the wives and the other for the brokers. The latter, commonly referred to as the Black Christmas party, rivaled Sodom and Gomorrah, asserts Randy. Despite a string of successes at the brokerage firm, Randy felt that he could do better. He quit on a Friday and started work at another firm the following Monday, taking his entire portfolio of clients with him. As if this weren't enough, Randy rubbed salt in the wound by attending seminars sponsored by his former employer with the intent of stealing even more clients. Around this time Randy, driving his Mercedes in an unsafe manner, struck a motorcyclist who later died of his injuries. Although he alleges that he did not know that he had hit someone until a day later, when he learned of his role in the death he tried to conceal evidence by hiding his slightly damaged Mercedes. Pleading guilty to vehicular homicide, Randy served evenings in jail for several months until he was released on parole. He is convinced that had his new employer not intervened on his behalf, he probably would have served several years in prison rather than a few months in jail. This only reinforced Randy's superoptimistic belief in his own invulnerability.

Shortly after his release from jail Randy quit his job to go into business for himself. He also bought a hair replacement franchise with plans of opening up several additional centers once the first franchise got off the ground. There was no doubt in Randy's mind that his hair replacement business would be as successful as his real estate and stock ventures. Regardless, the franchise cost in excess of $1 million beyond what he had available in liquid assets. Randy therefore decided to do what he had done so many times before when he had worked at the large brokerage houses—he "borrowed" more than $1 million from several different accounts, including two Catholic churches. Randy reasoned that one church didn't need the money for five or six years and the other didn't require a return for twenty years and rationalized that he would replace the money with interest long before it was needed. Surreptitiously, Randy stole the funds necessary to purchase the hair replacement franchise. However, the National Association of Security Dealers (NASD), alerted, he believes, by the national brokerage firm that he had quit several years earlier, stepped in. Created in 1938, the NASD is a national organization charged with regulating the securities industry. It was not long before the FBI was called in to investigate the case and ascertain whether any federal laws had been broken.

Around the time that Randy went into business for himself, he started an affair with a 17-year-old girl whom he met at a tanning salon. Randy had learned from his millionaire uncle the importance of image and took great pride in his physical appearance, projecting a successful persona by means of bodybuilding, cardiovascular exercise, weekly suntanning sessions, and hair replacement. Having a teenage girlfriend made him feel even younger. He grew increasingly overconfident and developed an unquenchable thirst for power. Using a variety of business contacts, Randy was able to get into restaurants, clubs, and events that were closed to the general public. This only fed Randy's rapidly expanding ego. While Randy's wife had always been a stabilizing influence in his life, his girlfriend catered to the more reckless and vicious side of his personality. As a result, Randy felt pulled in opposite directions, not unlike the central character in *Jekyll and Hyde*, a play that he reportedly attended on twenty-three separate occasions. By way of a growing resonance with the play's central character, Randy became convinced that the Jekyll and Hyde components of his self-image could coexist. He was Jekyll with his wife and Hyde with his girlfriend, but Hyde was slowly taking over.

Randy enjoyed the attention that he received from women and the power that he felt over men when he adopted the Hyde persona. In his mind Hyde was much more fun than Jekyll. While living out his Hydian fantasies, Randy began cheating on his girlfriend. He would routinely pick up women at biker bars or dancers performing at a local strip club, averring that he often left the club with two women. He was whirling out of control and headed for trouble; it was only a matter of time before he hit the wall. Randy's business decisions were growing increasingly more impulsive, and his behavior was becoming more erratic and unpredictable by the day. He was drinking more and had increased his consumption of cocaine. He was rude to friends and disrespectful toward superiors. Despite the fact that his wife would periodically confront him about his behavior, Randy's response was to show her the door, knowing full well that she was financially and emotionally dependent on him. Hyde became Randy's justification for breaking the rules and hurting others, whether the violations involved stealing from clients, entering into multiple affairs, or verbally abusing his wife.

The end came quickly for Randy. The FBI, aided by the NASD, was closing in and Randy, feeling the pressure, grew more arrogant. He superoptimistically believed that there was no way he would do any jail time, reassuring himself with such statements as "it isn't like I killed anyone." He would therefore taunt the FBI agents when they tried to interview him, which only made them that much more determined to build an airtight case against him. Randy had committed the fatal mistake of forgetting that he no longer had the backing of a large national brokerage firm. To the contrary, his former employer was doing everything within its power to hasten his demise. He had fallen from the high wire with no safety net. Many of the clients whom Randy had defrauded were allegedly willing to settle for restitution, but not the churches. A priest at one of the two Catholic churches that Randy defrauded stated that he was less interested in restitution than he was in making sure Randy was prosecuted to the fullest extent of the law; a priest at the other church characterized Randy as a modern-day Judas. Randy had learned a lesson that his uncle had neglected to teach him: never steal from the Catholic

Church. Charged with seven counts of mail fraud, two counts of wire fraud, one count of interstate transportation of stolen property, and one count of money laundering, Randy received a seventy-one-month sentence, of which he must serve at least sixty-one months in prison before returning to the community to serve three years of supervised release.

Lifestyle Assessment

Scores from the LCSF are reproduced in Table 6.1. A total score of 5 on the LCSF indicates that Randy manifests minimal involvement in, commitment to, and identification with the criminal lifestyle. The only LCSF subscale on which he achieves an elevated score (4) is self-indulgence, where he earned two points for substance abuse, one point for a divorce, and one point for a tattoo. Randy's high score on the self-indulgence subscale of the LCSF denotes his possible involvement, commitment, and identification with other lifestyles, in particular, the drug and sexual lifestyles. His identification with the business lifestyle is also apparent from his background. Thus, while Randy, as is typical of many white-collar offenders, does not consider himself a criminal, his affiliation with self-indulgent and corporate aims helps explain his descent into criminal behavior.

Randy completed the PICTS shortly after his arrival at the medium-security federal correctional facility where he began his sentence. Similar to the LCSF results, there is no evidence of significant criminal thinking on Randy's PICTS profile, which is depicted in Figure 6.3. The highest peaking scale on the protocol, sentimentality, falls below a T-score of 60, and is therefore of dubious value in accounting for his actions. Given Randy's vigorous sense of privilege and inconsistency (Jekyll and Hyde), it is surprising that he achieved such low scores on the entitlement and discontinuity scales. One possibility is that since Randy's entitlement and discontinuity stem from a lifestyle other than crime—a business or sexual lifestyle, perhaps—they do not register on the PICTS. What is clear is that Randy identifies more with a business than criminal lifestyle and sees himself as having been enticed by the glamour of the business world to defraud his investors. We should not lose sight of the fact that while the criminal, drug, and sexual lifestyles may have been ancillary to the business lifestyle, they still exercised a direct or indirect (through their interaction with the business lifestyle) effect on Randy's actions.

Table 6.1
Randy's Scores on the Lifestyle Criminality Screening Form (LCSF)

Irresponsibility	1
Self-Indulgence	4
Interpersonal Intrusiveness	0
Social Rule Breaking	0
TOTAL LCSF SCORE	5

Figure 6.3
Randy's Scores on the Psychological Inventory of Criminal Thinking Styles (PICTS)

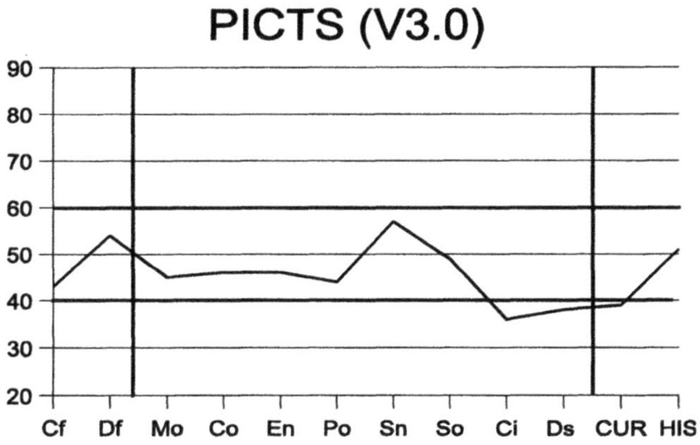

Note: Cf = confusion scale; Df = defensiveness scale; Mo = mollification scale; Co = cutoff scale; En = entitlement scale; Po = power orientation scale; Sn = sentimentality scale; So = superoptimism scale; Ci = cognitive indolence scale; Ds = discontinuity scale; CUR = current content scale; HIS = historical content scale.

Belief System Analysis

Self-View

The reflected appraisals that dominate Randy's self-view are those of his rich uncle and several business leaders whose opinions he respects. These individuals form an imaginary audience to which Randy plays as he acts out his Jekyll and Hyde life script. In his business ventures Randy is cunning, shrewd, and vicious, the inveterate Mr. Hyde. When slipping into a social relationship mode of interaction, Randy tries to imitate the sensitivity and caring of Dr. Jekyll, particularly in the presence of his wife. Waiting impatiently in the wings, nonetheless, is Dr. Jekyll's wicked alter ego, Mr. Hyde. Randy relates that Mr. Hyde can appear at any moment, especially when his girlfriend is there to serve as a discriminative stimulus or he is attempting to impress women other than his wife with his wit, charm, and prowess. The corridor that separates Randy's personal and professional lives gradually collapsed as he began playing to an imaginary audience that he believed preferred Hyde over Jekyll because Hyde was "more fun."

Corroboration can be found for Randy's involvement in all three modes of social comparison. At various points in his life he has used upward comparisons to compare himself to his uncle and respected business leaders in an effort to "improve" himself and become more like them. Randy also enacted parallel comparisons with other stockbrokers to determine his professional strengths and weaknesses relative to his competition. As important as upward and parallel comparisons have been in Randy's life, both pale in comparison to the downward comparisons that he made of others so that he could feel better about himself. Whether the target was a former coworker with whom he didn't get along, a potential suitor with whom he was in competition, or an ex-inmate from the county jail who approached him at a local mall, Randy made downward comparisons to feel superior to others. This reflects a basic insecurity that belies the narcissistic personality disorder with which he was diagnosed several years earlier by a psychologist during a pretrial evaluation. Randy may come across as narcissistic, but this is only because he feels insecure about himself and uses various lifestyles (drug, sexual, business) to enhance and bolster his deflated ego.

The self-representations that form Randy's self-view are generally dichotomized along the lines of the good Dr. Jekyll and the bad Mr. Hyde. Sensitivity, compassion, and sentimentality are coded for Dr. Jekyll, while tenacity, shrewdness, and ruthlessness are schemes from which the Hyde persona is constructed. Many people harbor a paradoxical mix of seeming incongruent personal characteristics and schemes. Those able to integrate and reconcile these discrepant parts are in a better position to reap the rewards of life in the sense that they are free to use more of their experience than people whose lives remain segmented and discontinuous. Profiting immensely from his exposure to the dialectic method, Randy learned to integrate the incompatibilities that plague all humans so that he might enlist his full repertoire of personal strengths, rather than relying on only a portion of his experience, in responding to, and solving, the problems of everyday living.

Male criminals and businessmen may share a strong masculine gender-role identity, of which Randy is a prime example. Taking heed of his uncle's credo that appearance is everything, Randy continues to work out daily. He not only lifts weights and walks obsessively, but when on the streets he would habitually imbibe large quantities of vitamins and steroids. Randy's gender-role identity is so masculine that one might wonder whether he protests too much. Hence, in addition to being insecure about his worthiness as a person, he may also be insecure about his own gender identity, for why else does he spend so much time cultivating this caricature of masculinity? Though Randy continues to reject the criminal role identity a year after his admission to a federal correctional institution, he is very comfortable with an image of himself as a cunning businessman. Nevertheless, he is becoming increasingly wary of this role identity for he fears that it could bring out the Hyde persona in him. In the past Randy used the business role to excuse and mollify his moral and legal transgressions in the belief that he was not truly responsible for actions that were simply in response to others' expectations of him in the fulfillment of a business role. If change is to occur, Randy must come to terms with the criminogenic nature of his business role identity.

Several fears have been instrumental in the construction of Randy's possible selves. In the past his fear of falling short of his goals drove him to pursue an ultra-successful future self. Fear of failure, a prime incentive for white-collar crime traceable to status concerns, appears to underlie Randy's highly competitive approach to life and his desire to defeat all comers, whether in business or in his personal life. Randy's fear for the present is that he will lose his intellectual and competitive edge after spending five years in prison. He has compensated for this feared self by working as a tutor in the institution's education department and offering real estate and stock classes to the inmate population. There is a realistic fear on Randy's part that he has lost critical opportunities for financial success that he may never be able to recover. This, coupled with the understanding that he may not be allowed to work as a stockbroker while on supervised release, has led to the formation of possible selves marked by the pursuit of alternative avenues of employment, from working as a luxury car salesman, to starting up his own hair replacement center.

World-View

Randy was able to describe his position on all four world-view dimensions, but as is often the case with those most heavily invested in lifestyle activities, he tends to vacillate between the two poles of each continuum. On the organismic-mechanistic dimension, for instance, Randy professes an organismic view of relationships and the business environment in the sense that he realizes that personal change in response to a continually self-altering relationship and business environment is necessary for success. At the same time, he is highly mechanistic when blocked in his efforts to achieve various relationship and business goals. Under circumstances such as these people are viewed as obstacles to be removed so that Randy can attain the objectives he has set for himself. The manipulation and intimidation that accompany such a mechanistic world-view are plainly evident in Randy's personal and business relationships. It is noteworthy that Coleman (1987) traces the "culture of competition" created in capitalistic societies to a seventeenth century mechanical, agentic world-view.

Randy's views on fatalism-agenticism also lack integration. As is commonly observed with white-collar crime (Trevino & Youngblood, 1990), Randy operates from an external locus of control. He fatalistically believes that his destiny is controlled by outside forces. Accordingly, he has developed an elaborate system of rituals and superstitions to which he attributes past successes and failures in both his personal and professional life. When getting ready for a date or preparing for an evening at the local strip club, Randy had a ritual that he would follow each time. The ritual began with a shower and ended with him driving to the liquor store, where he would purchase a specific brand of vodka, all the time listening to his favorite CD on the car stereo. Businesswise, he would sometimes spend as much as an hour circling the office until his "lucky" parking space opened up, and he was able to pull in. He further relates that he would never close a business deal without his "lucky" pen. In contrast to the fatalism contained in his rituals, Randy believes that a person makes his own luck. Even now, years later, Randy has trouble reconciling these two opposing aspects of his world-view.

The justice-inequity continuum is one dimension of Randy's world-view on which he demonstrates a clear preference. Randy actively rejects the view that the world is just and that people get what they deserve. As such, he staunchly supports the belief that the world is unjust. In the extreme, inequity views can precipitate depression, but in Randy's case they have inspired him to justify his own indiscretions. Like Mr. Hyde, he mollifies his destructive actions by pointing out the hypocrisy of coworkers who project a family man image in church while "banging their secretaries at work" or the priest who called Randy a modern-day Judas while arranging for cross-diocese transfers of "priests who had been caught molesting children." In Randy's mind the end justifies the means to the extent that life is not fair anyway. Machiavellianism, in truth, tends to be high in those convicted of white-collar crime (Baucus, 1994).

Nowhere does the Jekyll and Hyde metaphor play out more freely than on the malevolent-benevolent dimension of Randy's world-view. Though he makes allowances for good in the world, Randy is convinced that evil (Hyde) is more powerful than good (Jekyll) and will eventually win out in the end. It is human nature, says Randy, to take whatever you want and either deliberately or inadvertently harm others in the process. The growing segmentation of modern social life in industrialized culture may be partially responsible for the fragmented or discontinuous sense of self and reality witnessed in capitalistic societies (Bellah, Madsen, Sullivan, Swidler, & Tipton, 1985) and furnished Randy with the opportunity to follow one set of standards at work and another set of standards at home. Over time, however, the standards that Randy set for himself at work (Hyde) began to overtake his social life (Jekyll). Discontinuity is patently evident in Randy's world-view but is not reflected in his score on the Ds scale of the PICTS. This may be due to the fact that he uses discontinuity to support a business, rather than criminal, lifestyle.

The prototypes that fill Randy's world-view are rather simplistic and one-dimensional. Dividing the world into good and bad, as personified by the Jekyll and Hyde metaphor, has had a profound effect on Randy. There is also evidence that he was influenced by commercialism to purchase products, from cars to cologne, that made him feel successful. He further relates that he stole many of the ideas for his romantic interludes with his wife and girlfriend from daytime soap operas. Sadly, the schemes in Randy's world-view are borrowed almost exclusively from Broadway, Madison Avenue, and various Soap Operas. As is often the case, Randy's simplistic prototypes had a detrimental effect on the scope and sophistication of his self- and world-views. In an effort to look as good as he could and be larger than life, he had become a caricature of a person, in his own words, "a cartoon character." Before he can experience his own intrinsic power and humanity, Randy must develop more cognitively complex belief systems, possible selves, and prototypes.

Present-View

Randy, despite possessing above average intelligence, displays deficits in the perceptual and executive functions of the present-view. While in the midst of a preoccupation with power, drugs, and sex, Randy fell victim to a number of perceptual distortions. The entitlement and discontinuity that furthered these lifestyles were, in fact, constructed in a swamp of perceptual distortion. Adopting a mechanistic-inequitable world-view, Randy convinced himself that life was unjust and that others were out only for themselves. From Randy's perspective we live in a "dog-eat-dog" world and are accordingly justified in taking whatever measures are necessary to defend ourselves against sundry nefarious influences. Randy consequently felt entitled to take whatever he told himself he needed irrespective of how this might affect others. He accomplished this, in part, by distorting his perception so that he interpreted others' actions and intentions as malevolent. The discontinuity, which was both a reflection and precipitant of his obsession with "Jekyll and Hyde," likewise contributed to his perceptual distortions in the form of a dichotomous, black-and-white perspective.

Impulsivity began to infiltrate Randy's decisions after he went into business for himself. He didn't want to wait for the money required to buy the hair replacement franchise, and so he stole the money from investors. He didn't want to go through the effort of working on his marriage, and so he had one long-standing affair and a string of one-night stands. He didn't want to cooperate with the investigating officers and so chose to demean and act disrespectfully toward them. The impulsive manner in which Randy handled everyday problems in living was aggravating old problems and creating new ones. The growing difficulties and associated psychological distress served to skew his decision making further, which, in turn, hastened the downward spiral of his life. It is no wonder that right before his arrest Randy was fantasizing about a dramatic death, not unlike that of his hero Mr. Hyde. Incarceration, as much as he might not want to admit it, probably saved his life.

Past-View

The recollections that dominate Randy's past-view emerge as regrets over past decisions. First, he regrets having struck and killed the motorcyclist and laments his efforts to obstruct justice once he realized that he was responsible for the motorcyclist's death. Second, he regrets leaving the first major brokerage firm, the one from which he stole clients. Randy is convinced that had he remained at the firm, he would have received nothing more than a "slap on the wrist" for mishandling investors' money because the firm would have protected him. Third, Randy regrets cheating on his wife and ruining their relationship, for he now realizes that she was a vital stabilizing force in his life, keeping him grounded while his girlfriend complemented his reckless side. Interestingly, Randy feels little remorse for committing the current or instant offense. He has neutralized the guilt that he might have otherwise experienced with mollification ("the priest was a hypocrite"), entitlement ("I needed the money to start the business"), sentimentality ("I'm not a bad guy; I planned on paying the money back"), and discontinuity ("there are times when I am overwhelmed by Hyde") and does not identify himself as a criminal but as a businessman.

Future-View

A feature of the future-view instrumental in the formation of Randy's business/criminal lifestyle is the outcome expectancy that money is capable of eradicating one's basic insecurities in life. Money can be viewed as a kind of magical charm or talisman that wards off a person's darkest fears (Doyle, 1992). It is also the principal way that people in capitalist societies measure themselves against others and tally up the victories and losses in the competitive battles of life (Coleman, 1992). Randy believed that success in business and his conquest of women would enhance his status and ease his insecurities. As was mentioned in the section on the self-view, Randy was more concerned with self-enhancement than he was with either self-evaluation or self-improvement. His future-view was therefore dominated by anticipations of future wealth, recognition, and power. Randy and many other white-collar criminals eventually come to the realization that there is no end to greed. The more one gets, the more one wants; the accumulation of material wealth is a never-ending process in people who attempt to solve internal problems (insecurity and fear) with external palliatives (sex, drugs, power).

CONCLUSION

Randy, like many white-collar offenders, does not see himself as a criminal, nor does he view the actions leading up to his arrest, conviction, and incarceration as a crime. Rejecting a criminal identity is desirable; euphemistically reinterpreting law-violating behavior as something other than crime is not. As scholars, practitioners, and criminal justice policymakers, we want to make certain we are doing everything within our power to discourage self-labeling in those who violate societal laws. Labeling oneself a criminal is extremely destructive owing to the fact it creates a self-fulfilling prophecy that may be difficult for the individual to escape. The internal, stable, and global self-attributes that compose a label lock people into a negative pattern and interfere with their ability to consider alternative views and construct crime-incongruent belief systems. Refusing to acknowledge one's law-violating behavior as a crime, on the other hand, reduces one's felt responsibility for such actions and opens the door to future law-breaking opportunities. Those interested in promoting change in clients who have been convicted of white-collar crime must walk the thin line between discouraging self-labeling and encouraging acceptance of responsibility for one's law-violating behavior.

White-collar crime has traditionally been construed as less serious than street crime, and while this perception appears to be slowly changing, people living in capitalistic societies are still largely ignorant of the impact that white-collar crime has on their everyday lives. We find violent crime frightening, sexual crime disgusting, and drug trafficking frustrating. Whereas each of these crimes is significant in its own right and certainly not something to be ignored, the cumulative effect of these three crimes is probably less than the destructive potential of white-collar crime. One of the unwritten criteria of white-collar crime is that it is an offense for which personal injury is not intended, but how many people are harmed by white-collar crime, particularly when the crime is committed at the corporate-organizational level? If a corporation receives a small fine after contaminating a community's drinking supply because community leaders fear losing the company's tax base, should we be surprised when the business gets the impression that it is above the law? White-collar crime can bankrupt whole nations, compromise the health of countless citizens, and threaten the survival of the entire planet; it deserves a great deal more attention from criminal justice scholars, researchers, and policymakers than it has thus far received.

7

Belief Systems and Drug Trafficking

While it is commonly believed that America's war on drugs has failed to meet its stated objective of reducing the supply and demand of illicit psychoactive substances, it has been a boon to the prison industry. There are now three to four times as many Americans serving time in state and federal prisons for drug offenses than were imprisoned in 1989, when President George Bush declared his ill-fated war on drugs (BJS, 2000a, 2000b). It therefore seems fitting that this book include a chapter on belief systems congruent with drug trafficking. The term drug trafficking is intended to cover the importation, distribution, and sale of psychoactive substances that have been banned by the government. Furthermore, trafficking occurs at several different levels, from smuggling drugs across the border, to manufacturing them in illicit labs, to distributing them to dealers, to selling them to individual users. Repeating a point made in the chapters on violent crime, sexual assault, and white-collar crime, drug trafficking—the transportation, disbursement, and sale of illicit substances—will be defined by the offense rather than by the offender. This is based, in part, on the fact that many people who participate in drug trafficking also use drugs and commit a wide variety of nondrug offenses. Our journey begins, then, with a review of the extent and severity of drug trafficking.

EXTENT AND SEVERITY OF DRUG TRAFFICKING

There were 30,150 federal arrests for various drug crimes between October 1, 1997, and September 30, 1998 (BJS, 2000a). This was twice the number of federal arrests for property crime and six times the number of federal arrests for violent crime. Of those arrested on federal drug trafficking charges, 77% were prosecuted, 69% convicted, and 63% incarcerated, figures that are 45% to 103% higher than the rates of prosecution (53%), conviction (46%), and incarceration (31%) for other federal crimes. Although 60% of all federal prisoners are serving drug sentences, the number of state prisoners incarcerated for drugs is four times the number of federal inmates doing time for drug code violations. Juveniles tend not to appear on the federal registers, but surveys show that one in ten urban youth is involved in drug trafficking and government statistics indicate that between 1986 and 1991 juvenile arrests for drug dealing jumped dramatically, whereas juvenile arrests for drug use declined (Stanton & Galbraith, 1994). African American youth are particularly susceptible to incurring arrest for drug dealing. MacCoun and Reuter (1992) relate that one in six inner-city African American teenagers has been charged with peddling drugs. Since people often conduct thousands of drug transactions for every recorded arrest, the official numbers provide only a weak approximation of the true scope of the nation's drug problem. Drug trafficking may well be the most frequently committed criminal offense, more common perhaps than even simple property crimes.

Although it has been alleged that nearly half the illegal substances in the world are sold and consumed in the United States, drug trafficking is a world-wide problem. Canada chronicled 7,153 arrests for cocaine trafficking in 1990, a rate of 27 arrests per 100,000 people, while Italian authorities note that 42,104 drug offenses were reported to police in 1990, a per capita rate of 69.9 offenses per 100,000 population. There were 86,470 drug offenses reputed to have taken place in Australia in 1990 (per capita rate = 494.1), and statistics from Sweden show a 40% increase in violations of that country's Narcotic Drug Act between 1990 and 1993 (BJS, 1994). The difference between the United States and other Western nations may be less a matter of the absolute level of drug trafficking in American and Europe than how these two regions of the world have chose to respond to the drug problem. In a comparison of prison inmates in the United States and Great Britain it was determined that 24% of all inmates in the United States were serving time for drugs as opposed to 8% of all inmates in Great Britain. Additionally, 29% of the inmates incarcerated in American prisons for drugs were serving sentences in excess of ten years, whereas 6% of the drug offenders in Great Britain were serving sentences of this length (Lynch, Smith, Graziadei, & Pittayathikhun, 1994). More inmates serving longer sentences may simply mirror the political nature of the war on drugs in the United States.

The severity of drug trafficking is manifest in the violence that seems to go hand in hand with drug dealing. McBride, Burgman-Habermehl, Alpert, and Chitwood (1986) note that one-quarter of the homicides occurring in Dade County, Florida, between 1978 and 1982 could be traced to the importation, distribution, or sale of illicit substances. An even higher rate of violence was observed in New York City, where 43% of all homicides in 1988 were connected in some way to the drug trade (Goldstein, Brownstein, Ryan, & Bellucci, 1997). Violence is endemic to marijuana production and sales (Adler, 1993), heroin distribution (Ianni, 1974), and crack and cocaine dealing (Williams, 1989). One might go so far as to argue that violence has become an accepted and routine way of dealing with problems in neighborhoods where drug dealing is most visible (Sommers & Baskin, 1992). The question that this raises is whether violence is a trait of the individual who selects himself or herself into the drug trade or whether the drug trade itself fosters violence. Scrutinizing the well-publicized violence associated with the distribution and sale of crack cocaine, Fagan and Chin (1990) uncovered evidence in support of both propositions. The crack trade appears to call for higher levels of violence than other types of drug dealing, and violence-prone individuals are attracted to, and recruited into, the crack trade.

DEMOGRAPHICS OF DRUG TRAFFICKING

Statistics confirm that only about 630 persons 18 years of age and younger were arrested on federal drug charges in fiscal year 1997–1998 (BJS, 2000a), but the actual number of juveniles involved in drug trafficking is probably many times this figure. As Stanton and Galbraith (1994) point out, the rate of urban youth involvement in drug trafficking can be as high as 10%. Adult dealers realize that juveniles are less likely to be prosecuted by the authorities and have responded by actively recruiting teenagers and preadolescents into their drug organizations. Studies suggest that youth with limited options for legitimate financial success are at increased risk for being solicited and tutored by older individuals in the subtleties of drug trafficking at a relatively young age (Haberfeld, 1993; McCarthy, 1996). Prior to the mid-1980s, drug dealing was reserved for adults and older adolescents. Since that time the average age of persons participating in the drug trade has dropped steadily and the number of individuals confined in juvenile facilities for drug-related offenses has risen dramatically. Accordingly, the proportion of juveniles held in public and private juvenile facilities on drug-related charges rose from 5% in 1987 to 14% in 1998 (BJS, 1999).

Eighty-five percent of those arrested on federal drug charges in fiscal year 1997–1998 were male (BJS, 2000a). However, the rate of female involvement in drug trafficking is on the rise. The number of women arrested for drug offenses in New York state between 1983 and 1992 rose 142% compared to 40% for men over the same time period (New York State Division of Criminal Justice Services, 1993). The male–female disparity in the growth of drug offending persists, though the gap has narrowed; between 1991 and 1997 there was a nationwide increase in arrests for drug offenses in men of 36% as opposed to 45% in women (BJS, 1990, 1999). Bush and Weinfurt (1994) advise that while males are more often approached to sell drugs, females are 1.4 times more likely to report that they have assisted someone in performing a drug deal. There is a general belief among criminologists that females who take part in drug trafficking ordinarily assume a subordinate role, when in fact research shows that women occupy a variety of positions in drug organizations, to include taking leadership roles in which they depend on familial and quasi-familial relationships to create a positive work environment (Denton & O'Malley, 1999). As with males, violence is regularly encountered in the drug-dealing activities of females (Sommers & Baskin, 1997).

Minorities are arrested and incarcerated for drug trafficking at a rate three times their representation in American society. Inasmuch as African Americans and Hispanics constitute 24.6% of the U.S. population (U.S. Bureau of Census, 2001), they account for 78.2% of those imprisoned for drugs (Brownsberger, 2000). Racial disparity occurs even in districts where minorities are in the majority. African Americans make up 60% of the population of Baltimore, Maryland, yet account for 91% of the arrests for drugs in that city (Stanton & Galbraith, 1994). Between 1981 and 1991 the Maryland State Department of Education (1992) recorded a dramatic increase in the number of arrests for drug trafficking in African American youth, while the rate for white youth remained stable. This same study certified that African American youth are twice as likely to be approached about selling drugs than white youth. Disparity in the incarceration rates for white and minority subjects who participate in drug trafficking may reflect influences at any one of five levels: (1) the offense conduct (e.g., factors contributing to involvement in drug trafficking), (2) neighborhood enforcement (e.g., increased police presence in inner-city areas), (3) arrest (e.g., racial profiling), (4) prosecutorial and judicial decision making (e.g., postarrest racial bias), and (5) sentencing choices (e.g., harsher sentences for crack cocaine than powder cocaine or marijuana). Although analyses performed by Brownsberger (2000) generated modest backing for the neighborhood enforcement perspective, none of the five levels were able to fully explain the racial disparity observed in the rate of drug offense incarceration.

THEORIES OF DRUG TRAFFICKING

Social strain theory would seem well suited to unraveling the mysteries of drug dealing in inner-city youth. Administering surveys to 600 low-income African American males, Whitehead, Peterson, and Kaljee (1994) determined that nonmainstream activities like drug dealing were viewed by many of the interviewees as one of the few existing opportunities for economic advancement left open to them. Similar sentiments were expressed by a group of Puerto Rican gang members asked to describe their reasons for engaging in drug trafficking (Padilla, 1995). Agnew, Cullen, Burton, Evans, and Dunaway (1996) utilized dissatisfaction with one's monetary status as an index of social strain and discovered that this criterion correlated with both drug use and income-generating crime, including drug trafficking. These preliminary findings lend support to the proposition that stress and strain contribute to the development and maintenance of belief systems congruent with drug trafficking.

Differential association is the theory that has been applied most often to drug trafficking. African American juveniles who deal drugs report that their involvement was facilitated by the perception that their friends were actively involved in this activity (Li, Stanton, Feigelman, Black, & Romer, 1994). Holding positive views of persons affiliated with drug trafficking may exert an equally profound effect on young people's intentions to immerse themselves in the drug trade (Li & Feigelman, 1994). Another study finds that simply observing family and friends dealing drugs and being in an environment where drug trafficking is commonplace can significantly enhance a young person's future odds of dealing crack cocaine (Bush & Iannotti, 1994). The instructional role of older adolescents and adults in tutoring novice drug dealers has also been documented (Haberfeld, 1993). In fact, direct tutelage may be as crucial as associations and the cultivation of definitions favorable to violations of the law in promoting drug trafficking among teenagers (McCarthy, 1996). Alarid, Burton, and Cullen (2000) comment that associating with criminal friends and professing definitions favorable to violations of the law were predictive of drug offending in groups of young male and female felons.

Jacobs (1998) identified patterns of neutralization in the retrospective accounts of thirty-two former street-level heroin dealers intended to deflect responsibility for complaints of lower-quality drugs from their drug-using customers. Appeals to defensibility epitomize denial of responsibility in which dealers utilize excuses to absolve themselves of responsibility for lower quality heroin by blaming someone higher up in the distribution chain for tampering with the product and diluting its potency. These dealers also used counterdenunciations, a form of condemning the condemner, in which they hold the consumer responsible for the consequences of poor-quality heroin by diverting attention away from themselves and onto the user's honesty, manner of preparing the drug, or escalating tolerance to opiates. Curcione (1997) distinguished evidence of neutralization in the verbalizations of middle-class cocaine dealers indicating both denial of injury and condemnation of the condemners. Evaluations of Matza's (1964) drift hypothesis have proved more equivocal. Whereas it is likely that some drug traffickers drift in and out of the life-style (Adler, 1993; Curcione, 1997; Jacobs, 1998), desistance from drug dealing is oftentimes decisive, and the outcome definitive. Waldorf, Murphy, and Lauderback (1994) recount that 75% of their desisting cocaine dealers desisted the first time that they decided to do so.

Social control theory, the labeling perspective, and Thornberry's (1987) interactive approach have not been sufficiently studied to offer a conclusion on their applicability to drug offenses at this time. Rosenbaum (1987) ascertained that social control theory did an adequate job of accounting for drug offenses in a group of juveniles, although she collapsed drug dealing and drug use into a single category. Social control theory is partially corroborated by a study in which parental attachment and other indices of social control accounted for drug offending in female, but not male, young adult offenders (Alarid et al., 2000). Labeling theory finds sustenance in Haberfeld's (1993) notation that compared to youth incarcerated for nondrug offenses, youth imprisoned for drug trafficking were significantly more likely to perceive themselves as victimized by a criminal label and to perceive fewer legitimate options for themselves. Finally, Thornberry's interactive theory has been used to explain drug use behavior (Krohn, Lizotte, Thornberry, Smith, & McDowell, 1996; Paternoster, 1988) but has not yet been studied with respect to drug dealing. Thus, while these three criminological models show promise of advancing our understanding of drug trafficking, more research is required before their individual contribution can be gauged and assessed.

AN INTEGRATED-INTERACTIVE THEORY OF DRUG TRAFFICKING

Drug trafficking, according to the model presented in this book, is comprised of three primary elements: status, differential opportunity, and cognitive distortion. Each element is believed to interact reciprocally with its partners and with a number of other variables. Before the complex interactions that link these various components together are described, each major element is discussed.

Status

VanNostrand and Tewksbury (1999) identified three motives for drug trafficking in a group of twenty individuals arrested for dealing crack cocaine. The first motive, in line with social strain theory (Whitehead et al., 1994), concerned the perception that opportunities for gainful employment were closed off to them. Reasoning that they needed to support themselves and their families, these individuals turned to drug trafficking to make ends meet. A second motive mentioned by a number of the individuals interviewed by VanNostrand and Tewksbury was greed. Several of these individuals held legitimate jobs and were financially stable, though they wanted to supplement their incomes with illegal money so that they could purchase luxury items like opulent cars and designer clothes. Wanting a lavish lifestyle was cited by 60% of a group of Indian citizens as responsible for their involvement in drug sales (Sen & Pande, 1993). A third motive for drug trafficking, according to data gathered by VanNostrand and Tewksbury, is a sense of being addicted to the fast-paced lifestyle of selling drugs. Popularity, power, and status were benefits that the lifestyle promised and that many of the dealers had trouble giving up. Similar convictions are expressed by other individuals who report extensive involvement in the drug trade (Adler, 1993; Inciardi, Horowitz, & Pottieger, 1993; Weisheit, 1991). VanNostrand and Tewksbury note that in many cases motives changed over the course of a person's drug-trafficking career so that some individuals begin dealing drugs out of financial necessity but then continue selling out of greed or because of their preoccupation with the lifestyle.

Differential Opportunity

Differential opportunity to engage in drug trafficking means that certain factors serve to either increase or decrease a person's chances of becoming involved in drug trafficking by virtue of their ability to influence the person's access to specific learning contingencies and lifestyle materials. Children approached about selling drugs had been rated by their peers one year earlier as more impulsive, pugnacious, unfriendly, restless, and untrustworthy than children not approached to sell drugs (Bush & Weinfurt, 1994). Comparing fourteen juveniles charged with selling crack cocaine and nineteen juveniles charged with nondrug offenses, Schreiber (1992) detected greater problem solving, abstract reasoning, and affective identification deficits in the drug-dealing group relative to the non-drug-offending adolescents.

Situational factors are also pivotal in elevating risk for future involvement in drug trafficking. Several of the more salient situational influences on drug sales are drug-dealing friends and family members, residence in a neighborhood where drugs are plentiful (Bush & Iannotti, 1994), and familiarity with, and access to, situations where drugs are commonly sold, whether the situation is a crack house, bar, or street corner (Power, Green, Foster, & Stimson, 1995). Contacts and connections made in the course of conventional occupational and avocational pursuits can also furnish opportunities for drug dealing, as Curcione (1997) ascertained in a group of middle-class cocaine dealers.

Just as there are influences that enhance a person's opportunities for participation in drug trafficking, there are factors that limit trafficking opportunities as well. Parental monitoring can play a particularly potent role in reducing opportunities for drug trafficking. Li, Stanton, and Feigelman (2000) followed a group of 383 urban, African American 9- to 15-year-olds for four years at six-month intervals and discovered that the perception of being monitored by one's parents was stronger in females and younger subjects than it was in males and older subjects and that these perceptions were fairly stable over time. More importantly, cross-sectional and longitudinal analyses revealed that such monitoring had an inhibitory effect on drug use and trafficking. Although indirect parental control by way of attachment appeared to have little effect on the delinquent activities of a group of African American youth (Cernkovich, Giordano, & Rudolph, 2000), ties to conventional social organizations like school may have a stronger inhibitory effect on delinquency in general and drug use and trafficking in particular (Joseph, 1995). Drug use, as described later in this chapter, is commonly observed in those who deal drugs. In some cases the negative repercussions of drug use can provide an opportunity to desist from both drug use and drug trafficking, as reported in interviews held with a group of eighty former cocaine dealers and sellers (Waldorf et al., 1994).

Cognitive Distortion

In order to remain in a drug-selling lifestyle for any length of time one must distort one's thinking as a means of excusing and justifying one's actions. Such cognitive distortion is reflected in the use of common techniques of neutralization. Curcione (1997) discerned denial of responsibility ("they came to me; I didn't come to them"), denial of injury (pointing out that the majority of clients had used for years without ill effects), and condemnation of the condemners (highlighting fraudulent practices common to their pre-dealing conventional occupational world) in a group of middle-class cocaine dealers (250). Jacobs (1998) uncovered similar results in a group of inner-city heroin sellers. These individuals employed both denial of responsibility and condemnation of the condemners to divert attention away from themselves when customers complained about the quality of the heroin that they had purchased. Wishful thinking may also distort cognitive processes in ways congruent with drug trafficking (Schreiber, 1992). Cognitive distortion, therefore, serves a vital function in maintaining belief systems known to promote drug selling.

Overview

Figure 7.1 outlines the complex reciprocal relationships purported to exist between status, differential opportunity, and cognitive distortion in the evolution of a drug-trafficking lifestyle. Financial need, greed, lifestyle preoccupation, and strain are believed to supply the incentive for drug peddling, which is construed to be a desire for increased status. Status then interacts with differential opportunity to initiate the drug trafficking pattern. Outcome expectancies, which research indicates play a momentous role in young people's intentions to partake in drug-trafficking activities (Li, Stanton, Black, & Feigelman, 1996), are believed to affect a person's future propensity to engage in drug selling through their effect on the differential association and status-seeking processes. Differential association is believed to interact with expectancies, differential opportunities, and self-image. The priority of self-image in drug trafficking is validated by research proclaiming drug dealing as a way of enhancing one's self-view (Weisman, 1993) and constructing a masculine street identity (Collison, 1996). Self-image, in conjunction with cognitive distortion, serves to maintain the drug-trafficking pattern.

Figure 7.1
An Integrated-Interactive Model of Drug Trafficking

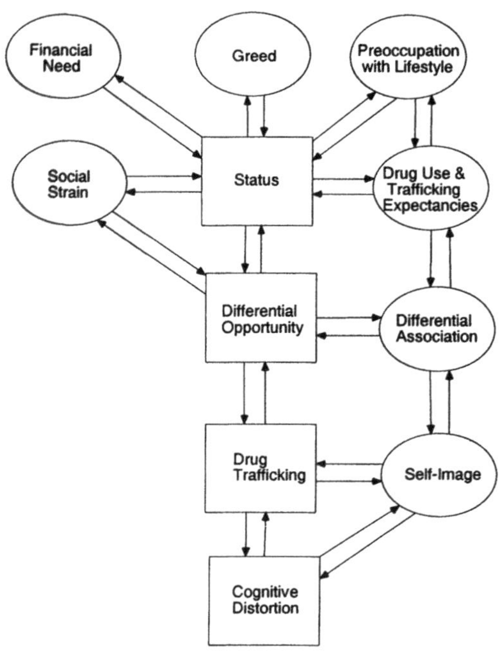

IS THERE A DIFFERENCE BETWEEN DRUG TRAFFICKING AND OTHER CRIMES?

High school students who deal drugs are more impulsive (Uribe & Ostrov, 1989) and more likely to follow a pattern of general delinquency (Smart, Adlaf, & Walsh, 1992) than high school students who do not deal drugs. Studying a group of 125 adult probationers, De Li, Priú, and MacKenzie (2000) determined that drug selling had a facilitative effect on property and violent crime, while drug use facilitated only property crime. Given the uncertain and potentially violent nature of drug trafficking, people involved in the drug trade are more apt to carry a gun than those who engage in other forms of criminality (Li & Feigelman, 1994). It therefore stands to reason that possession of a weapon increases opportunities for other types of offending. The overlap between drug and nondrug crime is not restricted to male offenders. Sommers and Baskin (1997) report that 38% of a group of 156 female drug dealers from two New York City neighborhoods admitted having committed a robbery in the past. Additionally, 33%, 17%, and 44% of the women participating in this study reported prior participation in assault, burglary, and prostitution, respectively.

Although drug trafficking overlaps extensively with other crimes, the crime category with which it seems most closely allied is violent crime (Fagan & Chin, 1990; Inciardi, 1990). Paul Goldstein (1985) examined three possible interpretations of the drug–violence connection. First, there is the psychopharmacological view that holds that ingesting certain types of chemicals fosters aggression in users predisposed to violence. Second, we have the economic view in which the high cost of street drugs causes some individuals to resort to economically oriented violent crimes (e.g., robbery) to support their habit. The third perspective entertained by Goldstein is the systemic view in which violence is regarded as intrinsic to the distribution and sale of illicit substances in the sense that aggression is used to settle disputes, gain territory, and punish transgressions. In a review of clinical and impressionistic studies Goldstein concludes that the systemic view does the best job of explaining the bulk of violence found in the drug trade. Research conducted on both male (Johnson, Williams, Dei, & Sanabria, 1990) and female (Sommers & Baskin, 1997) drug dealers verifies that the violence associated with the drug trade represents two distinct processes: (1) self- and social selection of violent people into the drug trade and (2) the encouragement of violence by the environments in which drug dealing takes place.

IS THERE A DIFFERENCE BETWEEN DRUG TRAFFICKING AND DRUG USE?

It is often assumed that those who sell drugs generally do not use drugs, and while there is some evidence to support this view, there are also data showing that many such individuals do, in fact, abuse drugs. Seventy percent of the drug-dealing adults interviewed by Reuter, MacCoun, and Murphy (1990) and 70% of the crack-dealing adolescents surveyed by Dembo, Hughes, Jackson, and Mieczkowski (1993) denied personal use of crack cocaine. Whereas a majority of the youthful crack dealers whose records were reviewed by Duncan, Kennedy, and Smith (2000) also denied the use of cocaine, most acknowledged habitual use of alcohol and marijuana. Perhaps drug dealers ingest substances other than the ones that they sell. In a large majority of cases, however, this also turns out to be untrue. All twenty crack cocaine dealers who spoke with VanNostrand and Tewksbury (1999) acknowledged a history of marijuana and cocaine abuse, although nineteen maintained that they were recreational users. Only one of the eighty distributors of cocaine participating in the Waldorf et al. (1994) investigation indicated that he did not use the product that he sold, and 60% of the sample stated that they believed they were addicted to an illicit substance. Seventy percent of a group of female dealers in crack cocaine and heroin acknowledged that they were regular users of crack (Sommers & Baskin, 1997). Drug use, it should be noted, is not confined to the lower echelons of drug distribution organizations. Both Adler (1993) and Curcione (1997) witnessed significant marijuana and cocaine usage in persons who engaged in marijuana and cocaine trafficking at the wholesale and international levels.

Conflicting results have been obtained in research examining the causal order of the drug use-drug trafficking relationship. Some studies suggest that drug use precedes drug dealing (Fagan & Chin, 1990; Inciardi, 1990), while other studies indicate that drug dealing precedes drug use (Bush & Iannotti, 1994; Whitehead et al., 1994). A longitudinal panel investigation of 383 urban African American youth followed up at six-month intervals for twenty-four months disclosed that of thirty-five youth initially involved in drug trafficking, twenty-two (67%) used illegal substances during a later wave, in contrast to nineteen to fifty-three (42%) drug-involved youth who continued ingesting illicit substances in subsequent waves (Li, Feigelman, Stanton, Galbraith, & Huang, 1998). A path analysis revealed that early drug trafficking predicted later drug trafficking and illicit drug use but that early illicit drug use failed to predict either subsequent illicit drug use or drug trafficking. Similar findings are reported by Sommers, Baskin, and Fagan (1996). Drug dealing may not only initiate drug use, but also interfere with the natural maturing out of drug misuse process observed in drug users as they age (Anglin, Brecht, Woodward, & Bonett, 1986). The reciprocal relationship that in all likelihood forms between drug dealing and drug use is reflected in the outcome of a large-scale study by Gossop, Marsden, and Stewart (2000) in which drug dealing was reduced to one-fifth its level at intake one year after enrollment in a residential or community program for substance misuse. In this study decreased drug trafficking correlated robustly with lower levels of heroin use.

LIFESTYLES CONGRUENT WITH DRUG TRAFFICKING

The criminal lifestyle is one of the patterns that underpins drug trafficking. Gangs that traffic in illicit substances often operate out of a criminal lifestyle.

Nearly two-thirds of the members of a Mexican-American gang heavily involved in drug trafficking reported that they wanted people to fear them (Becker, Felkenes, Magaña, & Huntley, 1997). Presumably, the power and control that a criminal lifestyle affords people, as well as the vast sums of money that can be accrued, were central to this group's decision to commit itself to the drug trade. Violence and disrespect for the law are additional elements of drug offending. For many of those who habitually engage in drug trafficking, violence is a way of life and an acceptable means of dealing with problems, disputes, and discipline (Fagan & Chin, 1990; Inciardi, 1990). Dembo et al. (1993) further remark that juvenile crack dealers did not consider arrest or long-term imprisonment as deterrents to continued involvement in the drug trade. Instead, they were more concerned with the immediate danger of violence or death that those who deal drugs on the streets face daily.

As described in the previous section, the drug lifestyle is a second lifestyle with relevance to drug trafficking. Contrary to popular belief, most drug dealers are also drug users, and many, in fact, misuse the same drugs that they sell. This occurs at all levels of the drug hierarchy, from wholesaler distributors to street dealers. Drug trafficking makes drugs available to the seller, which, in turn, increases opportunities for personal usage. There is controversy over the direction of the drug use–drug trafficking relationship, albeit the most likely scenario is that drug use and drug trafficking are reciprocally connected. Nevertheless, drug trafficking has been shown to have a stronger facilitative effect on future drug use than drug use has on future drug trafficking (Li et al., 1998; Sommers et al., 1996). Hence, a juvenile who enters the drug trade at age 10 or 11 has a greater chance of becoming a heavy drug user by age 13 or 14 than a juvenile who starts using drugs at age 10 or 11 has of becoming a drug dealer at age 13 or 14. The creation of a drug-use lifestyle through participation in drug-trafficking activities highlights the complex interrelationships that exist between variables in the formation of belief systems congruent with drug trafficking.

Even at the street or local level, drug trafficking operations are hierarchically ordered. Drug crews that are less well organized tend to be less successful and more vulnerable to arrest, competition, and predation than better-organized crews (Denton & O'Malley, 1999). In this way, drug organizations are like businesses. Responsibility, risk, and profit are not equally distributed but depend on a person's position in the hierarchy. We might go so far as to say that each level has its own job description and methods of entry and advancement (Adler, 1993; Curcione, 1997; Weisheit, 1991). It is overstating the case to conceptualize drug trafficking as an octopus with many arms, though a certain minimal degree of organization is required for success in the drug trade. As such, a business lifestyle is also frequently observed in those who habitually engage in drug dealing. The acquisition, preparation, packaging, and distribution of an illicit substance are not substantially different from how legitimate products are acquired, prepared, packaged, and distributed. This may be one reason why drugs have become such a hot political issue in many Western nations.

CASE ILLUSTRATION—ABOUT FACE

Background

Alfredo is a married Hispanic male serving a ninety-six-month sentence for drug distribution. The youngest of five children raised in an intact middle-class home environment in New York City, Alfredo had all of his basic needs taken care of as he was growing up. He attended a private high school and excelled in sports, earning a football scholarship to a Division 1A college in Pennsylvania. Alfredo had always been a good student, but by the time he got to college, his attitude had changed. Other students looked to him as a gangster when they learned that he had grown up in the Bronx. Playing the role of tough guy, he would bully weaker students and try to intimidate his teammates. He spent so much time partying that he had little time left for studying. After two and one-half years he left school when he was placed on academic probation because of poor grades. Moving back to New York City, he went to work at a grocery store. It was not long before he was approached by some friends from high school who asked if he would be interested in delivering a small quantity of drugs to sources in upstate New York.

Drug dealing went from an occasional trip to upstate New York for extra money to his primary means of support in a matter of months. Finding that he was able to intimidate others with his imposing 6'2", 250-pound frame, Alfredo became the perfect enforcer. He had known the organization's boss since high school and now served as his right-hand man. In no time Alfredo was neck-deep in the lifestyle. Due to good planning and good fortune the organization was an overnight success, selling cocaine wholesale to dealers at the rate of 100 kilograms a week. When he was not picking up kilos of cocaine from the airport, packaging the product, or counting money he could be found in bars and nightclubs. Although Alfredo did not use cocaine himself, he drank excessively. Staying out all night drinking at clubs soon began to take its toll. Alfredo's weight ballooned to over 400 pounds, and he was having problems with his stomach. He was married and had a young child but spent most of his time away from home. Living the lifestyle meant being out all night, drinking, and chasing women; it didn't mean being faithful, responsible, and respectful. It was not long before his wife sued for divorce.

About two years after he started dealing drugs, Alfredo wanted out. He began working at a car dealership, where he made reasonably good money. However, he could not avoid the lure of the streets, and it was not long before he was back in the lifestyle. After eight months away from the lifestyle he went back with a vengeance. He bought a grocery store into which he poured the majority of profits from his drug-dealing lifestyle, that is, whatever was left over after he paid for food, rent, partying, and a long list of luxury items that he was beginning to accumulate. Alfredo drove several different cars, all very expensive, and was acquiring a reputation as a big spender. He admits that he would think nothing of leaving a $60 tip for a barmaid, an amount greater than what he now earns in a month from his prison job. Once his divorce became final, he grew even more egocentric and self-destructive. Alfredo's weight was now nearly 500 pounds, and he was drinking every night. He knew that if things didn't change, he would soon be dead.

Alfredo decided to move out of New York City in hopes of saving his sanity and his life. Settling in a small town in Pennsylvania where drug trafficking was backward by New York standards, he recalls telling himself that he would own the town in a matter of weeks. He was not far off with respect to the town's drug trade. Importing cocaine and marijuana from his connections in New York, Alfredo set out to prove that he could run his own drug organization. With a large number of individual runners and drug dealers working for him, Alfredo soon became a fixture in the community. His reputation preceded him, and his size earned him the nickname "Big Al," an epithet of which he was proud. Treated with the utmost respect by nearly everyone in town, Alfredo would perform various good deeds, like sponsoring a youth basketball team, to endear himself to the townsfolk. He relates that he felt not unlike a movie star. Married for the second time, Alfredo thought that he had finally found his niche in life. In spite of this, he was trapped in a lifestyle of unbridled hedonism and despair. The partying and running around until three or four o'clock in the morning were wearing on his wife and their relationship. He would reserve Sunday to be with his wife, though he was so tired from running around all week that he would sleep through much of the day. After three years he returned to New York and his old drug crew.

In the three years that Alfredo had been away in Pennsylvania his old boss, Teddy, had retired to the Dominican Republic. Teddy's younger brother was put in charge of the New York operation but lacked Teddy's business savvy. Accordingly, the organization began to lose money for the first time since its inception. Alfredo, who had always been good with money, helped out by assuming responsibility for counting and allocating the money that the organization collected from its clients. Meanwhile, Teddy returned to New York in an attempt to salvage the drug empire that he had created and nurtured for seven years. Alfredo and the other crew members had always eschewed violence, relying more on finesse and intimidation to accomplish their goals. However, when Teddy's younger brother was kidnaped by a competing drug organization and held for ransom, the crew demonstrated a willingness and ability to use aggressive tactics to protect their assets and territory. Violence was the exception rather than the rule, and the members of the organization expressed great pride in their ability to make money without having to resort to "breaking heads." As the organization closed in on its tenth year of operation, there seemed to be nothing standing in the way of its becoming the top drug crew in the entire five boroughs.

When Alfredo first saw the car parked outside the warehouse where they stashed their drugs and counted money, he was unconcerned. There were no drugs in the house at the time, and he figured that the money they were counting was insufficient evidence for construction of a prosecutable case. As luck would have it, the house was under surveillance. Indeed, the target of the investigation was not Alfredo's organization but a drug crew that had sold heroin out of the same house several months earlier. Alfredo and his cohorts were unaware that another crew had been selling drugs from this same location when they rented the warehouse. Even though Alfredo's crew was not the target of the original investigation, a new investigation was initiated. One by one, crew members were stopped by the police as they left the premises. In several instances members were found to be in possession of kilogram-size packages of cocaine. Like a house of cards, the organization folded, and people who had allegedly been friends and associates for years began testifying against one another. Alfredo was fortunate. He was allowed to plead guilty in exchange for a 96-month prison sentence.

Since going to prison, Alfredo has lost over 200 pounds and has regained his zest for living. Attributing his change in attitude to a newfound interest in religion, the belief that he has a chance to start over, a desire to make his parents proud of him, and a sincere hope to make a better life for his wife, his son, and himself, Alfredo has turned over a new leaf to where money and power no longer direct his life. Alfredo's long-range goal is to own a restaurant, and his middle-range goal is to complete training programs in culinary arts and hotel and restaurant management while in prison. Nevertheless, Alfredo is realistic enough to understand to know that he will need to work for others before he runs his own business and that his first several years out of prison may be difficult. He is on good terms with his family and wife and is down to 250 pounds, half the weight that he carried when he was trafficking drugs. In many ways Alfredo has done an "about-face."

Lifestyle Assessment

Alfredo's total score on the LCSF (8) falls slightly below the standard cutoff of 10 used to demarcate significant involvement, commitment, and identification with a criminal lifestyle (see Table 7.1). This does not mean, however, that he is unfamiliar with the lifestyle. Despite getting a late start, Alfredo was a quick study who learned the ins and outs of the drug trade in relatively short order. Scores of 7 to 9 on the LCSF signal moderate risk for lifestyle involvement, as opposed to scores of 10 or higher which place the individual at high risk for lifestyle involvement (Walters, 1998c). Alfredo, it would seem, not only functioned in a criminal lifestyle, but also was heavily invested in the business and drug (alcohol) lifestyles in conducting his drug transactions. The link between the drug and criminal lifestyles may be particularly prominent in Alfredo's case. Self-indulgence, as represented by an orgy of food, alcohol, and women, accounts for half of Alfredo's score on the LCSF. Research suggests that self-indulgence is one of the factors that link the drug and criminal lifestyles (Walters, 1994). It was also a tightrope that Alfredo walked daily. Whether he burned out on the drug or the criminal lifestyle first is of little consequence, for in situations like Alfredo's, these lifestyles are so intertwined as to be virtually identical. The critical point is that Alfredo burned out on at least one of these lifestyles and that this assisted him with abandonment of the other lifestyle.

Table 7.1
Alfredo's Scores on the Lifestyle Criminality Screening Form (LCSF)

Irresponsibility	2
Self-Indulgence	4
Interpersonal Intrusiveness	1
Social Rule Breaking	1
TOTAL LCSF SCORE	8

Alfredo's PICTS profile (see Figure 7.2) displays peaks on the superoptimism (T-score = 64) and entitlement (T-score = 59) scales. Elevations on the superoptimism scale articulate Alfredo's belief that he can avoid the negative consequences of his actions. Administered shortly after his arrival in federal prison, Alfredo's scores on the PICTS denote that imprisonment and the desire to avoid future incarceration are often insufficient to stimulate change in people who have lived a criminal lifestyle for a period of ten years. Entitlement approached the T-score cutoff of 60 and reveals that Alfredo believes that he is a unique person who deserves special consideration. These scores have gradually declined in subsequent administrations of the PICTS with little or no appreciable change in the validity scales. Challenging Alfredo's superoptimism with the reality that he has been caught and imprisoned and will likely be caught again if he chooses to violate the law once he is released back to the community has been incorporated into a program of assisted change for Alfredo. His sense of entitlement has been challenged in daily interactions with other inmates whereby he has learned to respond to disputes and dares from other inmates in ways that he never would have imagined four years ago. In effect, Alfredo has become a new person, losing nearly 250 pounds and changing the way that he looks at himself and the world. As he himself has said more than once, he must learn to think of others before he thinks of himself.

Belief System Analysis

Self-View

The audience to which Alfredo played when he was trafficking drugs was his drug crew and the people with whom he came into contact who admired him for his prowess as a drug dealer. Alfredo's crews in New York and Pennsylvania were, in some respects, mutual admiration societies in which members reinforced and normalized each other's belief systems. Crew members saw themselves as smarter and slicker than other crews and felt as if there was no way that the police would ever catch them. There was also competition between crew members as each individual tried to put his own stamp on the organization. Alfredo was understandably concerned about how the other members of the crew viewed him, and these reflected appraisals became a central part of his self-view. He also saw

Figure 7.2
Alfredo's Scores on the Psychological Inventory of Criminal Thinking Styles (PICTS)

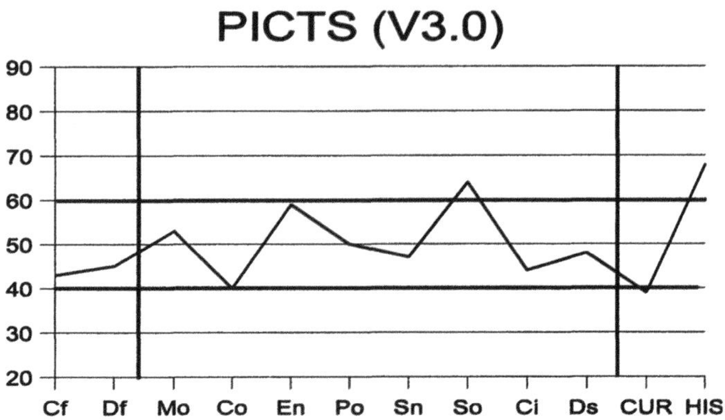

Note. Cf = confusion scale; Df = defensiveness scale; Mo = mollification scale; Co = cutoff scale; En = entitlement scale; Po = power orientation scale; Sn = sentimentality scale; So = superoptimism scale; Ci = cognitive indolence scale; Ds = discontinuity scale; CUR = current content scale; HIS = historical content scale.

himself as a "ghetto superstar" through the eyes of an admiring public whenever the crew would go to restaurants or nightclubs and spend huge sums of money. As "Big Al," he was not only feared, but also loved and respected, at least in his own mind, by people he hardly knew. The reflected appraisals upon which Alfredo based his self-view were biased toward perceptions of success and his efforts to project a good guy persona (sentimentality).

Alfredo regularly made upward social comparisons with the boss of the New York drug ring, Teddy. Friends since childhood and a year behind him in school, Alfredo had always looked up to Teddy and considered him a role model. Teddy was captain of the football team during Alfredo's junior year in high school. The next year Alfredo was captain. Teddy established the drug organization in New York. Alfredo tried to emulate him by moving to Pennsylvania and setting up a crew of his own. Whereas the Pennsylvania operation was financially viable, it never attained the success, notoriety, or mythical status of Teddy's New York operation. Eventually, Alfredo returned to New York and began working for Teddy once again. In making these upward social comparisons, Alfredo felt as if he could never get out from under his friend's shadow. Notwithstanding the arrogance of his move to Pennsylvania, Alfredo's loyalty was beyond reproach and his size and quick mind were assets that Teddy could not ignore. Consequently, Alfredo was welcomed back to the New York organization where he worked for another eighteen months until his arrest.

"Big Al" is the self-representation that best symbolizes how Alfredo thought of himself when he was most heavily involved in drug-trafficking activities. The crew as a whole saw themselves as the "biggest and best drug organization in New York." As such, they believed that they were entitled to take whatever they wanted. Money, says Alfredo, "gives you a feelings of invulnerability, as if you are wearing a bullet-proof vest." Explaining how his self-representations influenced how he treated others, he adds, "You manipulate because you can manipulate." Manipulation was done to achieve happiness, but as Alfredo soon discovered, manipulation only serves to make you more dependent on the lifestyle that it is designed to bolster. The attributions that contributed to Alfredo's self-representations during this period were, for the most part, internal, global, and stable. Negative outcomes, by comparison, were ascribed to external, global, and stable factors over which Alfredo had no control. Hence, he attributed success to the fact that he was a smart and resourceful businessman, and failure was blamed on nefarious outside influences or others' incompetence.

It has been argued that drug dealing is of cardinal significance in constructing a masculine street identity (Collison, 1996). Alfredo was a football star who earned a full scholarship to a Division 1A university to play football. However, because of his own irresponsibility and lack of maturity, he was unable to maintain his grades in class and interest in football. His hopes of completing college and playing in the National Football League were both dashed. In the process, his sense of masculinity and personal empowerment took a beating. Drug trafficking was not something that Alfredo set out to do when he left school, but once the opportunity presented itself, he took full advantage of it. A pattern as complex as drug trafficking can never be boiled down to a single cause. In any event, the opportunity to overcome his sense of failure and become a masculine hero once again, a "ghetto superstar," as he puts it, was instrumental in motivating him to continue with, and expand, his involvement in the fledgling drug organization that his friend Teddy had put together. His virility restored, Alfredo set out to prove to others that his macho image was something more than a mirage. Unfortunately, he never really believed in himself, and his lack of self-confidence helped keep him locked in the lifestyle upon which he depended to gain strength, pose, and purpose.

A feared self lay behind Alfredo's masculine protest. Afraid of being seen as weak, he did everything in his power to emit an air of invulnerability. He used his body, which grew to nearly 500 pounds, as a weapon to intimidate others so that he was not faced with the prospect of being put down and viewed by others as soft. Over time he created a wall to protect his fragile ego. This wall was constructed of many positively valenced global self-attributions that could turn into negatively valenced global self-attributions at a moment's notice because of their simplicity and lack of integration. Another feared self that assumed a central position in Alfredo's self-view was his fear of insignificance. There was nothing worse to him than being classified in the same category as everyone else, "an average Joe," in Alfredo's words. He had developed a positive possible self as a football hero to compensate for his fear of being average. When that dream disintegrated after he was asked to leave school due to poor grades, he needed to find another way to compensate for his fear of being irrelevant. The possible self as a millionaire drug dealer that others loved, feared, and respected soon replaced the old football possible self and seemed adequate compensation for the fear of being a nobody. As those who take the lifestyle route to self-improvement soon discover, lifestyle-based possible selves rarely deliver on their promises in the long run. In fact, they tend to do the exact opposite. Now Alfredo is just like the other 1,200 inmates who live in the federal prison where he is currently housed, and he is no different, in the eyes of society, from the 1.3 million state and federal prisoners currently incarcerated in the United States (BJS, 2000b).

World-View

Alfredo shows a clear predilection for the mechanical pole of the organismic-mechanistic dimension of the world-view. The drug organization in New York and the one that Alfredo operated in Pennsylvania are characterized by him as "well-oiled machines." There was a clear chain of command, and everyone had to efficiently perform his or her function for the overall mechanism to work properly. Owing to the fact that Alfredo and his crew were selling to other dealers rather than directly to users, they were able to manipulate the cocaine market in New York to some extent by selling to one dealer and not another or providing a more lucrative deal to a preferred seller. Alfredo remarks that when the leader of one of the crews with which Alfredo's organization dealt regularly was killed by a rival gang, the dead leader's crew stopped functioning and eventually disbanded as if it had been stripped of its gears. Mechanistic metaphors are not restricted to Alfredo's criminal activities, but also define his interactions with strangers, friends, and intimates. He was continually scheming in an effort to get over on others and justified his actions by convincing himself that "everything is a mind game."

In speaking with Alfredo, it is clear that he believes that he was destined to become a gangster. Alfredo acknowledges that he always enjoyed being in the limelight. When he was no longer receiving recognition for football, he was drawn to drug trafficking as a way of achieving admiration and hero status. Adopting a fatalistic world-view, Alfredo was able to relieve any guilt or misgivings that he had about involving himself in crime because "things are as they are supposed to be." Since his arrival in federal prison four years ago Alfredo has learned that he made a choice to enter into drug-trafficking activities and that he has the capacity to make different choices in the future. By achieving greater balance between fatalism and agenticism, Alfredo has put himself in a position to take firmer control of his life and do something more than passively accept whatever happens to him as fate.

Alfredo is a firm believer in a just world and lives according to the motto "You reap what you sow." Because they never killed anyone and were generally fair with customers, Alfredo and his crew believed that nothing bad would ever happen to them. Bad things happen only to those who deliberately hurt others, they reasoned. The crew had no illusions about society's reaction to their activities; they fully understood that conventional society looked down on their drug dealing. However, they rationalized that they were providing a service that was needed and desired and did not cause harm to a majority of customers. Those few users who experienced adverse reactions were perceived as somehow responsible for their own misery due to some unstated past wrong or simply because they were weak-minded. A strong belief in a just world made Alfredo less compassionate toward those who suffer sundry life hardships.

Despite his middle-class upbringing, the presence of two loving parents, and opportunities unavailable to most minorities, Alfredo adopted a malevolent world-view. He figured that since the world is a cruel and uncaring place, the only person you could count on is yourself. Loyalty aside, Alfredo didn't fully trust Teddy, and, as it turns out, he had good reason not to trust his old friend. Teddy allegedly approached Alfredo while the latter was in county jail waiting to be prosecuted for the instant offense and informed him that he would be happy to take care of his wife's sexual needs while Alfredo was away in prison. He apparently also approached Alfredo's wife with the same proposition. This reinforced the part of Alfredo's world-view that perceived people as selfish, uncaring, and untrustworthy. Today he still views the world as largely malevolent, but now he approaches the malevolence with "love in my heart." The "love in my heart" metaphor has helped Alfredo alter his world-view, opening him up to new information and making him more amenable to accepting assistance from others, neither of which he would never have done while he was trafficking drugs.

The prototypes that form Alfredo's world-view are overly simplistic and generally unresponsive to correction. One perspective that was of paramount significance in the construction of Alfredo's prototypes was the strength–weakness dichotomy, which is often the foundation of the power orientation thinking style. Alfredo appears to rely extensively on this dichotomy in sizing up people. In the past if he perceived someone as weak, he would seek to capitalize on, and take advantage of, these weaknesses for his own personal benefit. One should realize that inasmuch as this process may be automatic, it is by no means innate. Alfredo has spent a lifetime formulating his belief systems. His involvement in crime did not cause him to build simplistic prototypes, but merely aided, reinforced, and honed a tendency, which probably dates back to childhood, to evaluate the environment with dichotomous black-and-white categories that are rigidly constructed and poorly integrated with one another.

Present-View

Perceptual distortion is evident on the PICTS in the form of elevated scores on the superoptimism and entitlement scales. Superoptimism had a major bearing on Alfredo's present-view during the period in which he was involved in drug trafficking. He states that success in the drug trade reinforced the belief that you can do whatever you want without suffering negative repercussions. The resulting sense of invulnerability inspired more impulsive decision making which eventually led to his downfall. This illustrates the interactive nature of perceptual distortion in which immediate success and momentary avoidance of negative consequences precipitate cognitive distortion (superoptimism), followed by more arrogance and impetuous decision making, and while arrogance and impetuous decision making may foster success in the short-term, it courts disaster in the long-run. "You start to believe in your own superiority," says Alfredo. Perceptual distortions of this sort are a reflection of both superoptimism and entitlement. Down the line, success in drug trafficking encouraged Alfredo to conclude that he was entitled to do whatever he desired and treat people in whatever fashion he saw fit. In a very real sense, perceptual distortion played a key role in Alfredo's current legal troubles.

People involved in a pattern of drug trafficking often display weak problem solving and other executive function skills (Schreiber, 1992). From what can be gathered about Alfredo's background, he did not grow up with poor executive function skills. After ten years of dealing drugs, however, his judgment and problem-solving skills showed signs of atrophy. It was not that he did not see the mysterious car with tinted windows parked in front of the warehouse where he counted the proceeds of the crew's drug transactions; he just figured that since there were no drugs in the house at the time, there was nothing to worry about even if the house was under surveillance. In the early years the crew would have abandoned the building and set up shop elsewhere at the first sign of trouble. Continued success tends to breed superoptimism, and Alfredo and his cohorts truly believed that there was nothing that the police could do to them. They would soon learn otherwise, after Alfredo and several other members of the crew were arrested while leaving the premises and charged with trafficking in cocaine.

Past-View

As has already been mentioned, Alfredo grew up in a loving, middle-class home environment. He knew that his parents would never approve of his drug-dealing lifestyle. In an effort to keep them from unearthing his secret, he stayed away from them as much as possible. They suspected that something was wrong but never imagined that he was trafficking in controlled substances. They did not learn of his secret life until they accompanied him to court. Alfredo was smart enough to know that, unlike many individuals in the criminal justice system, he could not blame his criminal activity on his upbringing. He accordingly tried to block out many recollections from his past, as if doing so would magically expunge the harm that he was doing to himself and his family. Thus, his past-view was probably his least well developed belief system during the period in which he sold drugs. Since that time he has looked back on his life and believes that he has learned from past mistakes. His most important life lesson, contends Alfredo, is realizing that life is full of choices and that he can learn to make better choices in the future.

Future-View

Whereas Alfredo tried to block out his past, he was too busy making money in the present to be concerned about the future. With the exception of outcome expectancies that promised power, wealth, and status from continued participation in drug trafficking, Alfredo's future-view was, for the most part, barren. Furthermore, his time horizon was abbreviated in the sense that he was concerned only with selling the drugs that he had on him and counting and distributing the day's profits. When his wife begged him to stop trafficking for fear that he would be arrested and imprisoned, he told her not to worry because "when I go to jail, I'll be the one doing the time, not you." He now regrets making this statement in that he has come to realize that the entire family is affected when a member is sent to prison. Since his arrival in federal prison, Alfredo's future-view has expanded with anticipations of taking culinary arts and hotel and restaurant management courses and fulfilling his long-term goal of owning a restaurant. Unlike his mind-set during his drug-dealing days, Alfredo now understands that he must exercise patience to achieve his long-range goal of owning a restaurant and that in the meantime he will need to work hard and swallow his pride to remain free on the streets with his family, who has remained supportive of him.

CONCLUSION

As the demographic section of this chapter indicates, young people, minorities, and women have become increasingly more involved in drug trafficking over the last several years relative to older white males. The question is, what do these three demographic groups have in common? One possible connection between these three groups is that each contains a relatively high number of disfranchised individuals inflicted with low social power. Drug trafficking may therefore act as a social equalizer for those who find themselves in positions of low social-political status. Groups and people who believe that their opportunities for mainstream success are limited may be drawn to activities like drug dealing that promise huge profits over a relatively short period of time. These benefits are measured not only in dollars but in status, power, and respect as well. This lends strength to strain theory to the extent that people respond to decreased opportunities for success by finding alternative means to socially sanctioned goals. However, as we have learned in this book, it is unwise to reduce a pattern as complex as drug trafficking to a single cause. The majority of young people, minorities, and women do not participate in drug dealing. What, then, separates those who do and do not respond to strain by entering the drug trade?

In determining the factors responsible for people's involvement in drug trafficking, we begin with strain, necessity, and greed. However, we must look beyond these social structural and personal motivational influences to obtain a consummate picture of how drug trafficking develops into a pattern. For some, a budding interest in the lifestyle may be ignited by the presence of drug dealers in the neighborhood who appear to be benefitting financially and socially from their involvement in the drug trade. Through personal observation and the symbolic media, the person may become preoccupied with the anticipated rewards of a drug-selling lifestyle even before he or she sells his or her first gram of illegal substance. Outcome expectancies, some of which are the product of media and family socialization and some of which are shaped by personal experience, influence preoccupation, a person's desire for status, and his or her associations with drug-dealing peers. Strain and differential association then interact with differential opportunity to create conditions ripe for initial involvement in drug trafficking. Pattern maintenance occurs through continued association with drug-dealing peers, changes in self-image, and the cognitive distortions that maintain drug trafficking.

8

Belief Systems Incongruent with Crime

Each person constructs his or her own reality and then goes about defending this reality. In constructing and defending our beliefs, none of us believe that our particular version of reality is inaccurate or faulty. Otherwise, we would be motivated to change it. Before dismissing this tenet of integrated-interactive theory as pure tautology, it may be wise to examine the logic behind the argument. According to the perspective adopted in this book, people, as a consequence of existential fear, are driven to make sense of themselves and the surrounding environment. They do so by constructing belief systems designed to represent reality. Once these representations are no longer useful in explaining major aspects of one's experience, they are modified or discarded and replaced by more practical representations.

As Kelly (1955) observed nearly a half century ago, when people's belief systems fail to predict future events or are ineffective in clarifying the environment, people are confronted by anxiety, which serves as motivation to change the belief systems. Once initiated, the change process must make a transition toward system-wide application and then be maintained, nurtured, and reinforced to have a meaningful impact on behavior. However, before reviewing the phases of change, we must first define the core elements that facilitate the overall change process. These core elements, it is reasoned, can be identified through research on high-risk individuals who avoid future criminal involvement and in studies on high-rate offenders who eventually desist from crime. This, then, is where the present discussion begins.

IDENTIFYING BELIEF SYSTEMS INCONGRUENT WITH CRIME: RESILIENCE AND DESISTANCE

In an attempt to identify belief systems incongruent with crime research on resilience in high-risk individuals and desistance in high-rate offenders is reviewed.

Resilience in High-Risk Children and Adolescents

Risk factors place an individual at elevated risk for involvement in a pattern like crime or delinquency. Protective factors, on the other hand, insulate or shield the individual from the adverse effects of various risk factors and give rise to resilience. Perhaps the most famous study on resilience was Emmy Werner's (1986) survey of forty-nine high-risk youth born on the Hawaiian island of Kauai. All forty-nine children were raised in an impoverished home environment with at least one alcohol-abusing parent. Less than half (41%) the sample showed serious coping problems at age 18, suggesting that resilience was a fairly common occurrence in this group. There were no socioeconomic differences between resilient and problem 18-year-olds, although resilient subjects were more often described as "cuddly and affectionate" during the first year of life, had fewer episodes of serious family conflict during the first two years of life, earned higher IQ scores at age 10, and displayed greater responsibility and self-control by grade 12 than problem children. Throughout childhood resilient subjects enjoyed better relationships with adults, Werner argued that this is at least partly due to the fact that resilient children possessed temperaments that elicited positive attention from their primary caregivers.

Research on resilience as a means of averting future delinquency can be grouped into four broad categories of protection: structural or demographic variables, social-relational context, life course development, and cognitive factors, to include choice. Gender is a commonly studied structural variable in research on delinquency prevention, the consensus being that girls are more resistant to criminogenic influences than boys (Born, Chevalier, & Humblet, 1997; Henry, Caspi, Moffitt, Harrington, & Silva, 1999). Another structural variable with the capacity to protect against future delinquency is intelligence (Kandel et al., 1988; Lösel & Bliesener, 1994). High intelligence appears to protect otherwise vulnerable children from delinquent and criminogenic influences. Freitas and Downey (1998) determined that while high intelligence may protect against conduct disorder, they acknowledge that intelligence is a dynamic construct that interacts with conduct disorder in a manner that varies across both domain and context.

The intelligence–resilience relationship may be moderated by social factors in the sense that more intelligent children receive greater levels of social reinforcement than less intelligent children. Social factors may also exert a direct effect on resilience. Lösel and Bliesener (1994) discovered that resilient youth had more typically grown up in a positive social environment and expressed greater satisfaction with the social support that they received than nonresilient youth. Resilient children taking part in this study were also more likely to report a stable social relationship with someone outside the family; in approximately half the cases support came from a teacher, and in another one-third of the cases the source of support was an extended family member. In their sample of high-risk children, Born et al. (1997) likewise noted that more resilient children demonstrated greater social competence, more amiable interpersonal relations, and stronger emotional ties to parents and teachers than less resilient children. In all probability, these social contextual factors and resilience enter into a reciprocal relationship whereby more resilient children enjoy a wider array of positive social opportunities, and expanded positive social options nourish resilience.

Life course development is another contextual variable capable of protecting against future delinquency. Such life course contextual events as participation in school and church activities may very well foster resilience in vulnerable children. Boehnke, Hagan, and Merkens (1998) ascertained that a positive school experience and success in school prevented young adolescents from drifting into delinquency. Results from another study imply that school attendance may wield a protective effect, although perhaps only for male juveniles, even after controlling for social class, intelligence, family disruption, and adolescent delinquency (Henry et al., 1999). Pinkney (1987) writes that resilience in black children is associated with regular church attendance. In line with Hirschi's (1969) social control theory, children with attachments to conventional people and institutions exercise greater restraint and resilience in response to sundry opportunities and temptations to commit crime.

Choice and general cognitive factors may also promote resilience in children at risk for delinquent involvement. Resilience has been found to correlate with higher levels of self-esteem and self-efficacy (Garmezy, 1985; Lösel & Bliesener, 1994), heightened self-control (Born et al., 1997), an internal locus of control (O'Grady & Metz, 1987), and the use of more active and less avoidant coping styles (Lösel & Bliesener, 1994). Some studies reveal a positive relationship between resilience and either anxiety (Tremblay, Pihl, Vitaro, & Dobkin, 1994) or shyness (Blumstein, Farrington, & Moitra, 1985), while other studies denote that shyness may be a risk factor for future delinquency (Kellam, Simon, & Ensminger, 1983). This controversy was recently addressed in an investigation by Kerr, Tremblay, Pagani, and Vitaro (1997) whereby behavioral inhibition—defined as the tendency to react fearfully to strange or novel people, objects, and situations—successfully protected children against future delinquency, whereas social withdrawal served to elevate the child's odds of future delinquent involvement.

There has been speculation on the part of some developmental psychologists and educators that building competencies and reinforcing protective factors should be emphasized over interventions aimed at reducing risk since the latter approach emphasizes deficits rather than strengths (Benard, 1993; Benson, 1997). Delving into this issue further, Pollard, Hawkins, and Arthur (1999) witnessed a moderately strong inverse correlation between risk and protective factors. While these authors ascertained that protective factors were most efficacious in boosting resilience at higher levels of risk, it was not possible to completely eliminate problem behavior by focusing solely on protective factors. Pollard and his colleagues argue that prevention should seek to both reduce risk and promote protection. The science of risk reduction could perhaps be advanced and made more comprehensible if we were to direct our attention to the issue of desistance in people with previous involvement in serious delinquency and adult criminality.

Desistance in High-Rate Delinquents and Adult Offenders

Childhood and family-of-origin variables are reasonably effective in forecasting future antisocial involvement (Huesmann & Eron, 1992; Robins, 1978), though these structural-demographic measures are not particularly helpful in predicting desistance from crime (Laub, Nagin, & Sampson, 1998; Nagin, Farrington, & Moffitt, 1995). One structural variable with the capacity to augur crime initiation and cessation equally well is age. Hirschi and Gottfredson (1983) have called attention to the fact that the age-crime curve, which peaks in midadolescence and drops sharply after age 25, is invariant across time, culture, gender, and a whole host of other variables. Notwithstanding data showing that high-rate offenders desist later and record a less dramatic age-related decline in law-violating behavior than lower-rate offenders (Blumstein, Cohen, & Farrington, 1988), age remains one of the strongest correlates of cessation (Shover & Thompson, 1992). Gender is another structural variable that has proven its worth in forecasting future criminal involvement and termination. As expected, studies insinuate that females experience higher levels of crime suspension than males (Ayers et al., 1999; Elliott, Huizinga, & Menard, 1989). Despite the fact that past behavior is often one of the best predictors of future behavior, the degree of prior delinquency is overshadowed by relational and life course contextual variables in prognosticating future desistance (Sampson & Laub, 1993).

Often, criminal activity slows down before coming to a complete stop (Farrington, 1986; Le Blanc & Fréchette, 1989). In a series of interviews held with fifteen male ex-felons who decelerated and then desisted from crime, Irwin (1970) found that many of these individuals considered the formation of a satisfying intimate relationship a key factor in initiating and maintaining their desistance from crime. Adler (1993) also uncovered a social context effect in thirteen out of sixty-five drug smugglers who eventually exited crime in her long-term participant-observer study of drug trafficking. Relationships with people who helped them reintegrate back into conventional society were perceived as vital in precipitating cessation in many of these individuals. One of the factors motivating deceleration and desistance in thirty women with extensive histories of prior criminality was leaving old crime-centered associations behind and forming attachments to people unfamiliar with crime (Sommers, Baskin, & Fagan, 1994). Similar sentiments were echoed by a small group of Canadian robbers asked to discuss their reasons for leaving a criminal lifestyle after many years of active criminal involvement (Cusson & Pinsonneault, 1986). Ongoing social support from noncriminals (Hughes, 1998) and a public pronouncement or certification by conventional people that one has indeed abandoned the lifestyle (Meisenhelder, 1977; Sommers et al., 1994) may also be important in reinforcing one's initial decision to desist.

In a reanalysis of Glueck and Glueck's (1968) original 25-year follow-up study of 500 seriously delinquent boys, Laub et al. (1998) remark that marital and occupational status are both strongly associated with desistance. The quality of the marital bond and job stability from ages 25 to 32 identified participants who eventually desisted from crime. Whereas marriage (Rand, 1987) and employment (Graham & Bowling, 1995) do not always correlate with cessation, the quality of a marriage and the stability of employment are more reliably connected to eventual abandonment of a criminal lifestyle (Mischkowitz, 1994). The complexity of the marriage–crime relationship was featured in a study by Ouimet and Le Blanc (1996) to where cohabitation served as a risk factor for males between the ages of 18 and 21 and acted as a protective factor in men over the age of 21. Substance misuse, like marriage and job stability, is a life course event with relevance to deceleration and desistance in high-rate offenders. Researchers have verified an association between crime and heroin use, and there is now compelling evi-dence that attenuated use of this substance can lead to significant reductions in the commission of property crime (Anglin & Speckart, 1988; Nurco, Hanlon, Kinlock, & Duszynski, 1988). Finally, participation in conventional extravocational and extradomestic activities may also facilitate crime deceleration and desistance (Adler, 1993; Irwin, 1970).

Choice and general cognitive factors are just as pivotal as contextual factors in motivating crime cessation. Irwin (1970) discerned a growing fear of incarceration, diminished positive expectancies for crime, and a dawning realization of the futility of law-violating behavior in his small group of ex-felons who desisted after years of extensive criminal involvement. Interviews conducted with fifty desisting property offenders led Shover (1996) to conclude that decreased preoccupation with material success and expanding awareness of the futility of crime were central to their decision to decelerate and desist from criminal conduct. Mounting fear and a gradual wearing down of the criminal drive through repeated incarcerations and growing recognition of the pointlessness of crime were viewed as instrumental in motivating Canadian robbers to abandon a criminal lifestyle, as was the shock of seeing a crime partner killed or having a close brush with death oneself during the commission of a crime (Cusson & Pinsonneault, 1986). Eighty percent of the youthful desisters enrolled in a study administered by Hughes (1998) reported having been either shot or stabbed over the course of their criminal careers, with many of these individuals stating that such experiences greatly influenced their decision to abandon crime. Instead of drifting into desistance, women participating in the Sommers et al. (1994) study explicitly decided to stop committing crime and followed up this commitment with a public pronouncement of their intent to resist further law-breaking opportunities. Reassessing priorities (Leibrich, 1993) and disputing the perceived benefits of antisocial conduct (Ayers et al., 1999) also figure prominently in decisions to desist from delinquency and crime.

This review of the objective and subjective correlates of resilience and desistance intimates that attitudes and belief systems are critical in shielding vulnerable individuals from criminogenic influences and in promoting cessation once a criminal pattern begins. These correlates can be further subclassified into broad clusters, each cluster reflecting a different theme. Several correlates, for instance, converge around the theme of responsibility. Age, which tends to correlate with self-control and responsibility (Gottfredson & Hirschi, 1990), has a direct bearing on crime suspension (Shover & Thompson, 1992), while self-control manifests a positive relationship with resilience (Born et al., 1997). Choice, anoth-er correlate of responsibility, may also be a factor in terminating crime (Hughes, 1998; Sommers et al., 1994). A second cluster of resilience- and desistance-congruent themes form around the issue of confidence as marked by self-efficacy (Adler, 1993; Lösel & Bliesener, 1994), social competence (Born et al., 1997), and social skills (Ayers et al., 1999). Correlates joined by a common interest in altered life meaning show rarefied positive expectancies for crime (Ayers et al., 1999; Irwin, 1970; Shover, 1996), a growing fear of imprisonment (Ayers et al., 1999; Irwin, 1970), awareness of the futility of crime (Cusson & Pinsonneault, 1986; Irwin, 1970; Shover, 1996), and shifting priorities, goals, and values (Leibrich, 1993) in those who eventually decelerate and desist. A fourth theme is suggested by strong attachment to conventional activities (Sommers et al., 1994) and agents of socialization like school (Henry et al., 1999), marriage, and employment (Laub et al., 1998) in resilient and desisting individuals. This theme reflects a sense of community.

ORGANIZING BELIEF SYSTEMS INCONGRUENT WITH CRIME: CORE ELEMENTS OF CHANGE

The four core elements of change, as specified by research on resilience and desistance, are responsibility, confidence, meaning, and community. These elements can be used to enhance protection or reduce risk, though certain elements may be more useful for one purpose than the other. Confidence, by accentuating competence and encouraging skill development, is directed toward protection enhancement, whereas community acts to lessen risk factors by identifying criminogenic associations and activities that the person might want to avoid. Belief systems congruent with crime, it is reasoned, can be neutralized with the aid of both competence enhancement and risk reduction. Not only do responsibility, confidence, meaning, and community advance the causes of competence enhancement and risk reduction, but they also stimulate the self-organizational process believed to be the source of all change (Walters, 2000d). Altering the self-, world-, past-, present-, and future-views in order to make them less compatible with crime therefore requires ongoing attention to the four core elements of change.

Responsibility

Responsibility is defined as a willingness to be answerable for the choices that one makes in life. There are three subcomponents to this particular core element: choice, attributions, and accountability.

Choice

Both deterrence and economic theories of crime causation maintain that people evaluate the consequences of their actions before electing to commit a crime. Deterrence theory holds that people consider the severity and certainty of negative sanctions for criminal behavior prior to acting (Paternoster, 1989). Research affords modest corroboration of the perceived certainty of sanctions as inhibitors of crime, while there is no evidence that the perceived severity of sanctions has any effect on the criminal decision-making process (Niggli, 1994). Other theorists add a second dimension to the decision-making matrix by factoring the perceived benefits of crime into the economic utility equation (Becker, 1968; Piliavin, Gartner, Thornton, & Matsueda, 1986). A third approach is to weigh the relative costs and benefits of crime against the relative costs and benefits of noncrime. This approach is known as the satisfaction balance model (Gray & Tallman, 1984). Ward, Stafford, Gray, and Menke (1994) scrutinized risk taking on an analogue decision-making task and unearthed support for both the economic utility and satisfaction balance models, though the latter accounted for a substantially greater proportion of variance in risk taking than the former.

The decision to participate in a specific criminal act probably begins as a cursory cost-benefit analysis, irrespective of the fact that several nonutilitarian factors also play a leading role in the decision-making process. Studies carried out on juvenile delinquents (Cimler & Beach, 1981) and adult property offenders (Carroll & Weaver, 1986) reveal that choice is a psychological process subject to heuristics, shortcut decision-making, and errors of both omission and commission (Clarke & Cornish, 1985). Goals, values, and expectancies most certainly impact on criminal and noncriminal decision making as well (Walters, 2000d). Making clients aware of their capacity for choice and teaching them how to improve their decision-making competence by generating a wider array of options to problem situations and more thoroughly evaluating these options can go a long way toward establishing the necessary conditions for altering criminal belief systems. Hakeem had long believed that events in his life were outside his personal control and that there had never been a decision on his part to involve himself in crime. Through education on the choice process and training in problem solving and lateral thinking (creativity), he has assumed greater personal responsibility for his actions but still has a long way to go in terms of fulfilling his responsibilities.

Attributions

In an effort to understand our world, we infer attributes to ourselves and others based on our observations. These attributions can be ordered along several dimensions (Weiner, 1990), three of which are of prime significance in the integrated-interactive model: locus (internal vs. external), stability (stable vs. unstable), and specificity (global vs. specific). Conduct-disordered children (Powell & Rosén, 1999), incarcerated juvenile delinquents (Barriga, Landau, Stinson, Liau, & Gibbs, 2000), and adult sex offenders (Blumenthal, Gudjonsson, & Burns, 1999) all display a tendency to externalize responsibility for their behavior by projecting blame for the negative consequences of their actions onto other people and outside events. Where excuse making may protect physical and psychological well-being (Snyder & Higgins, 1988), externalizing responsibility for significant issues in one's personal life can corrupt the integrity of major life assumptions and culminate in overly simplistic belief systems (Thompson & Janigian, 1988). Internal attributions for negative personal events, while advancing the cause of responsibility, can also trigger a depressive reaction of sufficient strength to impede the decision-making process. In order to avoid precipitating a depressive reaction, attributions for negative events should be unstable and specific. Attributing negative outcomes to unstable and specific factors maintains hope for the future (Grove, Hanrahan, & McInman, 1991) and prevents the generalization of negative affect to related and unrelated situations (Mikulincer, 1986), respectively.

Reattribution is a technique that can be useful in altering self-defeating attributional patterns. By encouraging clients to reframe the causes of their own or another person's behavior, a helper can facilitate the process of reattribution and encourage clients to spurn belief systems congruent with crime. Morris, Alexander, and Turner (1991) note that reframing the behavior of individuals in a vignette depicting conflict between two brothers led to large decrements in blaming attributions. Unlike Hakeem, who in the past attributed his actions to external sources, Sid attributes negative events to internal, stable, and global factors. Positive events, on the other hand, are attributed to external, unstable, and specific causes. Helping Sid devise belief systems incongruent with crime means encouraging him to manufacture more stable and global attributions for success and more unstable and specific attributions for failure. The author has taken the opportunity to illustrate to Sid how his attributional style has contributed to his depression and loneliness. On several occasions Sid has been given the homework assignment of applying moderately stable and global attributions to ongoing success experiences and unstable and specific attributions to perceived failures in an effort to demonstrate precisely how his attributions influence his affective state.

Accountability

Attribution of responsibility for the consequences of one's actions is referred to as accountability. Deci and Ryan (1985) postulate that people who feel a strong sense of personal accountability for change are more apt to maintain that change. Reviewing the results of their own study on this issue, Davison, Tsujimoto, and Glaros (1973) comment that subjects attributing reduced levels of insomnia to their own efforts were better able to maintain the positive gains than subjects ascribing reduced insomnia to sleep medication. Likewise, habitual smokers receiving nicotine gum enjoyed better initial outcomes than smokers receiving a self-help manual with an intrinsic motivation orientation, but the intrinsic self-help (manual) group remained tobacco-abstinent twice as long as the nicotine gum condition in follow-ups spanning several months (Harackiewicz, Sansone, Blair, Epstein, & Manderlink, 1987). Accountability consists of making an internal attribution for both the positive and negative consequences of one's actions and assuming personal responsibility for these consequences.

As behaviorists are quick to point out, all actions have consequences. Some of these consequences are perceived to be positive, others are perceived to be negative, and still others are construed as neutral. A consequence can be momentous or barely noticeable. Consequences provide people with opportunities to learn from their mistakes and successes. The life lessons that consequences teach are one reason that most people exit crime-congruent lifestyles without professional assistance. Only when others step in and prevent the natural consequences of our actions from occurring, a process known as enabling, do consequences lose their self-correcting prerogative. Randy had been enabled most of his life. When he got in trouble as a youngster, he was bailed out by his parents and relatives; later when he worked as a stock broker his employers shielded him from the natural consequences of his illegal and quasi-legal conduct. The former enabled out of love; the latter out of a sense that Randy was an asset that needed to be protected. For perhaps the first time in his life Randy is facing the consequences of his actions. The author has instructed Randy to reframe his incarceration as a life lesson that can be used to change his belief systems to reflect attitudes less congruent with white-collar crime.

Confidence

Confidence entails faith and trust in one's abilities and a realistic sense of self-assurance. It is speculated that those who engage in crime habitually lack confidence in themselves and have come to rely almost exclusively on crime-congruent lifestyles to feel competent. Instilling confidence in people previously dependent on crime-congruent belief systems necessitates the introduction of three interrelated issues: human agency, social competence, and skill development.

Human Agency

The capacity to produce and regulate events in one's life is known as human agency. Human agency is further subdivided into self-efficacy and general confidence. Self-efficacy is the belief that one can competently cope with, and master, specific features of one's environment (Bandura, 1997). Structured inter-views conducted with one-hundred adolescents disclosed a meaningful link between self-efficacy for twelve problem situations and lower rates of self-reported delinquency (Allen, Leadbeater, & Aber, 1990). Ludwig and Pittman (1999) also detected an inverse association between self-efficacy for prosocial activities (self-mastery, trustworthiness) and delinquency. Efficacy in the form of personal power, on the other hand, correlated positively with delinquency. This implies that self-efficacy for crime (personal power) promotes belief systems congruent with crime, while self-efficacy for prosocial activities fosters belief systems incongruent with crime. General confidence can be as critical as self-efficacy and comes into play in situations for which the individual has yet to form efficacy expectancies. McCartney (1997) relates that general confidence in one's ability to maintain therapeutically derived changes correlated with the firmness of subjects' decisions to desist from problem drinking, smoking, eating, and gambling behavior.

Pollock (1996) espied that sex offenders enrolled in a twelve-session relapse prevention program exhibited augmented self-efficacy over the course of the program. One of the self-efficacy subscales, a scale that measured the expectancy that effective coping would be rewarded, predicted decreased recidivism in a three-year follow-up of group participants. Alfredo was drawn to drug trafficking as a means of regaining the past glory of his high school football days. He did not feel confident in his ability to gain recognition on his own. Knowledge obtained through active involvement in several groups run by the author as part of the Lifestyle Change Program, a forty-week relapse prevention group in particular, helped Alfredo attain self-efficacy for high-risk situations (boredom, disrespect) as well as a general sense of confidence capable of carrying him through situations for which he has not been trained. The relapse prevention group availed Alfredo of relevant skills, afforded him the opportunity to practice the skills in role plays, and supplied him with feedback, reinforcement, and encouragement upon completion of the role play.

Social Competence

Social competence is determined, in part, by a person's ability to translate desired selves into actual selves currently available in his or her social environment (Cantor, Mischel, & Schwartz, 1982). Those individuals at greatest risk for habitual criminality may view a delinquent- or crime-congruent lifestyle as an opportunity to create a possible self when more conventional possible selves are blocked by environmental constraints or low self-confidence (Oyserman & Markus, 1990). In a survey of inner-city African American youth, Oyserman and Saltz (1993) ascertained that low social competence placed adolescents at high risk for delinquent behavior. Delinquent youth possessed less balanced possible selves, lower social competence (albeit they were no less verbally proficient), and more deviant responses to the immediate opportunities furnished by the social environment than nondelinquent youth. Oyserman and Saltz discerned that delinquent youth participating in their study were more opportunistic and impulsive than nondelinquent youth to the extent that they pursued whatever identity materials were currently available to them, whereas nondelinquent youth were more deliberate and selective in searching for self-relevant goals and opportunities.

Proof of a connection between social competence and confidence is both compelling and complicated. Hurrelmann and Engel (1992) affirm that failure to meet performance standards in school can lead to a loss of confidence, which, in turn, may prompt a retreat into deviance as a means of achieving some semblance of self-respect. The child reasons, "if I can't be good at school, at least I can gain respect by robbing, stealing cars, or selling drugs." This is why personal power self-efficacy correlated positively with delinquency in the Ludwig and Pittman

(1999) study. Hakeem never felt accepted by his father or any representative of conventional society. Adopted by the neighborhood gang at a relatively early age, he was reinforced for being aggressive by the older members of the gang. He therefore learned to compensate for his lack of social competence in the conventional world by acquiring competence and high self-efficacy in a criminal lifestyle. The modeling of prosocial behavior and reasoned problem solving has been essential in the author's work with Hakeem, who seems to be moving in the direction of enlarged social competence for conventional activities (reading, scholarship, relationships) and who seems more willing to entertain possible selves other than those of gangster and hoodlum.

Skill Development

Bandura (1997) identifies four sources or wellsprings of self-efficacy. The least effective source, according to Bandura, is verbal persuasion, whereby the individual is encouraged to perform the skill in question with statements designed to induce confidence. A somewhat more effective approach is to arrange for the client to observe another person successfully performing the targeted task. This is referred to as vicarious experience. It is also possible to reduce the emotional arousal that could potentially interfere with successful execution of a complex task. Performance accomplishments, however, are the most effective means of inspiring confidence, says Bandura. Using this approach, the individual is afforded the opportunity to successfully perform the task, which, of course, requires skills training, practice, and feedback. In highlighting skills training as a mechanism for building confidence, it should be noted that social, coping, and problem-solving skill deficits are well documented in delinquent and criminal populations (Leadbeater, Hellner, Allen, & Aber, 1989; Ross & Fabiano, 1985). Even though there are no data showing that these deficits cause criminal involvement, it would seem prudent that we at least consider the possibility of a causal relationship between skills and crime.

With respect to skills training it is noteworthy that three of the six characteristics associated with successful intervention in a meta-analysis of forty-four controlled studies on officially adjudicated offenders published between 1970 and 1991 are skill-based: (1) targeting of "criminogenic needs" or skill deficits; (2) role playing and modeling, and (3) social cognitive skills training (Antonowicz & Ross, 1994). A follow-up of seventy-six child sex offenders processed through a comprehensive relapse prevention program indicated that the strongest predictor of freedom from future arrest was the individual's skill in applying the relapse prevention model (Marques, Nelson, West, & Day, 1994). Despite possessing superior verbal persuasion and sales skills, Randy lacks the ability to monitor and realistically appraise his own thinking and plans. To a certain extent his ex-wife helped him maintain control over his superoptimistic tendencies, but once his girlfriend entered the picture, Randy lost the benefit of this "auxiliary conscience." Randy is now learning how to exercise greater command over his thinking by self-monitoring and challenging the constructional errors—dichotomous reasoning and arbitrary inference—that serve as the foundation for his white-collar, crime-congruent belief systems.

Meaning

Meaning is conveyed in belief systems and dispensed in ways that foster personal growth, social relationships, and beliefs about success, hedonism, creativity, and legacy (Fiske & Chiriboga, 1990). The present discussion focuses on three fundamental features of meaning: identity transformation, goals and values, and cognitive complexity.

Identity Transformation

Those in search of an identity may deploy a lifestyle to breathe meaning and purpose into their lives. The problem that this presents is that a lifestyle can never do justice to the complexity of the human organism because it promotes self-labeling and, in turn, limits a person's options in life. Often the labeling process is initiated or reinforced by society. People who commit sexual crimes are variously described or diagnosed as rapists, child molesters, sexual perverts, and pedophiles. Controlling for the effects of prior record and the seriousness of the current offense, sex offenders referred to a psychiatrist and subsequently labeled with a psychiatric diagnosis were twice as likely to be incarcerated as nonreferred and nonlabeled sex offenders (Walsh, 1990). Tagging people convicted of sex crimes with a criminal rather than mental illness label, asserts Winick (1998), should provoke greater acceptance of responsibility for their law-violating behavior. Avoiding all forms of labeling nevertheless seems advisable, although a designation of mental illness is particularly nefarious for it conflicts with two of the core elements of change—responsibility and meaning. Labeling effects are not independent of the wider social or cultural context in which they occur. An early study on officially labeled U.S. delinquents found that labeling bred estrangement from parents but had no effect on the youth's relationships with peers and teachers (Foster, Dinitz, & Reckless, 1972). Applying the same research design to a group of officially labeled Chinese adolescent law-breakers, Zhang and Messner (1994) determined that criminal justice labeling had little impact on the child–parent bond but caused estrangement from friends and neighbors.

Identity transformation is one aspect of meaning known to facilitate the growth of belief systems incongruent with crime. A change in identity is commonly reported by those who desist from crime after years of law-violating behavior (Adler, 1993; Cusson & Pinsonneault, 1986; Irwin, 1970; Meisenhelder, 1977; Shover, 1996). Each of the four individuals whose cases were presented in this book had to alter his identity in order to construct belief systems incongruent with crime, but none are more notable in this regard than Sid. From the author's initial contact with Sid it was obvious that he saw himself as a pedophile and that this self-label was an intrinsic part of his identity and self-view. The internal, stable, and global self-attributions that contribute to Sid's practice of self-labeling have been challenged using a rational restructuring approach, although this has done little to change Sid's self-view. It is as if the pedophile label affords Sid the predictability that supports survival. After several months of direct confrontation Sid clung tenaciously to his self-view as a pedophile. The author decided to change directions and began reinforcing other aspects of Sid's life unrelated to his sexual interest in children. Topics as varied as reading, model trains, and the Civil War figured prominently in these discussions. The author then sought to encourage Sid to see himself as a person with many interests, only one of which was his sexual interest in children. The more daunting task of confronting Sid's sexual interest in young boys is ongoing. Cognitive reappraisal and rational restructuring are currently being used to dispel the sentimentality that supports Sid's contention that his sexual acting out was simply a matter of mentoring, the ultimate objective being to make pedophilia less feasible as his primary means of self-identification.

Goals and Values

Meaning also embodies the goals and values that direct a person's actions. Values are the standards by which we judge our actions, and goals are the outcomes that we pursue. Adolescents who lack prosocial values (Simons, Whitbeck, Conger, & Conger, 1991) and long-range goals (Wilson & Herrnstein, 1985) are at elevated risk for future delinquency. As with most relationships posed by integrated-interactive theory, the linkages between goals, values, and delinquency/crime are believed to be interactive and reciprocal. The nature of the relationship between values and self-efficacy appears to be additive rather than interactive, with prosocial values assuming an inverse relationship with delinquency in two different studies (Allen et al., 1990; Ludwig & Pittman, 1999). Goddard (1994) postulates that adolescents who engage in problem behavior possess a self-system grounded in values and goals that inhibit their decision-making ability and hinder their capacity to factor the rights and feelings of others into their decisions.

The integrated-interactive approach views adaptability as a matter of balance: balance between four value clusters (social, work, visceral, intellectual) and balance between long- and short-terms goals (Walters, 2000d). It is postulated that crime-congruent lifestyles emphasize visceral values over the other three value clusters and short-term goals over long-term objectives. Research conducted by Vohra and Ahmad (1993) demonstrates that delinquents score below nondelinquents on social and intellectual values, and findings from another study disclose a relationship between delinquency and the pursuit of hedonistic (visceral) values and short-term goals (Krueger, Caspi, Moffitt, White, & Stouthamer-Loeber, 1996). Alfredo displayed this very pattern during the ten-year period in which he sold drugs. Through values clarification and training in goal setting he has learned to balance his priorities (values) and expectancies (goals). Accordingly, he is now in a much better position to make purposeful and balanced decisions because he relies on a wider range of experience and considers both the long- and short-term consequences of his actions.

Cognitive Complexity

Belief systems congruent with crime are characteristically simple and weakly integrated. A change in a criminal belief system may therefore require a concomitant escalation in cognitive complexity. Cognitive complexity, which derives from George Kelly's (1955) personal construct theory of personality, relates to the number and organization of constructs that a person holds toward a particular subject. Research denotes that cognitive complexity portends increased adaptability as characterized by greater flexibility of thought (Hinze, Doster, & Joe, 1997), heightened awareness of others' emotional states (Beatty & Payne, 1984), superior communication skills (Denton, Burleson, & Sprenkle, 1995), and more accurate causal inferences (Fletcher, Rosanowski, Rhodes, & Lange, 1992). People high in cognitive complexity cope better with stress (Smith & Cohen, 1993), are less subject to anxiety (Dixon & Baumeister, 1991) and depression (Linville, 1985), and are more optimistic (Hinze & Doster, 1997) than people who attain low scores on measures of cognitive complexity. With respect to aggression and delinquency, McKeough, Yates, and Marini (1994) conclude that aggression in boys is associated with lower levels of cognitive complexity, and Orr and Ingersoll (1995) report that high-cognitive complexity students are less likely to commit minor delinquency than low-cognitive complexity students.

Augmenting cognitive complexity is a key to creating belief systems incongruent with crime. The first step of the complexity augmentation process is to invite the client to embrace complexity rather than avoid it (de Vries & Lehman, 1996). In this regard, Randy was asked to monitor his thinking in ten-minute segments over a period of several weeks. After participating in this exercise, Randy was in a position to better appreciate the complexity of his own thinking. Once the client comprehends the complexity of his or her thinking, the next step is to use dialectics (McGarry, 1996) or the Socratic method (Vitousek, Watson, & Wilson, 1998) or assume the position of devil's advocate (Walters, 2000d) to expand the complexity of the client's belief systems. Targeting the polarities evident in Randy's "Jekyll and Hyde" self-view, the author used the dialectic method to illustrate how these polarities could be reconciled and integrated with one another by means of the dialectic approach (thesis → antithesis → synthesis). The Socratic method was applied to Randy's thinking about his girlfriend whereby questions were posed in an effort to get him to think more deeply and complexly about the possible ramifications of remaining in a relationship with this young woman. Finally, the author would occasionally assume the position of devil's advocate by taking an exaggerated, simplistic view of some aspect of Randy's life and then encouraging him to evaluate and contest the validity of the author's argument.

Community

Humans are social animals and, as such, gather into groups for the purposes of affiliation, protection, and increased productivity. A sense of community, whereby we acknowledge our connectedness to people and events outside ourselves, is consequently vital to human survival. Connectedness and community give rise to three subgoals: informal social control, reciprocity, and transcendence.

Informal Social Control

Cross-cultural research on crime indicates that one of the principal factors separating high and low crime nations is informal social control (Adler, 1983). Informal social control is the supervision and direction rendered by the immediate social environment through reinforcement of selected customs, traditions, and rituals. Unlike the formal social control wielded by the criminal justice system, where transgressions are punished with probation or imprisonment, informal social control utilizes embarrassment, shame, and a person's innate desire for belonging to ensure conformity to the rules of the group. Citizens of nations like China and Japan abide by the rules of society because informal social controls, courtesy of a robust sense of familial and societal obligation, are in place (Allen, 1987). Even with the understanding that informal social control is stronger in Eastern than Western cultures, there is evidence, as exemplified by Hirschi's (1969) social control theory, that informal social control does play a role in preventing crime in the United States. Sampson and Laub (1993) offer an age-graded theory of informal social control in which social bonds in the form of ties to family and work are instrumental in preventing delinquency and facilitating crime deceleration and desistance. Preliminary research addressing this theory's underlying tenets has met with some success (Laub et al., 1998).

In addition to providing rules, guidance, and immediate negative sanctions for violations of culturally prescribed standards, informal social control also endows people with social support. A study done on a group of substance-abusing adolescent law-breakers determined that social support was indispensable in facilitating cessation of both drug use and crime (Hammersley, Forsyth, & Lavelle, 1990). Alfredo had grown up in a supportive home environment replete with informal social control and interpersonal support. For reasons best known to himself but that undoubtedly included personal ambition and low self-confidence, he chose to follow a path different from the one his parents had laid out for him and which his older siblings followed. Through introspection and a reevaluation of life goals and priorities, Alfredo is now prepared to abide by the informal social control furnished by his wife, parents, and other extended family members. Unlike competence or responsibility, informal social control is not something that a person learns but, rather, is something that a person accepts. To accept informal social control and support from others is to alter fundamental beliefs and attitudes about oneself and the world and construct belief systems incongruent with crime. Alfredo has made the decision to accept the informal social control and support supplied by his family in an effort to erect a sense of community designed to combat future crime-related urges.

Reciprocity

A communal attitude requires a sense of reciprocity. As such, the individual is as indebted to the wider community as the community is beholden to the individual. This sense of mutual obligation furthers the existence of the community and each of its members. Helping someone with whom one desires a communal relationship leads to increased levels of positive affect (Williamson & Clark, 1992), whereas refusing to assist someone with whom one desires a communal relationship is met by decreased levels of positive feelings (Williamson, Clark, Pegalis, & Behan, 1996). The reciprocity inherent in self-disclosure (Taylor & Belgrave, 1986) has been shown to reduce the long-term negative repercussions of a traumatic event (Donnelly & Murray, 1991) and is capable of stimulating cognitive complexity owing to the fact that the person is forced to consider a perspective different from his or her own (Clark, 1993). Reciprocity forms between individual people as well as between individuals and groups, and while a group's struggle for survival can bestow greater resilience on its members (Sonn & Fisher, 1996), an individual's struggle for survival contributes to the growth and well-being of the groups to which he or she belongs (Baumeister & Leary, 1995).

Group therapy can be a powerful means of effecting reciprocity in clients (Brisman & Siegel, 1985). This is one reason why the Lifestyle Change Program is conducted in groups. Another reason is that group members can serve as an external audience in the alteration of reflected appraisals that are maintaining crime-congruent belief systems. Sid has always felt alienated from mainstream society. Other than two psychologists, the only people with whom Sid has confided and felt any degree of reciprocity are those individuals who share his sexual interest in children and with whom he communicated over the Internet. Such a closed network of differential associations has helped Sid avoid the negative consequences of his actions and thwarted the self-corrective action of the natural self-organizational process. Surrounding himself with people who thought and acted as he did was something that Sid had in common with the other individuals whose case histories are presented in this book. Alfredo spent the majority of his time with his drug crew, Hakeem with fellow gang members, and Randy with brokers who, like him, believed that the end justifies the means. Group interaction, even if it is only with other convicted felons, can dissolve the isolation created by self-imposed differential association. Up to this point Sid has balked at the idea of participating in group sessions, even though he has been assured that his crime will not come up in discussions unless he himself brings it up. This is an issue that will likely continue to be worked on long after this book is published.

Transcendence

Traditional theories of psychology have generally neglected the issue of spirituality. With the exception of humanistic thinkers like Abraham Maslow (1971) and William Miller's (1999) recent book on integrating spiritual issues into psychotherapy, spirituality has been a topic largely confined to self-help groups like Alcoholics Anonymous. Transcendence is the term used in the integrated-interactive theory to account for spirituality and is defined as elevating oneself above one's current situation for the purpose of achieving harmony, union, and interaction with people, objects, events, and ideas outside oneself. Anderson (1994) coined the term relinquishment to describe a person's willingness to forsake familiar constructions and confront the alienation and fear that characterize the human condition. According to the integrated-interactive theory, one avenue of existential fear mastery is an evolving sense of community wherein the person recognizes his or her connectedness to the physical and interpersonal worlds in which we all live. Belief systems congruent with crime attain their power by promising to resolve existential fear, but the promise is false because criminal belief systems are so consumed with the lifestyle that they distance the person from the community and natural reservoirs of social support.

Forming belief systems incongruent with crime means seeing one's interconnectedness to the physical and interpersonal worlds. People who habitually enact lifestyles congruent with crime are often so wrapped up in their personal lives that they seem oblivious to what is going on around them. The solution is to gain a new perspective through self-transcendence. Within the integrated-interactive model there is something known as the transcendental self. Thus, besides a self-view, world-view, present-view, past-view, and future-view, there are also a self-in-the-world-view, self-in-the-present-view, self-in-the-past-view, self-in-the-future-view, and even a self-in-the-self-view. Formal religion is only one way people realize transcendence, and Hakeem's interest in Islam appears to have helped him get in touch with the spiritual side of himself. As a participant in the Lifestyle Change Program, Hakeem was asked to list and discuss the people whom he had hurt in a lifetime of criminal activity and violence. Cognitive restructuring was then used to challenge some of Hakeem's deep-seated attitudes about race and demonstrate to him that many of his prejudices and preconceptions are based on other people's prejudices and preconceived notions (mythical constructions) rather than on his own observations. Now, Hakeem has a much greater sense of his responsibilities to others, although a great deal more work needs to be done before he can enter the community as a contributing member instead of as a predator.

IMPLEMENTING BELIEF SYSTEMS INCONGRUENT WITH CRIME: PHASES OF ASSISTED CHANGE

Taking the four core elements of change described in the previous section, it is possible to construct an integrated-interactive model of assisted change. Research on crime desistance in conjunction with research on unassisted change from substance misuse (Walters, 2000e) indicates that most people get better without professional help. In fact, it could be argued that professional treatment impedes the natural change process in some instances by interfering with self-organization (Walters, 2000d). This section outlines a model of change that can be used by professional helpers to facilitate the natural change process believed to exist in all people and convert crime-congruent belief systems into crime-incongruent belief systems. The first three phases of the change process are the same as the first three phases of lifestyle development—initiation, transition, maintenance—with a fourth or change phase added.

Initiation

The initiation phase of change comprises three subphases: crisis, public pronouncement, and achieving perspective. A crisis occurs when the perceived costs of crime outweigh the perceived benefits in someone currently engaged in crime. The crisis can have an internal (e.g., sense of disgust) or external (e.g., nearly losing one's life during the commission of a crime) origin and may be motivated by a sense that crime is blocking one's approach to certain goals (e.g., desire to be a good role model for a newborn son or daughter) or producing negative consequences that the individual would sooner avoid (e.g., incarceration). Contrary to Matza's (1964) drift hypothesis, desisting female felons participating in the Sommers et al. (1994) study made a clear decision to terminate their criminal activities. This does not mean, however, that many individuals do not repeat this decision many times before committing themselves to it since deceleration often precedes desistance (Farrington, 1986; Le Blanc & Fréchette, 1989). It is important to understand that the helper need not invent a crisis because there are many crises in the lives of those who enact crime-congruent lifestyles. Instead, helpers can assist clients by asking them to describe the people whom they have harmed, opportunities that they have missed, possessions and relationships that they have lost, and embarrassing situations that they have encountered as a consequence of their involvement in crime and with the aid of imagery and discussion assist the client in defining and developing these naturally occurring crises.

The next subphase of the initiation phase is a public pronouncement of the individual's intention to change. A public pronouncement is integral to the process of unassisted change in substance abusers (Stall & Biernacki, 1986) and is viewed to be no less vital in desisting from crime. Sommers et al. (1994) advise that many of the desisting women in their sample made a public pronouncement to abandon crime, which corroborates an earlier study by Meisenhelder (1977) in which a public pronouncement solicited from an individual not currently involved in crime was a precursor of desistance. Tice (1992) reports that commitments made in front of an audience, even if the audience is imaginary, are more apt to precipitate a change in self-concept than commitments made alone. To expedite the public pronouncement process helpers can make use of a change plan (Walters, 1998d).

Unlike a treatment plan, the change plan is completed by the client and consists of a summary of (1) past involvements, commitments, and identifications the client would like to change, (2) present involvements, commitments, and identifications that have replaced the problematic pattern, and (3) future involvements, commitments, and identifications the client is currently pursuing. Whereas the change plan need not be completed in the presence of a helper, to satisfy the public pronouncement requirement of this subphase, the change plan should be shared with at least one other person.

The third subphase of the initiation phase of self-alteration is to effect a change in perspective. Symbolic healing encompasses the use of culture-specific symbols embedded in collective myth to redefine problems and offer culturally prescribed solutions to these problems (Dow, 1986). It is contingent upon the helper to convince the client that they share a sufficient number of world-view prototypes in common to permit the process of symbolic healing to take place. The shaman effect derives from the client-helper relationship or therapeutic alliance (Horvath, 1995) and takes note of the fact that 15% of the variance in outcome normally credited to psychotherapy is actually attributable to expectancy and placebo effects (Lambert, 1992). The shaman effect uses sensitivity, ritual, metaphor, dialectics, and the attribution triad (Walters, 2001b) to extend the arresting process initiated by various life crises and a public pronouncement of change. Sensitivity means striving to conceive of the client's problem from his or her own perspective or internal frame of reference. Like sensitivity, positive rituals contribute to the formation of a shaman effect by encouraging interpersonal communication and a general sense of community. Symbolic thought and meaning can be advanced and manipulated through metaphor where an abstract thought, feeling, or perception is transformed into a concrete object or situation (Seitz, 1998). The dialectic method, as previously described, makes use of the thesis → antithesis → synthesis sequence to discover more complex meanings. Finally, the attribution triad is composed of three interrelated beliefs instrumental in extending the lifestyle arresting process: (1) belief in the necessity of change, (2) belief in the possibility of change, (3) belief in one's ability to effect change.

Transition

The transitional phase of the assisted change process takes as its primary focus, modifying outcome expectancies and furnishing the client with skills training. As was pointed out in Chapter 3, outcome expectancies are critical in promoting a transition of belief systems congruent with crime. Outcome expectancies are equally pivotal in effecting a transition in belief systems incongruent with crime. Research on desistance from alcohol misuse shows that negative outcome expectancies for alcohol do a better job of predicting long-term outcome than positive alcohol expectancies (Fromme, Kivlahan, & Marlatt, 1986; Jones & McMahon, 1994). A rise in negative outcome expectancies for crime and a corollary reduction in positive crime expectancies have been observed in self-desisting former offenders

(Ayers et al., 1999; Cusson & Pinsonneault, 1986; Irwin, 1970). Highlighting the negative, long-term consequences of continued criminal involvement would seem a potentially effective strategy for amplifying negative crime expectancies. The expectancy challenge, on the other hand, may be useful in eviscerating positive outcome expectancies for crime, for it entails educating people about the hold that positive outcome expectancies have on their behavior. In research conducted on college students the expectancy challenge has been helpful in neutralizing the pattern-transitioning action of positive outcome expectancies for alcohol (Darkes & Goldman, 1993). The question at this juncture is whether the procedure can be effectively applied to outcome expectancies for crime.

As significant as outcome expectancies are in fostering the transition to belief systems incongruent with crime, one's helping efforts should also include skills training so that crime-congruent belief systems can be altered and new goals and values established. Skills covered during this particular subphase of the assisted change process will vary depending on the results of a thorough evaluation of the client's individual strengths and weaknesses. This evaluation should probably cover coping skills, problem-solving skills, social-communication skills, life skills, academic/educational skills, and thinking skills, at a minimum. Skill deficits are managed by (1) instructing the clients in the performance of the skill, (2) granting the client the opportunity to practice the skill in role plays and real-life situations, and (3) providing the client with corrective feedback designed to improve future use of the skill. Like any new behavior these skills will feel uncomfortable to the individual at first. It is therefore contingent upon the helper to encourage the client to work through the awkwardness and avoid giving up before the skill becomes habitual. A general rule of thumb is that it requires somewhere in the neighborhood of three to four months of repeated performance to convert a new behavior into a habit (Marlatt & George, 1984). Once acquired, however, the new skill has the power to engender feelings of confidence and self-efficacy.

Maintenance

Once established, belief systems incongruent with crime must be maintained if they are to hold dominion over a person's actions and decisions. The maintenance phase of the assisted change process is divided into three subphases: changing involvements, changing commitments, and changing identifications. For change to be maintained, involvements in the form of activities and associations must be altered. A person cannot expect to remain crime-free if he or she continues interacting with a criminogenic environment or insists on associating with criminal confederates. Identifying and avoiding people, places, and things likely to bring one into conflict with the criminal justice system are essential for changing involvements. Substitution is another technique with the strength to modify people's involvements by maintaining crime-incongruent belief systems. The inaugural step of the substitution process is to ask clients to list the perceived benefits of crime. Frequently mentioned benefits include power, respect, and excitement, although it may be necessary to advocate for increased specificity, particularly when money is mentioned because money represents different things to different people (e.g., control, status, freedom to do what you want). The next step is to identify socially acceptable substitute activities capable of achieving some of the benefits currently being satisfied by crime but without putting the individual at risk for incarceration. The third step is to have the client integrate these substitute activities into his or her daily routine.

Two requirements for belief system retention and maintenance are that (1) the individual should have faith in the belief system's overall accuracy and (2) the belief system should afford the individual a semblance of order and purpose (Thompson & Janigian, 1988). These two criteria need to be satisfied by any substitute set of beliefs to which the individual commits. Commitment to belief systems incongruent with crime demands that the client personally affirm the accuracy and meaningfulness of the underlying assumptions and tenets that mark his or her belief systems. Goals and values assume a central position in the formation of a commitment to belief systems incongruent with crime. Together, goals and values forge self-views, world-views, present-views, past-views, and future-views incongruent with crime and congruent with an interactive style that makes it significantly less likely that the individual will gain a sense of pride, identity, and priority from crime.

Altering identifications refers to the fact that the individual must actively reject labels commonly associated with crime and see such labels as irrelevant to himself or herself. The helper can assist clients in reaching this goal by resisting the urge to label the client. Instead of labeling the individual, the lifestyle should be labeled (i.e., talk about a criminal lifestyle rather than a lifestyle criminal). Once the old label-based identity has been repudiated, a new identity must be constructed if belief systems devised during the initiation and transitional phases are to be maintained. All four core elements should be represented in the new identity for it to be sufficiently adaptable to prevent the individual from reverting back to old criminal patterns. Accordingly, this identity must convey a sense of responsibility and accountability, confidence and self-efficacy, meaning and complexity, and community and connectedness. Clients are consequently encouraged to view themselves as people who have had problems with crime in the past but who can choose to act differently in the present with confidence, meaning, and community. In the absence of a change in identification, it is difficult to imagine that crime-incongruent belief systems could ever take root given the temptations and frustrations that people previously committed to crime-congruent lifestyles will inevitably encounter.

Change

Proposing a change phase for the change process may seem unnecessary and redundant. Every adaptation has the potential to become a pattern or lifestyle if the individual does not remain vigilant and flexible in the face of a continuously self-altering environment. It is consequently vital that the individual continue monitoring his or her belief systems as well as internal and external events for new information useful in constructing maximally adaptive belief systems. Though they do not mirror the external environment in every detail, belief systems should at least account for major environmental change. Doing so means that the belief systems of highly adaptive people are continually being rearranged and modified because change is an ongoing process. Without benefit of perpetual self-alteration, the individual will eventually fall victim to a pattern, if not a crime-congruent lifestyle, then perhaps some other variant or pattern that strips the individual of his or her adaptive potential and humanity.

CONCLUSION

The unbridled optimism of the 1960s that held that all criminal offenders were treatable was eventually replaced by the gloomy pessimism of the 1970s in which it was concluded that "nothing works" (Martinson, 1974). In the 1980s and 1990s the mood shifted once again to a position of tempered hopefulness in which intervention was viewed as effective within certain limits and parameters (Andrews et al., 1990; Garrett, 1985; Gendreau & Ross, 1987; Palmer, 1991). The resounding theme of the early twenty-first century, as outlined in this chapter, is that some programs work, other programs do not work, and still other programs make people worse. The characteristics of effective programming are (1) a sound conceptual model, (2) multifaceted procedures, (3) targeting of "criminogenic needs," (4) reliance on behavioral and social learning principles, (5) role playing and modeling, and (6) social cognitive skills training (Antonowicz & Ross, 1994). The integrated-interactive theory of crime-congruent lifestyles described in this book seeks to address each of these points in the creation of belief systems incongruent with crime. This approach employs an internally consistent, externally valid conceptual framework that rests heavily on behavioral and social learning principles to identify areas of strength and weakness and proposes the use of multifaceted interventions in which modeling, role playing, and social-cognitive skill development assume center stage.

It is the author's contention that the degree to which a program is effective, ineffective, or countereffective depends on whether it addresses the four core elements of change. Most people abandon crime-congruent lifestyles on their own and generally do so through accentuated responsibility, confidence, meaning, and community. Effective helping henceforth needs to emphasize these four elements. Each phase and subphase of the assisted change process makes use of all four elements. In any event, some elements assume greater prominence during certain phases or subphases of the change process than other elements. The guiding element for each phase and subphase of the assisted change process is outlined in Table 8.1. As helpful as Table 8.1 may be, it should be noted that core elements do more than direct the overall assisted change process; they also need to be considered as part of one's ongoing interactions with clients. Each time that a helper

Table 8.1
Core Elements That Guide the First Three Phases of the Assisted Change Process

Phase	Subphase and Procedures	Core Element(s)
INITIATION		
	Crises and the Motivation for Change	Responsibility
	Public Pronouncement	Responsibility
	Achieving Perspective: Shaman Effect	
	Sensitivity	Community
	Ritual	Community
	Metaphor	Meaning/Community
	Dialectics	Meaning
	Attribution Triad	
	Belief in the Necessity of Change	Responsibility
	Belief in the Possibility of Change	Meaning
	Belief in Ability to Effect Change	Confidence
TRANSITION		
	Altering Outcome Expectancies	Meaning
	Skill Development	Confidence
MAINTENANCE		
	Changing Involvements	Responsibility/Community
	Changing Commitments	Meaning/Community
	Changing Identifications	Confidence/Meaning

and client meet, the helper should make an effort to address the issues of responsibility, confidence, meaning, and community with the client. The core elements, therefore, direct the overall flow of the assisted change process as well as each individual interaction with clients. Keeping the four core elements of change foremost in one's mind is accordingly crucial in nurturing belief systems incongruent with crime.

This chapter has concentrated exclusively on micro-level strategies for altering belief systems congruent with crime. Messner and Rosenfeld (1997), on the other hand, offer a macro-level theory of crime that attributes America's crime problem to imbalance between major social institutions and nationwide acceptance of the "American Dream," defined as "a commitment to the goal of material success, to be pursued by everyone in society, under conditions of open, individual competition" (6). These influences have combined to create an obsession with achievement, a celebration of individuality, and glorification of material success, which, in turn, have contributed to a burgeoning crime rate relative to the rate recorded in other industrialized nations. The solution, say Messner and Rosenfeld, is to reduce the dominance of the capitalistic economy by rejuvenating major noneconomic social institutions like the family and schools and reevaluate the American Dream by tempering individual rights and ambition with collective responsibility and social obligation. Translated into the language of the four core elements of change, we as a society must rearrange our priorities (responsibility), feel pride beyond our ability to acquire and consume material goods (confidence), gain a true sense of the value of the person (meaning), and appreciate our obligaion to the past, present, and future of our world (community) if we are to have any chance of solving the problem of crime in the United States and abroad.

Epilogue

A wise man once said that theories that seek to explain everything end up explaining nothing. When I reflect on this sage advice, I am reminded of Gottfredson and Hirschi's (1990) general theory of crime. Gottfredson and Hirschi have been justly and deservedly rebuked for trying to reduce all crime, as well as a number of noncriminal behaviors, down to low self-control. The specific criticisms of self-control theory have been outlined elsewhere (Akers, 1991; Geis, 2000; Reed & Yeager, 1996) and need not be repeated here. Of concern to us in the final few pages of this book on belief systems congruent with crime is what, if anything, prevents the integrated-interactive theory from following the same path and suffering the same fate as Gottfredson and Hirschi's general theory of crime? I believe that several factors make the integrated-interactive approach less vulnerable to the limitations and problems that plague Gottfredson and Hirschi's model.

First, the integrated-interactive theory of crime-congruent lifestyles differs from Gottfredson and Hirschi's (1990) general theory of crime in its views on reductionism. In contrast to Gottfredson and Hirschi, the integrated-interactive theory holds firmly to the belief that crime cannot be reduced to a single process, whether that process be low self-control or a criminal lifestyle. A primary objective of this book has been to illustrate how different lifestyles interact with one another to create conditions conducive to crime. As Chapter 1 indicates, no single criminological theory is capable of explaining the wide diversity of crimes committed each year. By the same token, no single lifestyle can account for all varieties of criminal conduct. Not even the general lifestyle concept can explain all crime since some criminal events are the result of drift or specific situational forces.

Unlike Gottfredson and Hirschi's (1990) general theory of crime, the integrated-interactive theory does not assume that all forms of crime flow from the same source. As detailed in Chapters 4 through 7, violent crime, sexual assault, white-collar crime, and drug trafficking are each hypothesized to follow a different causal path. Whereas the four proposed pathways follow the same general format, incentive-opportunity-cognition, and share some of the same ancillary components, they are not blueprints that can be applied to all people or all crimes. The integrated-interactive theory makes allowances for broad individual differences both between and within patterns. Hence, while alcohol abuse is cited as an ancillary component of sexual assault, there is no evidence that Sid ever had a drinking problem. A belief system may give rise to crime by influencing human choice and decision making, but each decision is based on a person's perspective. Just as the same crime can arise from dissimilar belief systems, vastly different crimes can sometimes be traced to similar belief systems. Commonalities in crime exist, but we must never lose sight of the fact that people's means of perceiving and construing the various aspects of their experience is what determines how they interact with their internal and external environments and how they construct their criminal belief systems.

One of the many criticisms leveled against Gottfredson and Hirschi's (1990) general theory of crime is that it does a poor job of explaining crimes committed at the group level (Geis, 2000). The integrated-interactive theory, on the other hand, can be facilely applied to group-level violations through the nonlinear dynamical systems concept of fractals. In short, fractals demonstrate that relationships found at one level of a system are often replicated at other levels of that same system. Crowd violence, gang rape, organized crime, and corporate conspiracies can all be explained using principles outlined in this book. This is because belief systems cannot be reduced to interactions taking place within the organism. Belief systems join the individual and environment in a dynamic interaction of reciprocal forces. A similar process occurs in groups. Corporations and prison gangs profess collective belief systems that transcend the individual beliefs of their members. Personal beliefs can impact collective belief systems just as collective belief systems impact personal beliefs, albeit in large organizations the collective often exerts a more profound effect on the individual than the individual exerts on the collective. In the end, however, belief systems influence the criminal and noncriminal actions of groups as much as they influence the criminal and noncriminal activities of individuals.

A limitation not exclusive to Gottfredson and Hirschi's (1990) general theory of crime is that traditional criminological theory may not be fully applicable to female (Katz, 2000) and minority (Cernkovich, Giordano, & Rudolph, 2000) offending. Most theories of criminology have been developed and validated on teenage and young adult, white, male general delinquency and property crimes. The integrated-interactive theory may be in a unique position to address some of these under-studied groups, just as it has been shown to clarify different categories (violent, sexual, white-collar, drug) and levels (individual, group, organizational, societal) of crime. Belief systems are dramatically shaped and altered by cultural and socialization events. By stressing the cultural/socialization origins of the social comparison and role identity components of the self-view and the organic-mechanistic dimension of the world-view the integrated-interactive theory holds promise of elucidating the common and distinctive features that encourage criminal behavior in females and minorities.

In closing I would like to reiterate that crime is supported by lifestyles, which, in turn, are derived from belief systems. Lifestyles congruent with crime are varied but share at least one thing in common; all maintain that one is justified in violating the law. Whether people excuse their actions as necessary or rationalize them afterward as inevitable, those who commit crime believe that their version of reality is accurate and so rest comfortably in the knowledge that their behavior is justified. When working with clients, it is accordingly crucial that we highlight personal accountability, self-competence, cognitive complexity, and one's obligation to the larger community. It is difficult to ignore responsibility, confidence, meaning, and community as core elements of change when attempting to convert belief systems congruent with crime into belief systems incongruent with crime for they speak to the centrality of perception in lifestyle development and change. As I have come to realize after two decades of working with criminal offenders, perception is the key to understanding crime in that seeing is believing and believing is seeing; all else is illusion.

References

Abe, J. A., & Izard, C. E. (1999). The developmental functions of emotion: An analysis in terms of differential emotions theory. *Cognition and Emotion, 13*, 523–549.

Abel, G. G., Becker, J. V., Cunningham-Rathner, J. (1984). Complication, consent, and cognitions in sex between children and adults. *International Journal of Law and Psychiatry, 7*, 89–103.

Abel, G. G., Becker, J. V., Cunningham-Rathner, J., Mittelman, M., & Rouleau, J. L. (1988). Multiple paraphiliac diagnoses among sex offenders. *Bulletin of the American Academy of Psychiatry and Law, 16*, 153–168.

Abel, G. G., & Rouleau, J.-L. (1990). The nature and extent of sexual assault. In W. L. Marshall, D. R. Laws, & H. E. Barbaree (Eds.), *Handbook of sexual assault: Issues, theories, and treatment of the offender* (pp. 9–21). New York: Plenum.

Adams, M. S. (1996). Labeling and differential association: Towards a general social learning theory of crime and deviance. *American Journal of Criminal Justice, 20*, 147–164.

Adamson, L. B., & Bakeman, R. (1985). Affect and attention: Infants observed with mothers and peers. *Child Development, 56*, 582–593.

Adler, A. (1927). *The practice and theory of individual psychology*. New York: Harcourt, Brace, & World.

Adler, F. (1975). *Sisters in crime: The rise of the new female criminal*. New York: McGraw-Hill.

Adler, F. (1983). *Nations not obsessed with crime*. Littleton, CO: Fred B. Rothman.

Adler, P. A. (1993). *Wheeling and dealing: An ethnography of an upper-level drug dealing and smuggling community* (2nd ed.). New York: Columbia University Press.

Agnew, R. (1985). A revised strain theory of delinquency. *Social Forces, 64*, 151–167.

Agnew, R. (1990). The origins of delinquent events: An examination of offender accounts. *Journal of Research in Crime and Delinquency, 27*, 267–294.

Agnew, R. (1992). Foundations for a general strain theory of crime and delinquency. *Criminology, 30*, 47–87.

Agnew, R. (1993). Why do they do it? An examination of the intervening mechanisms between "social control" variables and delinquency. *Journal of Research in Crime and Delinquency, 30*, 245–266.

Agnew, R. (1994). The techniques of neutralization and violence. *Criminology, 32*, 555–580.

Agnew, R., & Brezina, T. (1997). Relational problems with peers, gender, and delinquency. *Youth and Society, 29*, 84–111.

Agnew, R., Cullen, F. T., Burton, V. S., Evans, T. D., & Dunaway, R. G. (1996). A new test of classic strain theory. *Justice Quarterly, 13*, 681–704.

Agnew, R., & Peters, A. A. (1986). The techniques of neutralization: An analysis of predisposing and situational factors. *Criminal Justice and Behavior, 13*, 81–97.

Agnew, R., & White, H. R. (1992). An empirical test of general strain theory. *Criminology, 30*, 475–499.

Agrawal, M., & Dalal, A. K. (1993). Beliefs about the world and recovery from myocardial infarction. *Journal of Social Psychology, 133*, 385–394.

Ainsworth, M.D.S. (1979). Infant–mother attachment. *American Psychologist, 34*, 932–937.

Ainsworth, M.D.S. (1989). Attachments beyond infancy. *American Psychologist, 44*, 709–716.

Ainsworth, M.D.S., Blehar, M., Waters, E., & Wall, S. (1978). *Patterns of attachment.* Hillsdale, NJ: Erlbaum.

Akers, R. L. (1977). *Deviant behavior: A social learning approach* (2nd ed.). Belmont, CA: Wadsworth.

Akers, R. L. (1991). Self-control as a general theory of crime. *Journal of Quantitative Criminology, 7*, 201–211.

Akers, R. L. (1994). *Criminological theories: Introduction and evaluation.* Los Angeles: Roxbury.

Akers, R. L. (1998). *Social learning and social structure: A general theory of crime and deviance.* Boston: Northeastern University Press.

Akers, R. L., Krohn, M. D., Lanza-Kaduce, L., & Radosevich, M. (1979). Social learning and deviant behavior: A special test of a general theory. *American Sociological Review, 44*, 636–655.

Akers, R. L., LaGreca, A., Cohran, J., & Sellers, C. (1989). Social learning theory and alcohol behavior among the elderly. *Sociological Quarterly, 30*, 625–638.

Alarid, L. F., Burton, V. S., & Cullen, F. T. (2000). Gender and crime among felony offenders: Assessing the generality of social control and differential association theories. *Journal of Research in Crime and Delinquency, 37*, 171–199.

Alexander, P. C. (1992). Applications of attachment theory to the study of sexual abuse. *Journal of Consulting and Clinical Psychology, 60*, 185–195.

Alexander, R., Jr. (1997). Reconstructing sex offenders as mentally ill: A labeling explanation. *Journal of Sociology and Social Welfare, 24*, 65–76.

Aljazireh, L. (1993). Historical, environmental, and behavioral correlates of sexual offending by male adolescents: A critical review. *Behavioral Science and the Law, 11*, 423–440.

Allen, C. M., & Pothast, H. L. (1994). Distinguishing characteristics of male and female child sex abusers. *Journal of Offender Rehabilitation, 21*, 73–88.

Allen, G. F. (1987). Where are we going in criminal justice? Some insights from the Chinese criminal justice system. *International Journal of Offender Therapy and Comparative Criminology, 31*, 101–110.

Allen, J. P., Leadbeater, B. J., & Aber, J. L. (1990). The relationship of adolescents' expectations and values to delinquency, hard drug use, and unprotected sexual intercourse. *Development and Psychopathology, 2*, 85–98.

Allport, G. (1961). *Pattern and growth in personality.* New York: Holt, Rinehart, & Winston.
Al-Talib, N., & Griffin, C. (1994). Labelling effect on adolescents' self-concept. *International Journal of Offender Therapy and Comparative Criminology, 38,* 47–57.
Altemeyer, B. (1988). Marching in step: A psychological explanation of state terror. *The Sciences, 28,* 30–38.
Anderson, C. A. (1987). Temperature and aggression: Effects on quarterly, yearly, and city rates of violent and nonviolent crime. *Journal of Personality and Social Psychology, 52,* 1161–1173.
Anderson, D. A. (1994). Transcendence and relinquishment in couple therapy. *Journal of Systemic Therapies, 13,* 36–41.
Anderson, S. M., Glassman, N. S., & Gold, D. A. (1998). Mental representations of the self, significant others, and nonsignificant others: Structure and processing of private and public aspects. *Journal of Personality and Social Psychology, 75,* 845–861.
Andrews, D. A., Zinger, I., Hoge, R. D., Bonta, J., Gendreau, P., & Cullen, F. T. (1990). Does correctional treatment work? A clinically-relevant and psychologically-informed meta-analysis. *Criminology, 28,* 369–404.
Andrews, J. H. (1994. August). Health-industry fraud eats up billions yearly. *Christian Science Monitor, 4,* p. 3.
Anglin, M. D., Brecht, M. L., Woodward, J. A., & Bonett, D. G. (1986). An empirical study of maturing out: Conditional factors. *International Journal of the Addictions, 21,* 233–246.
Anglin, M. D., & Speckart, G. (1988). Narcotics use and crime: A multisample, multimethod analysis. *Criminology, 26,* 197–234.
Antonowicz, D. H., & Ross, R. R. (1994). Essential components of successful rehabilitation programs for offenders. *International Journal of Offender Therapy and Comparative Criminology, 38,* 98–104.
Ardila, A., Pineda, D., & Rosselli, M. (2000). Correlation between intelligence test scores and executive function measures. *Archives of Clinical Neuropsychology, 15,* 31–36.
Arnett, J. J. (2000). High hopes in a grim world: Emerging adults' views of their futures and "Generation X." *Youth and Society, 31,* 267–286.
Arnkelsson, G. B., & Smith, W. P. (2000). The impact of stable and unstable attributes on ability assessment in social comparison. *Personality and Social Psychology Bulletin, 26,* 936–947.
Astington, J. W., & Jenkins, J. M. (1999). A longitudinal study of the relation between language and theory-of-mind development. *Developmental Psychology, 35,* 1311–1320.
Ayers, C. D., Williams, J. H., Hawkins, J. D., Peterson, P. L., Catalano, R. F., & Abbott, R. D. (1999). Assessing correlates of onset, escalation, deescalation, and desistance of delinquent behavior. *Journal of Quantitative Criminology, 15,* 277–306.
Babbage, D. R., & Ronan, K. R. (2000). Philosophical worldview and personality factors in traditional and social scientists: Studying the world in our own image. *Personality and Individual Differences, 28,* 405–420.
Badenes, L. V., Estevan, R.A.C., & Bacete, F.J.G. (2000). Theory of mind and peer rejection at school. *Social Development, 9,* 271–283.
Bahr, S. J. (1979). Family determinants and effects of deviance. In W. R. Burr, R. Hill, F. I. Nye, & I. L. Reiss (Eds.), *Contemporary theories about the family: Volume I. Research-based theories* (pp. 615–643). New York: Free Press.
Bakeman, R., & Adamson, L. B. (1986). Infants' conventionalized acts: Gestures and

words with mothers and peers. *Infant Behavior and Development, 9,* 215–230.
Baker, L. A., Vernon, P. O., & Ho, H. Z. (1991). The genetic correlation between intelligence and speed of information processing. *Behavior Genetics, 21,* 351–367.
Baldwin, M. W. (1992). Relational schemas and the processing of social information. *Psychological Bulletin, 112,* 461–484.
Ball, R. A. (1977). Emergent delinquency in a rurban area. In T. N. Ferdinand (Ed.), *Juvenile delinquency: Little brother grows up* (pp. 101–120). Beverly Hills, CA: Sage.
Ball, R. A. (1983). Development of basic norm violation. *Criminology, 21,* 75–94.
Ball, R. A., & Lilly, J. R. (1971). Juvenile delinquency in a rurban county. *Criminology, 9,* 69–85.
Ball-Rokeach, S. J. (1973). Values and violence: A test of the sub-culture of violence thesis. *American Sociological Review, 38,* 736–749.
Bandura, A. (1986). *Social foundations of thought and action: A social cognitive theory.* Englewood Cliffs, NJ: Prentice-Hall.
Bandura, A. (1997). *Self-efficacy.* New York: Freeman.
Barak, G. (1998). *Integrating criminologies.* Boston: Allyn & Bacon.
Barbaree, H. E., & Marshall, W. L. (1991). The role of male sexual assault in rape: Six models. *Journal of Consulting and Clinical Psychology, 59,* 621–630.
Barber, N. (2000). The sex ratio as a predictor of cross-national variation in violent crime. *Cross-Cultural Research, 34,* 264–282.
Barriga, A. Q., Landau, J. R., Stinson, B. L., Liau, A. K., & Gibbs, J. C. (2000). Cognitive distortion and problem behaviors in adolescents. *Criminal Justice and Behavior, 27,* 36–56.
Bartholomew, K. (1990). Avoidance of intimacy: An attachment perspective. *Journal of Social and Personal Relationships, 7,* 147–178.
Bartsch, K., & Wellman, H. M. (1995). *Children talk about mind.* New York: Oxford University Press.
Bartusch, D. J., & Matsueda, R. L. (1996). Gender, reflected appraisals, and labeling: A cross-group test of an interactionist theory of delinquency. *Social Forces, 75,* 145–177.
Bates, J. E., Maslin, C. A., & Frankel, K. A. (1985). Attachment security, mother–child interaction, and temperament as predictors of behavior-problem ratings at age three years. *Monographs of the Society for Research in Child Development, 50* (1–2, Serial No. 209).
Baucus, M. (1994). Pressure, opportunity and predisposition: A multivariate model of corporate illegality. *Journal of Management, 20,* 699–721.
Bauman, K. E., & Ennett, S. T. (1994). Peer influence on adolescent drug use. *American Psychologist, 49,* 820–822.
Baumeister, R. F. (1990). Suicide as escape from self. *Psychological Review, 97,* 90–113.
Baumeister, R. F., & Leary, M. R. (1995). The need to belong: Desires for interpersonal attachments as a fundamental human motivation. *Psychological Bulletin, 117,* 497–529.
Baumeister, R. F., Smart, L., & Boden, J. M. (1996). Relation of threatened egotism to violence and aggression: The dark side of high self-esteem. *Psychological Review, 103,* 5–33.
Beatty, M. J., & Payne, S. K. (1984). Listening comprehension as a function of cognitive complexity: A research note. *Communication Monographs, 51,* 85–89.
Beck, A. T., Wright, F. D., Newman, C. F., & Liese, B. S. (1993). *Cognitive therapy of substance abuse.* New York: Guilford.

Becker, G. S. (1968). Crime and punishment: An economic approach. *Journal of Political Economy, 76,* 169–217.
Becker, H. K., Felkenes, G. T., Magaña, L., & Huntley, J. (1997). A socioeconomic comparison of drug sales by Mexican-American and Mexican immigrant male gang members. *Journal of Gang Research, 4,* 37–47.
Becker, H. S. (1963). *Outsiders: Studies in the sociology of deviance.* New York: Free Press.
Becker, J. V. (1988). Adolescent sex offenders. *Behavior Therapist, 11,* 185–187.
Becker, J. V., Alpert, J. L., Bigfoot, D. S., Bonner, B. L., Geddie, L. F., Henggeler, S. W., Kaufman, K. L., & Walker, C. E. (1995). Empirical research on child abuse treatment: Report by the child abuse and neglect treatment working group, American Psychological Association. *Journal of Clinical Child Psychology, 24,* 23–46.
Beckett, R., Beech, A., Fisher, D., & Fordham, A. S. (1994). *Community-based treatment for sex offenders: An evaluation of seven treatment programs.* London: HMSO.
Bègue, L., & Fumey, V. (2000). Belief in a just world or self-serving strategy? *Social Behavior and Personality, 28,* 119–124.
Bell, R. Q. (1990). Neonatal behavior predictors of security of attachment. *Research and Clinical Center for Child Development, 12,* 3–13.
Bellah, R. N., Madsen, R., Sullivan, W. M., Swidler, A., & Tipton, S. M. (1985). *Habits of the heart.* Berkeley: University of California Press.
Bem, S. L. (1981). *Bem Sex-Role Inventory manual.* Palo Alto, CA: Mind Garden.
Benard, B. (1993, September). Resiliency paradigm validates craft knowledge. *Western Center News,* pp. 5–7.
Benda, B. B. (1997). An examination of a reciprocal relationship between religiosity and different forms of delinquency within a theoretical model. *Journal of Research in Crime and Delinquency, 34,* 163–186.
Benda, B. B., & Whiteside, L. (1995). Testing an integrated model of delinquency using LISREL. *Journal of Social Service Research, 21,* 1–32.
Bengtsson, H., & Johnson, L. (1992). Perspective taking, empathy, and prosocial behavior in late childhood. *Child Study Journal, 22,* 11–22.
Benn, R. K. (1986). Factors promoting secure attachment relationships between employed mothers and their sons. *Child Development, 57,* 1224–1231.
Benson, M. L. (1985). Denying the guilty mind: Accounting for involvement in a white-collar crime. *Criminology, 23,* 583–607.
Benson, M. L. (1989). The influence of class position on the formal and informal sanctioning of white-collar offenders. *Sociological Quarterly, 30,* 465–479.
Benson, M. L., & Moore, E. (1992). Are white-collar and common offenders the same? An empirical and theoretical critique of a recently proposed general theory of crime. *Journal of Research in Crime and Delinquency, 29,* 251–272.
Benson, P. L. (1997). *All kids are our kids: What communities must do to raise caring and responsible children and adolescents.* San Francisco: Jossey-Bass.
Berk, L. E. (1986). Relationship of elementary school children's private speech to behavioral accompaniment to task, attention, and task performance. *Developmental Psychology, 22,* 671–680.
Berk, L. E. (1992). Private speech: An overview of theory and the status of research. In R. M. Diaz & L. E. Berk (Eds.), *Private speech: From social interaction to self-regulation* (pp. 17-53). Hillsdale, NJ: Erlbaum.
Berk, L. E., & Garvin, R. A. (1984). Development of private speech among low-income Appalachian children. *Developmental Psychology, 20,* 271–286.

Berk, L. E., & Landau, S. (1997, April). *Private speech in the face of academic challenge: The failure of impulsive children to "get their act together."* Paper presented at the biennial meeting of the Society for Research in Child Development, Washington, DC.

Berk, L. E., & Potts, M. K. (1991). Development and functional significance of private speech among attention-deficit hyperactivity disordered and normal boys. *Journal of Abnormal Child Psychology, 19*, 357–377.

Berk, L. E., & Spuhl, S. T. (1995). Maternal interaction, private speech, and task performance in preschool children. *Early Childhood Research Quarterly, 10*, 145–169.

Berk, L. E., & Winsler, A. (1995). *Scaffolding children's learning: Vygotsky and early childhood education.* Washington, DC: National Association for the Education of Young Children.

Berkowitz, L. (1994). Guns and youth. In L. D. Eron, J. H. Gentry, & P. Schlegel (Eds.), *Reason to hope: A psychosocial perspective on violence and youth* (pp. 251–279). Washington, DC: American Psychological Association.

Bernard, T. J. (1987). Structure and control: Reconsidering Hirschi's concept of commitment. *Justice Quarterly, 44*, 409–424.

Bernburg, J. G., & Thorlindsson, T. (1999). Adolescent violence, social control, and the subculture of delinquency: Factors related to violent behavior and nonviolent delinquency. *Youth and Society, 30*, 445–460.

Berne, E. (1964). *Games people play.* New York: Grove.

Bigner, J. J. (1994). *Individual and family development: A life-span interdisciplinary approach.* Englewood Cliffs, NJ: Prentice-Hall.

Bjorkvist, K., Lagerspetz, K.M.J., & Kaukiainen, A. (1992). Do girls manipulate and boys fight? Developmental trends in regard to direct and indirect aggression. *Aggressive Behavior, 18*, 117–127.

Blachowicz, J. (1998). *Of two minds: The nature of inquiry.* Albany: State University of New York Press.

Blackford, J. U., & Walden, T. A. (1998). Individual differences in social referencing. *Infant Behavior and Development, 21*, 89–102.

Blair, R.J.R., Sellars, C., Strickland, I., Clark, F., Williams, A. O., Smith, M., & James, L. (1996). Theory of mind in the psychopath. *Journal of Forensic Psychiatry, 7*, 15–25.

Blaske, D. M., Borduin, C. M., Henggeler, S. W., & Mann, B. J. (1989). Individual, family and peer characteristics of adolescent sex offenders and assaultive offenders. *Developmental Psychology, 25*, 846–855.

Blumenthal, S., Gudjonsson, G., & Burns, J. (1999). Cognitive distortions and blame attribution in sex offenders against adults and children. *Child Abuse and Neglect, 23*, 129–143.

Blumstein, A., Cohen, J., & Farrington, D. P. (1988). Criminal career research: Its value for criminology. *Criminology, 26*, 1–35.

Blumstein, A., Farrington, D. P., & Moitra, S. (1985). Delinquency careers: Innocents, desisters, and persisters. In M. Tonry & N. Morris (Eds.), *Crime and justice: An annual review of research* (Vol. 6, pp. 187–219). Chicago: University of Chicago Press.

Boccia, M., & Campos, J. J. (1989). Maternal emotional signals, social referencing, and infants' reactions to strangers. *New Directions for Child Development, 44*, 25–49.

Boehnke, K., Hagan, J., & Merkens, H. (1998). Right-wing extremism among German adolescents: Risk factors and protective factors. *Applied Psychology: An International Review, 47*, 109–126.

Boeringer, S., Shehan, C. L., & Akers, R. L. (1991). Social contexts and social learning in sexual coercion and aggression: Assessing the contribution of fraternity membership.

Family Relations, 40, 558–564.

Boldizar, J. B., Perry, D. G., & Perry, L. C. (1989). Outcome values and aggression. *Child Development, 60*, 571–579.

Born, M., Chevalier, V., & Humblet, I. (1997). Resilience, desistance and delinquent career of adolescent offenders. *Journal of Adolescence, 20*, 679–694.

Borod, J. C., Pick, L. H., Hall, S., Sliwinski, M., Madigan, N., Obler, L., K., Welkowitz, J., Canino, E., Erhan, H. M., Goral, M., Morrison, C., & Talbert, M. (2000). Relationships among facial, prosodic, and lexical channels of emotional perceptual processing. *Cognition and Emotion, 14*, 193–211.

Boss, M. (1963). *Psychoanalysis and daseinanalysis*. New York: Basic Books.

Bowlby, J. (1980). *Attachment and loss: Vol. 3. Loss, sadness, and depression*. New York: Basic Books.

Bowlby, J. (1982). *Attachment and loss: Vol. 1. Attachment*. New York: Basic Books. (Original work published 1969)

Bradshaw, D. L., Goldsmith, H. H., & Campos, J. J. (1987). Attachment, temperament, and social referencing: Interrelationships among three domains of infant affective behavior. *Infant Behavior and Development, 10*, 223–231.

Braithwaite, J. (1989). Criminological theory and organizational crime. *Justice Quarterly, 6*, 333–358.

Bretherton, I. (1991). Intentional communication and development of an understanding of mind. In D. Frye & C. Moore (Eds.), *Children's theories of mind: Mental states and social understanding* (pp. 49–75). Hillsdale, NJ: Erlbaum.

Brewer, B. W. (1993). Self-identity and specific vulnerability to depressed mood. *Journal of Personality, 61*, 343–364.

Brezina, T. (1996). Adapting to strain: An examination of delinquent coping responses. *Criminology, 34*, 39–60.

Brezina, T. (1999). Teenage violence toward parents as an adaptation to family strain: Evidence from a national survey of male adolescents. *Youth and Society, 30*, 416–444.

Brisman, J., & Siegel, M. (1985). The bulimia workshop: A unique integration of group treatment approaches. *International Journal of Group Psychotherapy, 35*, 585–601.

Brown, H. J., & Gutsch, K. V. (1985). Cognitions associated with a delay of gratification task: A study with psychopaths and normal prisoners. *Criminal Justice and Behavior, 12*, 453–462.

Brown, J., & Smart, S. A. (1991). The self and social conduct: Linking self-representations to prosocial behavior. *Journal of Personality and Social Psychology, 60*, 368–375.

Brown, J. R., Doneland-McCall, N., & Dunn, J. (1996). Why talk about mental states? The significance of children's conversations with friends, siblings, and mothers. *Child Development, 67*, 836–849.

Brown, P., Keenan, J. M., & Potts, G. R. (1986). The self-reference effect with imagery encoding. *Journal of Personality and Social Psychology, 51*, 897–906.

Brownfield, D., & Sorenson, A. M. (1993). Self-control and juvenile delinquency: Theoretical issues and an empirical assessment of selected elements of a general theory of crime. *Deviant Behavior, 14*, 243–264.

Brownsberger, W. N. (2000). Race matters: Disproportionality of incarceration for drug dealing in Massachusetts. *Journal of Drug Issues, 30*, 345–374.

Bruhn, A. R., & Davidow, S. (1983). Earliest memories and the dynamics of delinquency. *Journal of Personality Assessment, 47*, 476–482.

Bumby, K. M. (1996). Assessing the cognitive distortions of child molesters and rapists: Development and validation of the MOLEST and RAPE scales. *Sexual Abuse: A*

Journal of Research and Treatment, 8, 37–54.

Bumby, K. M., & Marshall, W. L. (1994, October). *Loneliness and intimacy deficits among incarcerated rapists and child molesters.* Paper presented at the 13th annual research and treatment conference of the Association for the Treatment of Sexual Abusers, San Francisco, CA.

Bureau of Justice Statistics. (1990). *Sourcebook of criminal justice statistics—1989.* Washington, DC: U.S. Department of Justice.

Bureau of Justice Statistics. (1994). *The world factbook of criminal justice systems.* Washington, DC: U.S. Department of Justice.

Bureau of Justice Statistics. (1999). *Sourcebook of criminal justice statistics—1998.* Washington, DC: U.S. Department of Justice.

Bureau of Justice Statistics. (2000a, May). *Compendium of federal justice statistics, 1998* (NCJ 180258). Washington, DC: U.S. Department of Justice.

Bureau of Justice Statistics. (2000b, August). *Prisoners in 1999* (NCJ 183476). Washington, DC: U.S. Department of Justice.

Burkett, S. R., & Warren, B. O. (1987). Religiosity, peer associations, and adolescent marijuana abuse: A panel study of underlying causal structures. *Criminology, 25,* 109–131.

Burt, M. (1983). Justifying personal violence: A comparison of rapists and the general public. *Victimology, 8,* 131–150.

Burton, V. S., Cullen, F. T., Evans, T. D., & Dunaway, R. G. (1994). Reconsidering strain theory: Operationalism, rival theories, and adult criminality. *Journal of Quantitative Criminology, 10,* 213–239.

Bush, P. J., & Iannotti, R. J. (1993). Alcohol, cigarette, and marijuana use among fourth-grade urban school children in 1988/89 and 1990/91. *American Journal of Public Health, 83,* 111–114.

Bush, P. J., & Iannott, R. J. (1994, April). *Drug sales involvement in early adolescence.* Paper presented at the meeting of the Society for Behavioral Medicine, Boston.

Bush, P. J., & Weinfurt, K. P. (1994, October/November). *Early adolescents' participation in drug sales after being asked.* Paper presented at the annual meeting of the American Public Health Association, Washington, DC.

Bushman, B. J., & Cooper, H. M. (1990). Effects of alcohol on human aggression: An integrated research review. *Psychological Bulletin, 107,* 341–354.

Buss, A. N., & Plomin, R. (1984). *Temperament: Early developing personality traits.* Hillsdale, NJ: Erlbaum.

Butterworth, G., & Grover, L. (1990). Joint visual attention, manual pointing, and preverbal communication in human infancy. In M. Jeannerod (Ed.), *Attention and performance: XIII. Motor representation and control* (pp. 605–624). Hillsdale, NJ: Erlbaum.

Bynner, J. M., O'Malley, P. M., & Bachman, J. G. (1981). Self esteem and delinquency revisited. *Journal of Youth and Adolescence, 10,* 407–441.

Cadesky, E. B., Mota, V. L., & Schachar, R. J. (2000). Beyond words: How do children with ADHD and/or conduct problems process nonverbal information about affect? *Journal of the American Academy of Child and Adolescent Psychiatry, 39,* 1160–1167.

Cadinu, M. R., & Kiesner, J. (2000). Children's development of a theory of mind. *European Journal of Psychology of Education, 15,* 93–111.

Calavita, K., & Pontell, H. N. (1991). "Other people's money" revisited: Collective embezzlement in the savings and loan and insurance industries. *Social Problems, 38,* 94–112.

Calhoun, L. G., Cann, A., Tedeschi, R. G., & McMillan, J. (1998). Traumatic events and generational differences in assumptions about a just world. *Journal of Social Psychology, 138,* 789–791.

Campbell, A., Bibel, D., & Muncer, S. (1985). Predicting our own aggression: Person, subculture, or situation? *British Journal of Social Psychology, 24,* 169–180.

Campbell, C. S., MacKenzie, D. L., & Robinson, J. W. (1987). Female offenders: Criminal behavior and gender-role identity. *Psychological Reports, 60,* 867–873.

Canfield, R. L., Smith, E. G., Brezsynak, M. P., & Snow, K. L. (1997). Information processing through the first year of life: A longitudinal study using the visceral expectation paradigm. *Monographs on Social Research in Child Development, 62,* 1–145.

Cantor, N., Mischel, W., & Schwartz, J. (1982). A prototype analysis of psychological situations. *Cognitive Psychology, 14,* 45–77.

Caporael, L. R. (1997). The evolution of truly social cognition: The core configurations model. *Personality and Social Psychology Review, 1,* 276–298.

Carpenter, M., Nagell, K., & Tomasello, M. (1998). Social cognition, joint attention, and communicative competence from 9 to 15 months of age. *Monographs of the Society for Research in Child Development, 63(4),* Serial No. 255.

Carroll, J. S., & Weaver, F. (1986). Shoplifters' perceptions of crime opportunities: A process-tracing study. In D. B. Cornish & R. V. Clarke (Eds.), *The reasoning criminal: Rational choice perspectives on offending* (pp. 19–38). New York: Springer-Verlag.

Caspi, A., Elder, G. H., & Bem, D. J. (1987). Moving against the world: Life-course patterns of explosive children. *Developmental Psychology, 23,* 308–313.

Caspi, A., Elder, G. H., & Bem, D. J. (1988). Moving away from the world: Life-course patterns of shy children. *Developmental Psychology, 24,* 824–831.

Caspi, A., & Moffitt, T. E. (1993). When do individual differences matter? A paradoxical theory of personality coherence. *Psychological Inquiry, 4,* 247–271.

Caspi, A., Moffitt, T. E., Silva, P. A., Stouthamer-Loeber, M., Krueger, R. F., & Schmutte, P. S. (1994). Are some people crime prone? Replications of the personality-crime relationship across countries, genders, races, and methods. *Criminology, 32,* 163–195.

Cast, A. D., Stets, J. E., & Burke, P. J. (1999). Does the self conform to the views of others? *Social Psychology Quarterly, 62,* 68–82.

Catrambone, R., & Markus, H. (1987). The role of self-schemas in going beyond the information given. *Social Cognition, 5,* 349–368.

Cernkovich, S. A., Giordano, P. C., & Rudolph, J. L. (2000). Race, crime, and the American dream. *Journal of Research in Crime and Delinquency, 37,* 131–170.

Chao, R. K. (1995). Chinese and European American cultural models of the self reflected in mothers' childrearing beliefs. *Ethos, 23,* 328–354.

Chapell, M. S., & Takahashi, M. (1998). Differences in worldview of Japanese and Americans in young, middle-aged, and older cohorts. *Psychological Reports, 83,* 659–665.

Chassin, L., & Stager, S. F. (1984). Determinants of self-esteem among incarcerated delinquents. *Social Psychology Quarterly, 47,* 382–390.

Check, J. V. P., & Malamuth, N. M. (1983). Sex role stereotyping and reactions to depictions of stranger versus acquaintance rape. *Journal of Personality and Social Psychology, 45,* 344–356.

Cherek, D. R., Moeller, F. G., Dougherty, D. M., & Rhoades, H. (1997). Studies of violent and nonviolent male parolees: II. Laboratory and psychometric measurements of impulsivity. *Biological Psychiatry, 41,* 523–529.

Chomsky, N. (1968). *Language and mind.* New York: Harcourt Brace Jovanovich.

Cimler, E., & Beach, L. R. (1981). Factors involved in juveniles' decisions about crime. *Criminal Justice and Behavior, 8*, 275–286.
Clark, J. P., & Hollinger, R. C. (1983). *Theft by employees in work organizations*. Washington, DC: National Institute of Justice.
Clark, L. F. (1993). Stress and the cognitive-conversational benefits of social interaction. *Journal of Social and Clinical Psychology, 12*, 25–55.
Clarke, R. V., & Cornish, D. B. (1985). Modeling offenders' decisions: A framework for research and policy. In M. Tonry & N. Morris (Eds.), *Crime and justice: An annual review of research* (Vol. 6, pp. 147–185). Chicago: University of Chicago Press.
Clinard, M., & Quinney, R. (1986). *Criminal behavior systems: A typology*. Cincinnati, OH: Anderson.
Cloninger, C. R. (1987). A systematic method for clinical description and classification of personality variants. *Archives of General Psychiatry, 44*, 573–588.
Cloninger, C. R., Sigvardsson, S., & Bohman, M. (1988). Childhood personality predicts alcohol abuse in young adults. *Alcoholism: Clinical and Experimental Research, 12*, 494–505.
Cloward, R. A., & Ohlin, L. E. (1960). *Delinquency and opportunity*. New York: Free Press.
Cohen, A. K. (1955). *Delinquent boys*. New York: Free Press.
Coie, J. D., & Dodge, K. A. (1997). Aggression and antisocial behavior. In W. Damon & N. Eisenberg (Eds.), *Handbook of child psychology, Vol. 3: Social, emotional and personality development* (5th ed., pp. 779–862). New York: Wiley.
Coleman, J. W. (1987). Toward an integrated theory of white-collar crime. *American Journal of Sociology, 93*, 406–439.
Coleman, J. W. (1992). Crime and money: Motivation and opportunity in a monetarized economy. *American Behavioral Scientist, 35*, 827–836.
Coleman, J. W. (1994). *The criminal elite: The sociology of white collar crime* (3rd ed.). New York: St. Martin's Press.
Collins, J. M., & Schmidt, F. L. (1993). Personality, integrity, and white collar crime: A construct validity study. *Personnel Psychology, 46*, 295–311.
Collins, M. D. (1995). Neutralization theory: An empirical application and assessment (Doctoral dissertation, Oklahoma State University, 1994). *Dissertation Abstracts International, 56A*, 1531.
Collison, M. (1996). In search of the high life: Drugs, crime, masculinities, and consumption. *British Journal of Criminology, 36*, 428–444.
Colvin, M., & Pauly, J. (1983). A critique of criminology: Toward an integrated structural-Marxist theory of delinquency production. *American Journal of Sociology, 89*, 513–551.
Condy, S. R., Templer, D. I., Brown, R., & Veaco, L. (1987). Parameters of sexual contact of boys with women. *Archives of Sexual Behavior, 16*, 379–394.
Conners, J., & Heaven, P. C. (1990). Belief in a just world and attitudes toward AIDS sufferers. *Journal of Social Psychology, 130*, 559–560.
Cooley, C. H. (1964). *Human nature and the social order*. New York: Schocken. (Original work published 1902)
Copello, A. G., & Tata, P. R. (1990). Violent behaviour and interpretative bias: An experimental study of the resolution of ambiguity in violent offenders. *British Journal of Clinical Psychology, 29*, 417–428.
Costello, B. J. (1997). On the logical adequacy of cultural deviance theories. *Theoretical Criminology, 1*, 403–428.

Costello, B. J. (2000). Techniques of neutralization and self-esteem: A critical test of social control and neutralization theory. *Deviant Behavior, 21*, 307–329.
Cowen, E. L., Wyman, P. A., & Work, W. C. (1992). The relationship between retrospective reports of early child temperament and adjustment at ages 10–12. *Journal of Abnormal Child Psychology, 20*, 39–50.
Crane-Ross, D., Tisak, M. S., & Tisak, J. (1998). Aggression and conventional rule violation among adolescents: Social-reasoning predictors of social behavior. *Aggressive Behavior, 24*, 347–365.
Crawford, P. A., & Hade, D. H. (2000). Inside the picture, outside the frame: Semiotics and the reading of wordless picture books. *Journal of Research in Childhood Education, 15*, 66–80.
Cressey, D. R. (1971). *Other people's money: A study in social psychology of embezzlement*. Belmont, MA: Wadsworth. (Original work published 1953)
Crick, N. R. (1995). Relational aggression: The role of intent attributions, feelings of distress, and provocation type. *Developmental Psychopathology, 7*, 313–322.
Crick, N. R., & Dodge, K. A. (1994). A review and reformulation of social information-processing mechanisms in children's social adjustment. *Psychological Bulletin, 115*, 74–101.
Croall, H. (1989). Who is the white-collar criminal? *British Journal of Criminology, 29*, 157–174.
Cullen, F. T., Link, B. G., & Polanzi, C. W. (1982). The seriousness of crime revisited? *Criminology, 20*, 83–102.
Curcione, N. (1997). Suburban snowmen: Facilitating factors in the careers of middle-class coke dealers. *Deviant Behavior, 18*, 233–253.
Curran, D. J., & Renzetti, C. M. (1994). *Theories of crime*. Boston: Allyn & Bacon.
Curtis, L. A. (1975). *Violence, race, and crime*. Lexington, MA: D. C. Heath.
Cusson, M., & Pinsonneault, P. (1986). The decision to give up crime. In D. Cornish & R. Clarke (Eds.), *The reasoning criminal: Rational choice perspectives on offending* (pp. 72–82). New York: Springer-Verlag.
Cutting, A. L., & Dunn, J. (1999). Theory of mind, emotion understanding, language, and family background: Individual differences and interrelations. *Child Development, 70*, 853–865.
Dabney, D. (1995). Neutralization and deviance in the workplace: Theft of supplies and medicine by hospital nurses. *Deviant Behavior, 16*, 313–331.
Daly, K. (1989). Gender and varieties of white-collar crime. *Criminology, 27*, 769–794.
Daniels, D., & Plomin, R. (1985). Origins of individual differences in infant shyness. *Developmental Psychology, 21*, 118–121.
Darke, J. L. (1990). Sexual aggression: Achieving power through humiliation. In W. L. Marshall, D. R. Laws, & H. E. Barbaree (Eds.), *Handbook of sexual assault: Issues, theories, and treatment of the offender* (pp. 55–72). New York: Plenum.
Darkes, J., & Goldman, M. S. (1993). Expectancy challenge and drinking reduction: Experimental evidence for a mediational process. *Journal of Consulting and Clinical Psychology, 61*, 344–353.
Daugherty, M., White, C. S., & Manning, B. H. (1994). Relationship among private speech and creativity measurements of young children. *Gifted Child Quarterly, 38*, 21–26.
Davidow, S., & Bruhn, A. R. (1990). Earliest memories and the dynamics of delinquency: A replication study. *Journal of Personality Assessment, 54*, 601–616.
Davids, A., & Falkof, B. B. (1975). Juvenile delinquents then and now: Comparison of findings from 1959 and 1974. *Journal of Abnormal Psychology, 84*, 161–164.

Davis, M. H., Conklin, L., Smith, A., & Luce, C. (1996). Effect of perspective taking on the cognitive representation of persons. *Journal of Personality and Social Psychology, 70,* 713–726.

Davis, R. A. (1986). Testing Kohn's self-reliance hypothesis among high school adolescents. *Adolescence, 21,* 443–447.

Davison, G. C., Tsujimoto, R., & Glaros, A. (1973). Attribution and the maintenance of behavior change in falling asleep. *Journal of Abnormal Psychology, 82,* 124–135.

Dawkins, M. P. (1997). Drug use and violent crime among adolescents. *Adolescence, 32,* 395–405.

Deaux, K. (1992). Personalizing identity and socializing self. In G. Breakwell (Ed.), *Social psychology of identity and the self-concept* (pp. 9–33). London: Academic Press.

Deci, E., & Ryan, R. (1985). *Intrinsic motivation and self-determination in human behavior.* New York: Plenum.

DeKeseredy, W. S., & Kelly, K. (1995). Sexual abuse in Canadian university and college dating relationships: The contribution of male peer support. *Journal of Family Violence, 10,* 41–53.

de la Ossa, J. L., & Gauvain, M. (2001). Joint attention by mothers and children while using plans. *International Journal of Behavioral Development, 25,* 176–183.

De Li, S., Priú, H. D., & MacKenzie, D. L. (2000). Drug involvement, lifestyles, and criminal activities among probationers. *Journal of Drug Issues, 30,* 593–620.

Dembo, R., Hughes, P., Jackson, L., & Mieczkowski, T. (1993). Crack cocaine dealing by adolescents in two housing projects: A pilot study. *Human Organization, 52,* 89–96.

Deng, X. (1995). Toward a more comprehensive understanding of crime: An integrated model of self-control and rational choice theories (Doctoral dissertation, State University of New York, Buffalo, 1994). *Dissertation Abstracts International, 55A,* 3651.

Dennett, D. (1991). *Consciousness explained.* Boston: Little, Brown.

Denton, B., & O'Malley, P. (1999). Gender, trust, and business. *British Journal of Criminology, 39,* 513–530.

Denton, W. H., Burleson, B. R., & Sprenkle, D. H. (1995). Association of interpersonal cognitive complexity with communication skill in marriage: Moderating effects of marital distress. *Family Process, 34,* 101–111.

Deschenes, E. P., & Esbansen, F.-A. (1999). Violence and gangs: Gender differences in perceptions and behavior. *Journal of Quantitative Criminology, 15,* 63–96.

Desrochers, S., Ricard, M., Décarie, T. G., & Allard, L. (1994). Developmental synchrony between social referencing and Piagetian sensorimotor causality. *Infant Behavior and Development, 17,* 303–309.

de Vries, B., & Lehman, A. J. (1996). The complexity of personal narratives. In J. E. Birren & G. M. Kenyon (Eds.), *Aging and biography: Explorations in adult development* (pp. 149–166). New York: Springer.

Diaz, R. M., & Lowe, J. P. (1987). The private speech of young children at risk: A test of three deficit hypotheses. *Early Childhood Research Quarterly, 2,* 181–194.

Dietz, M. L. (1983). *Killing for profit: The social organization of felony homicide.* Chicago: Nelson-Hall.

Di Fazio, R., Kroner, D. G., & Forth, A. E. (1997). The Attribution Blame Scale with an incarcerated sample: Factor structure, reliability, and validity. *Criminal Behaviour and Mental Health, 7,* 153–164.

Dinovitzer, R. (1997). The myths of rapists and other normal men: The impact of psychiatric considerations on the sentencing of sexual assault offenders. *Canadian*

Journal of Law and Society, 12, 147–169.
Dinwiddie, S., Heath, A. C., Dunne, M. P., Bucholz, K. K., Madden, P. A. F., Slutske, W. S., Bierut, L. J., Statham, D. B., & Martin, N. G. (2000). Early sexual abuse and lifetime psychopathology: A co-twin-control study. *Psychological Medicine, 30*, 41–52.
Dishion, T. J., Patterson, G. R., Stoolmiller, M., & Skinner, M. L. (1991). Family, school, and behavioral antecedents to early adolescent involvement with antisocial peers. *Developmental Psychology, 27*, 172–180.
Dixon, T. M., & Baumeister, R. F. (1991). Escaping the self: The mediating effect of self-complexity. *Personality and Social Psychology Bulletin, 17*, 363–368.
Dodge, K. A. (1993). Social-cognitive mechanisms in the development of conduct disorder and depression. *Annual Review of Psychology, 44*, 559–584.
Dodge, K. A., & Frame, C. M. (1982). Social cognitive biases and deficits in aggressive boys. *Child Development, 53*, 620–635.
Dodge, K. A., Pettit, G. S., McClasky, G. S., & Brown, M. M. (1986). Social competence in children. *Monographs of the Society for Research in Child Development, 51*, 1–85.
Dodge, K. A., Price, J. M., Bachorowski, J., & Newman, J. P. (1990). Hostile attributional biases in severely aggressive adolescents. *Journal of Abnormal Psychology, 99*, 385–392.
Dodge, K. A., & Somberg, D. R. (1987). Hostile attributional biases among aggressive boys are exacerbated under conditions of threat to the self. *Child Development, 58*, 213–224.
Dodge, K. A., & Tomlin, A. (1983). *The role of cue-utilization in attributional biases among aggressive children*. Unpublished manuscript, Indiana University.
Dodge, K. A., & Tomlin, A. (1987). Utilization of self-schemas as a mechanism of interpersonal bias in aggressive children. *Social cognition, 5*, 280–300.
Dolan, B. (1995). The attribution of blame for criminal acts: Relationship with personality disorders and mood. *Criminal Behaviour and Mental Health, 5*, 41–51.
Donnelly, D. A., & Murray, E. J. (1991). Cognitive and emotional change in written essays and therapy interviews. *Journal of Social and Clinical Psychology, 10*, 334–350.
Donziger, S. R. (Ed.). (1996). *The real war on crime: The report of the National Criminal Justice Commission*. New York: Harper Perennial.
Dow, J. (1986). Universal aspects of symbolic healing: A theoretical synthesis. *American Anthropologist, 88*, 56–69.
Doyle, K. (1992). Toward a psychology of money. *American Behavioral Scientist, 35*, 708–724.
Dukes, R. L., & Lorch, B. D. (1989). Concept of self, mediating factors, and adolescence deviance. *Sociological Spectrum, 9*, 309–319.
Duncan, R. D., Kennedy, W. A., & Smith, D. W. (2000). Comparison of conduct-disordered behavior in crack-dealing versus nondealing juvenile offenders. *Psychological Reports, 86*, 1089–1096.
Dunn, J., Brown, J., Slomkowski, C., Tesla, C., & Youngblade, L. (1991). Young children's understanding of other people's feelings and beliefs: Individual differences and their antecedents. *Child Development, 62*, 1352–1366.
Dunn, J., & Kendrick, C. (1982). The speech of two- and three-year-olds to infant siblings: "Baby talk" and the context of communication. *Journal of Child Language, 9*, 579–595.
Durkheim, E. (1938). *The rules of sociological method* (S. A. Soloway & J. H. Mueller, Trans.). New York: Free Press.

Dutton, D. G. (1986). Wife assaulter's explanations for assault: The neutralization of self-punishment. *Canadian Journal of Behavioral Sciences, 18*, 381–390.

Eliason, S. L., & Dodder, R. A. (1999). Techniques of neutralization used by deer poachers in the western United States: A research note. *Deviant Behavior, 20*, 233–252.

Elizur, D. (1979). Values of personal well-being and of harming society among delinquent and non-delinquent youth. *Israel Annals of Psychiatry and Related Disciplines, 17*, 36–44.

Elliott, D. S., Huizinga, D., & Ageton, S. (1985). *Explaining delinquency and drug use.* Beverly Hills, CA: Sage.

Elliott, D. S., Huizinga, D., & Menard, S. (1989). *Multiple problem youth: Delinquency, substance use, and mental health problems.* New York: Springer-Verlag.

Elliott, D. S., Huizinga, D., & Morse, B. (1986). Self-reported violent offending: A descriptive analysis of juvenile violent offenders and their offending careers. *Journal of Interpersonal Violence, 1*, 472–514.

Elliott, D. S., Huizinga, D., & Morse, B. (1988). A career analysis of serious violent offenders. In *Violent crime.* Ann Arbor, MI: Center for the Study of Youth Policy.

Elliott, W. N., Fakouri, M. E., & Hafner, J. L. (1993). Early recollections of criminal offenders. *Individual Psychology, 49*, 68–75.

Ellis, L. (1987). Neurohormonal bases of varying tendencies to learn delinquent and criminal behavior. In E. K. Morris & C. J. Braukman (Eds.), *Behavioral approaches to crime and delinquency* (pp. 499–518). New York: Plenum.

Ellis, L., & Walsh, A. (1999, July/August). Criminologists' opinions about causes and theories of crime and delinquency. *The Criminologist, 24*, 1–6.

Emde, R. N., Biringen, Z., Clyman, R. B., & Oppenheim, D. (1991). The moral self of infancy: Affective care and procedural knowledge. *Developmental Review, 11*, 251–270.

Emler, N., & Reicher, S. (1995). *Adolescence and delinquency: The collective management of reputation.* Oxford, UK: Blackwell.

Empy, L. T., & Stafford, M. C. (1991). *American delinquency: Its meaning and construction* (3rd ed.). Belmont, CA: Wadsworth.

Enright, R. D., Olson, L. M., Ganiere, D., Lapsley, D. K., & Buss, R. R. (1984). A clinical model for enhancing adolescent ego identity. *Journal of Adolescence, 7*, 119–130.

Epstein, S. (1991). The self-concept , the traumatic neurosis, and the structure of personality. In D. Ozer, J. M. Healy, Jr., & A. J. Stewart (Eds.), *Perspectives in personality: Self and emotion* (Vol. 3, pp. 63–98). Greenwich, CT: JAI Press.

Erez, E. (1988). The myth of the new female offender: Some evidence from attitudes toward law and justice. *Journal of Criminal Justice, 16*, 499–509.

Erickson, K. G., Crosnoe, R., & Dornbusch, S. M. (2000). A social process model of adolescent deviance: Combining social control and differential association perspectives. *Journal of Youth and Adolescence, 29*, 395–425.

Erickson, P. G., & Goodstadt, M. S. (1979). Legal stigma for marijuana possession. *Criminology, 17*, 208–216.

Eron, L. D., & Huesmann, L. R. (1990). The stability of aggressive behavior: Even unto the third generation. In M. Lewis & S. M. Miller (Eds.), *Handbook of developmental psychopathology* (pp. 147–156). New York: Plenum.

Esbensen, F.-A., & Winfree, L. T. (1998). Race and gender between gang and non-gang youth: Results form a multisite survey. *Justice Quarterly, 15*, 505–526.

Esbensen, F.-A., Winfree, L. T., He, N., & Taylor, T. J. (2001). Youth gangs and definitional issues: When is a gang a gang, and why does it matter? *Crime and Delinquency, 47*, 105–130.

Fagan, J., & Chin, K. (1990). Violence as regulation and social control in the distribution of crack. *NIDA Research Monograph Series, 103,* 8–43.

Fagan, J., Piper, E., & Moore, M. (1986). Violent delinquents and urban youth: Correlates of survival and avoidance. *Criminology, 24,* 439–472.

Fagan, J., & Wexler, S. (1988). Explanations of sexual assault among violent delinquents. *Journal of Adolescent Research, 3,* 363–385.

Farnworth, M., & Leiber, M. J. (1989). Strain theory revisited: Economic goals, educational means, and delinquency. *American Sociological Review, 54,* 263–274.

Farrington, D. P. (1979). Longitudinal research on crime and delinquency. In N. Morris & M. Tonry (Eds.), *Crime and Justice: An annual review of research* (Vol. 1, pp. 289–348). Chicago: University of Chicago Press.

Farrington, D. P. (1986). Age and crime. In M. Tonry & N. Morris (Eds.), *Crime and Justice: An annual review of research* (Vol. 7, pp. 189–250). Chicago: University of Chicago Press.

Farrington, D. P. (1991). Childhood aggression and adult violence: Early precursors and later life outcomes. In D. J. Pepler & K. H. Rubin (Eds.), *The development and treatment of childhood aggression* (pp. 5–29). Hillsdale, NJ: Erlbaum.

Farrington, D. P., & Lambert, S. (1994). Differences between burglars and violent offenders. *Psychology, Crime and Law, 1,* 107–116.

Fehr, B., Baldwin, M., Collins, L., Patterson, S., & Benditt, R. (1999). Anger in close relationships: An interpersonal script analysis. *Personality and Social Psychology Bulletin, 25,* 299–312.

Feinman, S. (1985). Emotion expression, social referencing, and preparedness for learning in infancy—Mother knows best, but sometimes I know better. In G. Zivin (Ed.), *The development of expressive interactions* (pp. 191–318). Orlando, FL: Academic Press.

Feinman, S., & Lewis, M. (1983). Social referencing at ten months: A second order effect on infants' responses to strangers. *Child Development, 54,* 878–887.

Felson, R. B., Ribner, S. A., & Siegel, M. S. (1984). Age and the effect of third parties during criminal violence. *Sociology and Social Research, 68,* 452–462.

Felson, R. B., & Steadman, H. J. (1983). Situational factors in disputes leading to criminal violence. *Criminology, 21,* 59–74.

Festinger, L. (1954). A theory of social comparison processes. *Human Relations, 7,* 117–140.

Festinger, L. (1957). *A theory of cognitive dissonance.* Evanston, IL: Row, Peterson.

Field, T., Healy, B. T., Goldstein, S., & Guthertz, M. (1990). Behavior-state matching and synchrony in mother–infant interactions of nondepressed versus depressed dyads. *Developmental Psychology, 26,* 7–14.

Finkelhor, D., & Lewis, I. A. (1988). An epidemiological approach to the study of child molestation. *Annals of the New York Academy of Sciences, 528,* 64–78.

Fiske, M., & Chiriboga, D. A. (1990). *Change and continuity in adult life.* San Francisco: Jossey-Bass.

Fitts, W. H. (1965). *Tennessee Self Concept Scale manual.* Los Angeles: Western Psychological Services.

Flavell, J. H. (2000). Development of children's knowledge about the mental world. *International Journal of Behavioral Development, 24,* 15–23.

Flavell, J. H., Green, F. L., & Flavell, E. R. (1990). Developmental changes in young children's knowledge about the mind. *Cognitive Development, 5,* 1–27.

Fletcher, G. J. O., Rosanowski, J., Rhodes, G., & Lange, C. (1992). Accuracy and speed of causal processing: Experts versus novices in social judgement. *Journal of Experimen-*

tal Social Psychology, 28, 320–338.

Foglia, W. D. (2000). Adding an explicit focus on cognitions to criminological theory. In D. H. Fishbein (Ed.), *The science, treatment, and prevention of antisocial behavior: Application to the criminal justice system* (pp. 10.1–10.25). Kingston, NJ: Civic Research Institute.

Fondacaro, M. R., & Heller, K. (1990). Attributional style in aggressive adolescent boys. *Journal of Abnormal Child Psychology, 18*, 75–89.

Foster, J. D., Dinitz, S., & Reckless, W. C. (1972). Perceptions of stigma following public intervention for delinquent behavior. *Social Problems, 20*, 202–209.

Fowler, R. S., Bray, D. G., & Hollin, C. R. (1992). Young offenders' explanations of crime and preferred method of disposition. *International Journal of Offender Therapy and Comparative Criminology, 36*, 31–41.

Franklin, R. D., Allison, D. B., & Sutton, T. (1992). Alcohol, substance abuse, and violence among North Carolina prison admissions, 1988. *Journal of Offender Rehabilitation, 17*, 101–111.

Freitas, A. L., & Downey, G. (1998). Resilience: A dynamic perspective. *International Journal of Behavioral Development, 22*, 263–285.

Freud, S. (1962). *The neuro-psychosis of defense* (J. Strachey, Trans.). London: Hogarth. (Original work published 1894)

Friedman, J., & Rosenbaum, D. P. (1988). Social control theory: The salience of components by age, gender, and type of crime. *Journal of Quantitative Criminology, 4*, 363–381.

Frith, U., & Happé, F. (1999). Theory of mind and self-consciousness: What is it like to be autistic? *Mind and Language, 14*, 1–22.

Fromme, K., Kivlahan, D. R., & Marlatt, G. A. (1986). Alcohol expectancies, risk identification, and secondary prevention with problem drinkers. *Advances in Behaviour Research and Therapy, 8*, 237–251.

Furnham, A., & Boston, N. (1996). Theories of rape and the just world. *Psychology, Crime and Law, 2*, 211–229.

Furnham, A., & Gunter, B. (1984). Just world beliefs and attitudes toward the poor. *British Journal of Social Psychology, 23*, 265–269.

Garmezy, N. (1985). Stress resistant children: The search for protective factors. In J. E. Stevenson (Ed.), *Recent research in developmental psychopathology* (pp. 213–233). New York: Pergamon.

Garner, P. W. (1996). The relations of emotional role taking, effective/moral attributions, and emotional display rule knowledge to low-income school-age children's social competence. *Journal of Applied Developmental Psychology, 17*, 19–36.

Garrett, C. J. (1985). Effects of residential treatment on adjudicated delinquents: A meta-analysis. *Journal of Research in Crime and Delinquency, 22*, 287–308.

Gastil, R. D. (1971). Homicide and a regional culture of violence. *American Sociological Review, 36*, 412–427.

Gattegno, M.-P., Ionescu, S., Malvy, J., & Adrien, J.-L. (1999). Etude preliminaire de la recherche d'un lior specifique entre les troubles de l'attention conjointe et de la theorie de l'esprit dans l'autisme de l'enfant [Preliminary study about specific relationship between joint attention and "theory of mind" in infantile autism]. *Approche Neuropsychologique des Apprentissages Chez L'Enfant, 11*, 42–48.

Geis, G. (1977). The heavy electrical equipment cases of 1961. In G. Geis & R. F. Meier (Eds.), *White collar crime* (rev. ed., pp. 117–132). New York: Free Press.

Geis, G. (2000). On the absence of self-control as the basis for a general theory of crime: A

critique. *Theoretical Criminology, 4*, 35–53.
Gendreau, P., & Ross, R. R. (1987). Revivification of rehabilitation: Evidence from the 1980s. *Justice Quarterly, 4*, 349–407.
Gerstner, C. R., & Day, D. V. (1994). Cross-cultural comparison of leadership prototypes. *Leadership Quarterly, 5*, 121–134.
Giannini, A. J., & Fellows, K. W. (1986). Enhanced interpretation of nonverbal facial cues in rapists—A preliminary study. *Archives of Sexual Behavior, 15*, 153–156.
Gjone, H., & Stevenson, J. (1997). A longitudinal twin study of temperament and behavior problems: Common genetic or environmental influences? *Journal of the American Academy of Child and Adolescent Psychiatry, 36*, 1448–1456.
Glaser, B. A., Calhoun, G. B., & Horne, A. M. (1999). Cognitions and attributions of abused, aggressive, and control children. *Journal of Cognitive Psychotherapy, 13*, 107–119.
Glennon, F., Joseph, S., & Hunter, J. A. (1993). Just world beliefs in unjust societies: Northern Ireland. *Journal of Social Psychology, 133*, 591–592.
Gloger-Tippelt, G. S., & Huerkamp, M. (1998). Relationship change at the transition to parenthood and security of infant–mother attachment. *International Journal of Behavioral Development, 22*, 633–655.
Glueck, S., & Glueck, E. (1968). *Delinquents and nondelinquents in perspective*. Cambridge: Harvard University Press.
Gluhoski, V. L., & Wortman, C. B. (1996). The impact of trauma on world views. *Journal of Social and Clinical Psychology, 15*, 417–429.
Goddard, H. W. (1994, November). *Testing a social agreement theory of adolescent problem behavior*. Paper presented at the meeting of the National Council on Family Relations, Minneapolis.
Goethals, G. R., & Darley, J. M. (1977). Social comparison theory: The attributional approach. In J. Suls & R. L. Miller (Eds.), *Social comparison processes: Theoretical and empirical perspectives* (pp. 259–278). Washington, DC: Hemisphere.
Goff, C. H., & Nason-Clark, N. (1989). The seriousness of crime in Fredericton, New Brunswick: Perceptions toward white-collar crime. *Canadian Journal of Criminology, 31*, 19–34.
Goldsmith, H. H., & Alansky, J. A. (1987). Maternal and infant temperamental predictors of attachment: A meta-analytic review. *Journal of Consulting and Clinical Psychology, 55*, 805–816.
Goldsmith, H. H., & Campos, J. J. (1990). The structure of temperamental fear and pleasure in infants: A psychometric perspective. *Child Development, 61*, 1944–1964.
Goldstein, P. J. (1985). The drugs/violence nexus: A tripartite conceptual framework. *Journal of Drug Issues, 15*, 493–506.
Goldstein, P. J., Brownstein, H. H., Ryan, P. J., & Bellucci, P. A. (1997). Crack and homicide in New York City: A case study in the epidemiology of violence. In C. Reinarman & H. G. Levine (Eds.), *Crack in America: Demon drugs and social justice* (pp. 113–130). Berkeley: University of California Press.
Gomez, R., & Gomez, A. (2000). Perceived maternal control and support as predictors of hostile-biased attributions of intent and response selection in aggressive boys. *Aggressive Behavior, 26*, 155–168.
Gossop, M., Marsden, J., & Stewart, D. (2000). Drug selling among drug misusers before intake to treatment and at 1-year follow-up: Results from the National Treatment Outcome Research Study (NTORS). *Drug and Alcohol Review, 19*, 143–151.
Gottfredson, M. R., & Hirschi, T. (1990). *A general theory of crime*. Stanford, CA:

Stanford University Press.
Graham, J., & Bowling, B. (1995). *Young people and crime*. London: HMSO.
Grasmick, H. G., Tittle, C. R., Bursick, R. J., & Arneklev, B. J. (1993). Testing the core implications of Gottfredson and Hirschi's general theory of crime. *Journal of Research in Crime and Delinquency, 30*, 5–29.
Gray, L. N., & Tallman, I. (1984). A satisfaction balance model of decision making and choice behavior. *Social Psychology Quarterly, 47*, 146–159.
Greenwald, E., Leitenberg, H., Cado, S., & Tarran, M. J. (1990). Childhood sexual abuse: Long term effects on psychological and sexual functioning in a non-clinical and non-student sample of adult females. *Child Abuse and Neglect, 14*, 503–513.
Groth, A. N. (1979). *Men who rape: The psychology of the offender*. New York: Plenum.
Grove, J. R., Hanrahan, S. J., & McInman, A. (1991). Success/failure bias in attributions across involvement categories in sport. *Personality and Social Psychology Bulletin, 17*, 93–97.
Guerra, N. G. (1989). Consequential thinking and self-reported delinquency in high-school youth. *Criminal Justice and Behavior, 16*, 440–454.
Guerra, N. G., Huesmann, L. R., & Zelli, A. (1990). Attribution for social failure and adolescent aggression. *Aggressive Behavior, 19*, 421–434.
Guerra, N. G., & Slaby, R. G. (1989). Evaluative factors in social problem solving by aggressive boys. *Journal of Abnormal Child Psychology, 17*, 277–289.
Guralnick, M. J., & Paul-Brown, D. (1989). Peer-related communicative competence of preschool children: Developmental and adaptive characteristics. *Journal of Speech and Hearing Research, 32*, 930–943.
Haapanen, R. (1991). *Patterns of violent crime: A longitudinal investigation*. Sacramento: California Department of Youth Authority, Research Division.
Haapasalo, J., & Kankkonen, M. (1997). Self-reported childhood abuse among sex and violent offenders. *Archives of Sexual Behavior, 26*, 421–431.
Haberfeld, M. R. (1993). Criminal careers: Perceptions of adult offenders—The initiation and utilization of under-aged felons in organized criminal activity; drug distributing networks (Doctoral dissertation, City University of New York, 1992). *Dissertation Abstracts International, 53A*, 3683.
Hackney, S. (1969). Southern violence. *American Historical Review, 74*, 906–925.
Hagan, J., & Kay, F. (1990). Gender and delinquency in white-collar families: A power-control perspective. *Crime and Delinquency, 36*, 391–407.
Hagan, J., & Palloni, A. (1990). The social reproduction of a criminal class in work-class London, circa 1950–1980. *American Journal of Sociology, 96*, 265–300.
Hall, G. C. N., Shepherd, J. B., & Mudrak, P. (1992). MMPI taxonomies of child sexual and nonsexual offenders: A cross-validation and extension. *Journal of Personality Assessment, 58*, 127–137.
Hammersley, R., Forsyth, A., & Lavelle, T. (1990). The criminality of new drug users in Glasgow. *British Journal of Addiction, 85*, 1583–1594.
Hamparian, D. M., Davis, J. M., Jacobson, J. M., & McGraw, R. E. (1985). *The young criminal years of the violent few*. Washington, DC: U.S. Department of Justice.
Hankoff, L. D. (1987). The earliest memories of criminals. *International Journal of Offender Therapy and Comparative Criminology, 31*, 195–201.
Hanson, R. K. (1990). The psychological impact of sexual assault on women and children: A review. *Annals of Sex Research, 3*, 187–232.
Hanson, R. K., & Bussière, M. T. (1998). Predicting relapse: A meta-analysis of sexual offender recidivism studies. *Journal of Consulting and Clinical Psychology, 66*,

348–362.
Hanson, R. K., Gizzarelli, R., & Scott, H. (1994). The attitudes of incest offenders: Sexual entitlement and acceptance of sex with children. *Criminal Justice and Behavior, 21*, 187–202.
Hanson, R. K., & Scott, H. (1995). Assessing perspective-taking among sexual offenders, nonsexual criminals, and nonoffenders. *Sexual Abuse: A Journal of Research and Treatment, 7*, 259–277.
Hanson, R. K., & Scott, H. (1996). Social networks of sexual offenders. *Psychology, Crime, and Law, 2*, 249–258.
Hanson, R. K., Scott, H., & Steffy, R. A. (1995). A comparison of child molesters and nonsexual criminals: Risk predictors and long-term recidivism. *Journal of Research in Crime and Delinquency, 32*, 325–337.
Happé, F. (1995). The role of age and verbal ability in the theory of mind task performance of subjects with autism. *Child Development, 66*, 843–855.
Happé, F., & Frith, U. (1996). Theory of mind and social impairment in children with conduct disorder. *British Journal of Developmental Psychology, 14*, 385–398.
Harackiewicz, J. M., Sansone, C., Blair, L. W., Epstein, J. A., & Manderlink, G. (1987). Attributional processes in behavior change and maintenance: Smoking cessation and continued abstinence. *Journal of Consulting and Clinical Psychology, 55*, 372–378.
Hare, R. D. (1991). *The Hare Psychopathy Checklist-Revised manual.* Toronto, Ontario: Multi-Health Systems.
Hare, R. D., & McPherson, L. (1984). Violent and aggressive behavior by criminal psychopaths. *International Journal of Law and Psychiatry, 7*, 35–50.
Hare-Mustin, R. T., & Marecek, J. (1988). The meaning of difference: Gender theory, postmodernism, and psychology. *American Psychologist, 43*, 455–464.
Harris, G. T., Rice, M. E., & Quinsey, V. L. (1994). Psychopathy as a taxon: Evidence that psychopaths are a discrete class. *Journal of Consulting and Clinical Psychology, 62*, 387–397.
Harris, P. L. (1995). Commentary. *Monographs of the Society for Research in Child Development, 60* (1, Serial No. 243).
Harris, P., & Middleton, W. (1993). The illusion of control and optimism about health: On being less at risk but no more in control than others. *British Journal of Social Psychology, 33*, 369–386.
Hartnagel, T. F. (1980). Subculture of violence: Further evidence. *Pacific Sociological Review, 23*, 217–242.
Hartshorne, H., & May, M. A. (1928). *Studies in the nature of character: Studies in deceit.* New York: Macmillan.
Hatter, D. Y., & Ottens, A. J. (1998). Afrocentric world view and black students' adjustment to a predominately white university: Does worldview matter? *College Student Journal, 32*, 472–480.
Hayes, H. D. (1997). Using integrated theory to explain the movement into juvenile delinquency. *Deviant Behavior, 18*, 161–184.
Hazan, C., & Shaver, P. (1987). Romantic love conceptualized as an attachment process. *Journal of Personality and Social Psychology, 52*, 511–524.
Heath, A. C., Cloninger, C. R., & Martin, N. G. (1994). Testing a model for the genetic structure of personality: A comparison of the personality systems of Cloninger and Eysenck. *Journal of Personality and Social Psychology, 66*, 762–775.
Heath, L., Kruttschnitt, C., & Ward, D. (1986). Television and violent criminal behavior: Beyond the Bobo doll. *Victims and violence, 1*, 177–190.

Heather, N. (1979). The structure of delinquent values: A repertory grid investigation. *British Journal of Social and Clinical Psychology, 18*, 263–275.

Heimer, K. (1996). Gender, interaction, and delinquency: Testing a theory of differential social control. *Social Psychology Quarterly, 59*, 39–61.

Heimer, K. (1997). Socioeconomic status, subcultural definitions, and violent delinquency. *Social Forces, 75*, 799–833.

Heimer, K., & De Coster, S. (1999). The gendering of violent delinquency. *Criminology, 37*, 277–318.

Heimer, K., & Matsueda, R. L. (1994). Role-taking, role commitment, and delinquency: A theory of differential social control. *American Sociological Review, 59*, 365–390.

Heimer, K., & Matsueda, R. L. (1997). A symbolic interactionist theory of motivation and deviance: Interpreting psychological research. In D. W. Osgood (Ed.), *Motivation and delinquency: Nebraska Symposium on Motivation* (pp. 223–276). Lincoln: University of Nebraska Press.

Henderson, M., & Hewstone, M. (1984). Prison inmates' explanations for interpersonal violence: Accounts and attributions. *Journal of Consulting and Clinical Psychology, 52*, 789–794.

Henry, B., Caspi, A., Moffitt, T. E., Harrington, H., & Silva, P. A. (1999). Staying in school protects boys with poor self-regulation in childhood from later crime: A longitudinal study. *International Journal of Behavioral Development, 23*, 1049–1073.

Hideo, T. (1988). The role of law and lawyers in Japanese society. In O. I. Okimoto & T. P. Rohlen (Eds.), *Inside the Japanese system: Readings on contemporary society and political economy* (pp. 194–196). Stanford, CA: Stanford University Press.

Higgins, E. T. (2000). Social cognition: Learning about what matters in the social world. *European Journal of Social Psychology, 30*, 3–39.

Higgins, E. T., & Bargh, J. A. (1987). Social cognition and social perception. *Annual Review of Psychology, 38*, 369–425.

Hinze, T., & Doster, J. (1997). Relationship of construct relation and optimism. *Psychological Reports, 81*, 768–770.

Hinze, T., Doster, J., & Joe, V. C. (1997). The relationship of conservatism and cognitive complexity. *Personality and Individual Differences, 22*, 297–298.

Hirschi, T. (1969). *Causes of delinquency*. Berkeley: University of California Press.

Hirschi, T., & Gottfredson, M. (1983). Age and the explanation of crime. *American Journal of Sociology, 89*, 552–584.

Hirshberg, L. M., & Svejda, M. (1990). When infants look to their parents: Infants' social referencing of mothers compared to fathers. *Child Development, 61*, 1175–1186.

Hobson, R. P. (1991). Against the theory of "theory of mind." *British Journal of Developmental Psychology, 9*, 33–51.

Hoffman, J. P., & Cerbone, F. G. (1999). Stressful life events and delinquency escalation in early adolescence. *Criminology, 37*, 343–373.

Holland, R. C. (1995). Public perceptions of white collar crime seriousness: A survey of an Australian sample. *International Journal of Comparative and Applied Criminal Justice, 19*, 91–105.

Hollin, C. R., & Howells, K. (1987). Lay explanations of delinquency: Global or offence-specific? *British Journal of Social Psychology, 26*, 203–210.

Hollinger, R. C. (1991). Neutralization in the workplace: An empirical analysis of property theft and production deviance. *Deviant Behavior, 12*, 169–202.

Hollinger, R. C. (1992). Crime by computer: Correlates of software piracy and unauthorized account access. *Security Journal, 2*, 2–12.

Holton, C. L. (1995). Once upon a time served: Therapeutic application of fairy tales within a correctional environment. *International Journal of Offender Therapy and Comparative Criminology, 39*, 210–221.

Horley, J., & Quinsey, V. L. (1994). Assessing the cognitions of child molesters: Use of the semantic differential with incarcerated offenders. *Journal of Sex Research, 31*, 187–195.

Hornik, R., Risenhoover, N., & Gunnar, M. (1987). The effects of maternal positive, neutral, and negative affective communications on infant responses to new toys. *Child Development, 58*, 937–944.

Horowitz, A. V., & White, H. R. (1987). Gender role orientations and styles of pathology among adolescents. *Journal of Health and Social Behavior, 28*, 158–170.

Horvath, A. O. (1995). The therapeutic relationship: From transference to alliance. *In Session, 1*, 7–17.

Hsieh, C.-C., & Pugh, M. D. (1993). Poverty, income inequality, and violent crime: A meta-analysis of recent aggregate data studies. *Criminal Justice Review, 18*, 182–202.

Huber, P. B. (1972). Death and society among the Anggor of New Guinea. *Omega: Journal of Death and Dying, 3*, 233–243.

Hudson, S. M., Marshall, W. L., Wales, D. S., McDonald, E., Bakker, L. W., & McLean, A. (1993). Emotional recognition skills of sex offenders. *Annals of Sex Research, 6*, 199–211.

Hudson, S. M., & Ward, T. (1997a). Intimacy, loneliness, and attachment style in sexual offenders. *Journal of Interpersonal Violence, 12*, 323–339.

Hudson, S. M., & Ward, T. (1997b). Rape: Psychopathology and theory. In D. R. Law & W. T. O'Donahue (Eds.), *Handbook of sexual deviance: Theory and application* (pp. 332–355). New York: Guilford.

Huesmann, L. R., & Eron, L. D. (1992). Childhood aggression and adult criminality. In J. McCord (Ed.), *Facts, frameworks, and forecasts: Advances in criminological theory* (Vol. 3, pp. 137–156). New Brunswick, NJ: Transaction.

Hughes, C., & Dunn, J. (1997). "Pretend you didn't know": Young children's talk about mental states in pretend play. *Cognitive Development, 12*, 477–499.

Hughes, C., & Dunn, J. (1998). Understanding mind and emotion: Longitudinal associations with mental-state talk between young friends. *Developmental Psychology, 34*, 1026–1037.

Hughes, C., White, A., Sharpen, J., & Dunn, J. (2000). Antisocial, angry, and unsympathetic: "Hard-to-manage" preschoolers' peer problems and possible cognitive influences. *Journal of Child Psychology and Psychiatry, 41*, 169–179.

Hughes, M. (1998). Turning points in the lives of young inner-city men forgoing destructive criminal behaviors: A qualitative study. *Social Work Research, 22*, 143–151.

Humphrey, S. E., & Kahn, A. S. (2000). Fraternities, athletic teams, and rape: Importance of identification with a risky group. *Journal of Interpersonal Violence, 15*, 1313–1322.

Hurrelmann, K., & Engel, U. (1992). Delinquency as a symptom of adolescents' orientation toward status and success. *Journal of Youth and Adolescence, 21*, 119–138.

Huselid, R. F., & Cooper, M. L. (1994). Gender roles as mediators of sex differences in expressions of pathology. *Journal of Abnormal Psychology, 103*, 595–603.

Ianni, F. A. (1974). *Black Mafia: Ethnic succession in organized crime*. New York: Simon and Schuster.

Ickes, W., & Gonzalez, R. (1994). "Social" cognition and social cognition: From the subjective to the intersubjective. *Small Group Research, 25*, 294–315.

Inciardi, J. A. (1990). The crack-violence connection within a population of hard-core adolescent offenders. In M. De La Rosa, E. Y. Lambert, & B. Gropper (Eds.), *Drugs and violence: Causes, correlates, and consequences* (pp. 92–111). Rockville, MD: National Institute on Drug Abuse.

Inciardi, J. A., Horowitz, R., & Pottieger, A. (1993). *Street kids, street drugs, street crime.* Belmont, CA: Wadsworth.

Irwin, J. (1970). *The felon.* Englewood Cliffs, NJ: Prentice-Hall.

Izard, C. E., Fantauzzo, C. A., Castle, J. M., Haynes, O. M., Rayias, M. F., & Putnam, P. H. (1995). The ontogeny and significance of infants' facial expressions in the first nine months of life. *Developmental Psychology, 31*, 997–1013.

Jacobs, B. A. (1998). Drug dealing and negative reciprocity. *Deviant Behavior, 19*, 29–49.

Jacobs, W. L., Kennedy, W. A., & Meyer, J. B. (1997). Juvenile delinquents: A between-group comparison study of sexual and nonsexual offenders. *Sexual Abuse: A Journal of Research and Treatment, 9*, 201–217.

Jang, S. J., & Smith, C. A. (1997). A test of reciprocal causal relationships among parental supervision, affective ties, and delinquency. *Journal of Research in Crime and Delinquency, 34*, 307–336.

Jang, S. J., & Thornberry, T. P. (1998). Self-esteem, delinquent peers, and delinquency: A test of the self-enhancement thesis. *American Sociological Review, 63*, 586–598.

Jankowski, M. S. (1991). *Islands in the street: Gangs and American urban society.* Berkeley: University of California Press.

Janoff-Bulman, R. (1989). Assumptive worlds and the stress of traumatic events: Applications of the schema construct. *Social Cognition, 7*, 113–136.

Janoff-Bulman, R. (1991). Understanding people in terms of their assumptive worlds. In D. Ozer, J. Healy, & A. Stewart (Eds.), *Perspectives in personality: Self and emotion* (Vol. 3, pp. 99–116). London: Kingsley.

Janoff-Bulman, R., & Timko, C. (1987). Coping with traumatic events: The role of denial in light of people's assumptive worlds. In C. R. Snyder & C. E. Ford (Eds.), *Coping with negative life events: Clinical and social psychological perspectives* (pp. 135–159). New York: Plenum.

Janoff-Bulman, R., & Wortman, C. B. (1977). Attributions of blame and coping in the "real world": Severe accident victims react to their lot. *Journal of Personality and Social Psychology, 35*, 351–363.

Jenkins, P. H. (1997). School delinquency and the school social bond. *Journal of Research in Crime and Delinquency, 34*, 337–367.

Jensen, G. F. (1980). Labeling and identity: Toward a reconciliation of divergent findings. *Criminology, 18*, 121–129.

Jensen, G. F. (1995). Salvaging structure through strain: A theoretical and empirical critique. In F. Adler & W. S. Laufer (Eds.), *Advances in criminological theory* (pp. 139–158). New Brunswick, NJ: Transaction.

Jensen, G. F., & Rojek, D. G. (1992). *Delinquency and youth crime* (2nd ed.). Prospect Heights, IL: Waveland.

Jensen, L. A. (1997). Different worldviews, different morals: America's culture war divide. *Human Development, 40*, 325–344.

Jeyasingh, J. V. (1985). Inside white collar crime. *Social Defence, 21*, 17–24.

Johnson, B., Williams, T., Dei, K., & Sanabria, H. (1990). Drug abuse in the inner city: Impact on hard-drug users and the community. In J. Q. Wilson & M. Tonry (Eds.), *Crime and justice: An annual review of research* (Vol. 13, pp. 9–66). Chicago: University of Chicago Press.

Johnson, B. R., Jang, S. J., De Li, S., & Larson, D. (2000). The "invisible institution" and black youth crime: The church as an agency of local social control. *Journal of Youth and Adolescence, 29*, 479–498.

Johnson, J. A., Germer, C. K., Efran, J. S., & Overton, W. F. (1988). Personality as the basis for theoretical predilections. *Journal of Personality and Social Psychology, 55*, 824–835.

Johnson, M. H., & Dziurawiec, S., Bastrip, J., & Morton, J. (1992). The effects of movement of internal features on infants' preferences for face-like stimuli. *Infant Behavior and Development, 15*, 129–136.

Johnson, R. E. (1987). Mother's versus father's role in causing delinquency. *Adolescence, 22*, 305–315.

Johnston, W. A., & Hawley, K. J. (1994). Perceptual inhibition of expected inputs: The key that opens closed minds. *Psychonomic Bulletin and Review, 1*, 56–72.

Jones, B. T., & McMahon, J. (1994). Negative alcohol expectancy predicts post-treatment abstinence survivorship: The whether, when, and why of relapse to a first drink. *Addiction, 89*, 1653–1665.

Jones, E. E., & Nisbett, R. E. (1971). *The actor and the observer: Divergent perceptions of the causes of behavior*. Morristown, NJ: General Learning Press.

Joseph, J. (1995). Juvenile delinquency among African Americans. *Journal of Black Studies, 25*, 475–491.

Junger, M., & Marshall, I. H. (1997). The interethnic generalizability of social control theory: An empirical test. *Journal of Research in Crime and Delinquency, 34*, 79–112.

Junger, M., & Tremblay, R. E. (2000). Self-control, accidents, and crime. *Criminal Justice and Behavior, 26*, 485–501.

Kagan, J., & Snidman, N. (1991). Temperamental factors in human development. *American Psychologist, 46*, 856–862.

Kail, R., & Salthouse, T. A. (1994). Processing speed as a mental capacity. *Acta Psychologica, 86*, 199–225.

Kalichman, S. C., Kelly, J. A., Morgan, M., & Rompa, D. (1997). Fatalism, current life satisfaction, and risk for HIV infection among gay and bisexual men. *Journal of Consulting and Clinical Psychology, 65*, 542–546.

Kandel, E., & Freed, D. (1989). Frontal-lobe dysfunction and antisocial behaviour: A review. *Journal of Clinical Psychology, 45*, 404–413.

Kandel, E., Mednick, S. A., Kirkegaard-Sorensen, L., Hutchings, B., Knop, J., Rosenberg, R., & Schulsinger, F. (1988). IQ as a protective factor for subjects at high risk for antisocial behavior. *Journal of Consulting and Clinical Psychology, 56*, 224–226.

Kaplan, H. B. (1980). *Deviant behavior in defense of self.* New York: Academic Press.

Kaplan, H. B., & Lin, C.-H. (2000). Deviant identity as a mediator of the relation between negative self-feelings and deviant behavior. *Journal of Early Adolescence, 20*, 150–177.

Kaplan, H. B., Martin, S. S., & Johnson, R. J. (1986). Self rejection and the explanation of deviance: Specification of the structure among latent constructs. *American Journal of Sociology, 92*, 384–411.

Karniol, R., & Ben-Moshe, R. (1991). Drawing inferences about others' cognitions and affective reactions: A test of two models for representing affect. *Cognition and Emotion, 5*, 241–253.

Kasari, C., Freeman, S., Mandy, P., & Sigman, M. D. (1995). Attention regulation by children with Down syndrome: Coordinated joint attention and social referencing looks. *American Journal on Mental Retardation, 100*, 128–136.

Katz, R. S. (2000). Explaining girls' and women's crime and desistance in the context of their victimization experiences: A developmental test of revised strain theory and the life course perspective. *Violence Against Women, 6*, 633–660.

Keenan, J. M., Golding, J. M., & Brown, P. (1992). Factors controlling the advantage of self-reference over other-reference. *Social Cognition, 10*, 79–94.

Kellam, S. G., Simon, M. B., & Ensminger, M. E. (1983). Antecedents in first grade of teenage substance use and psychological well-being: A two-year community-wide prospective study. In D. F. Ricks & B. S. Dohrenwend (Eds.), *Origins of psychopathology* (pp. 17–42). New York: Cambridge University Press.

Kelly, G. A. (1955). *The psychology of personal constructs*. New York: Norton.

Kennedy, H. G., & Grubin, D. H. (1992). Patterns of denial in sex offenders. *Psychological Medicine, 22*, 191–196.

Kerbo, H. R., & Inoue, M. (1990). Japanese social structure and white collar crime: Recruit cosmos and beyond. *Deviant Behavior, 11*, 139–154.

Kerr, M., Tremblay, R. E., Pagani, L., & Vitaro, F. (1997). Boys' behavioral inhibition and the risk of later delinquency. *Archives of General Psychiatry, 54*, 809–816.

Khoo, A.C.E., & Oakes, P. J. (2000). The variability of the delinquent self: Anti-authority attitudes and endorsement of neutralization techniques among incarcerated delinquents in Singapore. *Asian Journal of Social Psychology, 3*, 125–132.

Kirkpatrick, L. A., & Shaver, P. (1988). Fear and affiliation reconsidered from a stress and coping perspective: The importance of cognitive clarity and fear reduction. *Journal of Social and Clinical Psychology, 7*, 214–233.

Klein, M. (1986). Labeling theory and delinquency policy: An experimental test. *Criminal Justice and Behavior, 13*, 47–79.

Klein, S. B., & Loftus, J. B. (1988). The nature of self-referent encoding: The contributions of elaborative and organizational processes. *Journal of Personality and Social Psychology, 55*, 5–11.

Klemke, L. W. (1978). Does apprehension for shoplifting amplify or terminate shoplifting activity? *Law and Society Review, 12*, 391–403.

Klinnert, M. D., Emde, R. N., Butterfield, P., & Campos, J. J. (1986). Social referencing: The infant's use of emotional signals from a friendly adult with mother present. *Developmental Psychology, 22*, 427–432.

Kohn, M. L., & Schooler, C. (1982). Job conditions and personality: A longitudinal assessment of their reciprocal effects. *American Journal of Sociology, 87*, 1257-1286.

Kono, S. (1994). Why don't juvenile delinquents anticipate results of future events according to past evidence? A study of discontinuity of time perspective and causal attributes. *Japanese Journal of Criminal Psychology, 32*, 1–10.

Kosson, D. S., Smith, S. S., & Newman, J. P. (1990). Evaluation of the construct validity of psychopathy in black and white inmates: Three preliminary studies. *Journal of Abnormal Psychology, 99*, 250–259.

Krafft, K. C., & Berk, L. E. (1998). Private speech in two preschools: Significance of open-ended activities and make-believe play for verbal self-regulation. *Early Childhood Research Quarterly, 13*, 637–658.

Krauss, R. M., & Fussell, S. R. (1996). Social psychological models of interpersonal communication. In E. T. Higgins & R. W. Krugkinski (Eds.), *Social Psychology: Handbook of Basic Principles* (pp. 655–701). New York: Guilford.

Krippner, S. (1986). Dreams and development of personal mythology. *Journal of Mind and Behavior, 7*, 449–461.

Krohn, M., Lizotte, A. J., Thornberry, T. P., Smith, C., & McDowell, D. (1996). Reciprocal causal relationships among drug use, peers, and beliefs: A five-wave panel model. *Journal of Drug Issues, 26*, 405–428.

Krohn, M., & Massey, C. (1980). Social control and delinquent behavior: An examination of the elements of the social bond. *Sociological Quarterly, 21*, 544–559.

Krohn, M. L., Skinner, W. F., Massey, J. L., & Akers, R. (1985). Social learning theory and adolescent cigarette smoking: A longitudinal study. *Social Problems, 32*, 455–473.

Krueger, R. F., Caspi, A., Moffitt, T. E., White, J., & Stouthamer-Loeber, M. (1996). Delay of gratification, psychopathology, and personality: Is low self-control specific to externalizing problems? *Journal of Personality, 64*, 107–129.

Kruttschnitt, C. (1994). Gender and interpersonal violence. In A. J. Reiss Jr. & J. A. Roth (Eds.), *Understanding and preventing violence, Vol. 3: Social influences* (pp. 293–376). Washington, DC: National Academy Press.

Kulik, J. A., & Mahler, H. I. (1989). Stress and affiliation in a hospital setting: Preoperative roommate preferences. *Personality and Social Psychology Bulletin, 15*, 183–193.

Kupersmidt, J. B., & Coie, J. D. (1990). Preadolescent peer status, aggression, and school adjustment as predictors of externalizing problems in adolescence. *Child Development, 61*, 1350–1362.

Lambert, M. J. (1992). Psychotherapy outcome research: Implications for integrative and eclectic therapists. In J. C. Norris & M. R. Goldfried (Eds.), *Handbook of psychotherapy integration* (pp. 94–129). New York: Basic Books.

Landsheer, J. A., Hart, H. Y., & Kox, W. (1994). Delinquent values and victim damage: Exploring the limits of neutralization theory. *British Journal of Criminology, 34*, 44–53.

Langan, P. A., & Farrington, D. P. (1998). *Crime and justice in the United States and in England and Wales, 1981–96* (NCJ-169284). Washington, DC: Bureau of Justice Statistics.

Langevin, R., & Lang, R. A. (1990). Substance abuse among sex offenders. *Annals of Sex Research, 3*, 397–424.

Larsen, J., Hudson, S. M., & Ward, T. (1995). Evaluation of attributional change in relapse prevention programme for child molesters. *Behaviour Change, 12*, 127–138.

Larzelere, R. E., & Patterson, G. R. (1990). Parental management: Mediator of the effect of socioeconomic status on early delinquency. *Criminology, 28*, 301–324.

Lasley, J. R. (1988). Toward a control theory of white-collar offending. *Journal of Quantitative Criminology, 4*, 347–362.

Lattimore, P. K., Visher, C. A., & Linster, R. L. (1995). Predicting rearrest for violence among serious youthful offenders. *Journal of Research in Crime and Delinquency, 32*, 54–83.

Laub, J. H., Nagin, D. S., & Sampson, R. J. (1998). Trajectories of change in criminal offending: Good marriages and the desistance process. *American Sociological Review, 63*, 225–238.

Leadbeater, B J., Hellner, I., Allen, J. P., & Aber, J. L. (1989). Assessment of interpersonal negotiation strategies in youth engaged in problem behaviors. *Developmental Psychology, 25*, 465–472.

Le Blanc, M. (1997). Socialization or propensity: A test of an integrative control theory with adjudicated boys. *Studies in Crime and Crime Prevention, 6*, 200–224.

Le Blanc, M., & Fréchette, M. (1989). *Male criminal activity, from childhood through youth: Multilevel and developmental perspectives*. New York: Springer-Verlag.

Lecky, P. (1945). *Self-consistency: A theory of personality*. New York: Island.

Leibrich, J. (1993). *Straight to the point: Angles on giving up crime*. Otago, NZ: University of Otago Press.

Lemert, E. M. (1951). *Social pathology.* New York: McGraw-Hill.

Lerner, M. J. (1980). *The belief in a just world: A fundamental delusion.* New York: Plenum.

Letkemann, P. (1973). *Crime as work.* Englewood Cliffs, NJ: Prentice-Hall.

Leung, K., & Lau, S. (1989). Effects of self-concept and perceived disapproval of delinquent behavior in school children. *Journal of Youth and Adolescence, 18,* 345–359.

Levant, M. D., & Bass, B. A. (1991). Parental identification of rapists and pedophiles. *Psychological Reports, 69,* 463–466.

Levi, K. (1981). Becoming a hit man: Neutralization in a very deviant career. *Urban Life, 10,* 47–63.

Levy, K. N., Blatt, S. J., & Shaver, P. R. (1998). Attachment styles and parental representations. *Journal of Personality and Social Psychology, 74,* 407–419.

Levy, K.S.C. (1997). Multifactorial self-concept and delinquency in Australian adolescents. *Journal of Social Psychology, 137,* 277–283.

Lewis, M., & Brooks-Gunn, J. (1979). *Social cognition and the acquisition of the self.* New York: Plenum.

Li, X., & Feigelman, S. (1994). Recent and intended drug trafficking among male and female urban African-American early adolescents. *Pediatrics, 93,* 1044–1049.

Li, X., Feigelman, S., Stanton, B., Galbraith, J., & Huang, W. (1998). Drug trafficking and drug use among urban African-American adolescents: A causal analysis. *Journal of Adolescent Health, 23,* 280–288.

Li, X., Stanton, B., Black, M. M., & Feigelman, S. (1996). Persistence of drug trafficking behaviors and intentions among urban African American early adolescents. *Journal of Early Adolescence, 16,* 469–487.

Li, X., Stanton, B., & Feigelman, S. (2000). Impact of perceived parental monitoring on adolescent risk behavior over 4 years. *Journal of Adolescent Health, 27,* 49–56.

Li, X., Stanton, B., Feigelman, S., Black, M. M., & Romer, D. (1994). Drug trafficking and drug use among urban African American early adolescents. *Journal of Early Adolescence, 14,* 491–508.

Lillard, A. (1999). Developing a cultural theory of mind: The CIAO approach. *Current Directions in Psychological Science, 8,* 57–61.

Lillard, A. S., Zeljo, A., & Harlan, D. (1998). *Developing cultural schemas.* Unpublished manuscript, University of Virginia, Charlottesville.

Linquest, C. A., Smusz, T. D., & Doerner, W. (1985). Causes of conformity: An application of control theory to adult misdemeanant probationers. *International Journal of Offender Therapy and Comparative Criminology, 29,* 1–14.

Linville, P. W. (1985). Self-complexity and affective extremity: Don't put all of your eggs in one cognitive basket. *Social Cognition, 3,* 94–120.

Lipton, D. N., McDonel, E. C., & McFall, R. M. (1987). Heterosocial perception in rapists. *Journal of Consulting and Clinical Psychology, 55,* 17–21.

Liska, A. E., & Bellair, P. E. (1995). Violent-crime rates and racial composition: Convergences over time. *American Journal of Sociology, 101,* 578–610.

Liska, A. E., & Reed, M. D. (1985). Ties to conventional institutions and delinquency: Estimating reciprocal effects. *American Sociological Review, 50,* 547–560.

Locke, K. D., & Nekich, J. C. (2000). Agency and communion in naturalistic social comparisons. *Personality and Social Psychology Bulletin, 26,* 864–874.

Loeber, R., Farrington, D. P., Stouthamer-Loeber, M., Moffitt, T. E., & Caspi, A. (1998). The development of male offending: Key findings from the first decade of the

Pittsburgh youth study. *Studies on Crime and Crime Prevention, 7,* 141–171.
Loeber, R., & Hay, D. (1997). Key issues in the development of aggression and violence from childhood to early adulthood. *Annual Review of Psychology, 48,* 371–410.
Loehlin, J. C. (1989). Partitioning environmental and genetic contributions to behavioral development. *American Psychologist, 44,* 1285–1292.
Longshore, D., & Turner, S. (1998). Self-control and criminal opportunity: Cross-sectional test of the general theory of crime. *Criminal Justice and Behavior, 25,* 81–98.
Lopez, V. A., & Emmer, E. T. (2000). Adolescent male offenders: A grounded theory study of cognition, emotion, and delinquent crime contexts. *Criminal Justice and Behavior, 27,* 292–311.
Lösel, F., & Bliesener, T. (1994). Some high-risk adolescents do not develop conduct problems: A study of protective factors. *International Journal of Behavioral Development, 17,* 753–777.
Loza, W., & Clements, P. (1991). Incarcerated alcoholics' and rapists' attributions of blame for criminal acts. *Canadian Journal of Behavioural Science, 23,* 76–83.
Lucy, J. A. (1997). Linguistic relativity. *Annual Review of Anthropology, 26,* 291–312.
Ludwig, K. B., & Pittman, J. F. (1999). Adolescent prosocial values and self-efficacy in relation to delinquency, risky sexual behavior, and drug use. *Youth and Society, 30,* 461–482.
Luminet, O., Bouts, P., Delie, F., Manstead, A. S. R., & Rimé, B. (2000). Social sharing of emotion following exposure to a negatively valenced situation. *Cognition and Emotion, 14,* 661–688.
Lupfer, M. B., Doan, K., & Houston, D. A. (1998). Explaining unfair and fair outcomes: The therapeutic value of attributional analyses. *British Journal of Social Psychology, 37,* 495–511.
Lynch, J. P., Smith, S. K., Graziadei, H. A., & Pittayathikhun, T. (1994). *Profile of inmates in the United States and in England and Wales, 1991* (NCJ–145863). Washington, DC: Bureau of Justice Statistics.
Lytton, H. (1990). Child and parent effects on boys' conduct disorder: A reinterpretation. *Developmental Psychology, 26,* 683–697.
MacCoun, R., & Reuter, P. (1992). Are the wages of sin $30.00/hour?: Economic aspects of street level drug dealing. *Crime and Delinquency, 38,* 477–491.
Mak, A. S. (1990). Testing a psychosocial control theory of delinquency. *Criminal Justice and Behavior, 17,* 215–230.
Malamuth, N. M., & Brown, L. M. (1994). Sexually aggressive men's perceptions of women's communications: Testing three explanations. *Journal of Personality and Social Psychology, 67,* 699–712.
Malinosky-Rummell, R., & Hansen, D. J. (1993). Long term consequences of childhood physical abuse. *Psychological Bulletin, 114,* 68–79.
Mandelbröt, B. (1990). Fractals—A geometry of nature. *New Scientist, 15,* 38–43.
Manning, B. H., White, C. S., & Daugherty, M. (1994). Young children's private speech as a precursor to metacognitive strategy use during task engagement. *Discourse Processes, 17,* 191–211.
Markus, H. (1980). Self-schemata and processing information about the self. *Journal of Personality and Social Psychology, 35,* 63–78.
Markus, H., & Nurius, P. (1986). Possible selves. *American Psychologist, 41,* 954–969.
Markus, H., & Wurf, E. (1987). The dynamic self-concept: A social psychological perspective. *Annual Review of Psychology, 38,* 299–337.
Marlatt, G. A., & George, W. J. (1984). Relapse prevention: Introduction and overview of

the model. *British Journal of Addiction, 79,* 261–275.

Marques, J., Nelson, C., West, A., & Day, D. M. (1994). The relationship between treatment goals and recidivism among child molesters. *Behaviour Research and Therapy, 32,* 577–588.

Marshall, W. L. (1997). The relationship between self-esteem and deviant sexual arousal in nonfamilial child molesters. *Behavior Modification, 21,* 86–96.

Marshall, W. L., Barbaree, H. E., & Fernandez, Y. M. (1995). Some aspects of social competence in sexual offenders. *Sexual Abuse: A Journal of Research and Treatment, 7,* 113–127.

Marshall, W. L., Champagne, F., Brown, C., & Miller, S. (1997). Empathy, intimacy, loneliness, and self-esteem in nonfamilial child molesters: A brief report. *Journal of Child Sexual Abuse, 6,* 87–98.

Marshall, W. L., Hudson, S. M., Jones, R., & Fernandez, Y. M. (1995). Empathy in sex offenders. *Clinical Psychology Review, 15,* 99–113.

Marshall, W. L., Serran, G. A., & Cortoni, F. A. (2000). Childhood attachments, sexual abuse, and their relationship to adult coping in child molesters. *Sexual Abuse: A Journal of Research and Treatment, 12,* 17–26.

Martin, F. P., & Osgood, D. W. (1987). Autonomy as a source of pro-social influence among incarcerated adolescents. *Journal of Applied Social Psychology, 17,* 97–107.

Martin, J. E. (1999). Assessment of executive functions in sexual offenders (Doctoral dissertation, Adler School of Professional Psychology, 1998). *Dissertation Abstracts International, 59B,* 5580.

Martinson, R. (1974). What works?—Questions and answers about prison reform. *The Public Interest, 35,* 22–54.

Marusza, J. (1997). Urban white working-class males and the possibilities of collective anger: Patrolling Riley Road. *Urban Review, 29,* 97–112.

Maryland State Department of Education. (1992). *Maryland adolescent drug survey.* Baltimore: Author.

Mas, C. H., Alexander, J. F., & Turner, C. W. (1991). Dispositional attributions and defensive behavior in high- and low-conflict delinquent families. *Journal of Family Psychology, 5,* 176–191.

Maslow, A. H. (1971). *The farther reaches of human nature.* New York: Viking.

Mason, R., & Calvin, L. D. (1978). A study of admitted income tax evasion. *Law and Society Review, 3,* 73–89.

Matsueda, R. L. (1992). Reflected appraisals, parental labeling, and delinquency: Specifying a symbolic interactionist theory. *American Journal of Sociology, 97,* 1577–1611.

Matthys, W., Cuperus, J. M., & Van Engeland, H. (1999). Deficient social problem-solving in boys with ODD/CD, with ADHD, and with both disorders. *Journal of the American Academy of Child and Adolescent Psychiatry, 38,* 311–321.

Matza, D. (1964). *Delinquency and drift.* New York: Wiley.

Mauro, C. F., & Harris, Y. R. (2000). The influence of maternal child-rearing attitudes and teaching behaviors on preschoolers' delay of gratification. *Journal of Genetic Psychology, 161,* 292–306.

May, D. C. (1999). Scared kids, unattached kids, or peer pressure: Why do students carry firearms to school? *Youth and Society, 31,* 100–127.

Mazerolle, P. (1998). Gender, general strain, and delinquency: An empirical examination. *Justice Quarterly, 15,* 65–91.

Mazerolle, P., Burton, V. S., Cullen, F. T., Evans, T. D., & Payne, G. L. (2000). Strain,

anger, and delinquent adaptations: Specifying general strain theory. *Journal of Criminal Justice, 28,* 89–101.
Mazerolle, P., & Piquero, A. (1997). Violent responses to strain: An examination of conditioning influences. *Violence and Victims, 12,* 323–343.
McBride, D. C., Burgman-Habermehl, C., Alpert, J., & Chitwood, D. (1986). Drugs and homicide. *Bulletin of the New York Academy of Medicine, 62,* 497–508.
McCall, P. L., Land, K. C., & Cohen, L. E. (1992). Violent criminal behavior: Is there a general and continuing influence of the South? *Social Science Research, 21,* 286–310.
McCarthy, B. (1996). The attitudes and actions of others: Tutelage and Sutherland's theory of differential association. *British Journal of Criminology, 36,* 135–147.
McCartney, J. (1997). Between knowledge and desire: Perceptions of decision-making in the addictive behaviors. *Substance Use and Misuse, 32,* 2061–2092.
McClelland, J. L., McNaughton, B. L., & O'Reilly, R. C. (1995). Why there are complementary learning systems in the hippocampus and neocortex: Insights from the successes and failures of connectionist models of learning and memory. *Psychological Review, 102,* 419–437.
McGarry, J. (1996). Applications of Eastern and naturalistic philosophy in the modification of Western belief systems. *Australian Journal of Clinical Hypnotherapy and Hypnosis, 17,* 79–90.
McKay, M. M., Chapman, J. W., & Long, N. R. (1996). Causal attributions for criminal offending and sexual arousal: Comparison of child sex offenders with other offenders. *British Journal of Clinical Psychology, 35,* 63–75.
McKeough, A., Yates, T., & Marini, A. (1994). Intentional reasoning: A developmental study of behaviorally aggressive and normal boys. *Development and Psychopathology, 6,* 285–304.
Mead, G. H. (1934). *Mind, self, and society.* Chicago: University of Chicago Press.
Mead, G. H. (1982). Class lectures in social psychology. In D. L. Miller (Ed.), *The individual and the social self: Unpublished works of George Herbert Mead* (pp. 27–105). Chicago: University of Chicago Press. (Original work published 1914)
Mears, D. P., Ploeger, M., & Warr, M. (1998). Explaining the gender gap in delinquency: Peer influence and moral evaluations of behavior. *Journal of Research in Crime and Delinquency, 35,* 251–266.
Mednick, S. A., Brennan, P., & Kandel, E. (1988). Predisposition to violence. *Aggressive Behavior, 14,* 25–33.
Meins, E., Fernyhough, C., Russell, J., & Clark-Carter, D. (1998). Security of attachment as a predictor of symbolic and mentalizing abilities: A longitudinal study. *Social Development, 7,* 1–24.
Meisenhelder, T. (1977). An exploratory study of exiting from criminal careers. *Criminology, 15,* 319–334.
Menard, S. (1995). A developmental test of Mertonian anomie theory. *Journal of Research in Crime and Delinquency, 32,* 136–174.
Menard, S., & Elliott, D. S. (1994). Delinquency bonding, moral beliefs, and illegal behavior: A three-way panel model. *Justice Quarterly, 11,* 173–188.
Merriam-Webster. (Ed.). (2000). *Webster's third new international dictionary: Unabridged.* Springfield, MA: Author.
Merton, R. K. (1957). *Social theory and social structure* (rev. ed.). Glencoe, IL: Free Press.
Messerschmidt, J. W. (1993). *Masculinities and crime.* Lanham, MD: Rowman and Littlefield.
Messner, S. F. (1988). Research on cultural and socioeconomic factors in criminal violence.

Psychiatric Clinics of North America, 11, 511–525.
Messner, S. F., & Rosenfeld, R. (1997). *Crime and the American dream*. Belmont, CA: Wadsworth.
Miccio-Fonseca, L. C. (2000). Adult and adolescent female sex offenders: Experiences compared to other female and male sex offenders. *Journal of Psychology and Human Sexuality, 11*, 75–88.
Mikulincer, M. (1986). Attributional processes in the learned helplessness paradigm: Behavioral effects of global attributions. *Journal of Personality and Social Psychology, 51*, 1248–1256.
Mikulincer, M. (1995). Attachment style and the mental representation of the self. *Journal of Personality and Social Psychology, 69*, 1203–1215.
Mikulincer, M. (1997). Adult attachment style and information processing: Individual differences in curiosity and cognitive closure. *Journal of Personality and Social Psychology, 72*, 1217–1230.
Milgram, S. (1974). *Obedience to authority*. New York: Harper & Row.
Miller, J. G. (1984). Culture and the development of everyday social explanation. *Journal of Personality and Social Psychology, 46*, 961–978.
Miller, W. R. (1999). *Integrating spirituality into treatment: Resources for practitioners*. Washington, DC: American Psychological Association.
Minor, W. W. (1984). Neutralization as a hardening process: Considerations in the modeling of change. *Social Forces, 62*, 995–1019.
Mischel, W. (1968). *Personality and assessment*. New York: Wiley.
Mischel, W., Shoda, Y., & Rodriguez, M. I. (1989). Delay of gratification in children. *Science, 26*, 933–938.
Mischkowitz, R. (1994). Desistance from a delinquent way of life? In E.G.M. Whitekamp & H. J. Kerner (Eds.), *Cross-national longitudinal research on human development and criminal behaviour* (pp. 303–327). London: Kluwer.
Mitchell, J., Dodder, R. A., & Norris, T. D. (1990). Neutralization and delinquency: A comparison by sex and ethnicity. *Adolescence, 25*, 487–497.
Moffitt, T. E. (1993a). Adolescent-limited and life-course-persistent antisocial behavior: A developmental taxonomy. *Psychological Review, 100*, 674–701.
Moffitt, T. E. (1993b). The neuropsychology of conduct disorders. *Developmental Psychopathology, 5*, 135–151.
Moffitt, T. E., Gabrielli, W. F., Mednick, S. A., & Schulsinger, F. (1981). Socioeconomic status, IQ, and delinquency. *Journal of Abnormal Psychology, 90*, 152–156.
Moffitt, T. E., & Silva, P. A. (1988). Self-reported delinquency, neuropsychological deficits and history of attention deficit disorder. *Journal of Abnormal Child Psychology, 16*, 553–569.
Monahan, J. (1984). The predictors of violent behavior: Toward a second generation of theory and policy. *American Journal of Psychiatry, 141*, 10–15.
Monson, C. M., Jones, L. M., Rivers, P. C., & Blum, S. B. (1998). Alcohol and sex offending: What do child sex offenders think about drinking? *Journal of Addictions and Offender Counseling, 19*, 15–27.
Montgomery, D. E., Fine, M. A., & James-Meyers, L. (1990). The development and validation of an instrument to assess an optimal Afrocentric world view. *Journal of Black Psychology, 17*, 37–54.
Moore, D. G., Hobson, R. P., & Anderson, M. (1995). Person perception: Does it involve IQ-independent perceptual processing? *Intelligence, 20*, 65–86.
Moore, E., & Mills, M. (1990). The neglected victims and unexamined costs of white-collar

crime. *Crime and Delinquency, 36,* 408–418.

Morin, A. (1995). Preliminary data on a relation between self-talk and complexity of the self-concept. *Psychological Reports, 76,* 267–272.

Morissette, P., Ricard, M., & Gouin-Décarie, T. (1995). Interactions between shared attention during the preverbal period and the development of verbal references. *International Journal of Psychology, 30,* 481–498.

Morris, S. B., Alexander, J. F., & Turner, C. W. (1991). Do reattributions of delinquent behavior reduce blame? *Journal of Family Psychology, 5,* 192–203.

Mosher, D. L., & Tomkins, S. S. (1988). Scripting the macho man: Hypermasculine socialization and enculturation. *Journal of Sex Research, 25,* 60–84.

Mothersead, P. K., Kivlighan, D. M., & Wynkoop, T. F. (1998). Attachment, family dysfunction, parental alcoholism, and interpersonal distress in late adolescence: A structural model. *Journal of Counseling Psychology, 45,* 196–203.

Mueller, B. (1987, June/July). Reflections of culture: An analysis of Japanese and American advertising appeals. *Journal of Advertising Research,* pp. 51–59.

Mussweiler, T., Gabriel, S., & Bodenhausen, G. V. (2000). Shifting social identities as a strategy for deflecting threatening social comparisons. *Journal of Personality and Social Psychology, 79,* 398–409.

Nagin, D. S., Farrington, D. P., & Moffitt, T. E. (1995). Life course trajectories of different types of offenders. *Criminology, 33,* 111–139.

Nagin, D. S., & Paternoster, R. (1994). Personal capital and social control: The deterrence implications of a theory of individual differences in criminal offending. *Criminology, 32,* 581–606.

Nagin, D. S., & Tremblay, R. E. (1999). Trajectories of boys' physical aggression, opposition, and hyperactivity on the path to physically violent and nonviolent juvenile delinquency. *Child Development, 70,* 1181–1196.

Neidigh, L., & Tomiko, R. (1991). The coping strategies of child sex abusers. *Journal of Sex Education and Therapy, 17,* 103–110.

Newcomb, A. F., & Bagwell, C. L. (1996). The developmental significance of children's friendship relations. In W. M. Bukowski, A. F. Newcombe, & W. W. Hartup (Eds.), *The company they keep: Friendship in childhood and adolescence* (pp. 289–321). New York: Cambridge University Press.

Newcomb, T. M. (1929). *Consistency of certain extrovert-introvert behavior patterns in 51 problem boys.* New York: Columbia University Teachers College, Bureau of Publications.

New York State Division of Criminal Justice Services. (1993). *Crime and justice annual report, 1983–1992.* Albany, NY: Author.

Niggli, M. A. (1994). Rational choice theory and crime prevention. *Studies on Crime and Crime Prevention, 3,* 83–103.

Nurco, D. N., Hanlon, T. E., Kinlock, T. W., & Duszynski, K. R. (1988). Differential criminal patterns of narcotic addicts over an addiction career. *Criminology, 26,* 407–424.

O'Carroll, T. (1980). *Paedophilia: The radical case.* London: Owen.

O'Connor, M. J., Sigman, M., & Brill, N. (1987). Disorganization of attachment in relation to maternal alcohol consumption. *Journal of Consulting and Clinical Psychology, 55,* 831–836.

O'Connor, T. R. (1994). Inequity and crime: An empirical assessment of general strain theory (Doctoral dissertation, Indiana University of Pennsylvania, 1993). *Dissertation Abstracts International, 54A,* 3384.

O'Grady, D., & Metz, J. R. (1987). Resilience in children at high risk for psychological disorder. *Journal of Pediatric Psychology, 12*, 3–23.

Okamoto, H. (1998). A study on the juvenile delinquent's self-efficacy and outcome expectancy for jobs and delinquency. *Japanese Journal of Criminal Psychology, 36*, 1–22.

Okimoto, D. I., & Rohlen, T. P. (Eds.). (1988). *Inside the Japanese system: Readings on contemporary society and political economy*. Stanford, CA: Stanford University Press.

Olmstead, R. E., Guy, S. M., O'Mally, P. M., & Bentler, P. M. (1991). Longitudinal assessment of the relationship between self-esteem, fatalism, loneliness, and substance use. *Journal of Social Behavior and Personality, 6*, 749–770.

Olweus, D. (1979). Stability of aggressive reaction patterns in males: A review. *Psychological Bulletin, 86*, 852–875.

Olweus, D. (1980). Familial and temperamental determinants of aggressive behavior in adolescent boys: A causal analysis. *Developmental Psychology, 16*, 644–660.

Omata, K. (1995). Territoriality in the house and its relationship to the use of rooms and the psychological well-being of Japanese married women. *Journal of Environmental Psychology, 15*, 147–154.

O'Quin, K., & Volger, C. C. (1989). Effects of just world beliefs on perceptions of crime perpetrators and victims. *Social Justice Research, 3*, 47–56.

Orcutt, J. (1987). Differential association and marijuana use: A closer look at Sutherland (with a little help from Becker). *Criminology, 25*, 341–358.

Ornduff, S. R. (2000). Childhood maltreatment and malevolence: Quantitative research findings. *Clinical Psychology Review, 20*, 997–1018.

Orr, D. P., & Ingersoll, G. M. (1995). The contribution of level of cognitive complexity and pubertal timing to behavioral risk in young adolescents. *Pediatrics, 95*, 528–533.

Oswald, P. A. (1996). The effects of cognitive and affective perspective taking on empathic concern and altruistic helping. *Journal of Social Psychology, 136*, 613–623.

Ouimet, M., & Le Blanc, M. (1996). The role of life experiences in the continuation of the adult criminal career. *Criminal Behaviour and Mental Health, 6*, 73–97.

Overholser, C., & Beck, S. (1986). Multimethod assessment of rapists, child molesters, and three control groups on behavioral and psychological measures. *Journal of Consulting and Clinical Psychology, 54*, 682–687.

Owens, T. J. (1994). Two dimensions of self-esteem: Reciprocal effects of positive self-worth and self-deprecation on adolescent problems. *American Sociological Review, 59*, 391–407.

Oyserman, D. (1993). Adolescent identity and delinquency in interpersonal context. *Child Psychiatry and Human Development, 23*, 203–214.

Oyserman, D., & Markus, H. (1990). Possible selves and delinquency. *Journal of Personality and Social Psychology, 59*, 712–725.

Oyserman, D., & Saltz, E. (1993). Competence, delinquency, and attempts to attain possible selves. *Journal of Personality and Social Psychology, 65*, 360–374.

Padilla, F. (1995). The working gang. In M. W. Klein, C. L. Maxson, & J. Miller (Eds.), *The modern gang reader* (pp. 53–61). Los Angeles: Roxbury.

Palmer, T. (1991). The effectiveness of intervention: Recent trends and current issues. *Crime and Delinquency, 37*, 330–346.

Parrott, C. A., & Strongman, K. T. (1984). Locus of control and delinquency. *Adolescence, 19*, 459–471.

Paternoster, R. (1988). Examining three-wave deterrence models: A question of temporal order and specification. *Journal of Criminal Law and Criminology, 79*, 135–179.

Paternoster, R. (1989). Absolute and restrictive deterrence in a panel of youth: Explaining the onset, persistence/desistance, and frequency of delinquent offending. *Social Problems, 36*, 289–309.

Paternoster, R., & Iovanni, L. (1989). The labeling perspective and delinquency: An elaboration of the theory and assessment of evidence. *Justice Quarterly, 6*, 359–394.

Paternoster, R., & Mazerolle, P. (1994). General strain theory and delinquency: A replication and extension. *Journal of Research in Crime and Delinquency, 31*, 235–263.

Paternoster, R., Saltzman, L., Waldo, G., & Chircos, T. (1983). Perceived risk and social control: Do sanctions really deter? *Law and Society Review, 17*, 457–479.

Patrick, E., & Abravanel, E. (2000). The self-regulatory nature of preschool children's private speech in a naturalistic setting. *Applied Psycholinguistics, 21*, 45–61.

Patterson, G. R. (1996). *Some characteristics of a developmental theory for early onset delinquency*. New York: Oxford University Press.

Payne, D. C., & Gough, L. A. (1995). Treatment of dysfunctional adult reaction to being called abusive names: A cybernetic sociofeedback approach. *Journal of Family Psychotherapy, 6*, 47–61.

Pepper, S. (1942). *World hypotheses*. Berkeley: University of California Press.

Perner, J. (1991). *Understanding the representational mind*. Cambridge: MIT Press.

Perner, J., & Howes, D. (1992). "He thinks he knows": And more developmental evidence against the simulation (role taking) theory. *Mind and Language, 7*, 72–86.

Perner, J., Ruffman, T., & Leekam, S. R. (1994). Theory of mind is contagious: You catch it from your sibs. *Child Development, 65*, 1228–1238.

Perry, D. G., Perry, L. C., & Rasmussen, P. (1986). Cognitive and social leaning mediators of aggression. *Child Development, 52*, 700–711.

Peterson, C. C., & Siegel, M. (2000). Insights into theory of mind from deafness and autism. *Mind and Language, 15*, 123–145.

Phelen, P. (1995). Incest and its meaning: The perspectives of fathers and daughters. *Child Abuse and Neglect, 19*, 7–24.

Piaget, J. (1952). *The origins of intelligence in children*. New York: International Universities Press.

Pietromonaco, P. R., Manis, J., & Markus, H. (1986). The relationship of employment to self-perception and well-being in women: A cognitive analysis. *Sex Roles, 17*, 467–477.

Piliavin, I., Gartner, R., Thornton, C., & Matsueda, R. (1986). Crime, deterrence, and rational choice. *American Sociological Review, 51*, 101–119.

Pinkney, A. (1987). *Black Americans* (3rd ed.). Englewood Cliffs, NJ: Prentice-Hall.

Piper, E. S. (1985). Violent recidivism and chronicity in the 1958 Philadelphia cohort. *Journal of Quantitative Criminology, 1*, 319–344.

Pithers, W. D. (1990). Relapse prevention with sexual aggressors: A method for maintaining therapeutic gain and enhancing external supervision. In W. L. Marshall, D. R. Laws, & H. E. Barbaree (Eds.), *Handbook of sexual assault: Issues, theories and treatment of the offender* (pp. 343–361). New York: Plenum.

Pithers, W. D., Beal, L. S., Armstrong, J., & Petty, J. (1989). Identification of risk factors through clinical interviews and analysis of records. In D. R. Laws (Eds.), *Relapse prevention with sex offenders* (pp. 77–87). New York: Guilford.

Plomin, R., & Rowe, D. C. (1977). A twin study of temperament in young children. *Journal of Psychology, 97*, 107–113.

Pogrebin, M., Poole, E., & Martinez, A. (1992). Accounts of professional misdeeds: The sexual exploitation of clients by psychotherapists. *Deviant Behavior, 13*, 229–252.

Polk, K. (1991). Review of "A General Theory of Crime" by Michael R. Gottfredson and Travis Hirschi. *Crime and Delinquency, 37*, 575–581.

Pollack, G., Gilmore, C., Stewart, J., & Mattison, S. (1989). A follow-up of aggressive behavior in children. *Educational Review, 41*, 263–270.

Pollard, J. A., Hawkins, J. D., & Arthur, M. W. (1999). Risk and protection: Are both necessary to understand diverse behavioral outcomes in adolescence? *Social Work Research, 23*, 145–158.

Pollock, N. L., & Hashmall, J. M. (1991). The excuses of child molesters. *Behavioral Sciences and the Law, 9*, 53–59.

Pollock, P. H. (1996). Self-efficacy and sexual offending against children: Construction of a measure and changes following relapse prevention treatment. *Legal and Criminological Psychology, 1*, 219–228.

Porter, J. F., & Critelli, J. W. (1994). Self-talk and sexual arousal in sexual aggression. *Journal of Social and Clinical Psychology, 13*, 223–239.

Porter, S. (1990). Adolescent sex offenders: A study of the relationship between self-concept and sexual behavior in adolescent males. *American Journal of Forensic Psychology, 8*, 61–73.

Povinelli, D. J., Landau, K. R., & Perilloux, H. K. (1996). Self-recognition in young children using delayed versus live feedback: Evidence of a developmental asynchrony. *Child Development, 67*, 1540–1554.

Powell, K. M., & Rosén, L. A. (1999). Avoidance of responsibility in conduct disordered adolescents. *Personality and Individual Differences, 27*, 327–340.

Power, R., Green, A., Foster, R., & Stimson, G. (1995). A qualitative study of the purchasing and distribution patterns of cocaine and crack users in England and Wales. *Addiction Research, 2*, 363–379.

Prager, E., & Solomon, Z. (1995). Perceptions of world benevolence, meaningfulness, and self-worth among elderly Israeli Holocaust survivors and non-survivors. *Anxiety, Stress and Coping: An International Journal, 8*, 265–277.

Prentky, R. A., Knight, R. A., Sims-Knight, J. E., Straus, H., Rokous, F., & Cerce, D. (1989). Developmental antecedents of sexual aggression. *Developmental Psychopathology, 1*, 153–169.

Proulx, J., McKibben, A., & Lusignan, R. (1996). Relationships between affective components and sexual behaviors in sexual aggressors. *Sexual Abuse: A Journal of Research and Treatment, 8*, 279–289.

Pryor, J. B., & Stoller, L. M. (1994). Sexual cognition processes in men high in likelihood to sexually harass. *Personality and Social Psychology Bulletin, 20*, 163–169.

Pyszczynski, T., Greenberg, J., & Solomon, S. (1997). Why do we need what we need? A terror management perspective on the roots of human social motivation. *Psychological Inquiry, 8*, 1–20.

Pyszczynski, T., Greenberg, J., & Solomon, S. (1998). A terror management perspective on the psychology of control: Controlling the uncontrollable. In M. Kofta, G. Weary, & G. Sedek (Eds.), *Personal control in action: Cognitive and motivational mechanisms* (pp. 85–108). New York: Plenum.

Quiggle, N., Garber, J., Panak, W., & Dodge, K. A. (1992). Social-information processing in aggressive and depressed children. *Child Development, 63*, 1305–1320.

Racey, B. D., Lopez, N. L., & Schneider, H. G. (2000). Sexually assaultive adolescents: Cue perception, interpersonal competence and cognitive distortions. *International Journal of Adolescence and Youth, 8*, 229–239.

Raine, A., Venables, P. H., & Williams, M. (1990). Autonomic orienting responses in 15-

year-old male subjects and criminal behavior at age 24. *American Journal of Psychiatry, 147*, 933–937.
Rand, A. (1987). Transitional life events and desistance from delinquency and crime. In M. E. Wolfgang, T. P. Thornberry, & R. M. Figlio (Eds.), *From boy to man, from delinquency to crime* (pp. 134–162). Chicago: University of Chicago Press.
Reed, G. E., & Yeager, P. C. (1996). Organizational offending and neoclassical criminology: Challenging the reach of "A General Theory of Crime." *Criminology, 34*, 357–382.
Reed, M. D., & Rose, D. R. (1998). Doing what Simple Simon says? Estimating the underlying causal structures of delinquent associations, attitudes, and serious theft. *Criminal Justice and Behavior,* 25, 240–274.
Regoli, R. M., & Poole, E. D. (1978). The commitment of delinquents to their misdeeds: A re-examination. *Journal of Criminal Justice, 6*, 261–268.
Reicher, S., & Emler, N. (1985). Delinquent behaviour and attitudes to formal authority. *British Journal of Social Psychology, 24*, 161–168.
Reid, A., & Deaux, K. (1996). Relationship between social and personal identities: Segregation or integration? *Journal of Personality and Social Psychology, 71*, 1084–1091.
Rennison, C. M. (1999). *Criminal victimization 1998; Changes 1997–98 with trends 1993–98.* Washington, DC: Bureau of Justice Statistics.
Resick, P. A. (1993). The psychological impact of rape. *Journal of Interpersonal Violence, 8*, 223–255.
Retowski, S. (1995). Psychological correlates of long-term unemployment. *Przeglad Psycholiczny, 38*, 141–160.
Reuter, P., MacCoun, R., & Murphy, P. (1990). *Money from crime: A study of the economics of drug dealing in Washington, DC.* Santa Monica, CA: Rand Corporation.
Richardson, D. R., Green, L. R., & Lago, T. (1998). The relationship between perspective-taking and nonaggressive responding in the face of an attack. *Journal of Personality, 66*, 235–256.
Richardson, D. R., Hammock, G. S., Smith, S. M., Gardner, W., & Signo, M. (1994). Empathy as a cognitive inhibitor of interpersonal aggression. *Aggressive Behavior, 20*, 275–289.
Roberts, R. E., Roberts, C. R., & Chen, R. Y. (1998). Suicidal thinking among adolescents with a history of attempted suicide. *Journal of the American Academy of Child and Adolescent Psychiatry, 37*, 1294–1300.
Robins, L. N. (1978). Sturdy childhood predictors of adult antisocial behavior: Replication from longitudinal studies. *Psychological Medicine, 8*, 611–622.
Robinson, T. L., & Howard-Hamilton, M. (1994). An Afrocentric paradigm: Foundation for a healthy self-image and healthy interpersonal relationships. *Journal of Mental Health Counseling, 16*, 327–337.
Rogers, R., Salekin, R. T., Sewell, R. W., & Cruise, K. R. (2000). Prototypical analysis of antisocial personality disorder: A study of inmate samples. *Criminal Justice and Behavior, 27*, 234–255.
Rogers, T. B., Kuiper, N. A., & Kirker, W. S. (1977). Self-reference and the encoding of personal information. *Journal of Personality and Social Psychology, 35*, 677–688.
Roggman, L. A., Langlois, J. H., & Hubbs-Tait, L. (1987). Mothers, infants, and toys: Social play correlates of attachment. *Infant Behavior and Development, 10*, 233–237.
Roitberg, T., & Menard, S. (1995). Adolescent violence: A test of integrated theory. *Studies on Crime and Crime Prevention, 4*, 177–196.

Rokeach, M. (1973). *The nature of human values*. New York: Free Press.

Rokeach, M. (1983). A value approach to the prevention and reduction of drug abuse. *NIDA Research Monograph Series, 47*, 172–194.

Romero, J., & Williams, J. (1985). Recidivism among convicted sex offenders: A 10-year follow-up study. *Federal Probation, 49*, 58–64.

Rosen, W. D., Adamson, L. B., & Bakeman, R. (1992). An experimental investigation of infant social referencing: Mothers' messages and gender differences. *Developmental Psychology, 28*, 1172–1178.

Rosenbaum, J. (1987). Social control, gender, and delinquency: An analysis of drug, property, and violent offenders. *Justice Quarterly, 4*, 117–132.

Rosenberg, M. (1986). Self-concept from middle childhood through adolescence. In J. Suls & A. G. Greenwald (Eds.), *Psychological perspectives on the self* (Vol. 3, pp. 107–135). Hillsdale, NJ: Erlbaum.

Rosenberg, M., Schooler, C., & Schoenbach, C. (1989). Self-esteem and adolescent problems. *Sociological Review, 54*, 1004–1018.

Ross, M., & Wilson, A. E. (2000). Constructing and appraising past selves. In D. Schacter (Ed.), *Memory and belief* (pp. 231–258). Cambridge: Harvard University Press.

Ross, R. R., & Fabiano, E. A. (1985). *Time to think: A cognitive model of delinquency prevention and offender rehabilitation*. Johnson City, TN: Institute of Social Sciences & Art.

Rossi, P. H., Waite, R., Bose, C. E., & Berk, R. E. (1974). The seriousness of crimes: Normative structure and individual differences. *American Sociological Review, 39*, 224–237.

Roth, H., & Nicholson, C. L. (1990). Earliest school recollections as a diagnostic device for identifying successfully or unsuccessfully mainstreamed violent and assaultive youth. *Journal of Offender Counseling, Services and Rehabilitation, 15*, 117–129.

Rutter, M., & Giller, H. (1984). *Juvenile delinquency: Trends and perspectives*. New York: Guilford.

Rychlak, J. F. (1992). A teleologist's reactions to "On Private Events and Theoretical Terms." *Journal of Mind and Behavior, 13*, 347–358.

Sampson, R. J., & Laub, J. H. (1993). *Crime in the making: Pathways and turning points through life*. Cambridge: Harvard University Press.

Sappington, A. A. (1996). Relationships among prison and adjustment, beliefs, and cognitive coping style. *International Journal of Offender Therapy and Comparative Criminology, 40*, 54–62.

Sappington, A. A., Pharr, R., Tunstall, A., & Rickert, E. (1997). Relationships among child abuse, date abuse, and psychological problems. *Journal of Clinical Psychology, 53*, 1–11.

Saxon, T. F., Frick, J. E., & Colombo, J. (1997). A longitudinal study of maternal interactional styles and infant visual attention. *Merrill-Palmer Quarterly, 43*, 48–66.

Schachter, S. (1959). *The psychology of affiliation*. Stanford, CA: Stanford University Press.

Schimel, J., Arndt, J., Pyszczynski, T., & Greenberg, J. (2001). Being accepted for who we are: Evidence that social validation of the intrinsic self reduces general defensiveness. *Journal of Personality and Social Psychology, 80*, 35–52.

Schmitz, S., Saudino, K. J., Plomin, R., Fulker, D. W., & De Fries, J. C. (1996). Genetic and environmental influences on temperament in middle childhood: Analyses of teacher and tester ratings. *Child Development, 67*, 409–423.

Schoenfeld, C. G. (1988). Blacks and violent crime: A psychoanalytical oriented analysis.

Journal of Psychiatry and Law, 16 269–301.
Scholl, B. J., & Leslie, A. M. (1999). Modularity, development and "theory of mind." *Mind and Language, 14,* 131–153.
Schreiber, K. (1992). The adolescent crack dealer: A failure in the development of empathy. *Journal of the American Academy of Psychoanalysis, 20,* 1561–1571.
Schur, E. M. (1971). *Labeling and deviant behavior.* New York: Harper & Row.
Schwartz, M. D., & DeKeseredy, W. S. (1997). *Sexual assault on the college campus: The role of male peer support.* Thousand Oaks, CA: Sage.
Schweizer, K. (1998). Complexity of information processing and the speed-ability relationship. *Journal of General Psychology, 125,* 89–102.
Scourfield, J., Martin, N., Lewis, G., & McGuffin, P. (1999). Heritability of social cognitive skills in children and adolescents. *British Journal of Psychiatry, 175,* 559–564.
Scully, D. (1988). Convicted rapists' perceptions of self and victim: Role taking and emotions. *Gender and Society, 2,* 200–213.
Sedikides, C., & Brewer, M. B. (Eds.). (2001). *Individual self, relational self, collective self.* Philadelphia: Taylor & Francis.
Séguin, J. R., Pihl, R. O., Harden, P. W., Tremblay, R. E., & Boulerice, B. (1995). Cognitive and neuropsychological characteristics of physically aggressive boys. *Journal of Abnormal Psychology, 104,* 614–624.
Seibert, J. M., Sliwin, L, & Hogan, A. E. (1986). Social and cognitive bases of early comprehension of object reference. *Cognitive Development, 14,* 391–404.
Seidman, B. T., Marshall, W. L., Hudson, S. M., & Robertson, P. J. (1994). An examination of intimacy and loneliness in sex offenders. *Journal of Interpersonal Violence, 9,* 518–534.
Seitz, J. A. (1998). Nonverbal metaphor: A review of theories and evidence. *Genetic, Social, and General Psychological Monographs, 124,* 95–119.
Sen, A., & Pande, P. (1993). Perception of the drug peddlers: Role identification, role norms and their general approach toward life. *Social Science International, 9,* 61–71.
Serin, R. C., & Kuriychuk, M. (1994). Social and cognitive processing deficits in violent offenders: Implications for treatment. *International Journal of Law and Psychiatry, 17,* 431–441.
Sewall, L. (1998). Looking for a worldview: Perceptual practice in an ecological age. *Humanistic Psychologist, 26,* 163–178.
Shapiro, C. E., Schwartz, C. E., & Astin, J. A. (1996). Controlling ourselves, controlling our world: Psychology's role in understanding positive and negative consequences of seeking and gaining control. *American Psychologist, 51,* 1213–1230.
Shapiro, S. P. (1990). Collaring the crime, not the criminal: Reconsidering the concept of white-collar crime. *American Sociological Review, 55,* 346–365.
Sherwin, R. (1963). White-collar crime, conventional crime and Merton's deviant behavior theory. *Wisconsin Sociologist, 2,* 7–10.
Shields, I. W., & Whitehall, G. C. (1994). Neutralization and delinquency among teenagers. *Criminal Justice and Behavior, 21,* 223–235.
Shoda, Y., Mischel, W., & Wright, J. C. (1993). The role of situational demands and cognitive competencies in behavior organization and personality coherence. *Journal of Personality and Social Psychology, 65,* 1023–1035.
Shover, N. (1996). *Great pretenders: Pursuits and careers of persistent thieves.* Oxford, UK: Westview.
Shover, N., Norland, S., James, J., & Thorton, W. (1979). Gender roles and delinquency.

Social Forces, 58, 162–175.

Shover, N., & Thompson, C. (1992). Age, differential expectations, and crime desistance. *Criminology, 30*, 89–104.

Sigvardsson, S., Bohman, M., & Cloninger, C. R. (1987). Structure and stability of childhood personality: Prediction of later social adjustment. *Journal of Child Psychology, Psychiatry, and Allied Disciplines, 28*, 929–946.

Silverberg, S. B., Vazsonyi, A. T., Schlegel, A. E., & Schmidt, S. (1998). Adolescent apprentices in Germany: Adult attachment, job expectations, and delinquent attitudes. *Journal of Adolescent Research, 13*, 254–271.

Simons, R. L., Whitbeck, L. B., Conger, R. D., & Conger, K. J. (1991). Parenting factors, social skills, and value commitments as precursors to school failure, involvement with deviant peers, and delinquent behavior. *Journal of Youth and Adolescence, 20*, 645–664.

Skinner, B. F. (1953). *Science and human behavior.* New York: Macmillan.

Skinner, W. F., & Fream, A. M. (1997). A social learning theory analysis of computer crime among college students. *Journal of Research in Crime and Delinquency, 34*, 495–518.

Slaby, R. G., & Guerra, N. G. (1988). Cognitive mediators of aggression in adolescent offenders: I. Assessment. *Developmental Psychology, 24*, 580–588.

Slavney, P. R. (1992). Belief and behavior: The role of "folk psychology" in psychiatry. *Comprehensive Psychiatry, 33*, 166–172.

Smallbone, S. W., & Dadds, M. R. (2000). Attachment and coercive sexual behavior. *Sexual Abuse: A Journal of Research and Treatment, 12*, 3–15.

Smart, R. G., Adlaf, E. M., & Walsh, G. W. (1992). Adolescent drug sellers: Trends, characteristics and profiles. *British Journal of Addiction, 87*, 1561–1570.

Smith, C. B., Adamson, L. B., & Bakeman, R. (1988). Interactional predictors of early language. *First Language, 8*, 143–156.

Smith, D. A., & Paternoster, R. (1990). Formal processing and future delinquency: Deviance amplification as selection artifact. *Law and Society Review, 24*, 1109–1131.

Smith, H. S., & Cohen, L. H. (1993). Self-complexity and reactions to a relationship break-up. *Journal of Social and Clinical Psychology, 12*, 367–384.

Smith, L. (1995). Self-organizing processes in learning to learn words: Development is not induction. In C. A. Nelson (Eds.), *Basic and applied perspectives on learning, cognition, and development* (Minnesota Symposium on Child Psychology, Vol. 28, pp. 1–32). Mahwah, NJ: Erlbaum.

Smith, W. P., & Sachs, P. (1997). Social comparison and task prediction: Ability similarity and the use of a proxy. *British Journal of Social Psychology, 36*, 587–602.

Smithmyer, C. M., Hubbard, J. A., & Simons, R. F. (2000). Proactive and reactive aggression in delinquent adolescents: Relations to aggression outcome expectancies. *Journal of Clinical Child Psychology, 29*, 86–93.

Snyder, C. R., & Higgins, R. L. (1988). Excuses: Their effective role in the negotiation of reality. *Psychological Bulletin, 101*, 23–35.

Snyder, M. (1983, May). *The self in action.* Paper presented at the 55th annual meeting of the Midwestern Psychological Association, Chicago.

Snyder, M. L., Stephan, W. G., & Rosenfield, D. (1978). Attributional egoism. In J. H. Harvey, W. Ickes, & R. F. Kidd (Eds.), *New directions in attributional research* (Vol. 2, pp. 91–120). Hillsdale, NJ: Erlbaum.

Sommers, I., & Baskin, D. R. (1992). Sex, race, age, and violent offending. *Violence and Victims, 7*, 191–201.

Sommers, I., & Baskin, D. R. (1994). Factors related to female adolescent initiation into violent street crime. *Youth and Society, 25*, 468–489.

Sommers, I., & Baskin, D. R. (1997). Situational or generalized violence in drug dealing networks. *Journal of Drug Issues, 27*, 833–849.

Sommers, I., Baskin, D. R., & Fagan, J. (1994). Getting out of the life: Crime desistance by female street offenders. *Deviant Behavior, 15*, 125–149.

Sommers, I., Baskin, D. R., & Fagan, J. (1996). The structural relationship between drug use, drug dealing, and other income supporting activities among women drug sellers. *Journal of Drug Issues, 26*, 975–1006.

Sonn, C. C., & Fisher, A. T. (1996). Sense of community: Community resilient response to oppression and change. *Journal of Community Psychology, 26*, 457–472.

Sorce, J., Emde, R. N., Campos, J. J., & Klinnert, M. (1985). Maternal emotional signalings: Its effects on the visual cliff behavior of 1-year-olds. *Developmental Psychology, 21*, 195–200.

Spinath, F. M., & Angleitner, A. (1998). Contrast effects in Buss and Plomin's EAS questionnaire: A behavioral-genetic study on early developing personality traits assessed through parental ratings. *Personality and Individual Differences, 25*, 947–963.

Stahl, S. S., & Sacco, W. P. (1995). Heterosocial perception in child molesters and rapists. *Cognitive Therapy and Research, 19*, 695–706.

Stall, R., & Biernacki, P. (1986). Spontaneous remission from the problematic use of substances: An inductive model derived from a comparative analysis of the alcohol, opiate, tobacco, and food/obesity literatures. *International Journal of the Addictions, 21*, 1–23.

Stamp, G. H., & Sabourin, T. C. (1995). Accounting for violence: An analysis of male spousal abuse narratives. *Journal of Applied Communication Research, 23*, 284–307.

Stanton, B., & Galbraith, J. (1994). Drug trafficking among African-American early adolescents: Prevalence, consequences and associated behaviors and beliefs. *Pediatrics, 93*, 1039–1043.

Stenberg, G., & Hagekull, B. (1997). Social referencing and mood modification in 1-year-olds. *Infant Behavior and Development, 20*, 209–217.

Stermac, L. E., & Segal, Z. V. (1989). Adult sexual contact with children: An examination of cognitive factors. *Behavior Therapy, 20*, 573–584.

Stevenson, R. J., Lind, B., & Weatherburn, D. (1999). The relationship between alcohol sales and assault in New South Wales, Australia. *Addiction, 94*, 397–410.

Stolzenberg, L., & D'Alessio, S. J. (2000). Gun availability and violent crime: New evidence from the National Incident-Based Reporting System. *Social Forces, 78*, 1461–1482.

Stone, M. H., & Thompson, E. H. (2001). Executive function impairment in sexual offenders. *Journal of Individual Psychology, 57*, 51–59.

Sutherland, E. H. (1939). *Principles of criminology* (3rd ed.). Philadelphia: Lippincott.

Sutherland, E. H. (1983). *White collar crime: The uncut version.* New Haven, CT: Yale University Press. (Original work published 1949)

Sutherland, E. H., & Cressey, D. R. (1978). *Principles of criminology* (10th ed.). Philadelphia: Lippincott.

Suzuki, Y. (1990). A study of seat-taking in seminar classes: Data analysis of three seminar classes in a woman's university. *Japanese Journal of Psychology, 61*, 127–132.

Svrakic, N. M., Svrakic, D. M., & Cloninger, C. R. (1996). A quantitative theory of psychological development: Fundamentals of a self-organizing psychobiological complex. *Development and Psychopathology, 8*, 247–272.

Swann, W. B., Jr. (1987). Identity negotiation: Where two roads meet. *Journal of Personality and Social Psychology, 53*, 1038–1051.

Swann, W. B., Jr., Hixon, J. G., Stein-Seroussi, A., & Gilbert, D. T. (1990). The fleeting gleam of praise: Behavioral reactions to self-relevant feedback. *Journal of Personality and Social Psychology, 43*, 59–66.

Swann, W. B., Jr., Pelham, B. W., & Krull, D. S. (1989). Agreeable fancy or disagreeable truth? How people reconcile their self-enhancement and self-verification needs. *Journal of Personality and Social Psychology, 57*, 782–791.

Swann, W. B., Jr., Wenzlaff, R. M., Krull, D. S., & Pelham, B. W. (1992). Allure of negative feedback: Self-verification strivings among depressed persons. *Journal of Abnormal Psychology, 101*, 293–306.

Sykes, G., & Matza, D. (1957). Techniques of neutralization: A theory of delinquency. *American Sociological Review, 22*, 664–670.

Tanaka, K. (1999). Judgments of fairness by just world believers. *Journal of Social Psychology, 139*, 631–638.

Tannenbaum, F. (1938). *Crime and community*. New York: Ginn.

Tarde, G. (1912). *Penal philosophy*. Boston: Little, Brown.

Tarshis, E., & Shore, B. M. (1991). Perspective taking in high and above average IQ preschool children. *European Journal for High Ability, 2*, 201–211.

Taylor, D. A., & Belgrave, F. Z. (1986). The effects of perceived intimacy and valence on self-disclosure reciprocity. *Personality and Social Psychology Bulletin, 12*, 247–255.

Teasdale, J. D. (1993). Emotion and two kinds of meaning: Cognitive therapy and applied cognitive science. *Behaviour Research and Therapy, 31*, 339–354.

Tedeschi, J. T., & Felson, R. B. (1994). *Violence, aggression, and coercive actions*. Washington, DC: American Psychological Association.

Thompson, L., & Fine, G. A. (1999). Socially shared cognition, affect, and behavior: A review and integration. *Personality and Social Psychology Review, 3*, 278–302.

Thompson, S. C., & Janigian, A. S. (1988). Life schemes: A framework for understanding the search for meaning. *Journal of Social and Clinical Psychology, 7*, 260–280.

Thornberry, T. P. (1987). Toward an interactional theory of delinquency. *Criminology, 25*, 863–891.

Thornberry, T. P., Lizotte, A. J., Krohn, M. D., Farnworth, M., & Jang, S. J. (1991). Testing interactional theory: An examination of reciprocal causal relationships among family, school, and delinquency. *Journal of Criminal Law and Criminology, 82*, 3–33.

Thornberry, T. P., Lizotte, A. J., Krohn, M. D., Farnworth, M., & Jang, S. J. (1994). Delinquent peers, beliefs, and delinquent behavior: A longitudinal test of interactional theory. *Criminology, 32*, 47–83.

Thornberry, T. P., Moore, M., & Christenson, R. L. (1985). The effect of dropping out of high school on subsequent criminal behavior. *Criminology, 23*, 3–18.

Thrasher, F. M. (1927). *The gang*. Chicago: University of Chicago Press.

Thurman, Q. C. (1984). Deviance and the neutralization of moral commitment: An empirical analysis. *Deviant Behavior, 5*, 291–304.

Tice, D. M. (1992). Self-concept change and self-presentation: The looking glass self is also a magnifying glass. *Journal of Personality and Social Psychology, 63*, 435–451.

Tittle, C., Burke, M., & Jackson, E. (1986). Modeling Sutherland's theory of differential association: Toward an empirical clarification. *Social Forces, 65*, 405–432.

Tittle, C. R., Villemez, W. T., & Smith, D. A. (1978). The myth of social class and criminality: An empirical assessment of the empirical evidence. *American Sociological Review, 43*, 643–656.

Toch, H. (1993). *Violent men: An inquiry into the psychology of violence*. Washington, DC: American Psychological Association. (Original work published 1969)
Tomasello, M. (1999). The human adaptation for culture. *Annual Review of Anthropology, 28*, 509–529.
Torgersen, S. (1985). Hereditary differentiation of anxiety and affective neuroses. *British Journal of Psychiatry, 146*, 530–534.
Toupin, J., Déry, M., Pauzé, R., Mercier, H., & Fortin, L. (2000). Cognitive and familial contributions to conduct disorder in children. *Journal of Child Psychology and Psychiatry, 41*, 333–344.
Trafimow, D., Silverman, E. S., Fan, R.M.-T., & Law, J.S.F. (1997). The effects of language and priming on the relative accessibility of the private self and the collective self. *Journal of Cross-Cultural Psychology, 28*, 107–123.
Trafimow, D., Triandis, H. C., & Goto, S. C. (1991). Some tests of the distinction between the private self and the collective self. *Journal of Personality and Social Psychology, 60*, 649–655.
Tremblay, R. E., Pihl, R. O., Vitaro, F., & Dobkin, P. L. (1994). Predicting early onset of male antisocial behavior from preschool behavior. *Archives of General Psychiatry, 51*, 732–738.
Trevino, L., & Youngblood, S. (1990). Bad apples in bad barrels: A causal analysis of ethical decision-making behavior. *Journal of Applied Psychology, 78*, 378–385.
Triandis, H. C., McCusker, C., & Hui, C. H. (1990). Multimethod probes of individualism and collectivism. *Journal of Personality and Social Psychology, 59*, 1006–1020.
Trice, A. D., & Lamb, M. (1996). Sex-role orientation among incarcerated women. *Psychological Reports, 79*, 92–94.
Triplett, R., & Jarjoura, G. R. (1994). Theoretical and empirical specification of a model of informal labeling. *Journal of Quantitative Criminology, 10*, 241–276.
U. S. Bureau of Census. (2001). *Census 2000—Population by race and Hispanic or Latino origin for the United States: 1990 and 2000*. Washington, DC: Author.
Uribe, V. M., & Ostrov, E. (1989). Correlations of substance abuse and self-image among socially diverse groups of adolescents and clinical implications. *Hillside Journal of Clinical Psychiatry, 11*, 25–34.
VanNostrand, L.-M., & Tewksbury, R. (1999). The motives and mechanisms of operating an illegal drug enterprise. *Deviant Behavior, 20*, 57–83.
Vaughn, D. (1983). *Controlling unlawful organizational behavior: Social structure and corporate misconduct*. Chicago: University of Chicago Press.
Vazsonyi, A. T., Pickering, L. E., Junger, M., & Hessing, D. (2001). An empirical test of a general theory of crime: A four-nation comparative study of self-control and the prediction of deviance. *Journal of Research in Crime and Delinquency, 38*, 91–131.
Venables, P. H. (1987). Autonomic nervous system factors in criminal behavior. In S. A. Mednick, T. E. Moffitt, & S. A. Stack (Eds.), *The causes of crime: New biological approaches* (pp. 110–136). New York: Cambridge University Press.
Vitousek, K., Watson, S., & Wilson, G. T. (1998). Enhancing motivation for change in treatment-resistant eating disorders. *Clinical Psychology Review, 18*, 391–420.
Vohra, S., & Ahmad, H. (1993). Personality and value patterns of delinquents and nondelinquents—A comparative study. *Journal of Personality and Clinical Studies, 9*, 31–37.
Vold, G. B., Bernard, T. J., & Snipes, J. B. (1998). *Theoretical criminology* (4th ed.). New York: Oxford University Press.
von Broembsen, F. (1989). Transformation of identity: Referent location, agency, and

levels of integration in the progress from potential self to existential identity. *American Journal of Psychoanalysis, 49*, 329–338.
Vowell, P. R., & May, D. C. (2000). Another look at classic strain theory: Poverty, status, perceived blocked opportunity, and gang membership as predictors of adolescent violent behavior. *Sociological Inquiry, 70*, 42–60.
Vygotsky, L. S. (1986). *Thought and language* (A. Kozulin, Trans.). Cambridge: MIT Press. (Original work published 1934)
Waas, G. A. (1988). Social attributional bias of peer-rejected and aggressive children. *Child Development, 59*, 969–975.
Waegel, W. B., Ermann, M. D., & Horowitz, A. M. (1981). Organizational responses to imputations of deviance. *Sociological Quarterly, 22*, 43–55.
Walden, T. A., & Baxter, A. (1989). The effect of context and age on social referencing. *Child Development, 60*, 1511–1518.
Waldorf, D., Murphy, S., & Lauderback, D. (1994). Middle class cocaine sellers: Self-reported reasons for stopping sales. *Addiction Research, 2*, 109–126.
Walsh, A. (1990). Twice labeled: The effect of psychiatric labeling on the sentencing of sex offenders. *Social Problems, 37*, 373–389.
Walsh, B. J., & Middleton, J. R. (1984). *The transforming vision: Shaping a Christian world view.* Downers Grove, IL: InterVarsity Press.
Walters, G. D. (1990). *The criminal lifestyle: Patterns of serious criminal conduct.* Newbury Park, CA: Sage.
Walters, G. D. (1992). *Foundations of criminal science: 2. The use of knowledge.* New York: Praeger.
Walters, G. D. (1994). *Drugs and crime in lifestyle perspective.* Thousand Oaks, CA: Sage.
Walters, G. D. (1995). The Psychological Inventory of Criminal Thinking Styles: Part I. Reliability and preliminary validity. *Criminal Justice and Behavior, 22*, 307–325.
Walters, G. D. (1996a). The Psychological Inventory of Criminal Thinking Styles: Part III. Predictive validity. *International Journal of Offender Therapy and Comparative Criminology, 40*, 105–112.
Walters, G. D. (1996b). Sexual preoccupation as a lifestyle. *Sexual and Marital Therapy, 11*, 373–382.
Walters, G. D. (1997). Predicting short-term release outcome using the LCSF and PICTS. *Journal of Mental Health in Corrections Consortium, 43*, 18–25.
Walters, G. D. (1998a). The alcohol expectancy process: Origins, structure, and change. *Alcoholism Treatment Quarterly, 16*, 25–38.
Walters, G. D. (1998b). *Changing lives of drugs and crime: Intervening with substance-abusing offenders.* Chichester, UK: Wiley.
Walters, G. D. (1998c). The Lifestyle Criminality Screening Form: Psychometric properties and practical utility. *Journal of Offender Rehabilitation, 27*, 9–23.
Walters, G. D. (1998d). Planning for change: An alternative to treatment planning with sexual offenders. *Journal of Sex and Marital Therapy, 24*, 217–229.
Walters, G. D. (1999). Human survival and the self-destruction paradox: An integrated theoretical model. *Journal of Mind and Behavior, 20*, 57–78.
Walters, G. D. (2000a). *Beyond behavior: Constructing an overarching psychological theory of lifestyles.* Westport, CT: Praeger.
Walters, G. D. (2000b). Disposed to aggress? In search of the violence-prone personality. *Aggression and Violent Behavior, 5*, 177–190.
Walters, G. D. (2000c). Outcome expectancies for crime: Their relationship to fear and the negative consequences of criminal involvement. *Legal and Criminological Psychol-*

ogy, 5, 261–272.
Walters, G. D. (2000d). *The self-altering process: Exploring the dynamic nature of lifestyle development and change*. Westport, CT: Praeger.
Walters, G. D. (2000e). Spontaneous remission from alcohol, tobacco, and other drug abuse: Seeking quantitative answers to qualitative questions. *American Journal of Drug and Alcohol Abuse, 26*, 443–460.
Walters, G. D. (2001a). The relationship between masculinity, femininity, and criminal thinking in male and female offenders. *Sex Roles, 45*, 677–689.
Walters, G. D. (2001b). The shaman effect in counseling clients with alcohol problems. *Alcoholism Treatment Quarterly, 19*, 31–43.
Walters, G. D. (in press-a). Changes in criminal thinking and identity in novice and experienced inmates: Prisonization revisited. *Criminal Justice and Behavior*.
Walters, G. D. (in press-b). The Psychological Inventory of Criminal Thinking Styles (PICTS): A review and meta-analysis. *Assessment*.
Walters, G. D., & Elliott, W. N. (1999). Predicting release and disciplinary outcome with the Psychological Inventory of Criminal Thinking Styles: Female data. *Legal and Criminological Psychology, 4*, 15–21.
Walters, G. D., Elliott, W. N., & Miscoll, D. (1998). Use of the Psychological Inventory of Criminal Thinking Styles in a group of female offenders. *Criminal Justice and Behavior, 25*, 125–134.
Walters, G. D., & Geyer, M. D. (2002). *Criminal thinking and identity in white-collar offenders*. Manuscript submitted for publication.
Walters, G. D., Trgovac, M., Rychlec, M., Di Fazio, R., & Olson, J. R. (2002). Assessing change with the Psychological Inventory of Criminal Thinking Styles: A controlled analysis and multisite cross-validation. *Criminal Justice and Behavior, 29*, 308–331.
Walters, G. D., White, T. W., & Denney, D. (1991). The Lifestyle Criminality Screening Form: Preliminary data. *Criminal Justice and Behavior, 18*, 406–418.
Ward, D. A., Stafford, M. C., Gray, L. N., & Menke, B. A. (1994). Deterrence, opportunity, and choice. *Journal of Applied Social Psychology, 24*, 1777–1793.
Ward, T. (2000). Sexual offenders' cognitive distortions as implicit theories. *Aggression and Violent Behavior, 5*, 491–507.
Ward, T., Hudson, S. M., Johnston, L., & Marshall, W. L. (1997). Cognitive distortions in sex offenders: An integrative review. *Clinical Psychology Review, 17*, 479–507.
Ward, T., Hudson, S. M., & Marshall, W. L. (1995). Cognitive and affective deficits in sexual aggression: A cognitive deconstructionist analysis. *Sexual Abuse: A Journal of Research and Treatment, 7*, 67–83.
Ward, T., Hudson, S. M., & Marshall, W. L. (1996). Attachment style in sex offenders: A preliminary study. *Journal of Sexual Research, 33*, 17–26.
Ward, T., & Keenan, T. (1999). Child molesters' implicit theories. *Journal of Interpersonal Violence, 14*, 821–838.
Webster, S. D., & Beech, A. R. (2000). The nature of sexual offenders' affective empathy: A grounded theory analysis. *Sexual Abuse: A Journal of Research and Treatment, 12*, 249–261.
Weiner, B. (1990). Attribution in personality psychology. In L. A. Pervin (Ed.), *Handbook of personality: Theory and research* (pp. 465–485). New York: Guilford.
Weiner, N. A. (1989). Violent criminal careers and violent career criminals: An overview of the research literature. In N. A. Weiner & M. E. Wolfgang (Eds.), *Violent crime, violent criminals* (pp. 35–138). Newbury Park, CA: Sage.
Weinrott, M. A., & Saylor, M. (1991). Self-reports of crimes committed by sex offenders.

Journal of Interpersonal Violence, 6, 286–300.
Weinstein, N., & Klein, W. M. (1996). Unrealistic optimism: Present and future. *Journal of Social and Clinical Psychology, 15*, 1–8.
Weisburd, D., Chayet, E. F., & Waring, E. J. (1990). White-collar crime and criminal careers: Some preliminary findings. *Crime and Delinquency, 36*, 342–355.
Weisburd, D., Waring, E., & Chayet, E. (1995). Specific deterrence in a sample of offenders convicted of white-collar crimes. *Criminology, 33*, 587–607.
Weisheit, R., (1991). The intangible rewards from crime: The case of domestic marijuana cultivation. *Crime and Delinquency, 37*, 506–527.
Weisman, G. K. (1993). Adolescent PTSD and the developmental consequences of crack dealing. *American Journal of Orthopsychiatry, 63*, 553–561.
Welch, M. (1990). The value systems of incarcerated embezzlers compared to other inmates and the general population. *Journal of Offender Counseling, Services and Rehabilitation, 15*, 155–176.
Wellford, C., & Triplett, R. (1993). The future of labeling theory: Foundations and promises. In F. Adler & W. S. Laufer (Eds.), *New directions in criminological theory* (pp. 1–22). New Brunswick, NJ: Transaction.
Wellman, H. M. (1990). *The child's theory of mind.* Cambridge, MA: Bradford.
Wellman, H. M., & Gelman, S. A. (1998). Knowledge acquisition in functional domains. In D. Kuhn & R. S. Siegler (Eds.), *Handbook of child psychology: Vol 2. Cognition, perception, and language* (5th ed., pp. 523–573). New York: Wiley.
Wells, E. L., & Rankin, J. H. (1988). Direct parental controls and delinquency. *Criminology, 26*, 263–285.
Wells, J. T. (1994, October). The billion dollar clip. *Internal Auditor*, pp. 32–37.
Welsh, W. N., & Gordon, A. (1991). Cognitive mediators of aggression: Test of a causal model. *Criminal Justice and Behavior, 18*, 125–145.
Werner, E. E. (1986). Resilient offspring of alcoholics: A longitudinal study from birth to age 19. *Journal of Studies on Alcohol, 47*, 34–40.
West, D. J. (2000). The sex crime situation: Deterioration more apparent than real? *European Journal of Criminal Policy and Research, 8*, 399–422.
Whalen, C. K., Henker, B., & Granger, D. A. (1990). Social judgment processes in hyperactive boys: Effects of methylphenidate and comparisons with normal peers. *Journal of Abnormal Child Psychology, 18*, 297–316.
Wheeler, S., Weisburd, D., Waring, E., & Bode, N. (1988). White collar crimes and criminals. *American Criminal Law Review, 25*, 331–357.
Whitehead, T. L., Peterson, J., & Kaljee, L. (1994). Socioeconomic deprivation, urban drug trafficking and low-income African-American male gender identity. *Pediatrics, 3*, 1050–1054.
Wiatrowski, M., & Anderson, K. L. (1987). The dimensionality of the social bond. *Journal of Quantitative Criminology, 3*, 65–81.
Widom, C. S. (1989). Does violence beget violence?: A critical examination of the literature. *Psychological Bulletin, 106*, 3–28.
Wieckowski, E., Hartsoe, P., Mayer, A., & Shortz, J. (1998). Deviant sexual behavior in children and young adults: Frequency and patterns. *Sexual Abuse: A Journal of Research and Treatment, 10*, 293–303.
Will, S., Pontell, H. N., & Cheung, R. (1998). Risky business revisited: White-collar crime and the Orange County bankruptcy. *Crime and Delinquency, 44*, 367–387.
Willerman, L., & Plomin, R. (1973). Activity level in children and their parents. *Child Development, 44*, 854–858.

Williams, T. (1989). *The cocaine kids: The inside story of a teenage drug ring*. New York: Addison-Wesley.

Williamson, G. M., & Clark, M. S. (1992). Impact of desired relationship type on affective reactions to choosing and being required to help. *Personality and Social Psychology Bulletin, 18*, 10–18.

Williamson, G. M., Clark, M. S., Pegalis, L. J., & Behan, A. (1996). Affective consequences of refusing to help in communal and exchange relationships. *Personality and Social Psychology Bulletin, 22*, 34–47.

Williamson, S., Harpur, T. J., & Hare, R. D. (1991). Abnormal processing of affective words by psychopaths. *Psychophysiology, 28*, 260–273.

Wilson, A. E., & Ross, M. (2000). The frequency of temporal-self and social comparisons in people's personal appraisals. *Journal of Personality and Social Psychology, 78*, 928–942.

Wilson, J. Q., & Herrnstein, R. (1985). *Crime and human nature*. New York: Simon & Schuster.

Windle, R. C., & Windle, W. (1995). Longitudinal patterns of physical aggression: Associations with adult social, psychiatric, and personality functioning and testosterone levels. *Development and Psychopathology, 7*, 563–585.

Winick, B. J. (1998). Sex offender law in the 1990s: A therapeutic jurisprudence analysis. *Psychology, Public Policy, and Law, 4*, 505–570.

Winsler, A. (1998). Parent–child interaction and private speech in boys with ADHD. *Applied Developmental Science, 2*, 17–39.

Winsler, A., Diaz, R. M., McCarthy, E. M., Atencio, D. J., & Chabay, L. A. (1999). Mother–child interaction, private speech, and task performance in preschool children with behavior problems. *Journal of Child Psychology and Psychiatry, 40*, 891–904.

Wolfgang, M. E., & Ferracuti, F. (1967). *The subculture of violence*. London: Tavistock.

Wolfgang, M. E., Thornberry, T. P., & Figlio, R. M. (1987). *From boy to man, from delinquency to crime*. Chicago: University of Chicago Press.

Wong, S. K. (1998). Peer relations and Chinese-Canadian delinquency. *Journal of Youth and Adolescence, 27*, 641–659.

Wood, J. V. (1989). Theory and research concerning social comparisons of personal attributes. *Psychological Bulletin, 22*, 520–537.

Wood, J. V., Giordano-Beech, M., & Ducharme, M. J. (1999). Compensating for failure through social comparison. *Personality and Social Psychology Bulletin, 25*, 1370–1386.

Wood, J. V., Giordano-Beech, M., Taylor, K. L., Michela, J. L., & Gaus,V. (1994). Strategies of social comparison among people with low self-esteem: Self-protection and self-enhancement. *Journal of Personality and Social Psychology, 67*, 713–731.

Wood, P. B. (1993). Risk-taking and self-control: Social psychological correlates of delinquency. *Journal of Crime and Justice, 16*, 111–130.

Wright, B.R.E., Caspi, A., Moffitt, T. E., & Silva, P. A. (1999). Low self-control, social bonds, and crime: Social causation, social selection, or both? *Criminology, 37*, 479–514.

Wright, J. D., Sheley, J. F., & Smith, M. D. (1992). Kids, guns, and killing fields. *Society, 30*, 84–89.

Young, J. (1971). The role of the police as amplifiers of deviancy, negotiators of reality, and translators of fantasy. In S. Cohen (Ed.), *Images of deviance* (pp. 27–61). Hammondsworth, UK: Penguin.

Young, M. de (1988). The indignant page: Techniques of neutralization in the publications of pedophile organizations. *Child Abuse and Neglect, 12*, 583–591.

Youngblade, L. M., & Dunn, J. (1995). Individual differences in young children's pretend play with mother and sibling: Links to relationships and understanding of other people's feelings and beliefs. *Child Development, 66*, 1472–1492.

Zaitchick, M. C., & Mosher, D. L. (1993). Criminal justice implications of the macho personality constellation. *Criminal Justice and Behavior, 20*, 227–239.

Zarbatany, L., & Lamb, M. E. (1985). Social referencing as a function of information source: Mothers versus strangers. *Infant Behavior and Development, 8*, 25–33.

Zeitlin, L. R. (1971, June). A little larceny can do a lot for company morale. *Psychology Today, 14*, pp. 22, 24, 26, 64.

Zelazo, P. D., Carter, A., Reznick, J. S., & Frye, D. (1997). Early development of executive function: A problem-solving framework. *Review of General Psychology, 1*, 198–226.

Zelazo, P. D., Sommerville, J. A., & Nichols, S. (1999). Age-related changes in children's use of external representations. *Developmental Psychology, 35*, 1059–1071.

Zhang, L., & Messner, S. F. (1994). The severity of official punishment for delinquency and change in interpersonal relations in Chinese society. *Journal of Research in Crime and Delinquency, 31*, 416–433.

Zimbardo, P. G. (1972). Pathology of imprisonment. *Society, 6*, pp. 4, 6, 8.

Index

About the Author

GLENN D. WALTERS is a Clinical Psychologist and Coordinator of the Drug Abuse Program, Psychology Services, Federal Correctional Institute, Schuylkill.

www.ingramcontent.com/pod-product-compliance
Ingram Content Group UK Ltd.
Pitfield, Milton Keynes, MK11 3LW, UK
UKHW021027041026
15470UKWH00013B/198

9 780275 978204